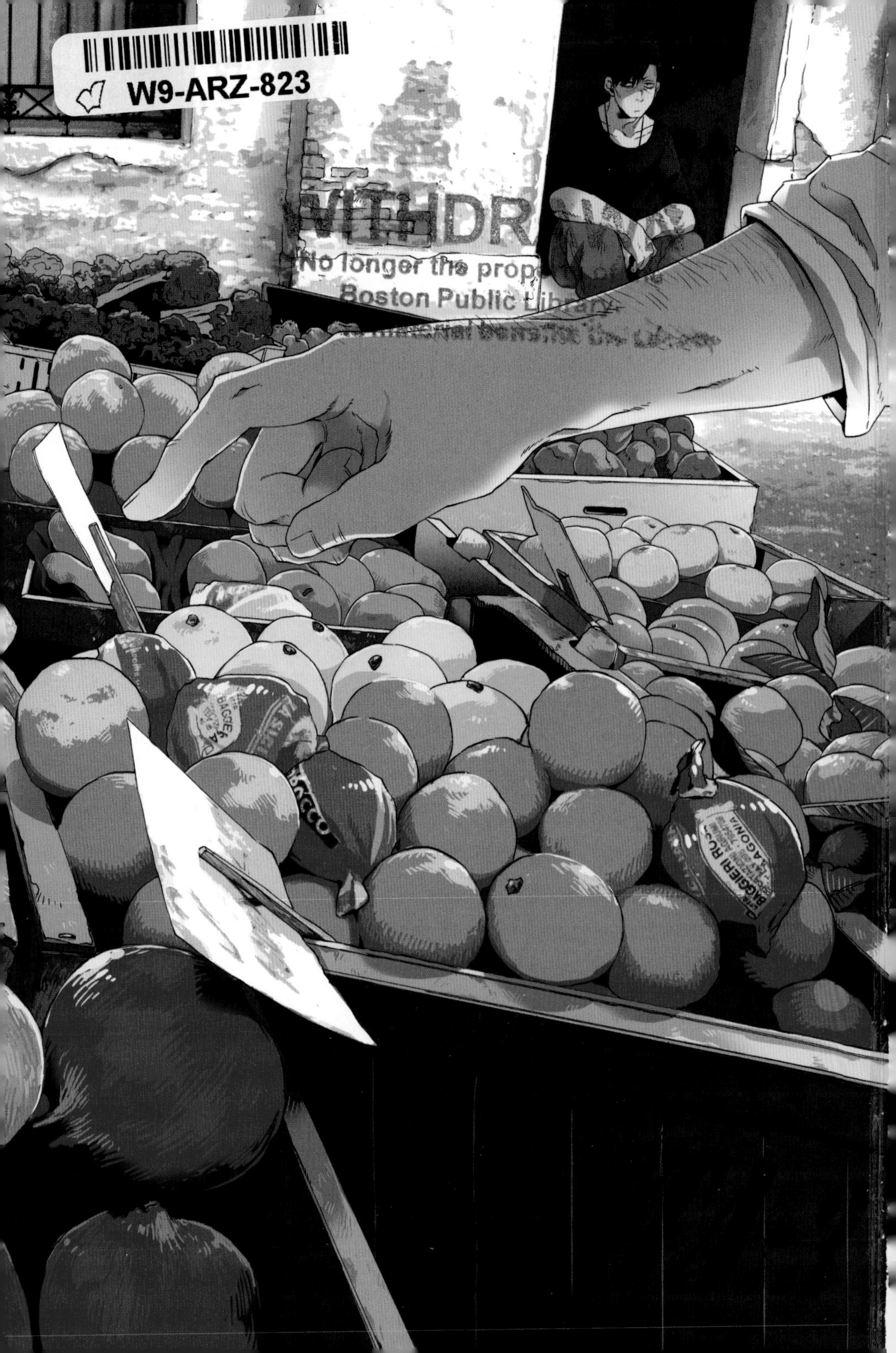

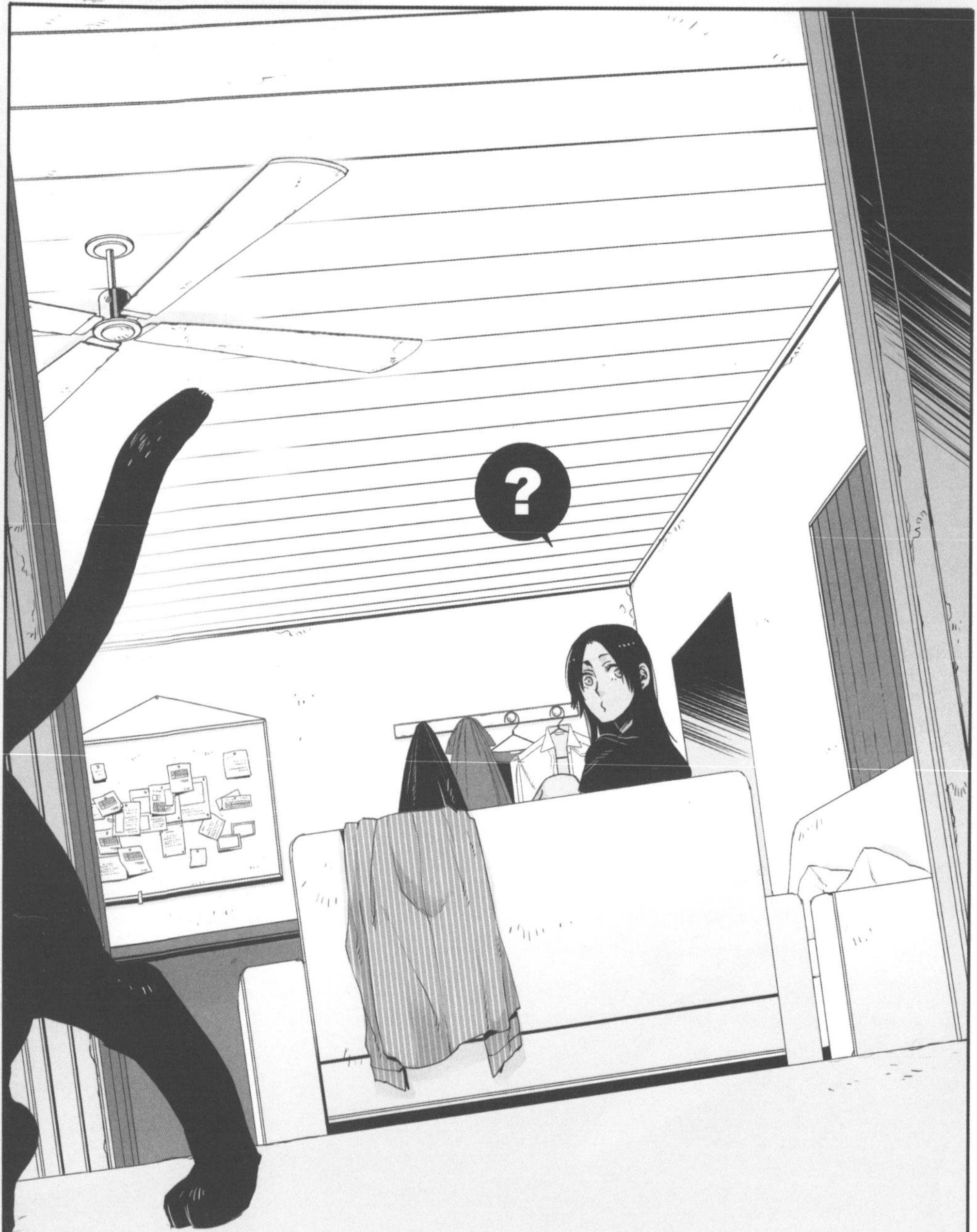
?

ENTER!

GANGSTA

3

KOHSKE

THE HANDYMEN

WORICK ARCANGELO

NICOLAS BROWN

THEO'S CLINIC

DR. THEO

THE POLICE

ALEX BENEDETTO

NINA

CODY BALFOUR

CHAD ADKINS

CRISTIANO FAMILY

MARCO ADRIANO

PAULKLEE GUILD

STORY

GANGSTA._NO_003

2012070900003

In Ergastulum, a tough town run by the Mafia, the "Handymen" Nicolas and Worick make a living doing odd jobs for their clients, from routine deliveries to extrajudicial killings. The men are respected by both the police brass and the Mafia bosses, not least because Nicolas is a "Twilight," an ex-mercenary possessing extraordinary abilities. The hidden history of how the scion of an elite family and a boy soldier of the Twilight ranks formed an unbreakable bond now comes to light.

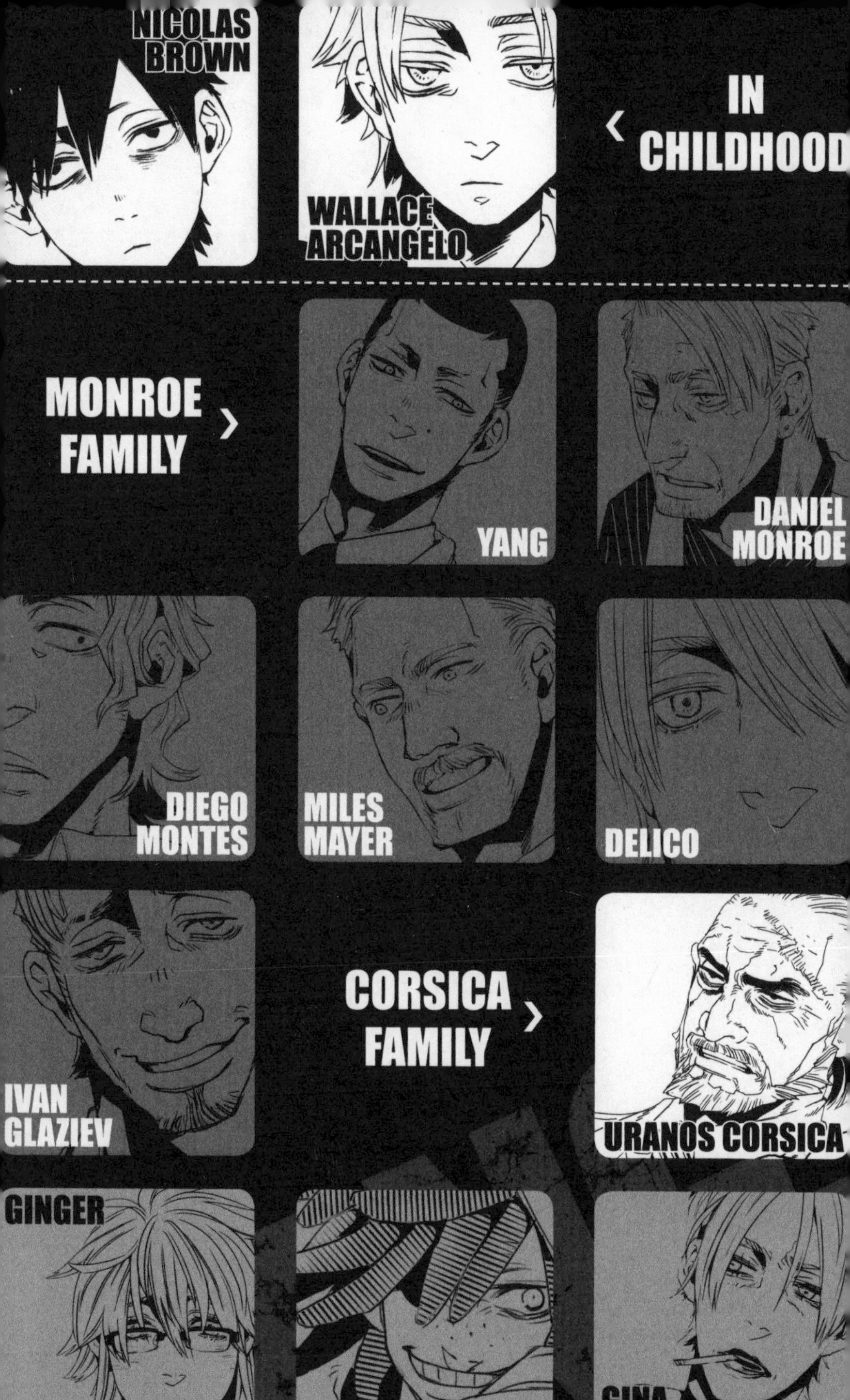

IN CHILDHOOD
WALLACE ARCANGELO
NICOLAS BROWN
DANIEL MONROE
YANG
MONROE FAMILY
DELICO
MILES MAYER
DIEGO MONTES
URANOS CORSICA
CORSICA FAMILY
IVAN GLAZIEV
GINA PAULKLEE
DOUG
GINGER

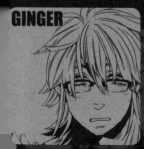

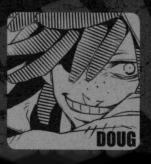

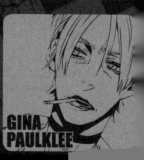

GANGSTA

CONTENTS

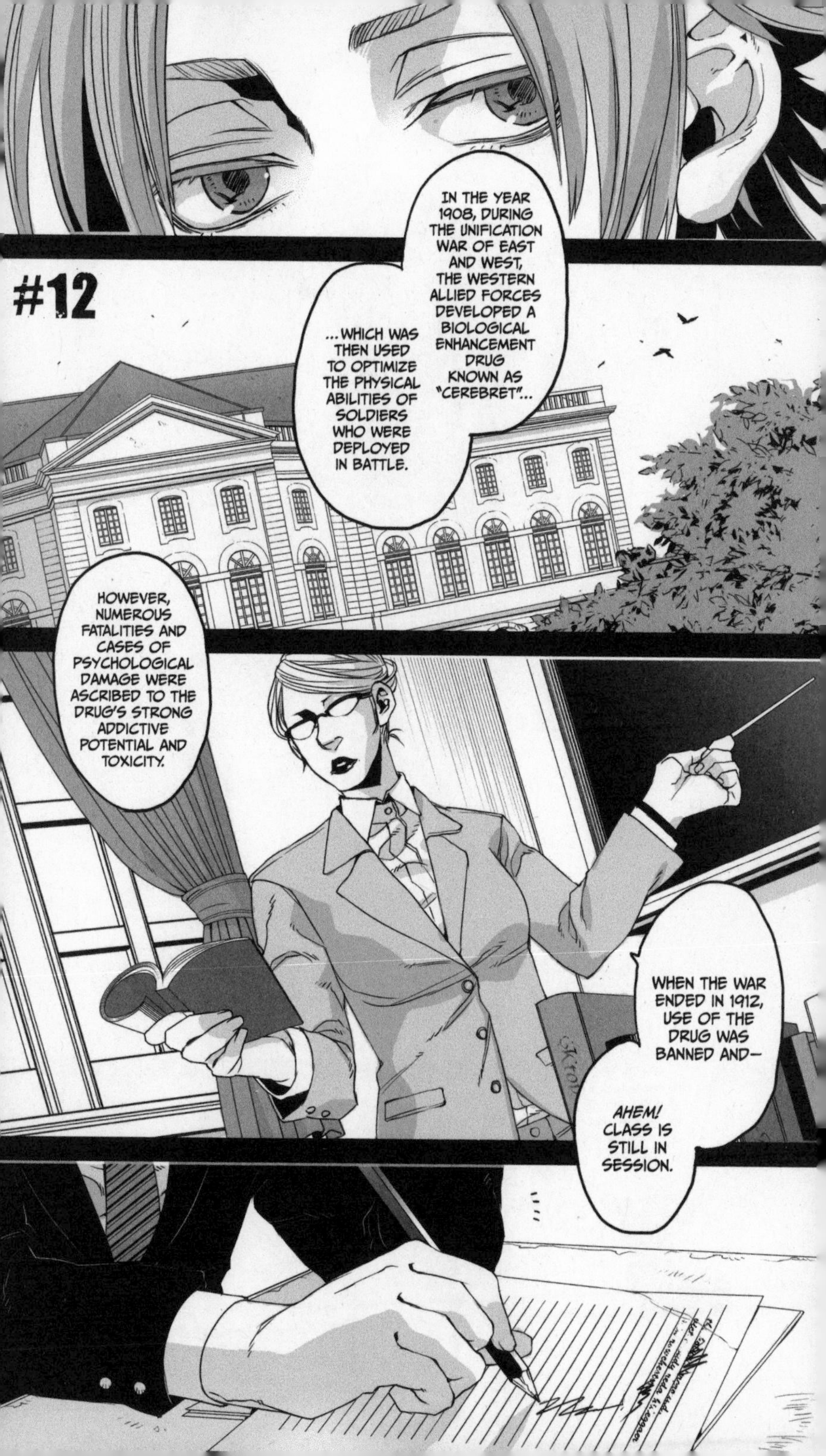
#12
IN THE YEAR 1908, DURING THE UNIFICATION WAR OF EAST AND WEST, THE WESTERN ALLIED FORCES DEVELOPED A BIOLOGICAL ENHANCEMENT DRUG KNOWN AS "CEREBRET"...
...WHICH WAS THEN USED TO OPTIMIZE THE PHYSICAL ABILITIES OF SOLDIERS WHO WERE DEPLOYED IN BATTLE.
HOWEVER, NUMEROUS FATALITIES AND CASES OF PSYCHOLOGICAL DAMAGE WERE ASCRIBED TO THE DRUG'S STRONG ADDICTIVE POTENTIAL AND TOXICITY.
WHEN THE WAR ENDED IN 1912, USE OF THE DRUG WAS BANNED AND—
AHEM! CLASS IS STILL IN SESSION.

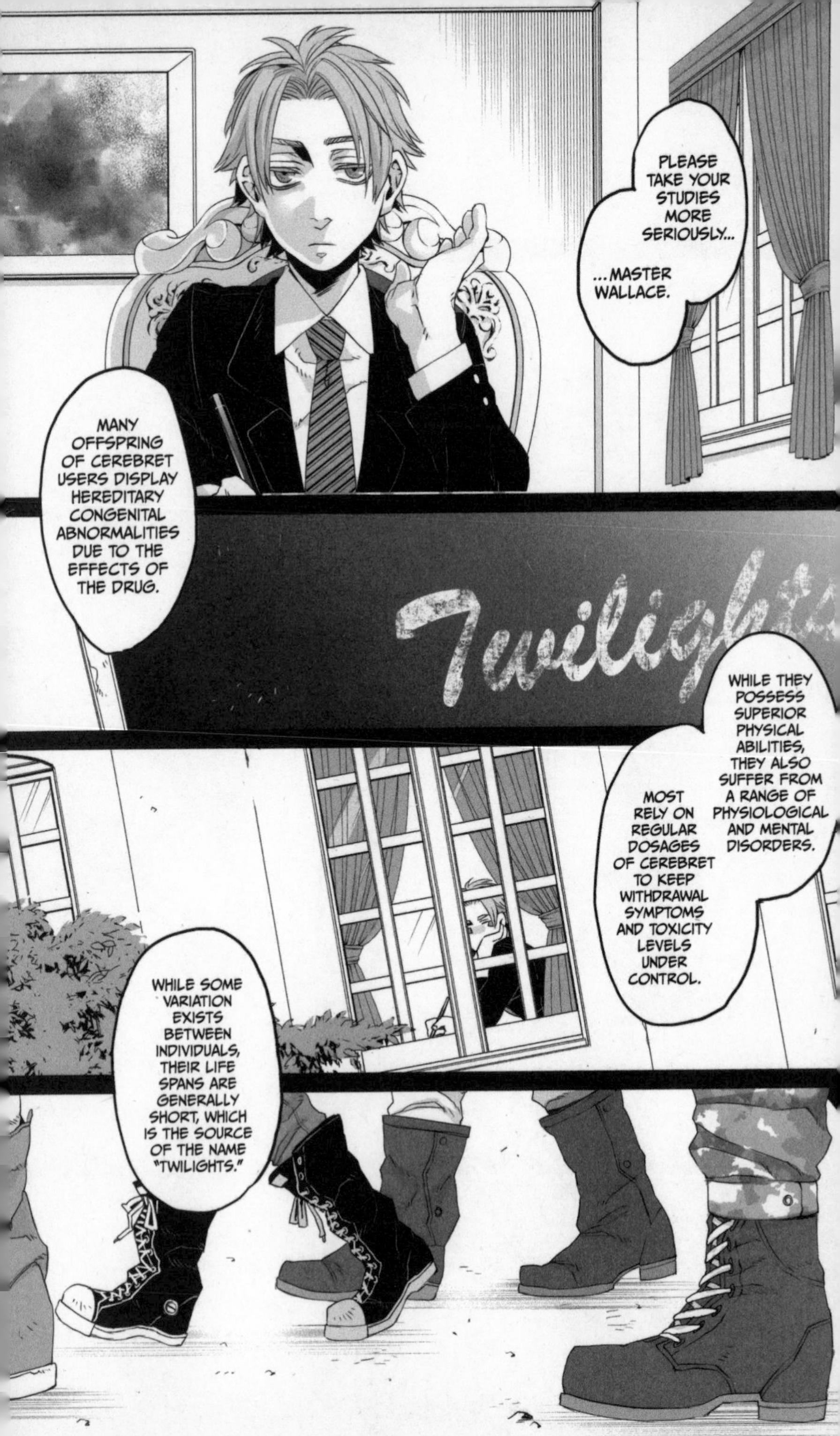
PLEASE TAKE YOUR STUDIES MORE SERIOUSLY...
...MASTER WALLACE.
MANY OFFSPRING OF CEREBRET USERS DISPLAY HEREDITARY CONGENITAL ABNORMALITIES DUE TO THE EFFECTS OF THE DRUG.
Twilight
WHILE THEY POSSESS SUPERIOR PHYSICAL ABILITIES, THEY ALSO SUFFER FROM A RANGE OF PHYSIOLOGICAL AND MENTAL DISORDERS.
MOST RELY ON REGULAR DOSAGES OF CEREBRET TO KEEP WITHDRAWAL SYMPTOMS AND TOXICITY LEVELS UNDER CONTROL.
WHILE SOME VARIATION EXISTS BETWEEN INDIVIDUALS, THEIR LIFE SPANS ARE GENERALLY SHORT, WHICH IS THE SOURCE OF THE NAME "TWILIGHTS."

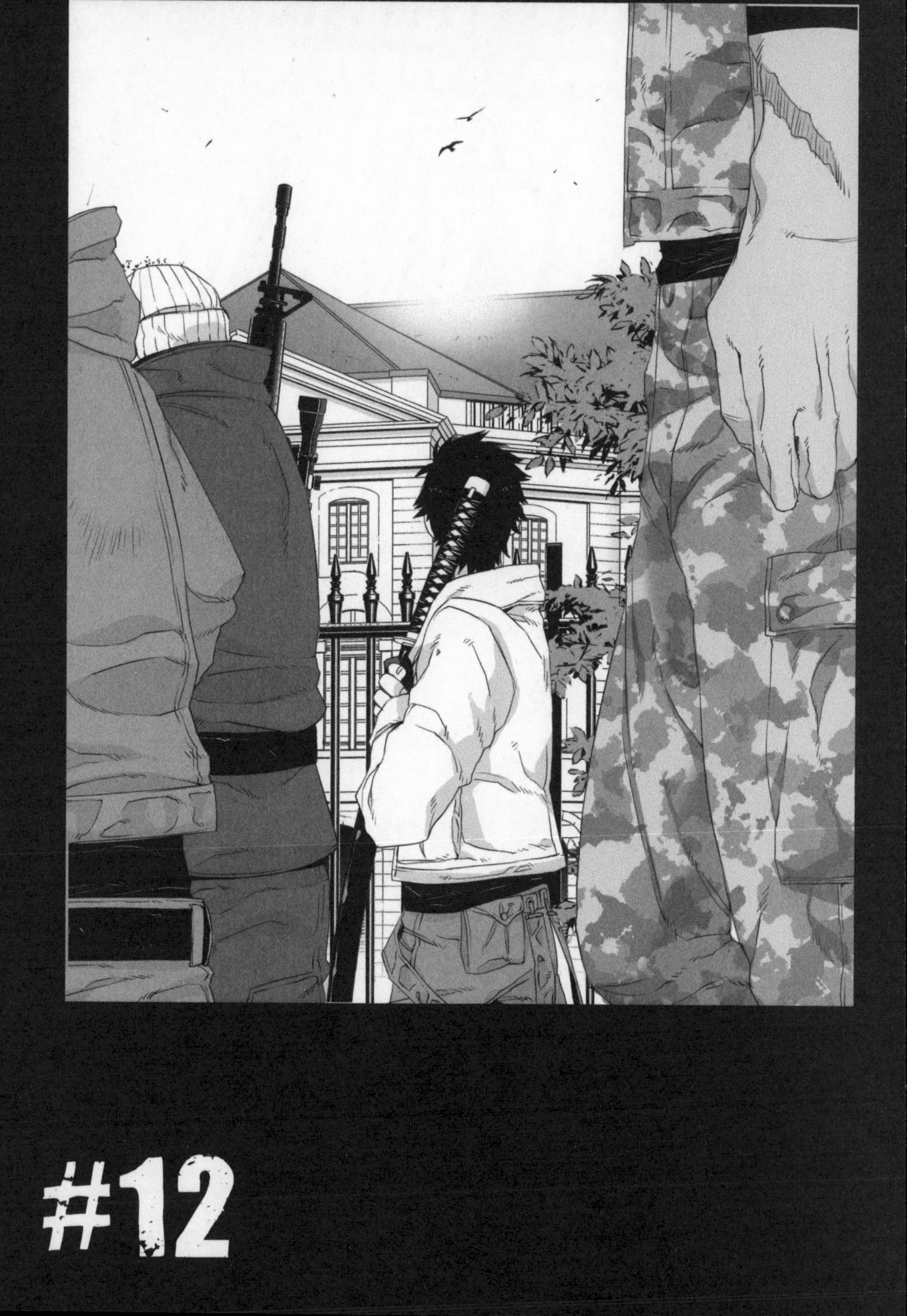

#12

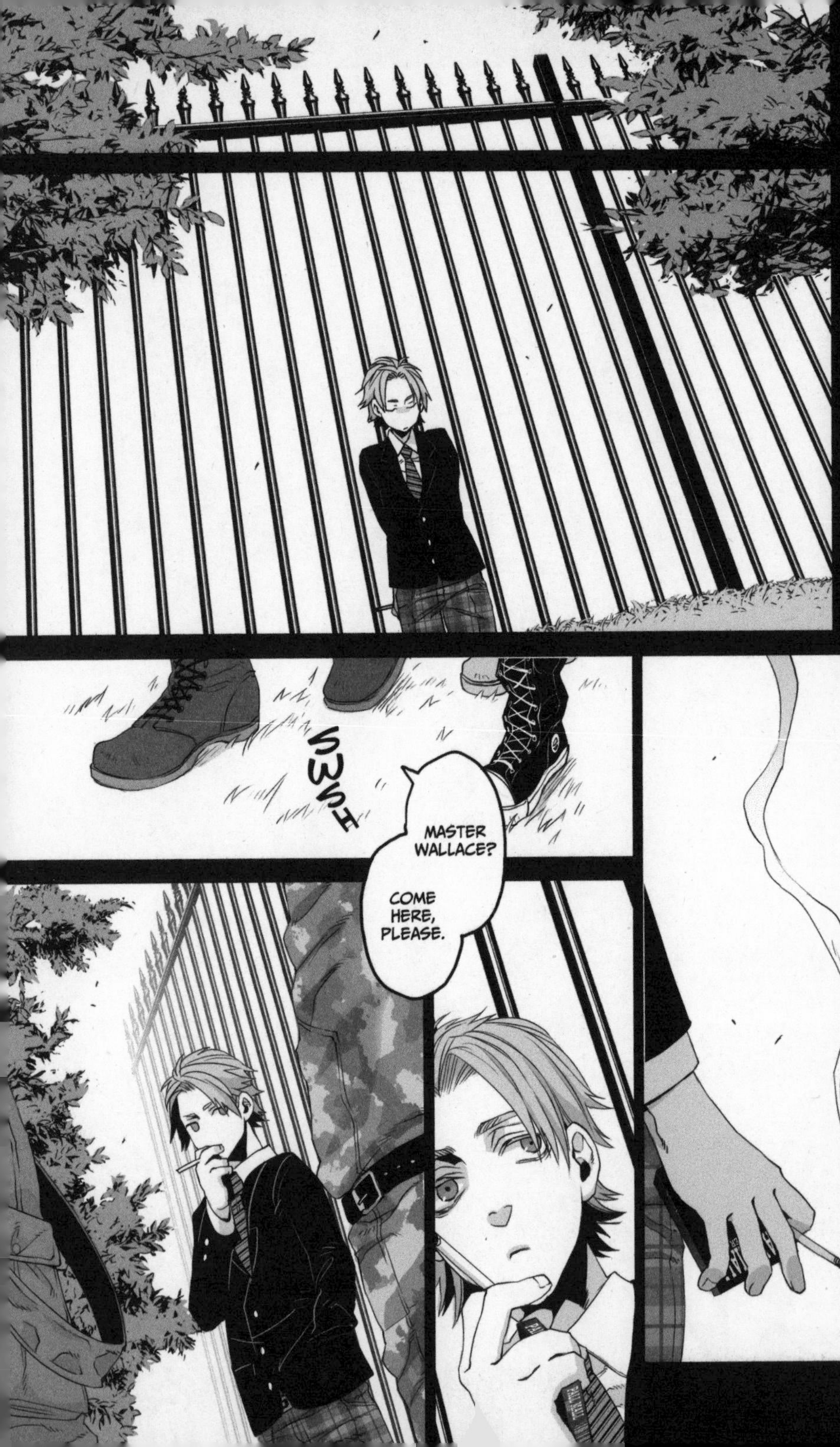
SWSH
MASTER WALLACE? COME HERE, PLEASE.

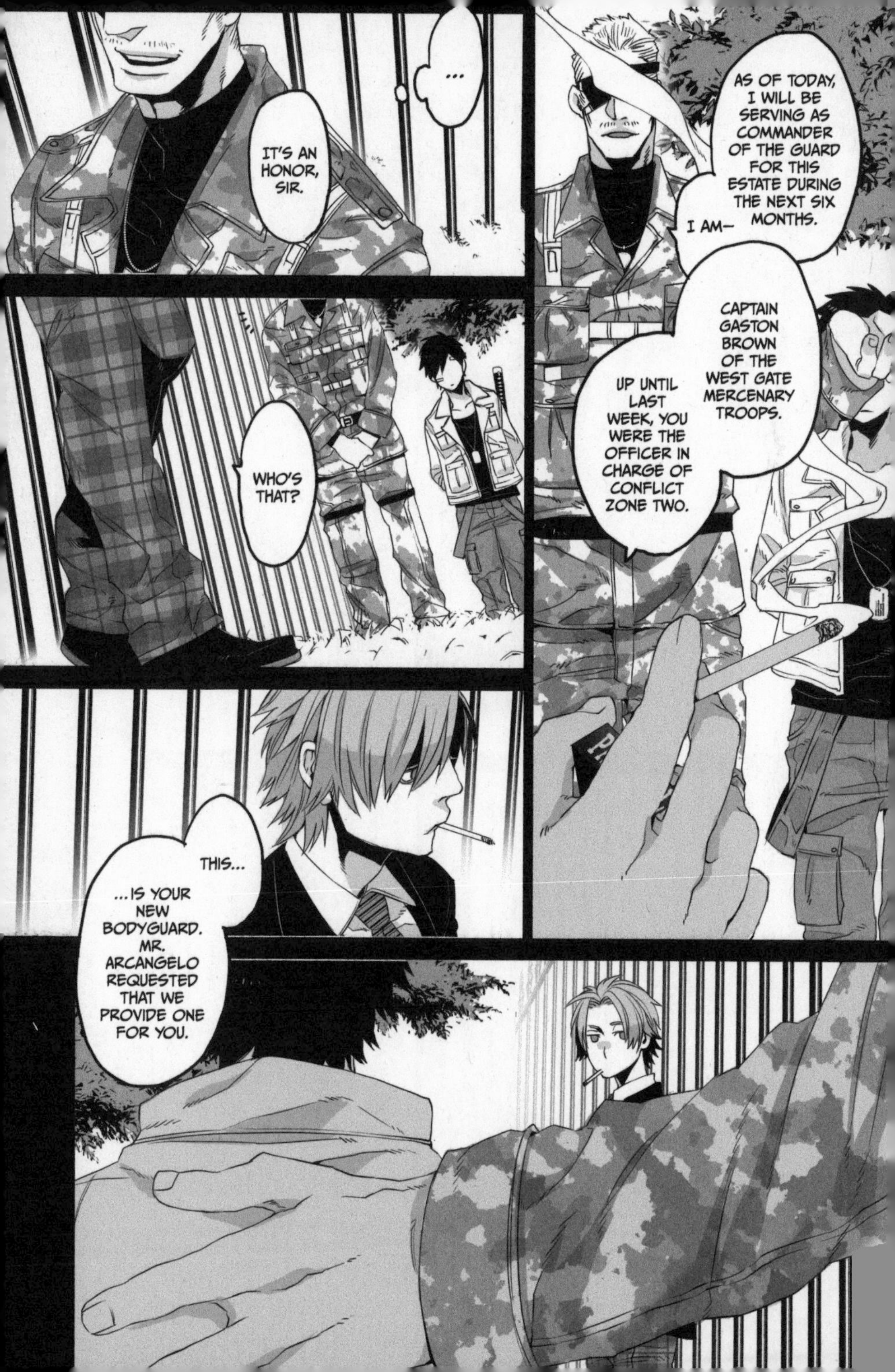

AS OF TODAY, I WILL BE SERVING AS COMMANDER OF THE GUARD FOR THIS ESTATE DURING THE NEXT SIX MONTHS.
I AM—
CAPTAIN GASTON BROWN OF THE WEST GATE MERCENARY TROOPS.
UP UNTIL LAST WEEK, YOU WERE THE OFFICER IN CHARGE OF CONFLICT ZONE TWO.
...
IT'S AN HONOR, SIR.
WHO'S THAT?
THIS...
...IS YOUR NEW BODYGUARD. MR. ARCANGELO REQUESTED THAT WE PROVIDE ONE FOR YOU.

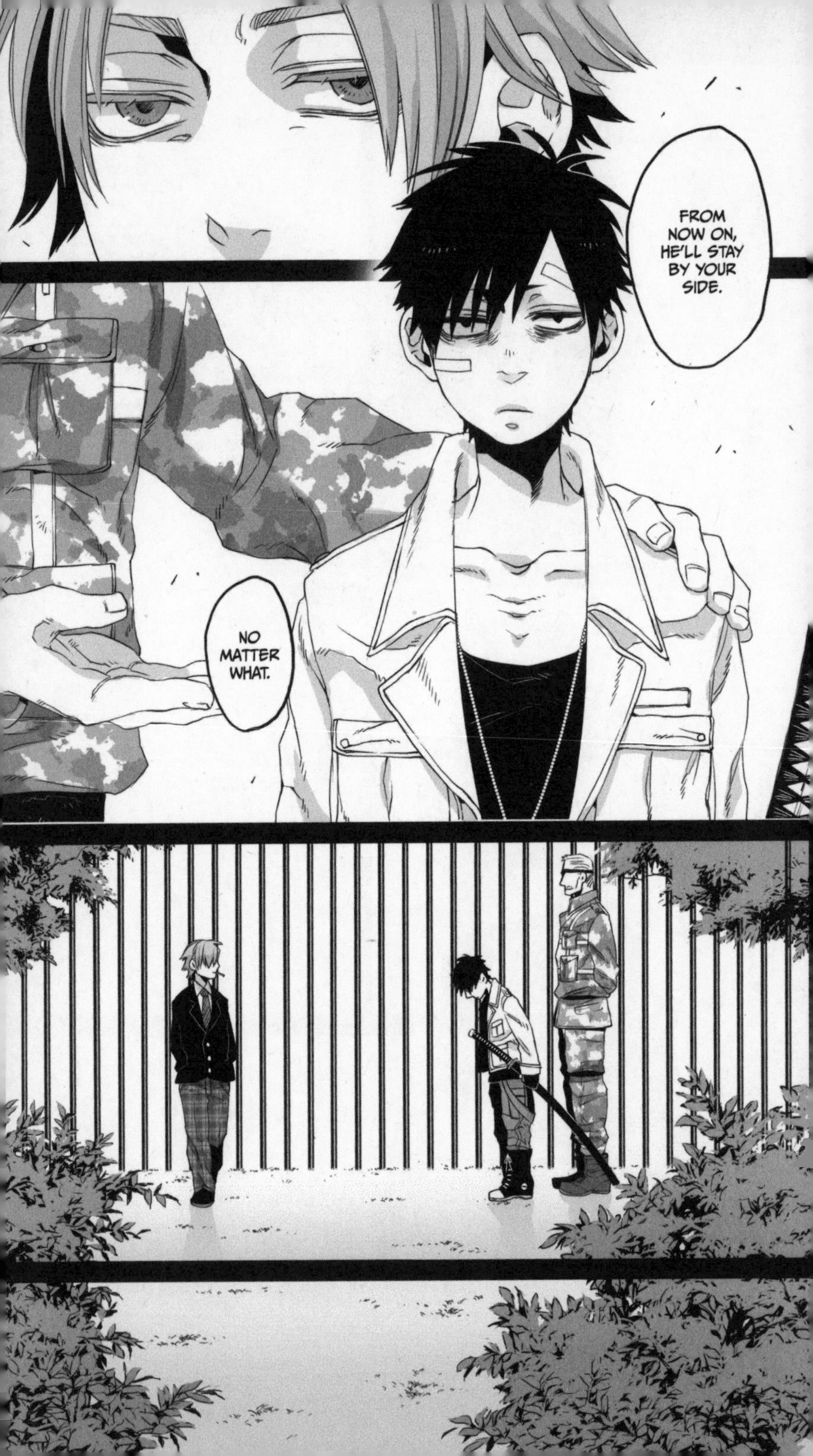
FROM NOW ON, HE'LL STAY BY YOUR SIDE.
NO MATTER WHAT.

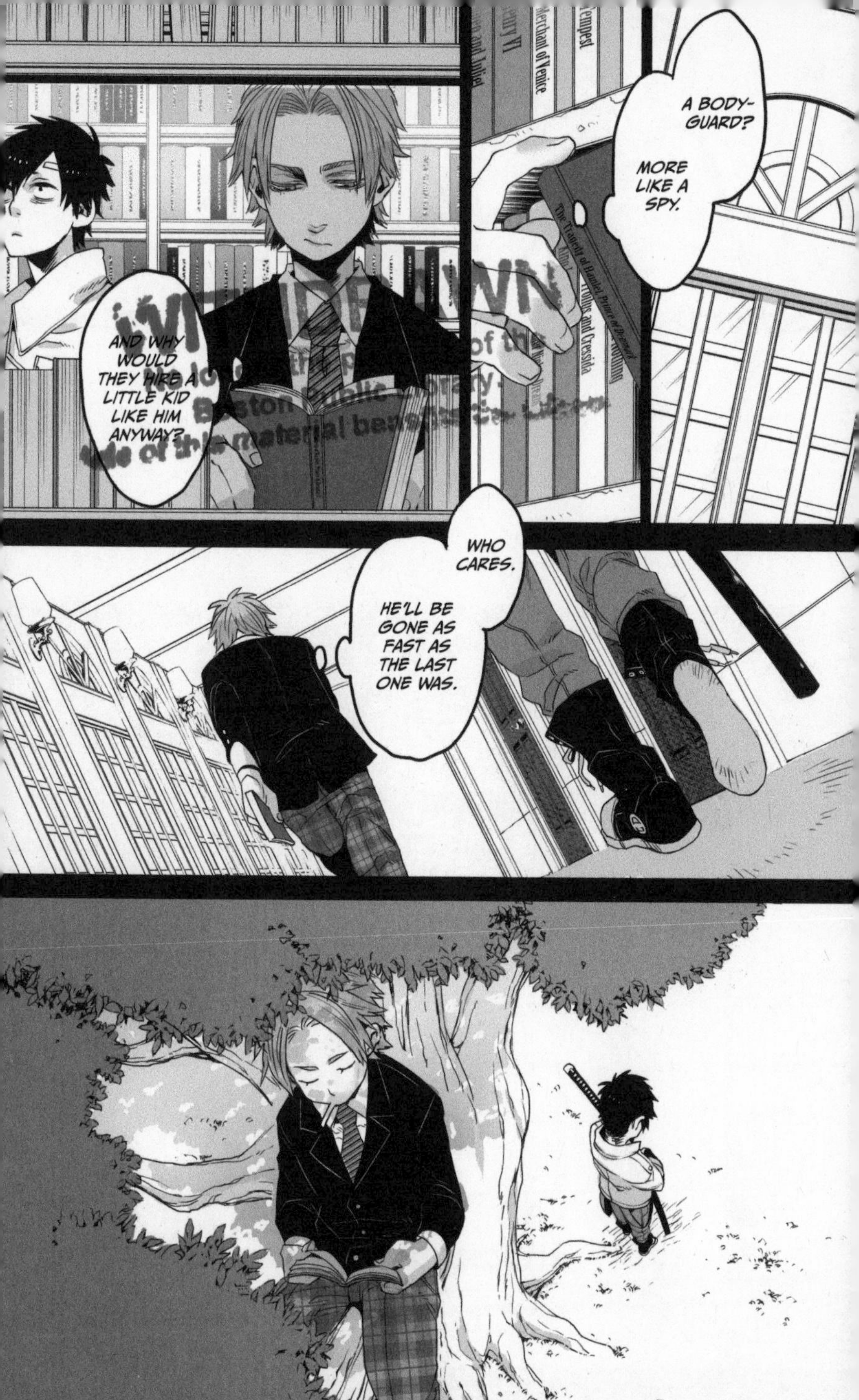
A BODY-GUARD?
MORE LIKE A SPY.
AND WHY WOULD THEY HIRE A LITTLE KID LIKE HIM ANYWAY?
WHO CARES.
HE'LL BE GONE AS FAST AS THE LAST ONE WAS.

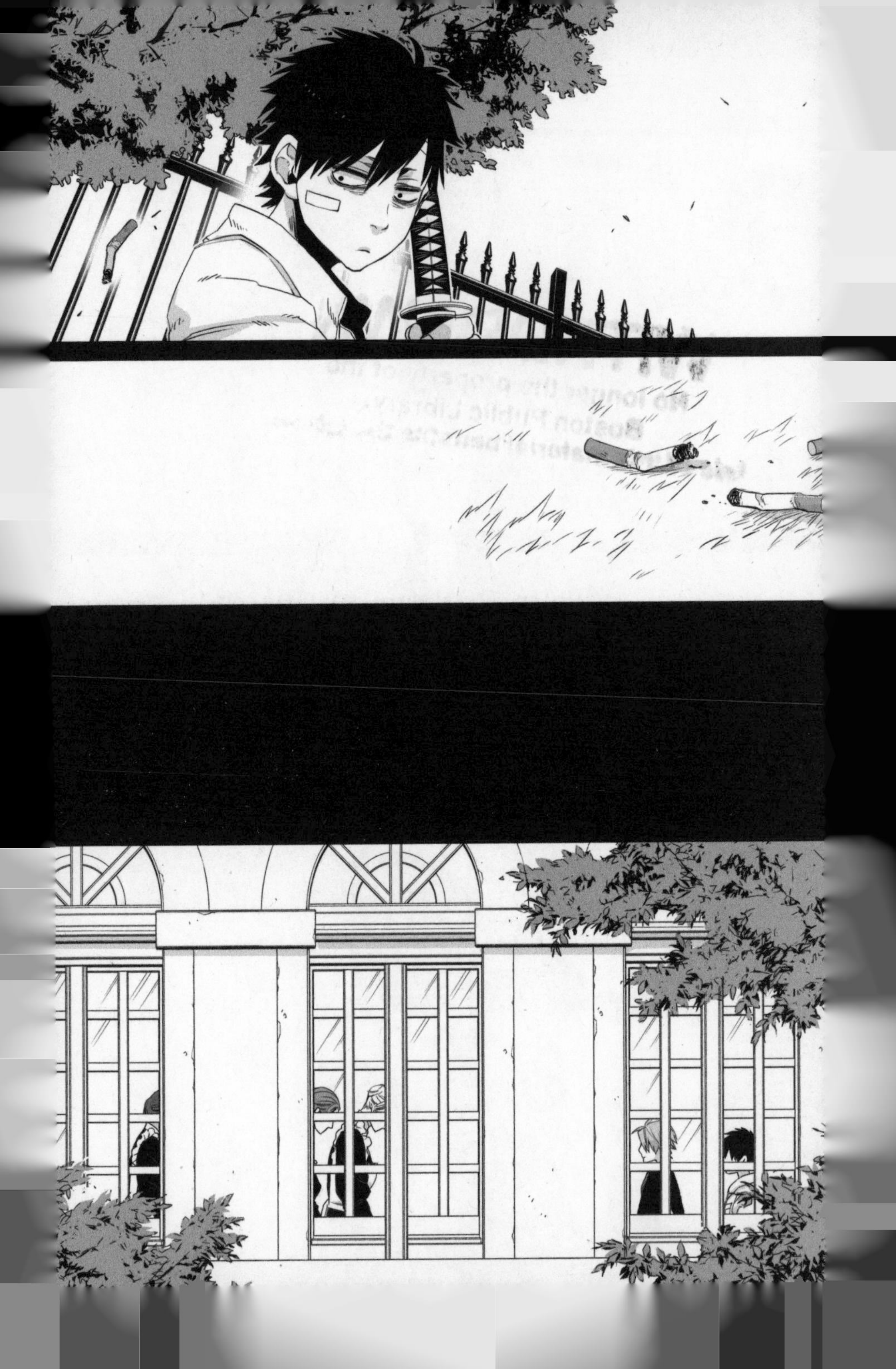

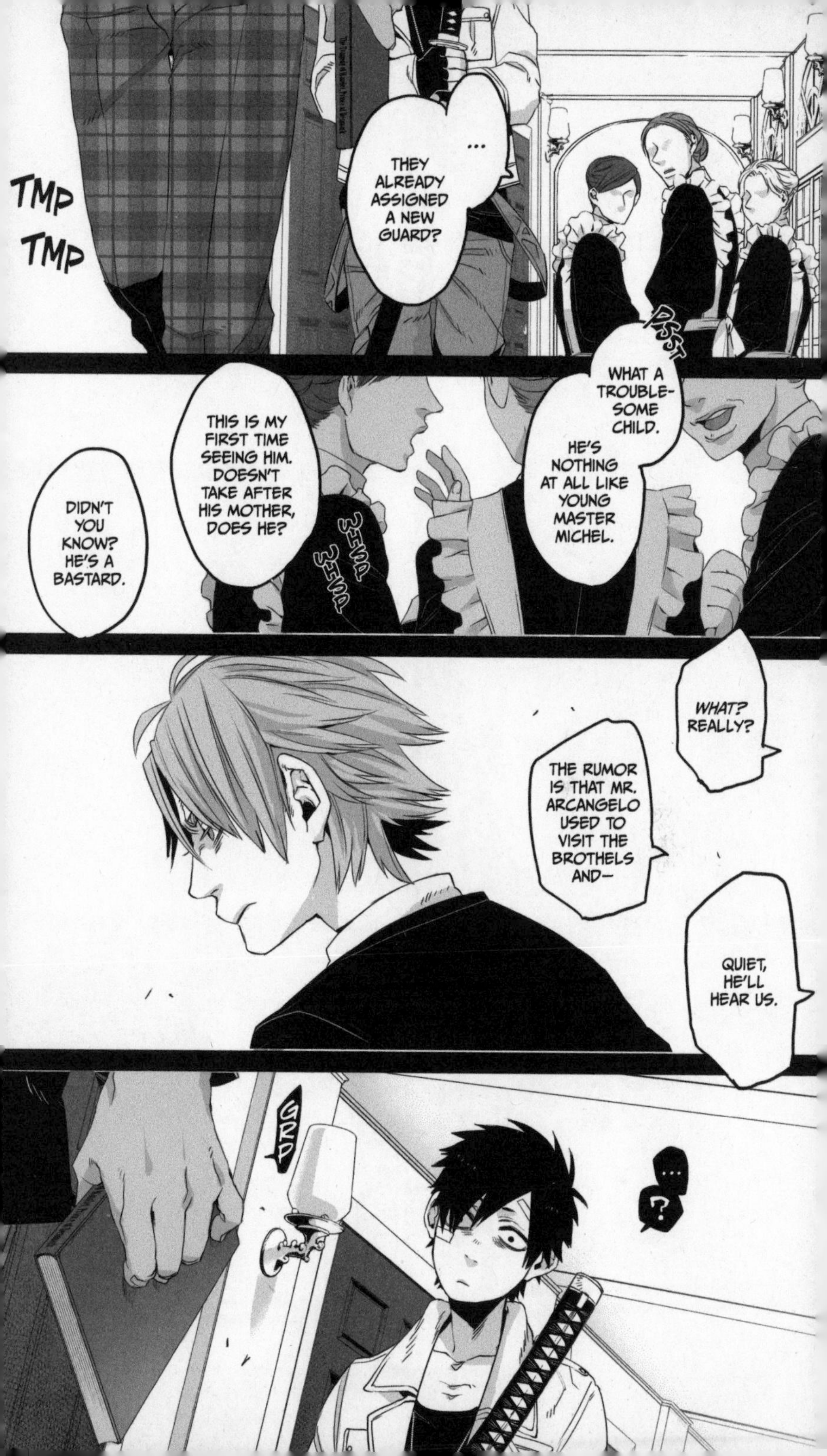
...
THEY ALREADY ASSIGNED A NEW GUARD?
TMP TMP
PSST
WHAT A TROUBLE-SOME CHILD.
HE'S NOTHING AT ALL LIKE YOUNG MASTER MICHEL.
THIS IS MY FIRST TIME SEEING HIM. DOESN'T TAKE AFTER HIS MOTHER, DOES HE?
WHSP WHSP
DIDN'T YOU KNOW? HE'S A BASTARD.
WHAT? REALLY?
THE RUMOR IS THAT MR. ARCANGELO USED TO VISIT THE BROTHELS AND—
QUIET, HE'LL HEAR US.
...
?
GRP

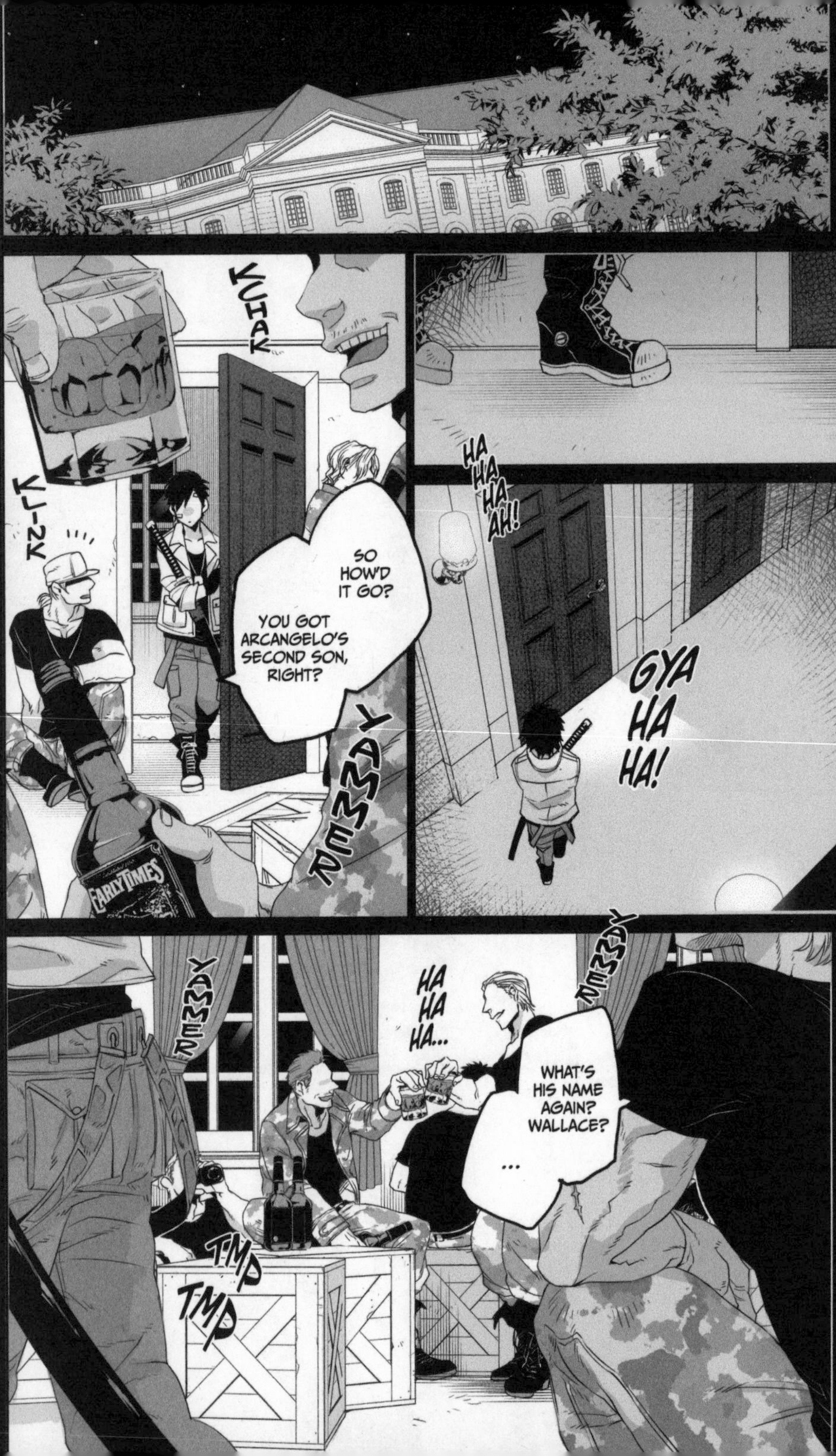
HA HA HA AH!
GYA HA HA HA!
KCHAK
SO HOW'D IT GO?
YOU GOT ARCANGELO'S SECOND SON, RIGHT?
KLINK
YAMMER
EARLY TIMES
YAMMER
WHAT'S HIS NAME AGAIN? WALLACE?
...
HA HA HA HA...
YAMMER
TMP TMP

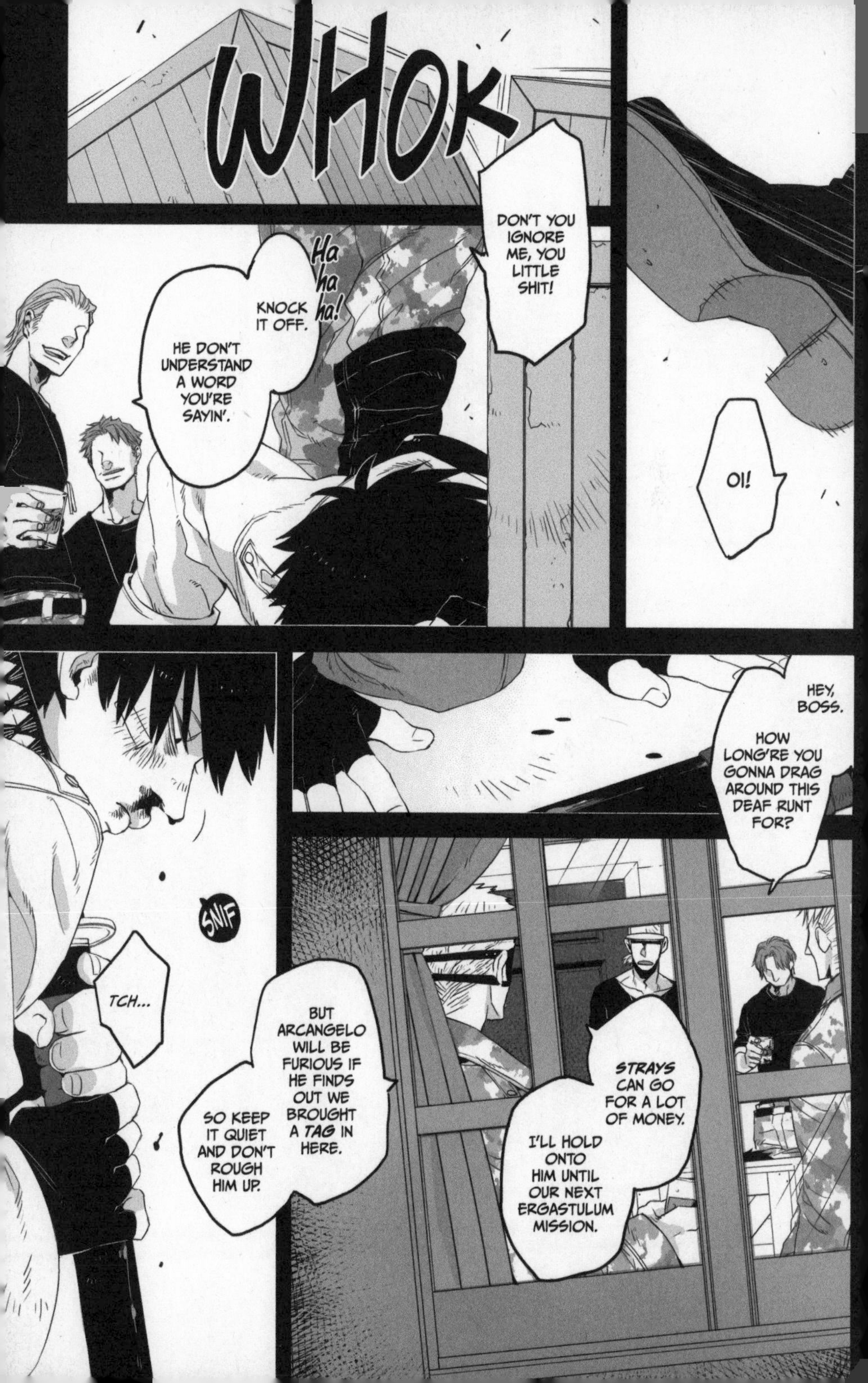
OI!
WHOK
DON'T YOU IGNORE ME, YOU LITTLE SHIT!
Ha ha ha!
KNOCK IT OFF.
HE DON'T UNDERSTAND A WORD YOU'RE SAYIN'.
HEY, BOSS.
HOW LONG'RE YOU GONNA DRAG AROUND THIS DEAF RUNT FOR?
STRAYS CAN GO FOR A LOT OF MONEY.
I'LL HOLD ONTO HIM UNTIL OUR NEXT ERGASTULUM MISSION.
BUT ARCANGELO WILL BE FURIOUS IF HE FINDS OUT WE BROUGHT A TAG IN HERE.
SO KEEP IT QUIET AND DON'T ROUGH HIM UP.
SNIF
TCH...

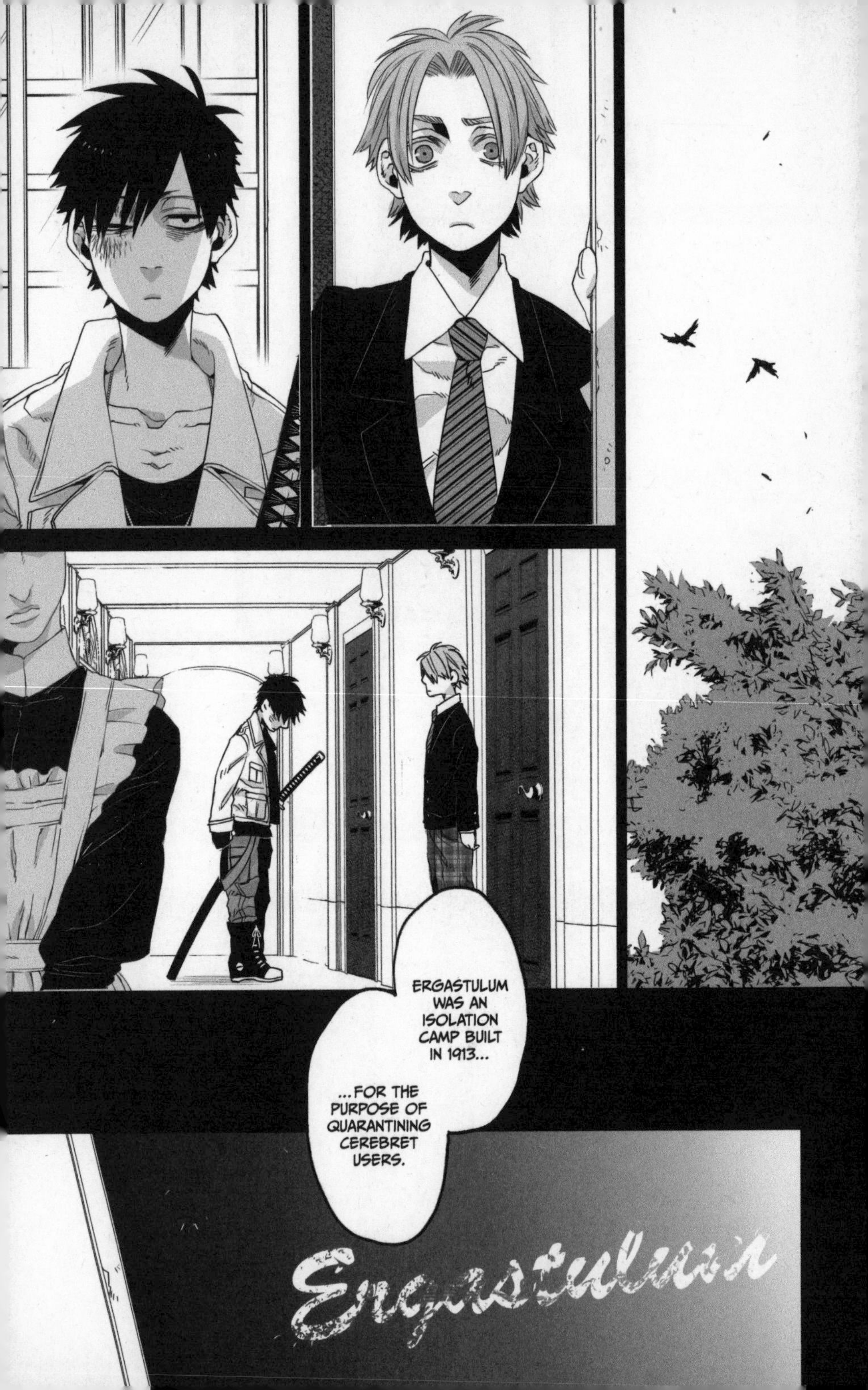
ERGASTULUM WAS AN ISOLATION CAMP BUILT IN 1913...
...FOR THE PURPOSE OF QUARANTINING CEREBRET USERS.
Ergastulum

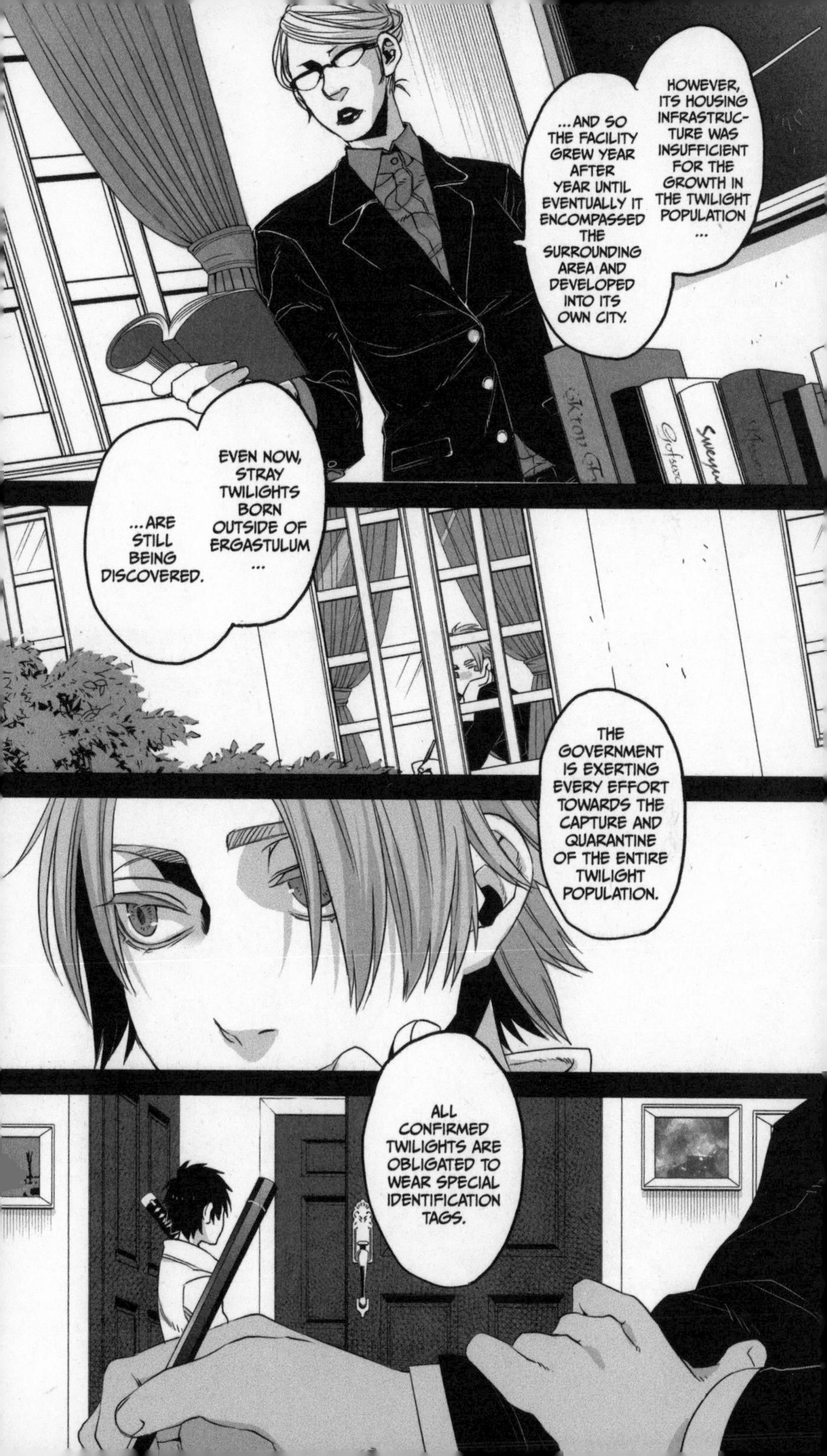
HOWEVER, ITS HOUSING INFRASTRUCTURE WAS INSUFFICIENT FOR THE GROWTH IN THE TWILIGHT POPULATION ...
...AND SO THE FACILITY GREW YEAR AFTER YEAR UNTIL EVENTUALLY IT ENCOMPASSED THE SURROUNDING AREA AND DEVELOPED INTO ITS OWN CITY.
EVEN NOW, STRAY TWILIGHTS BORN OUTSIDE OF ERGASTULUM ...
...ARE STILL BEING DISCOVERED.
THE GOVERNMENT IS EXERTING EVERY EFFORT TOWARDS THE CAPTURE AND QUARANTINE OF THE ENTIRE TWILIGHT POPULATION.
ALL CONFIRMED TWILIGHTS ARE OBLIGATED TO WEAR SPECIAL IDENTIFICATION TAGS.

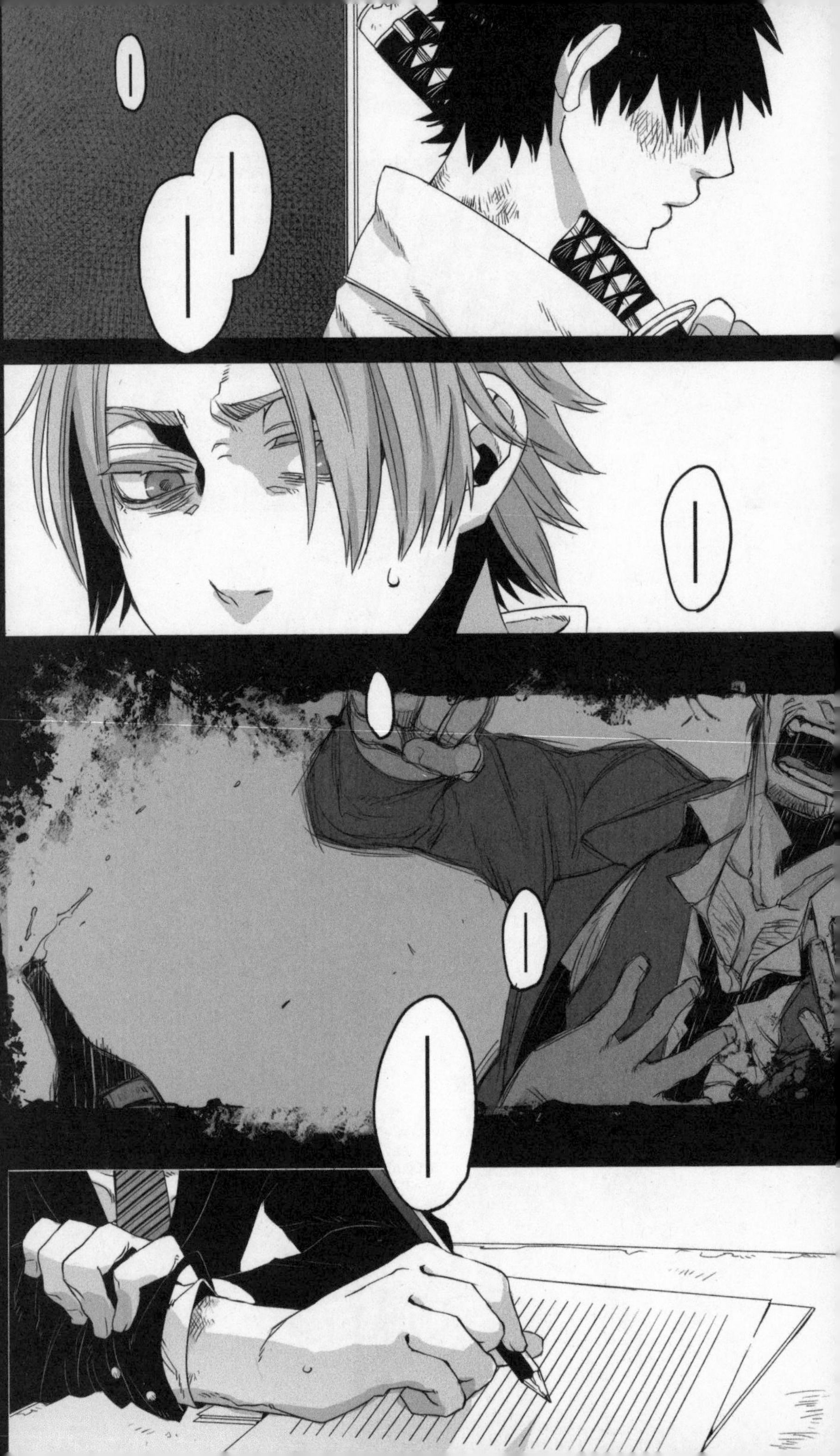

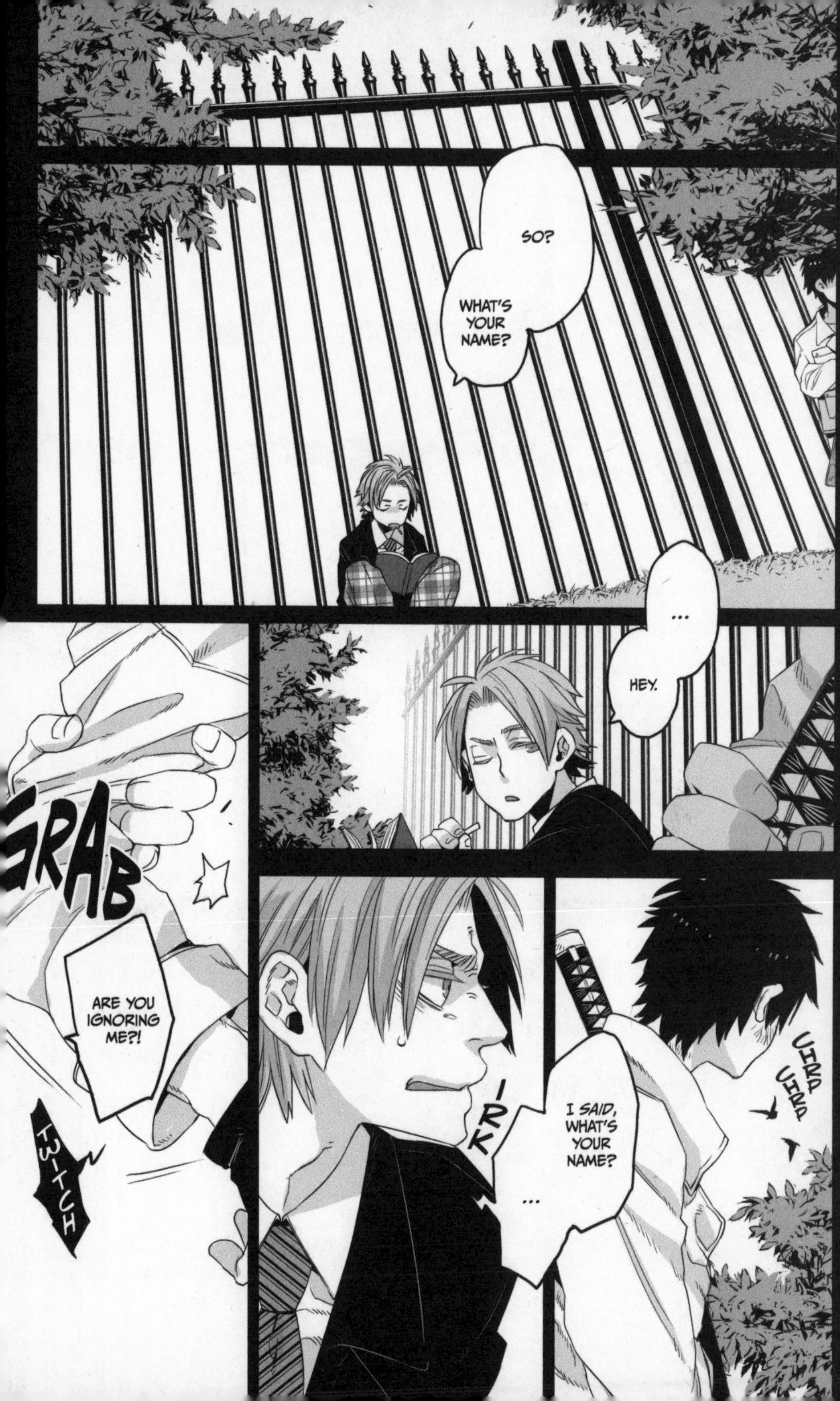
SO?
WHAT'S YOUR NAME?
...
HEY.
CHRP CHRP
I SAID, WHAT'S YOUR NAME?
IRK
...
GRAB
ARE YOU IGNORING ME?!
TWITCH

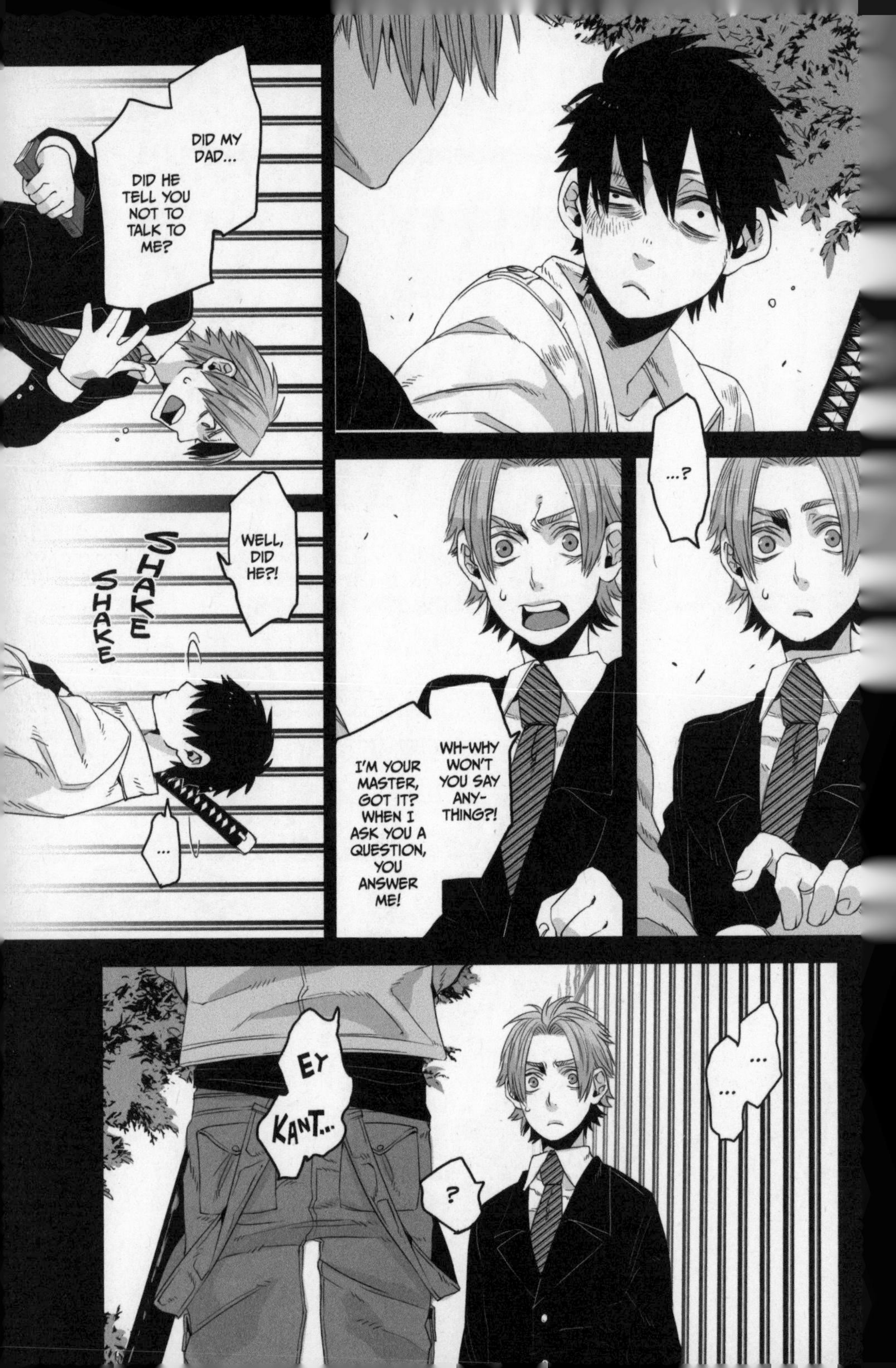

DID MY DAD... DID HE TELL YOU NOT TO TALK TO ME?
...?
WH-WHY WON'T YOU SAY ANY-THING?!
I'M YOUR MASTER, GOT IT? WHEN I ASK YOU A QUESTION, YOU ANSWER ME!
WELL, DID HE?!
SHAKE SHAKE
...
EY KANT...
?
... ...

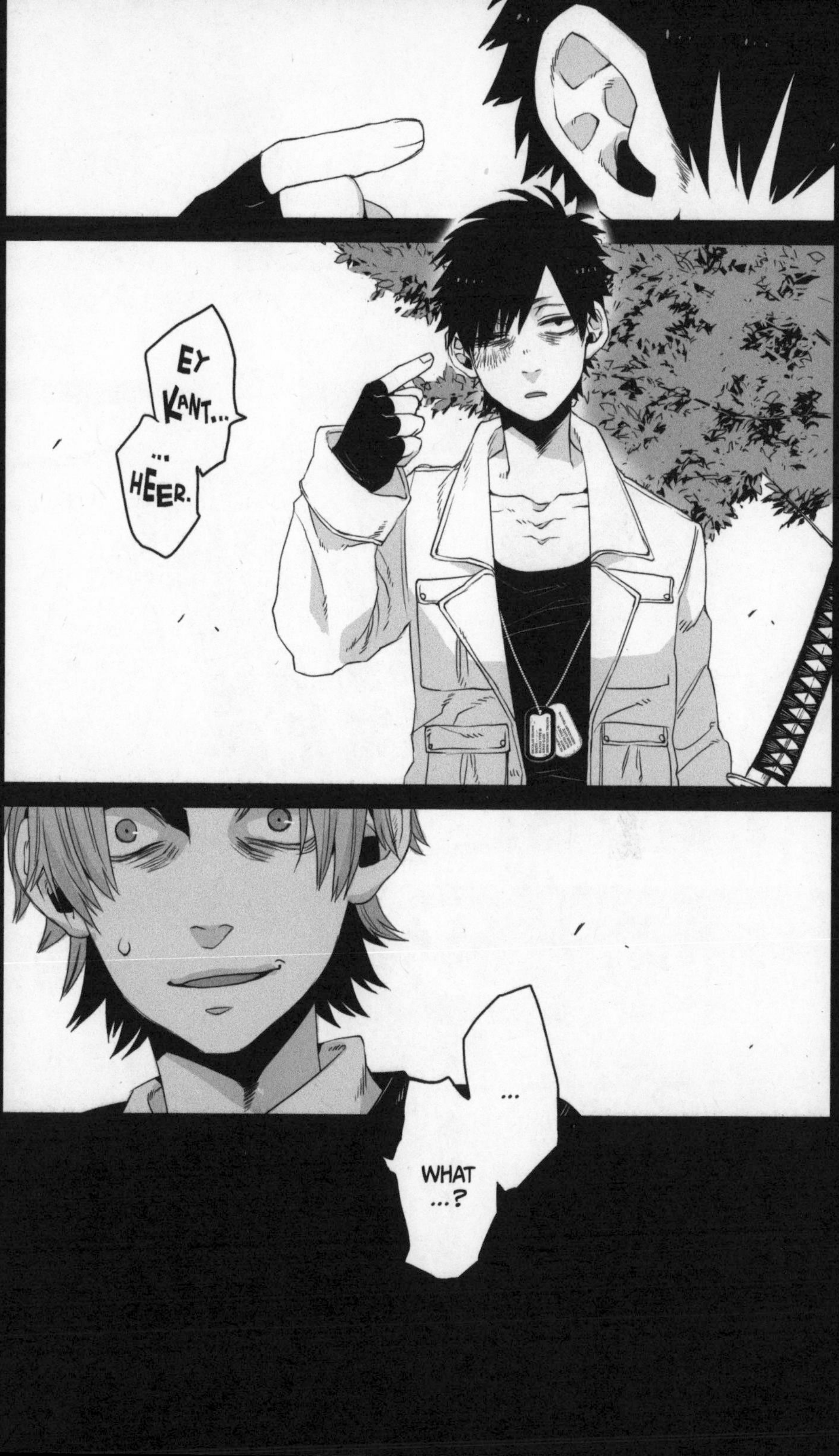
EY KANT...
... HEER.
...
WHAT ...?

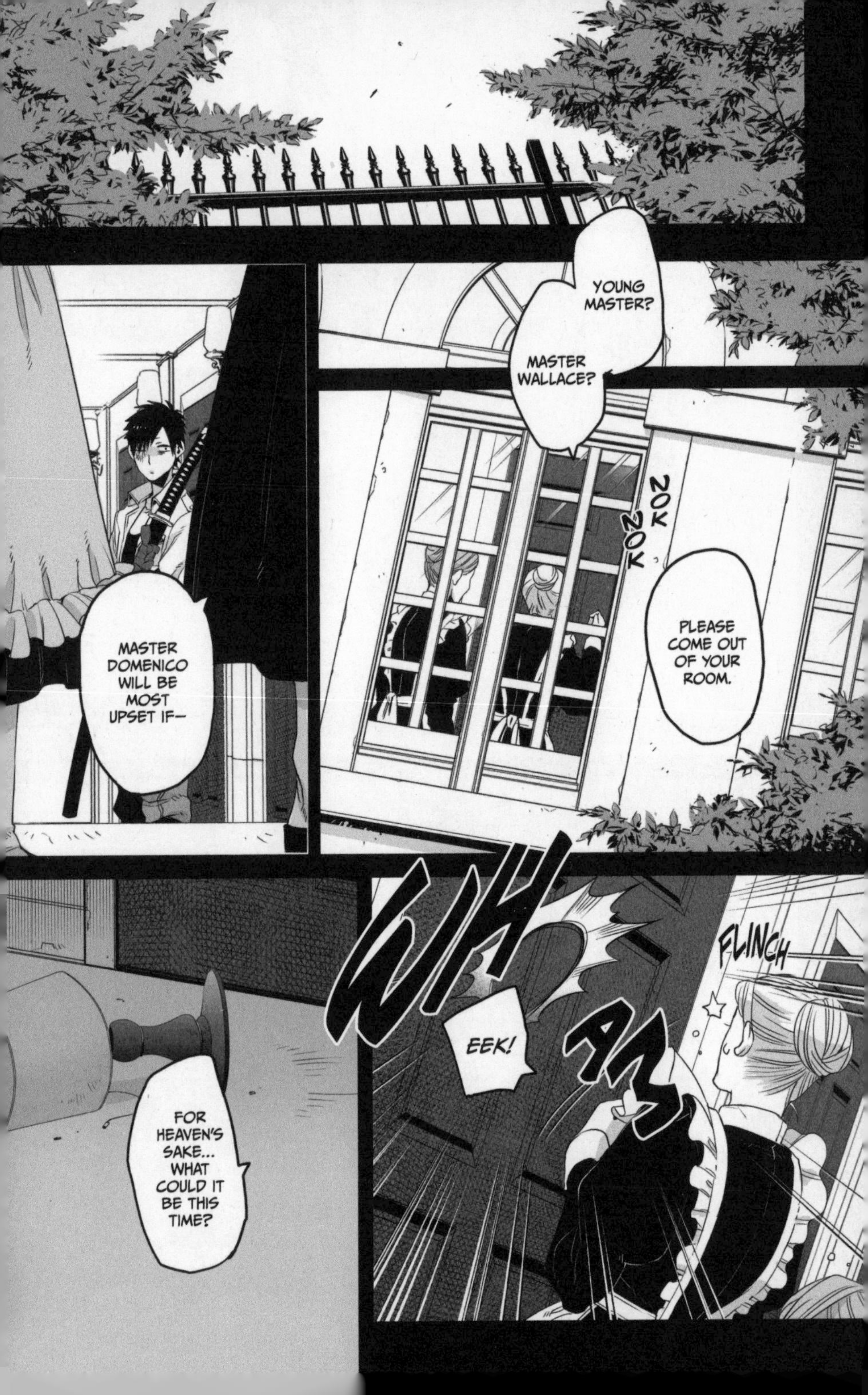
YOUNG MASTER?
MASTER WALLACE?
NOK NOK
PLEASE COME OUT OF YOUR ROOM.
MASTER DOMENICO WILL BE MOST UPSET IF—
FLINCH
WHAM
EEK!
FOR HEAVEN'S SAKE... WHAT COULD IT BE THIS TIME?

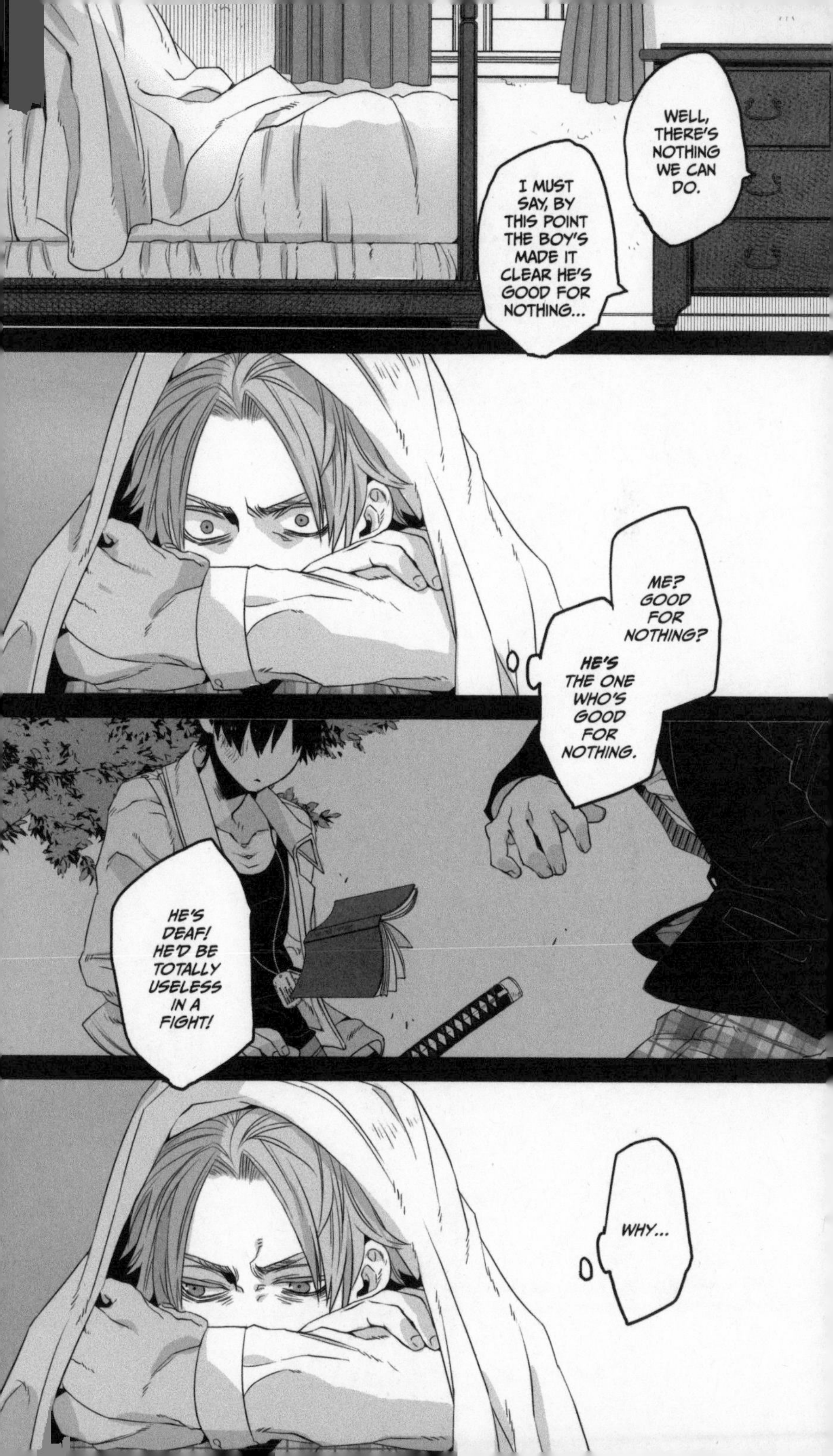
WELL, THERE'S NOTHING WE CAN DO.
I MUST SAY, BY THIS POINT THE BOY'S MADE IT CLEAR HE'S GOOD FOR NOTHING...
ME? GOOD FOR NOTHING? HE'S THE ONE WHO'S GOOD FOR NOTHING.
HE'S DEAF! HE'D BE TOTALLY USELESS IN A FIGHT!
WHY...

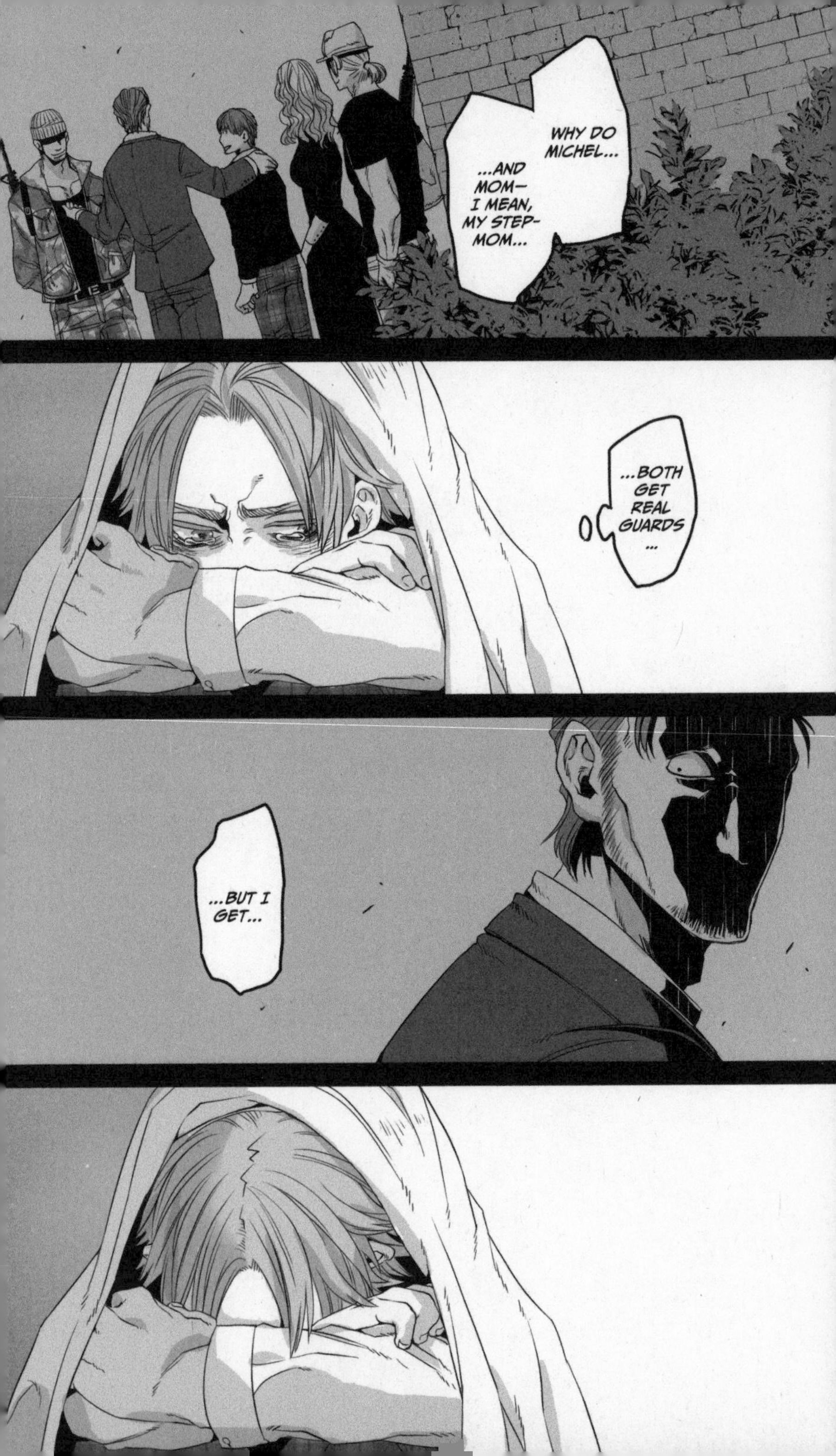
WHY DO MICHEL...
...AND MOM— I MEAN, MY STEP-MOM...
...BOTH GET REAL GUARDS ...
...BUT I GET...

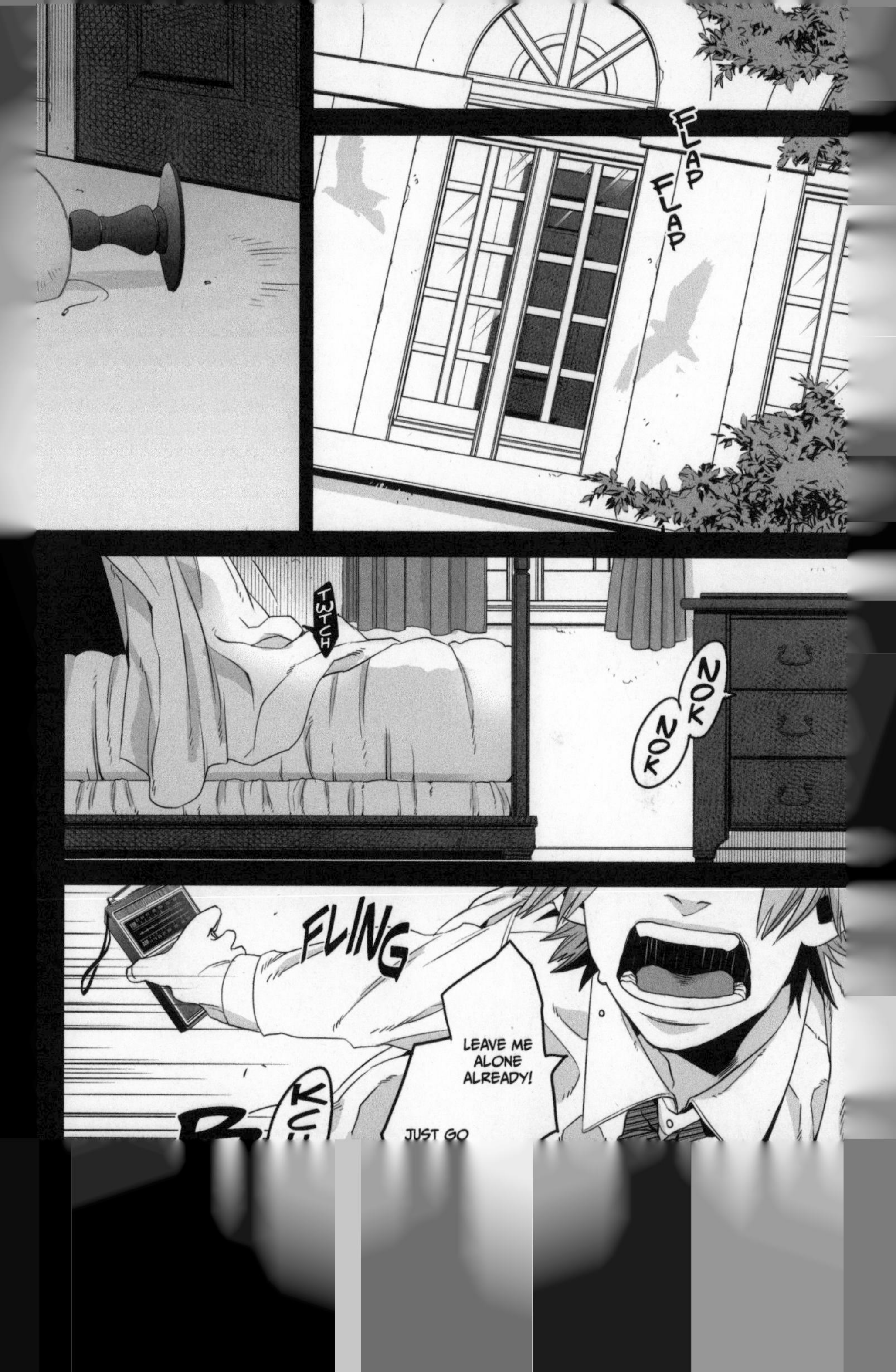
FLAP FLAP
NOK NOK
TWITCH
FLING
LEAVE ME ALONE ALREADY!
JUST GO

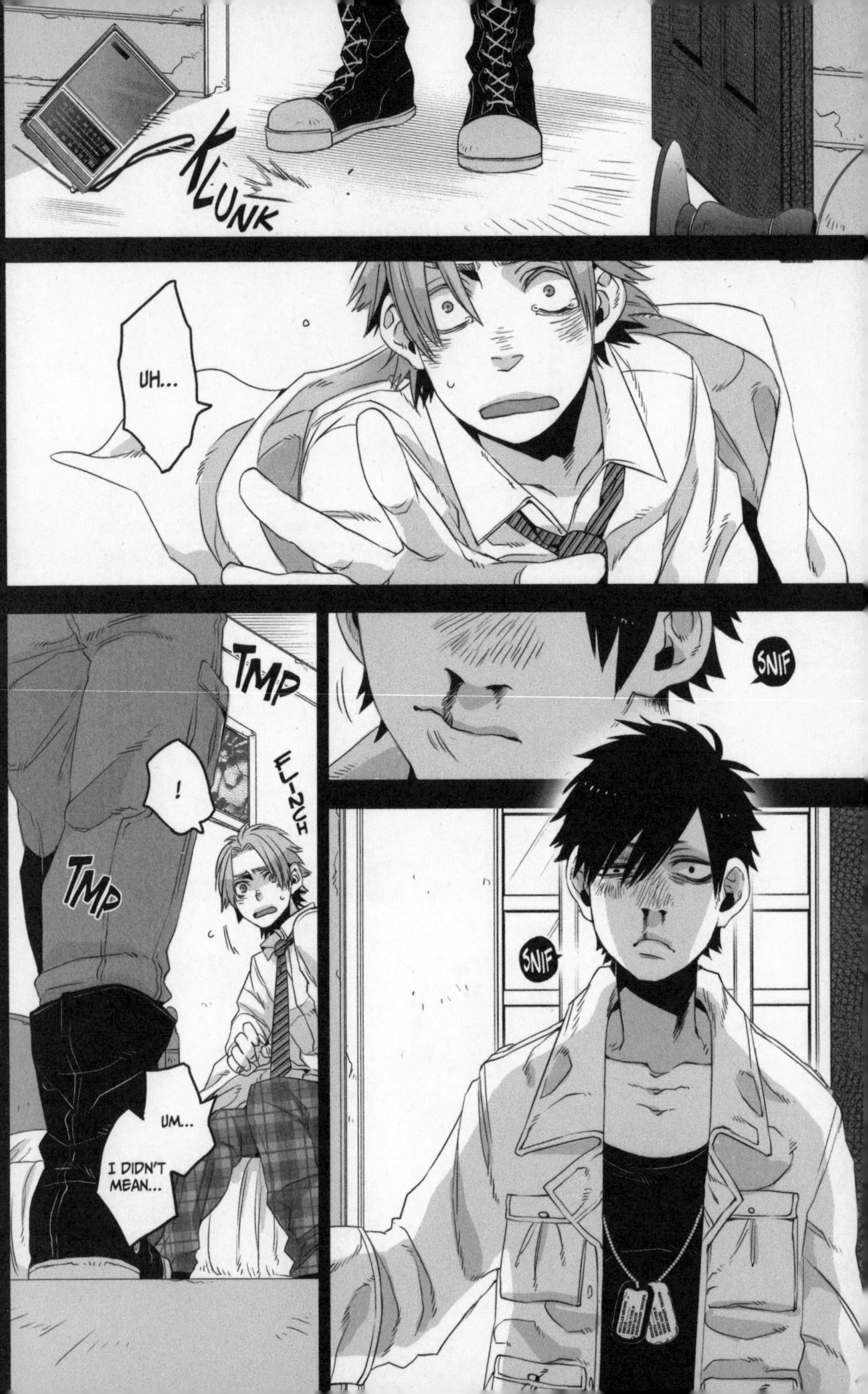
KLUNK
UH...
SNIF
SNIF
TMP
FLINCH
!
TMP
UM...
I DIDN'T MEAN...

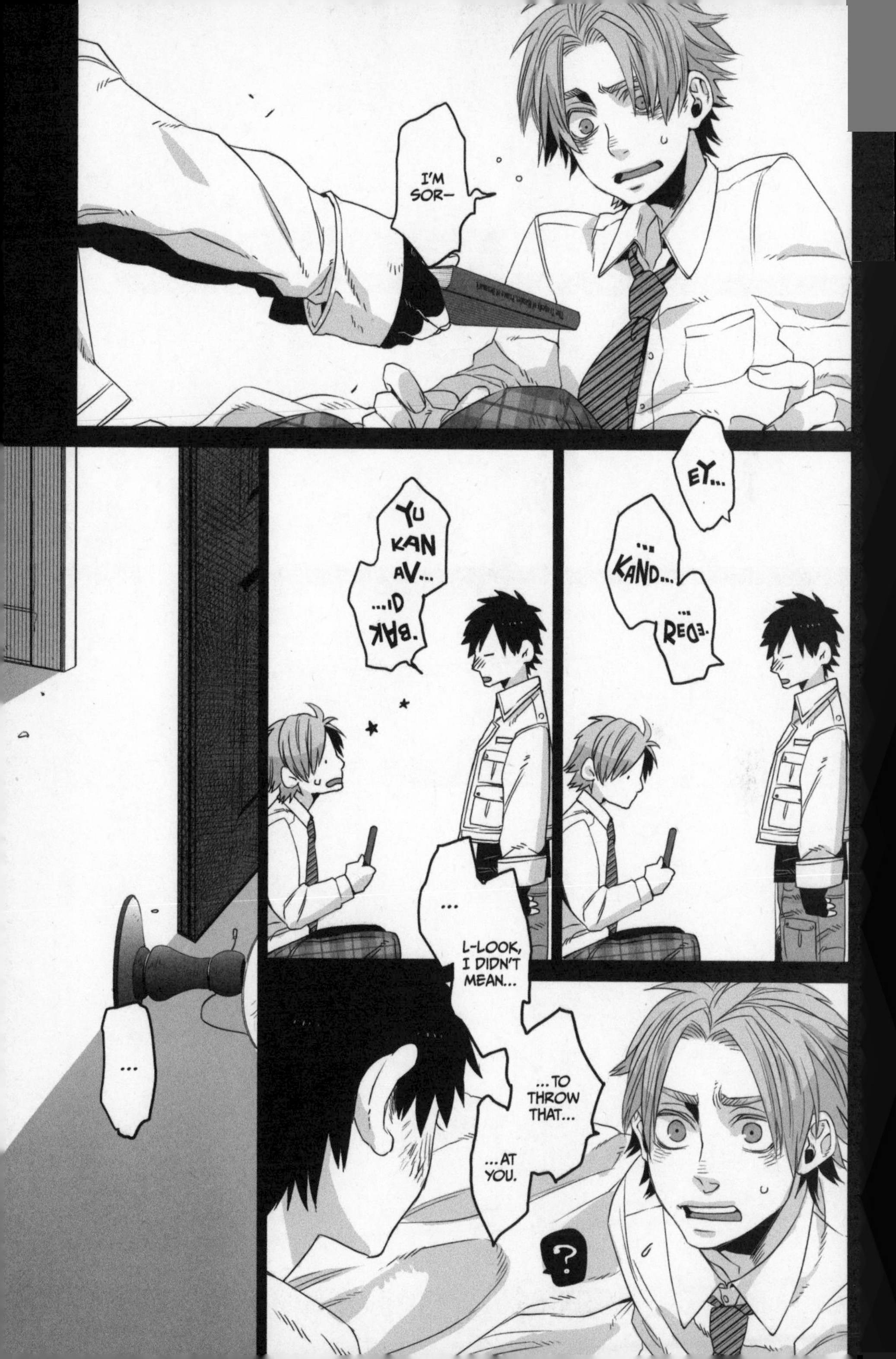
I'M SOR—
EY...
...KAND... ...REDE.
YU KAN AV... DI... BAK.
...
L-LOOK, I DIDN'T MEAN...
...TO THROW THAT...
...AT YOU.
?
...

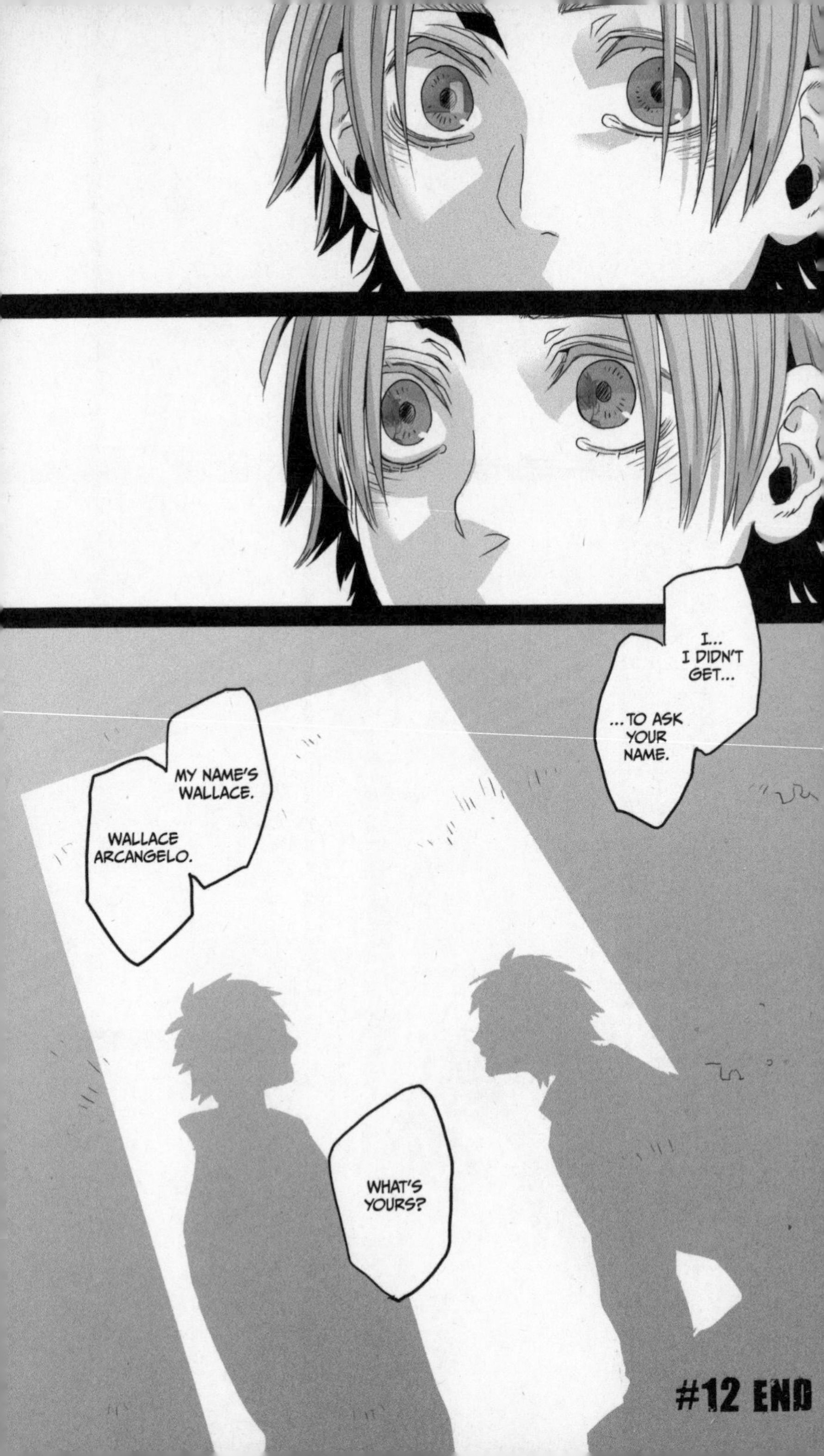
I... I DIDN'T GET...
...TO ASK YOUR NAME.
MY NAME'S WALLACE.
WALLACE ARCANGELO.
WHAT'S YOURS?
#12 END

GANGST

#13

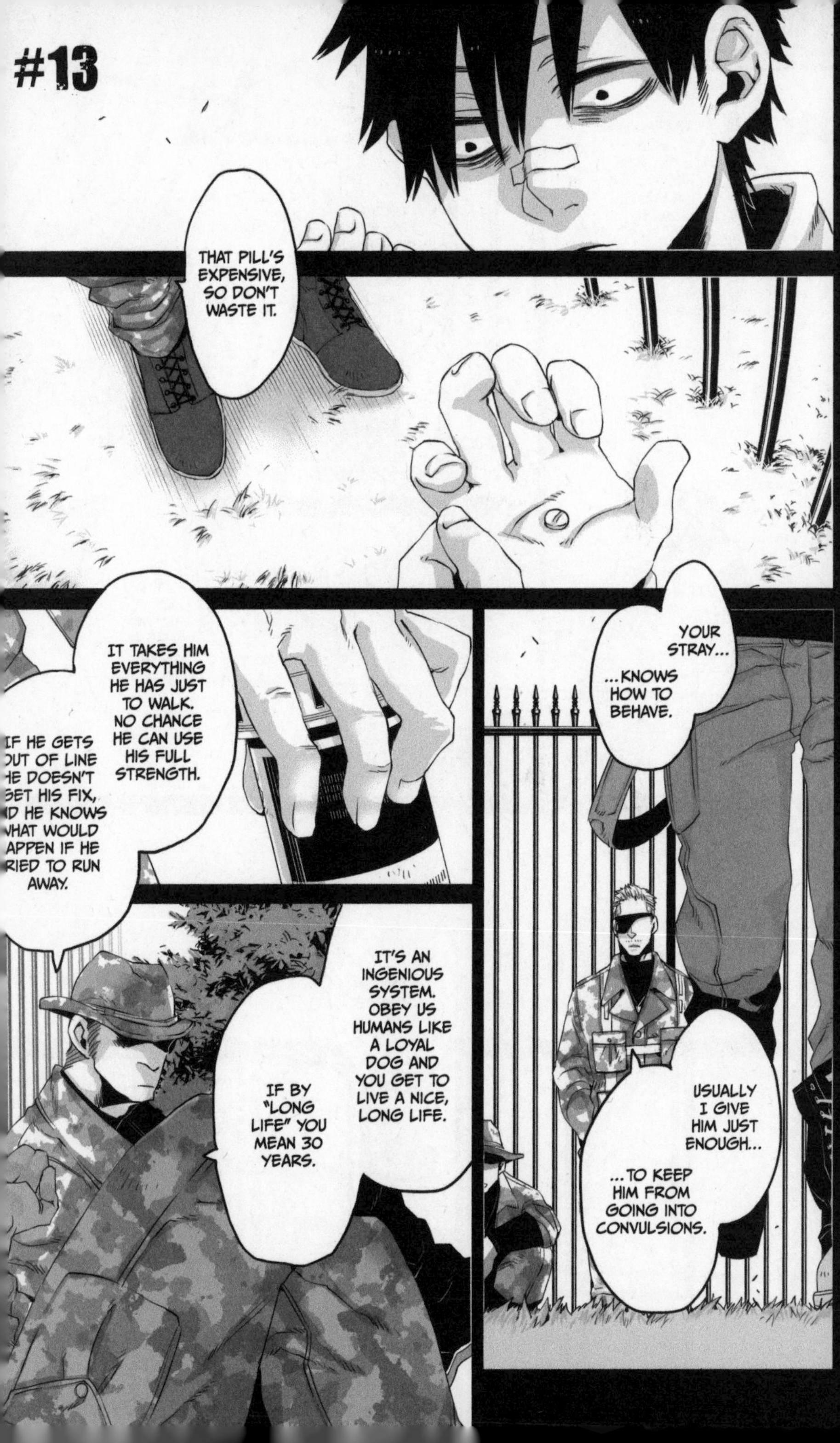
THAT PILL'S EXPENSIVE, SO DON'T WASTE IT.
YOUR STRAY...
...KNOWS HOW TO BEHAVE.
USUALLY I GIVE HIM JUST ENOUGH...
...TO KEEP HIM FROM GOING INTO CONVULSIONS.
IT TAKES HIM EVERYTHING HE HAS JUST TO WALK. NO CHANCE HE CAN USE HIS FULL STRENGTH.
IF HE GETS UT OF LINE HE DOESN'T ET HIS FIX, D HE KNOWS HAT WOULD APPEN IF HE RIED TO RUN AWAY.
IT'S AN INGENIOUS SYSTEM. OBEY US HUMANS LIKE A LOYAL DOG AND YOU GET TO LIVE A NICE, LONG LIFE.
IF BY "LONG LIFE" YOU MEAN 30 YEARS.

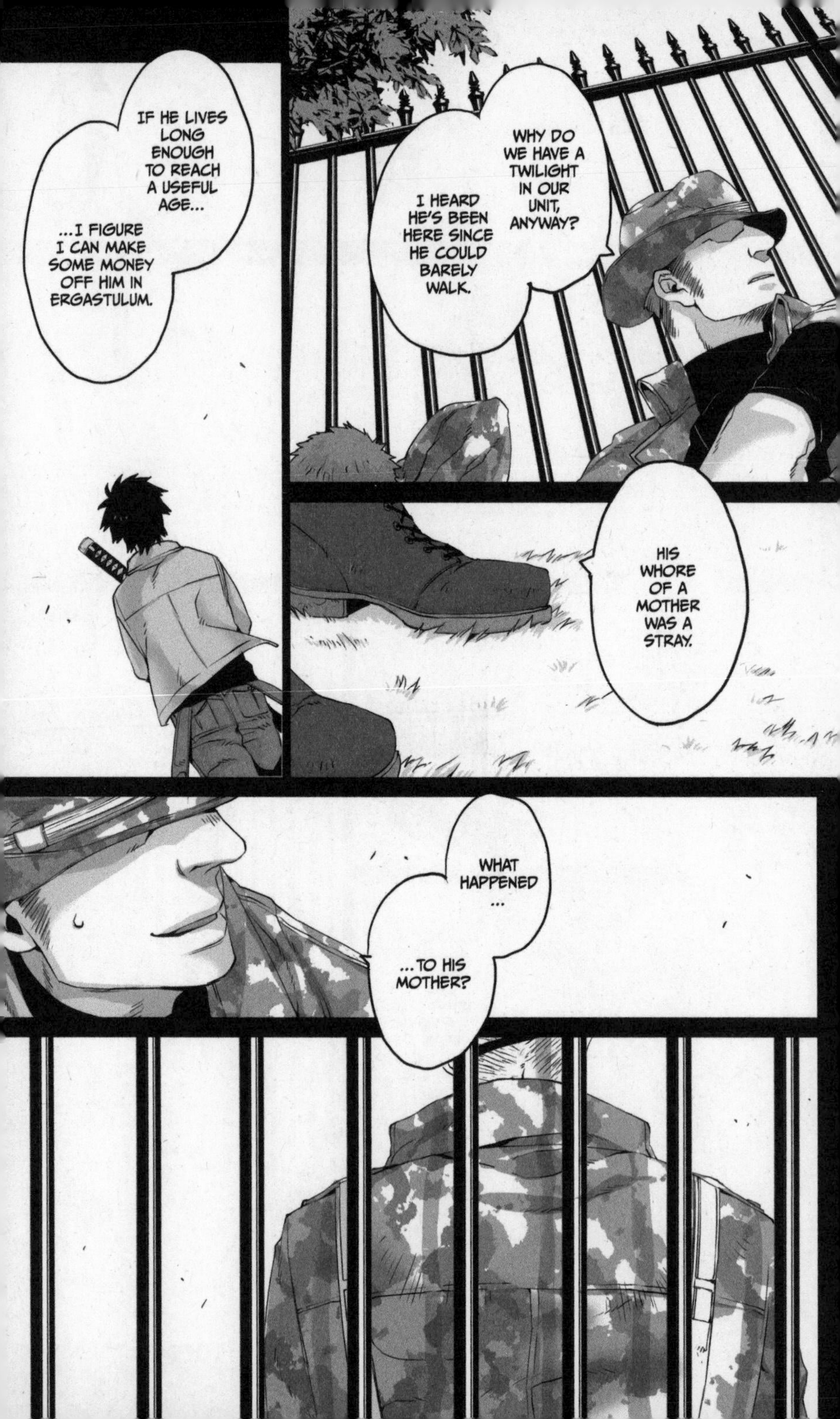
WHY DO WE HAVE A TWILIGHT IN OUR UNIT, ANYWAY?
I HEARD HE'S BEEN HERE SINCE HE COULD BARELY WALK.
HIS WHORE OF A MOTHER WAS A STRAY.
IF HE LIVES LONG ENOUGH TO REACH A USEFUL AGE...
...I FIGURE I CAN MAKE SOME MONEY OFF HIM IN ERGASTULUM.
WHAT HAPPENED ...
...TO HIS MOTHER?

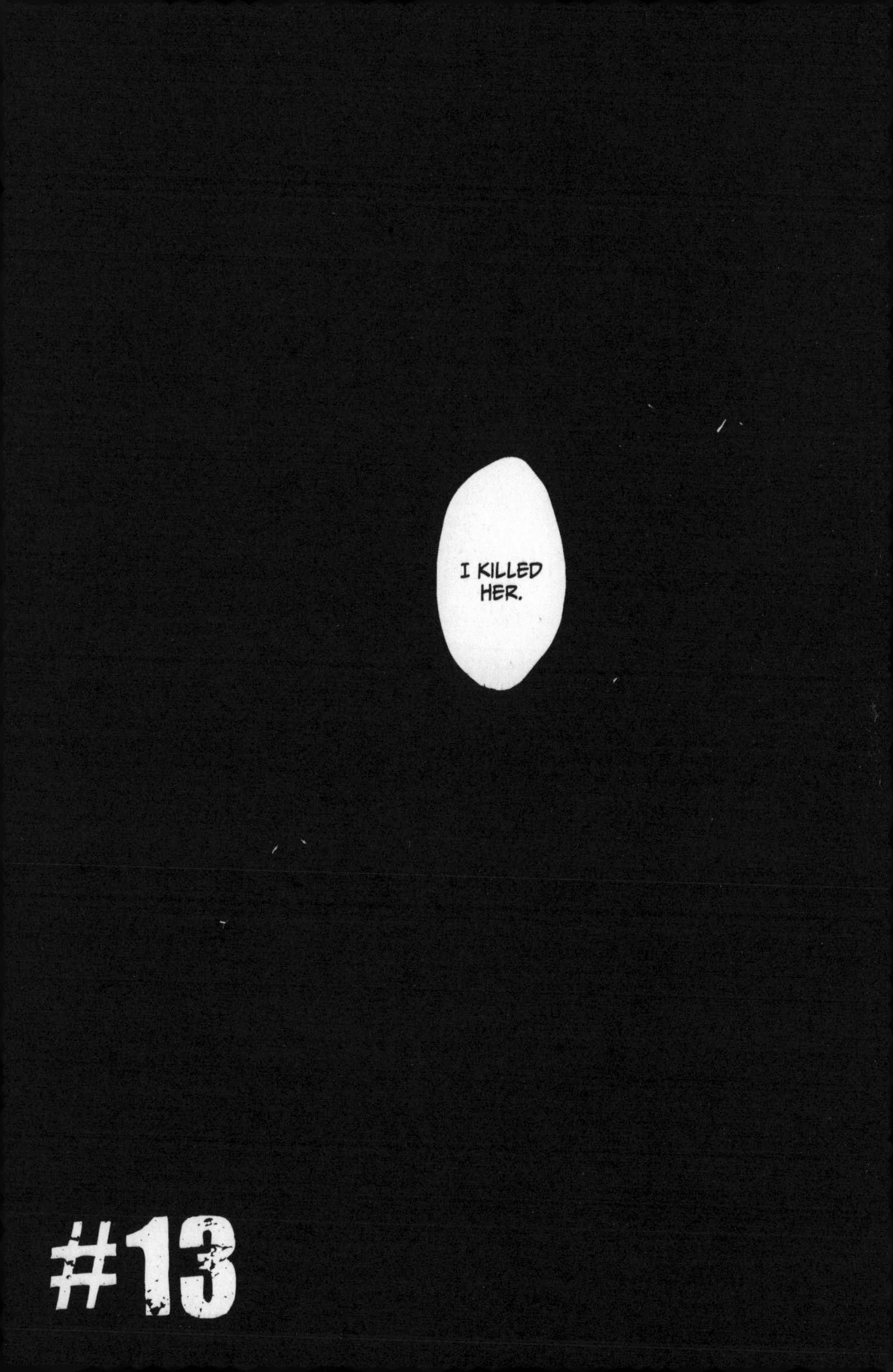
I KILLED HER.
#13

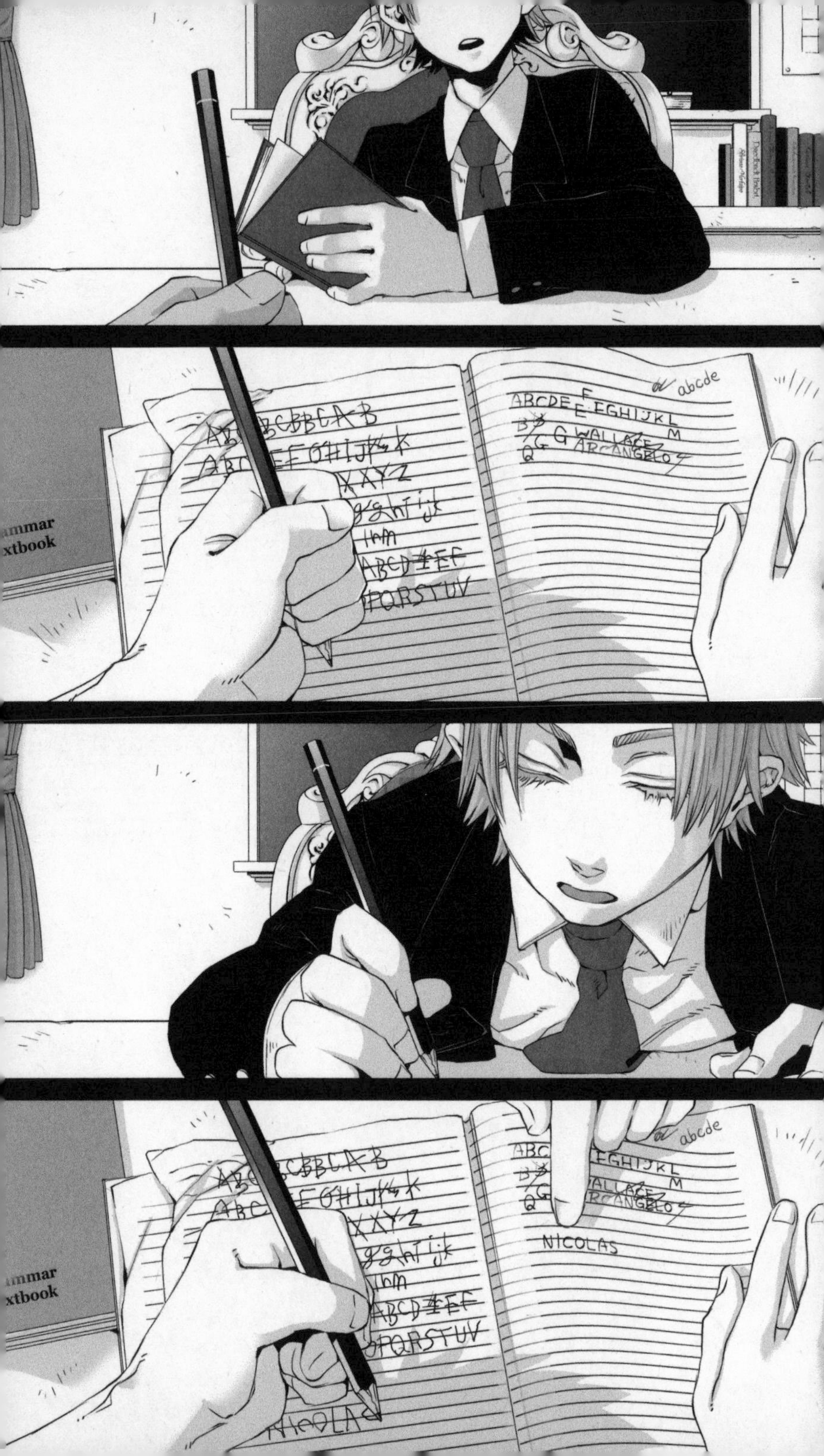
ammar
xtbook
abcde
ABCDE
EFGHIJKL
WALLACE
ARCANGELO
abcde
NICOLAS

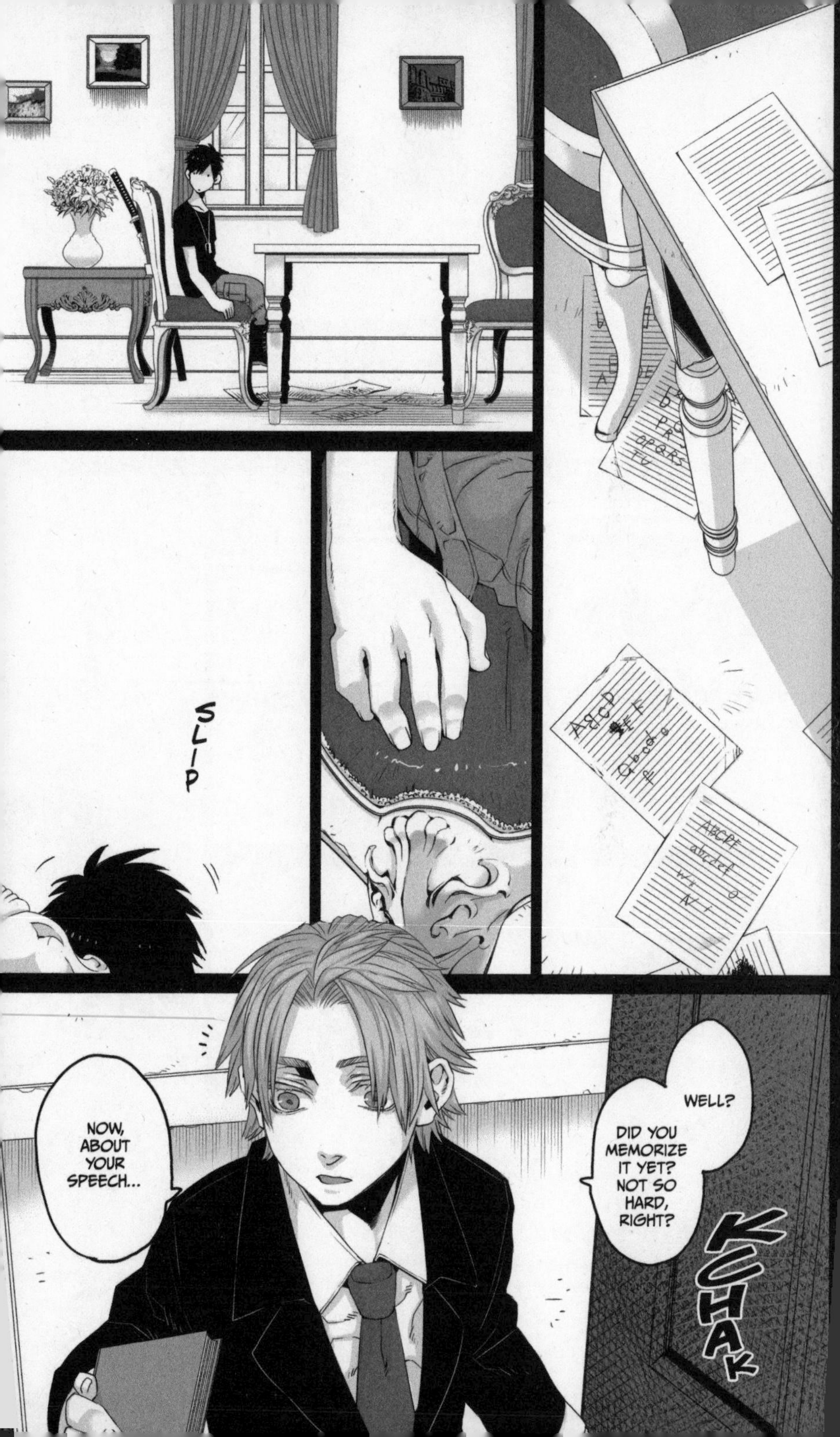
SLIP
WELL?
DID YOU MEMORIZE IT YET? NOT SO HARD, RIGHT?
KCHAK
NOW, ABOUT YOUR SPEECH...

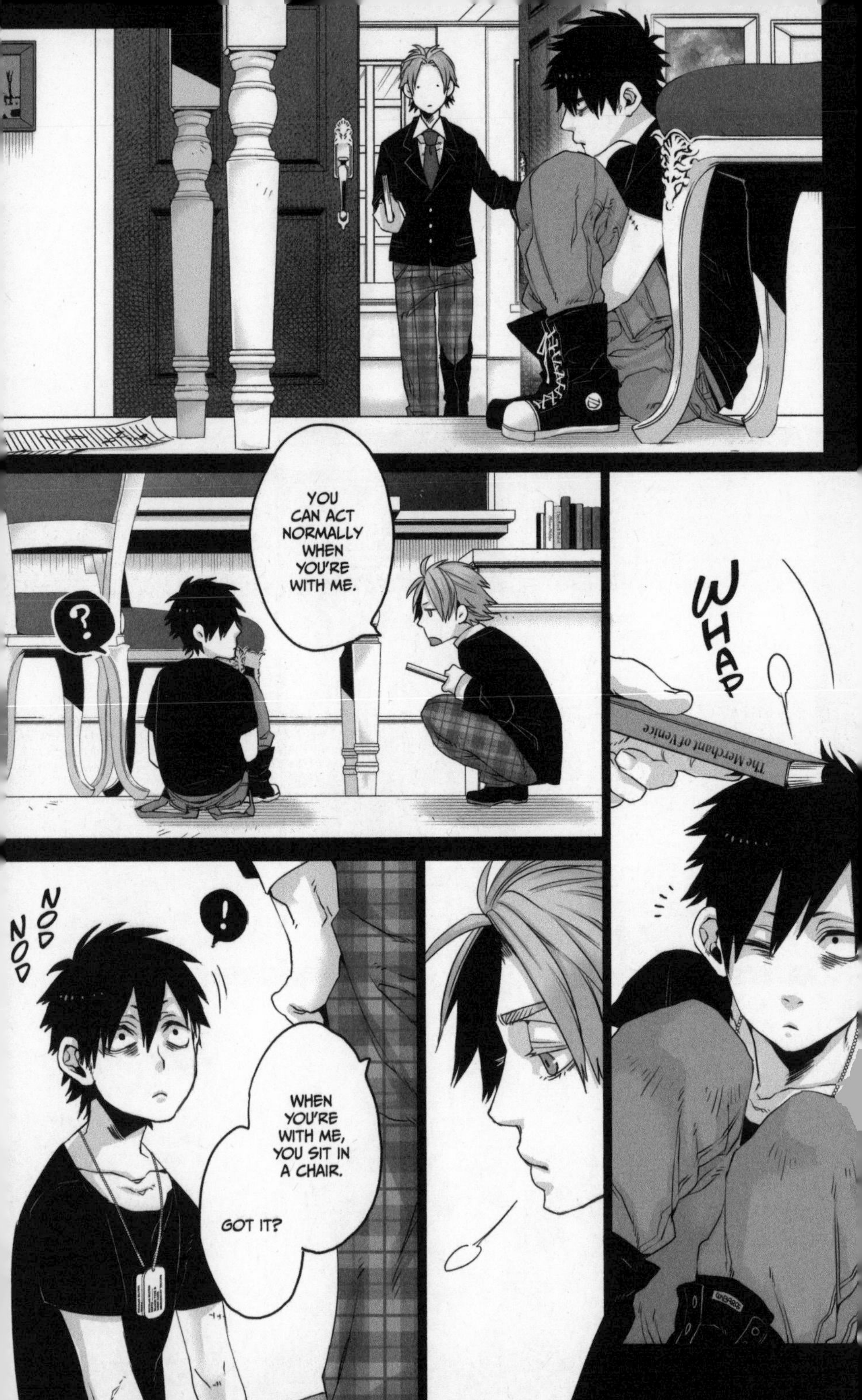
WHAP
The Merchant of Venice
YOU CAN ACT NORMALLY WHEN YOU'RE WITH ME.
?
!
NOD NOD
WHEN YOU'RE WITH ME, YOU SIT IN A CHAIR.
GOT IT?

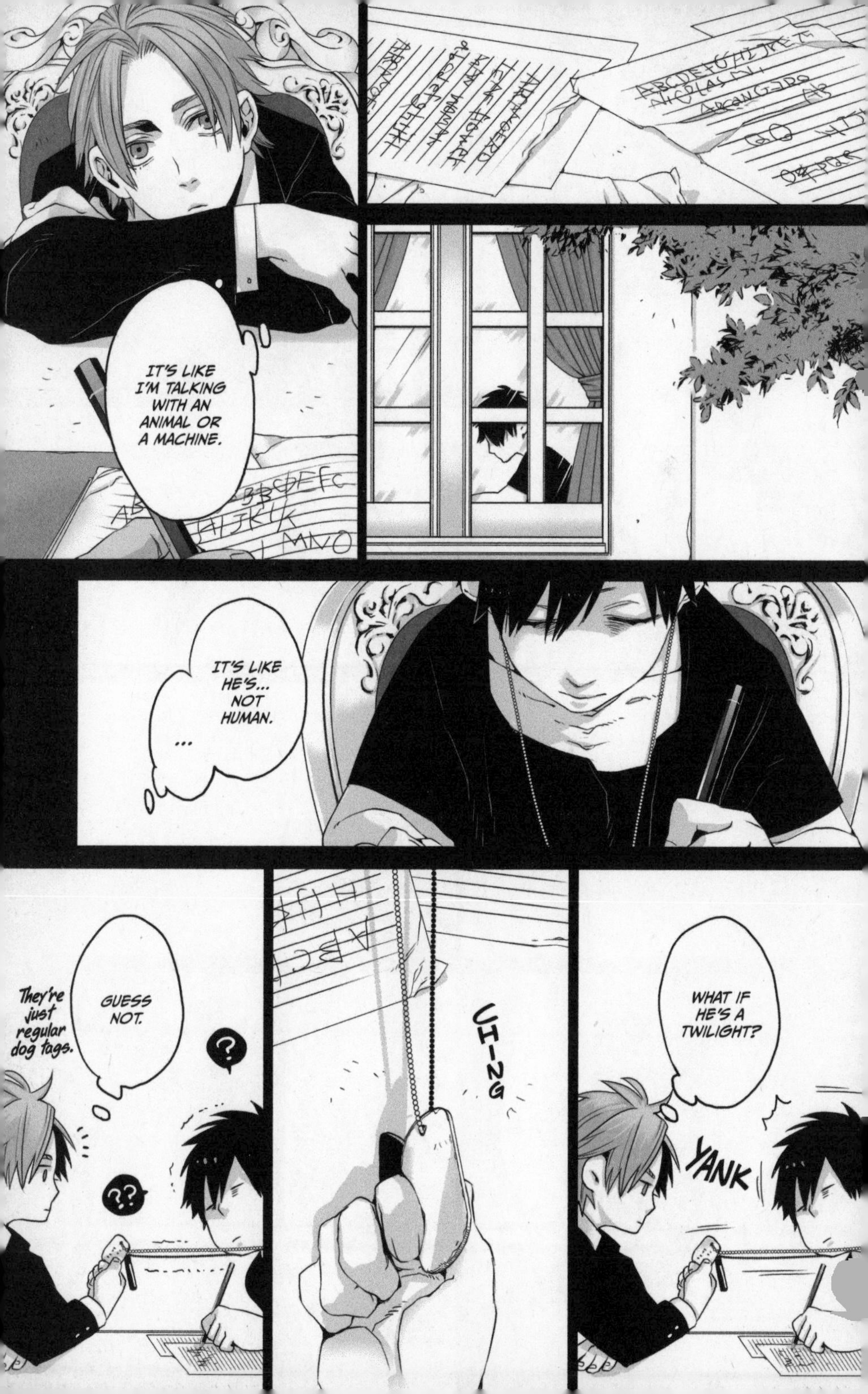
IT'S LIKE I'M TALKING WITH AN ANIMAL OR A MACHINE.
IT'S LIKE HE'S... NOT HUMAN.
...
WHAT IF HE'S A TWILIGHT?
YANK
CHING
GUESS NOT.
They're just regular dog tags.
?
??

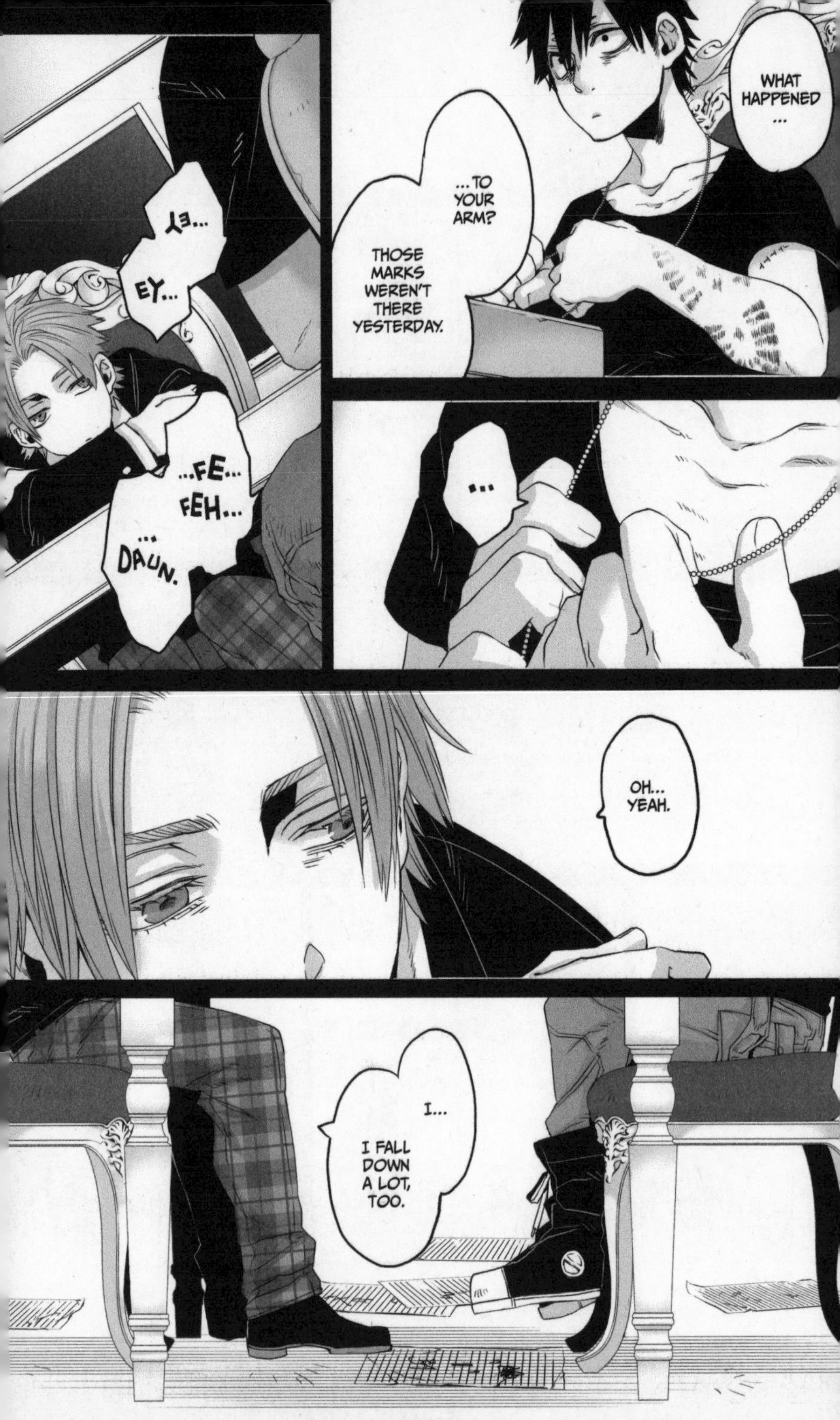
WHAT HAPPENED ...
...TO YOUR ARM?
THOSE MARKS WEREN'T THERE YESTERDAY.
...
...EY...
EY...
...FE... FEH... ...DAUN.
OH... YEAH.
I... I FALL DOWN A LOT, TOO.

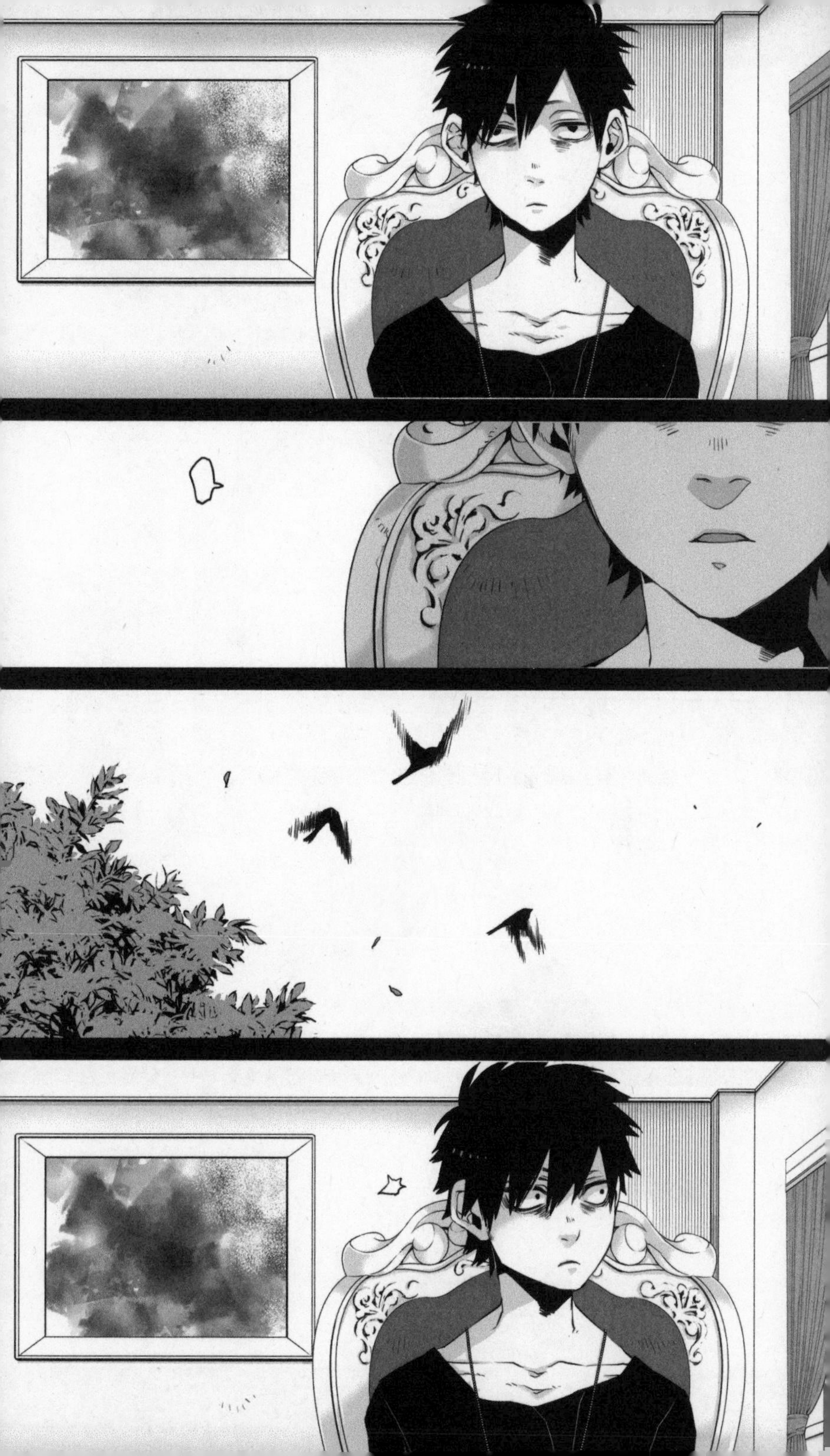

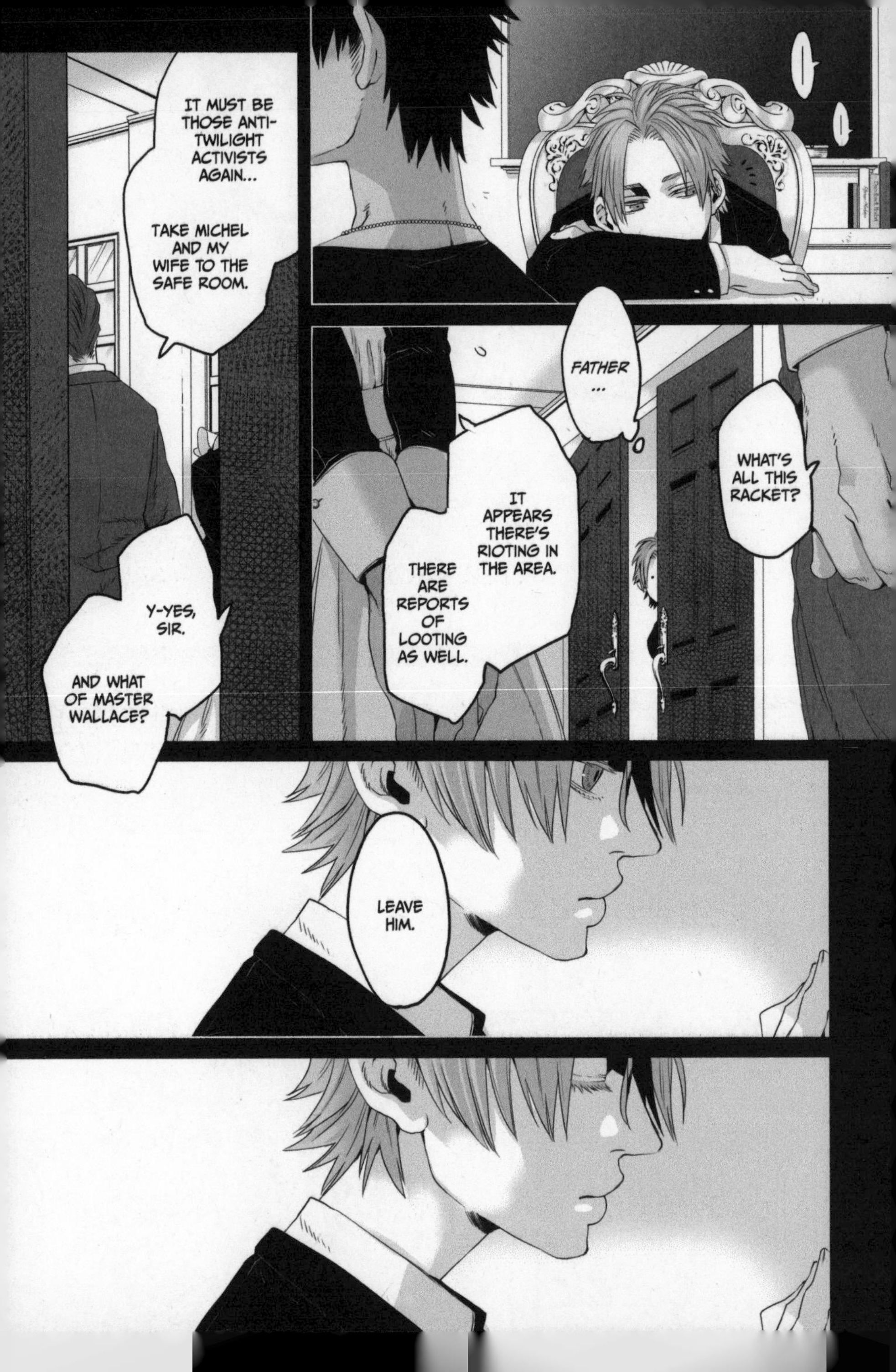
WHAT'S ALL THIS RACKET?
FATHER ...
IT APPEARS THERE'S RIOTING IN THE AREA.
THERE ARE REPORTS OF LOOTING AS WELL.
IT MUST BE THOSE ANTI-TWILIGHT ACTIVISTS AGAIN...
TAKE MICHEL AND MY WIFE TO THE SAFE ROOM.
Y-YES, SIR.
AND WHAT OF MASTER WALLACE?
LEAVE HIM.

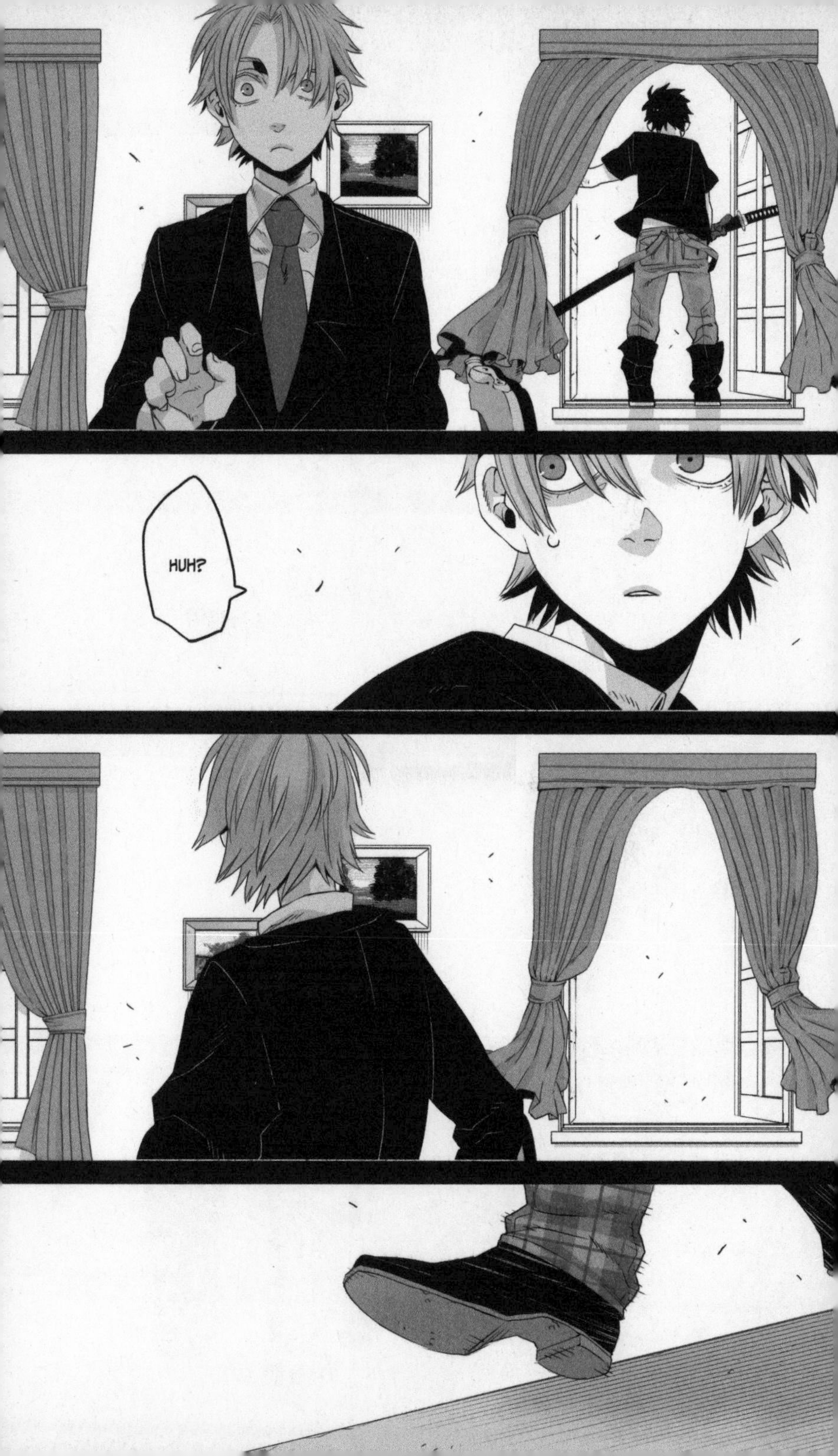
HUH?

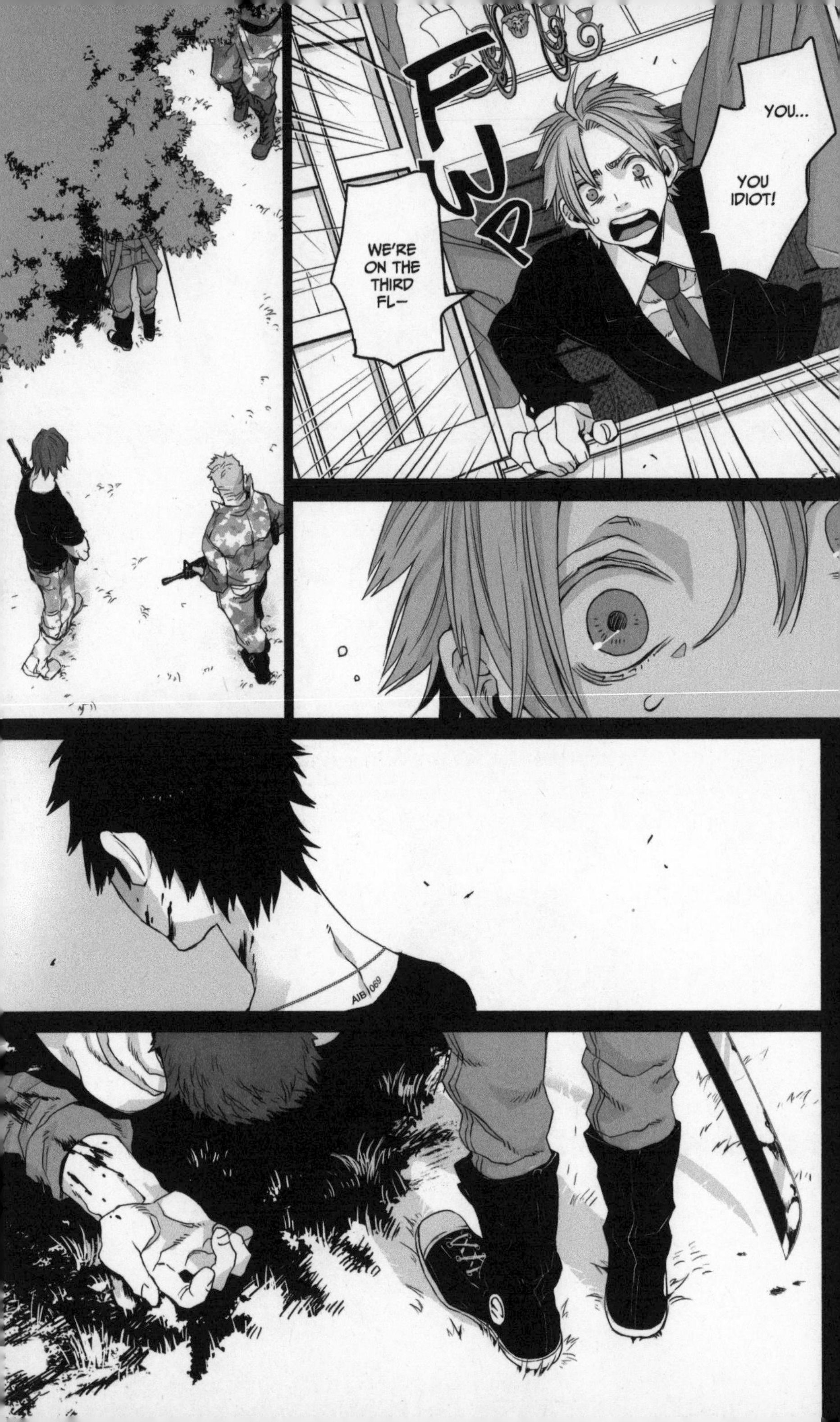
YOU...
YOU IDIOT!
FWP
WE'RE ON THE THIRD FL—
AIB 069

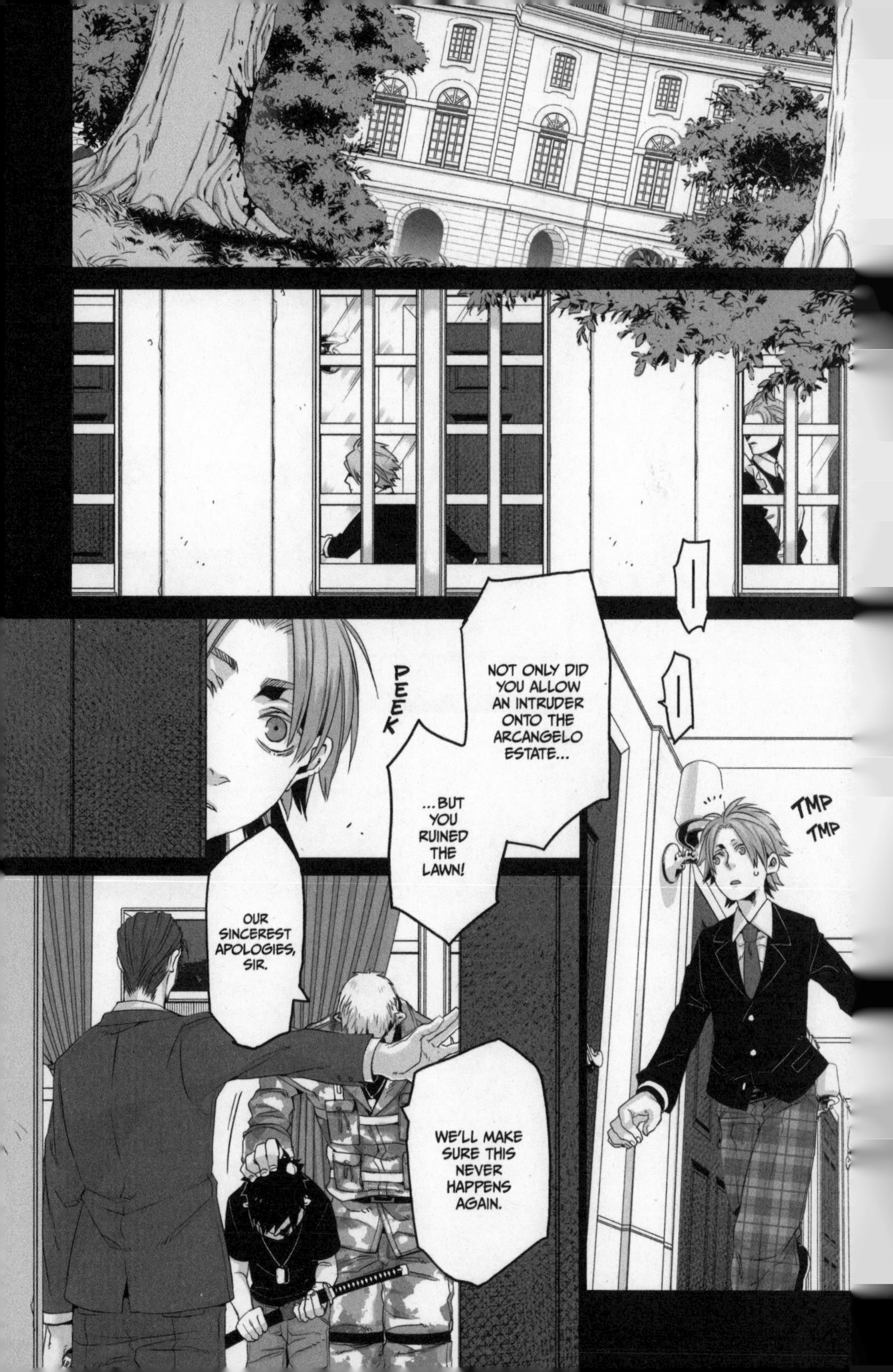
NOT ONLY DID YOU ALLOW AN INTRUDER ONTO THE ARCANGELO ESTATE...
TMP TMP
...BUT YOU RUINED THE LAWN!
PEEK
OUR SINCEREST APOLOGIES, SIR.
WE'LL MAKE SURE THIS NEVER HAPPENS AGAIN.

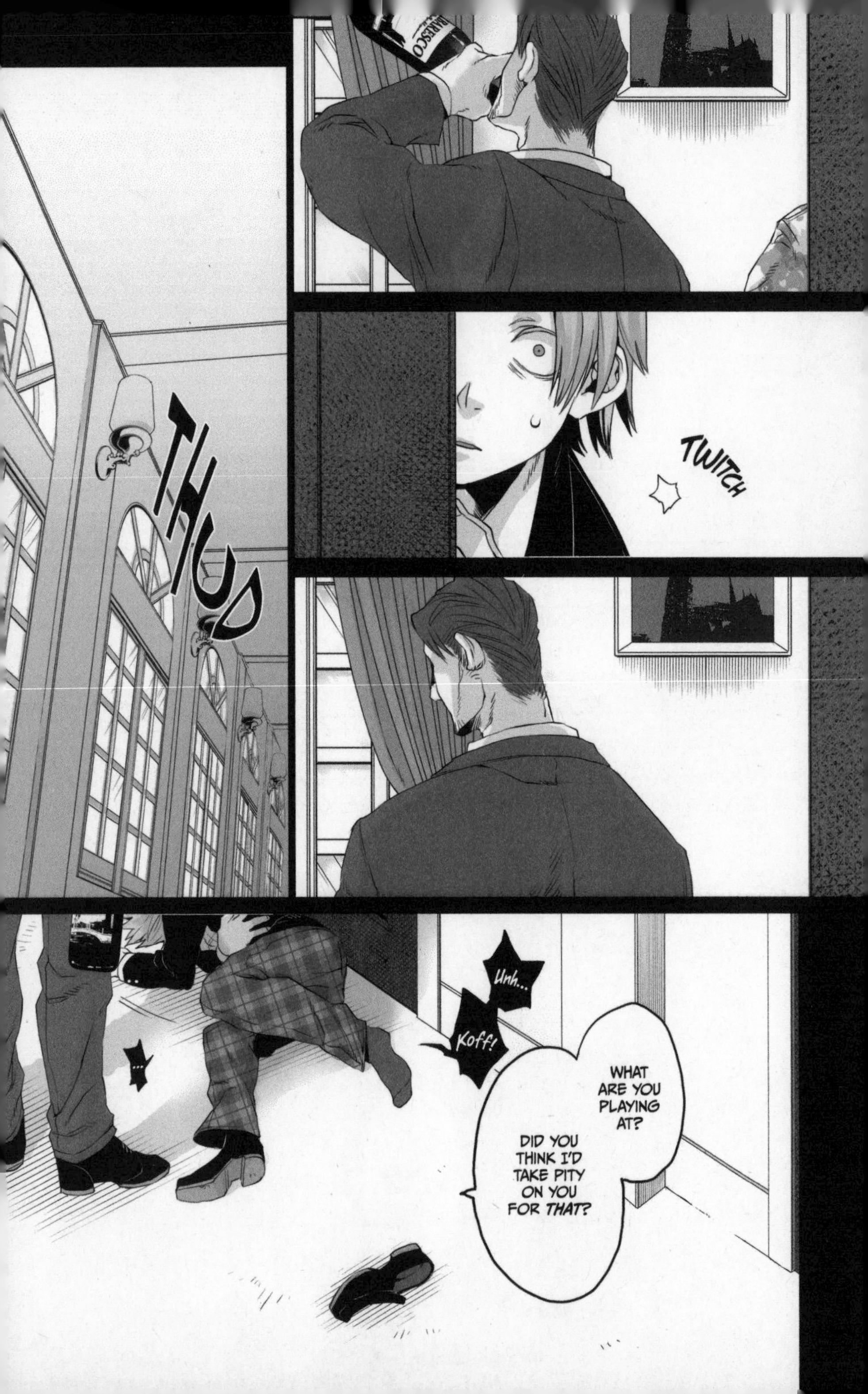
TWITCH
THUD
Unh...
Koff!
WHAT ARE YOU PLAYING AT?
DID YOU THINK I'D TAKE PITY ON YOU FOR *THAT*?
...

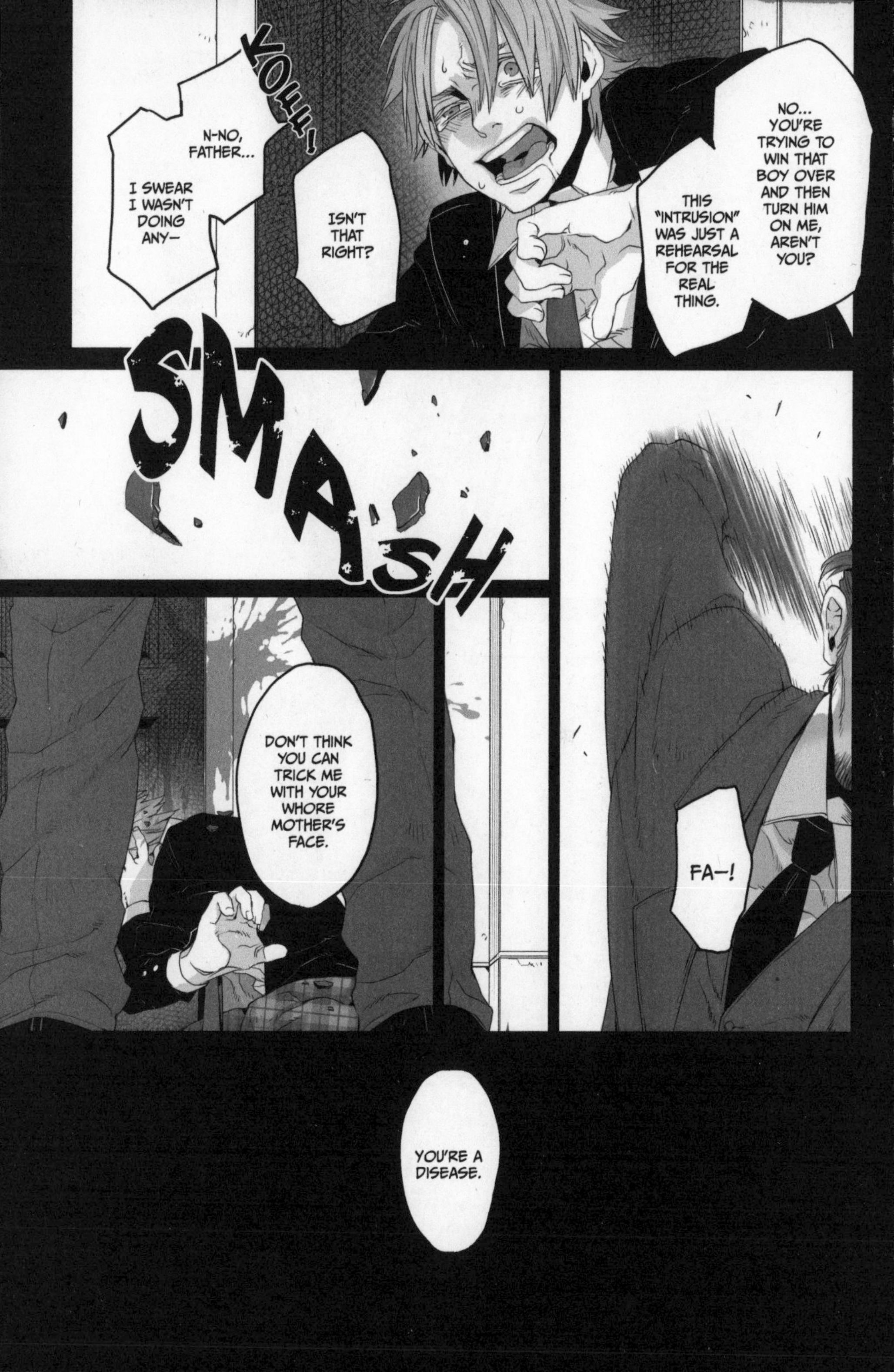
NO... YOU'RE TRYING TO WIN THAT BOY OVER AND THEN TURN HIM ON ME, AREN'T YOU?
THIS "INTRUSION" WAS JUST A REHEARSAL FOR THE REAL THING.
ISN'T THAT RIGHT?
KOFF!
N-NO, FATHER...
I SWEAR I WASN'T DOING ANY—
FA—!
SMASH
DON'T THINK YOU CAN TRICK ME WITH YOUR WHORE MOTHER'S FACE.
YOU'RE A DISEASE.

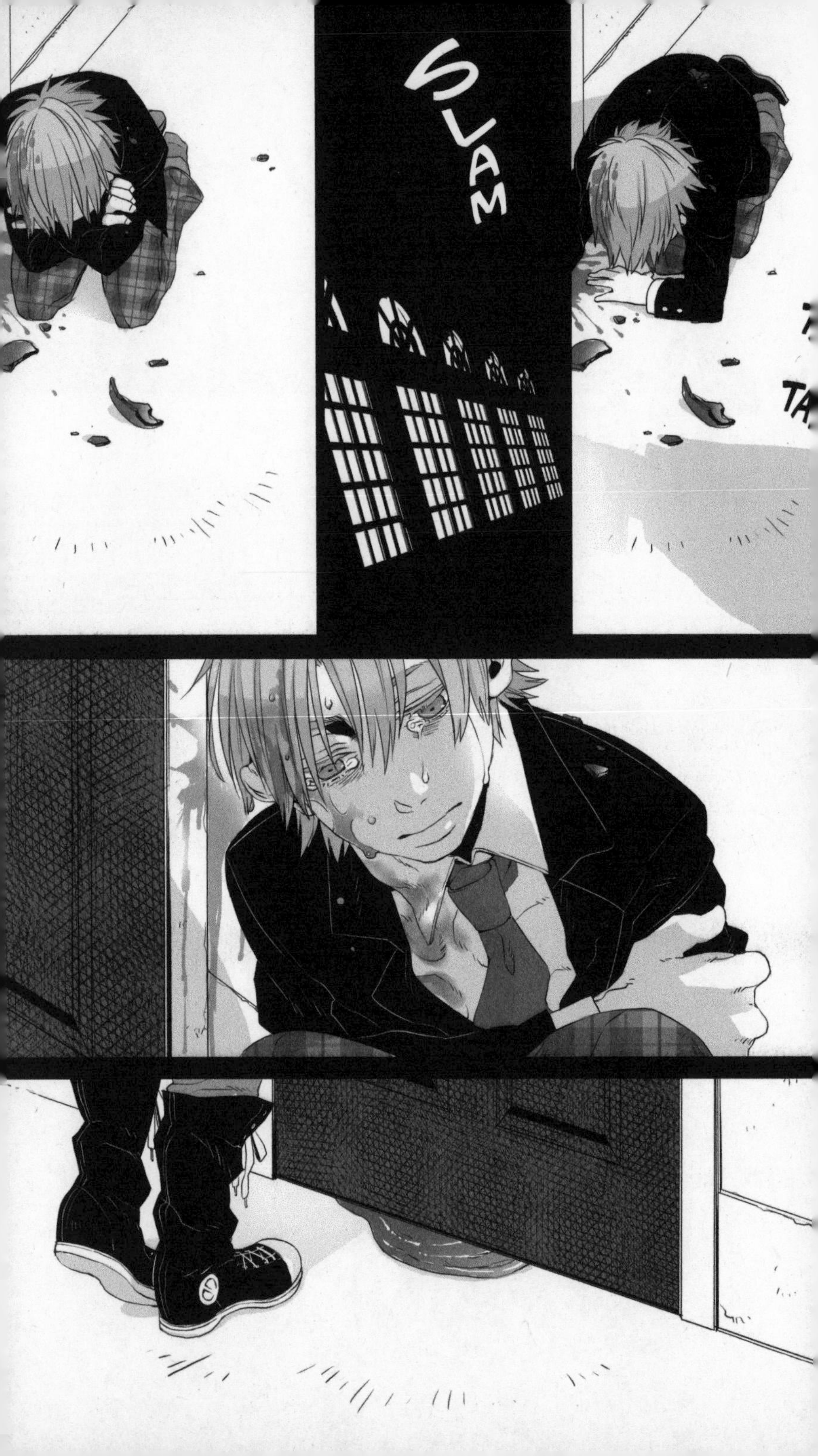
TA
SLAM

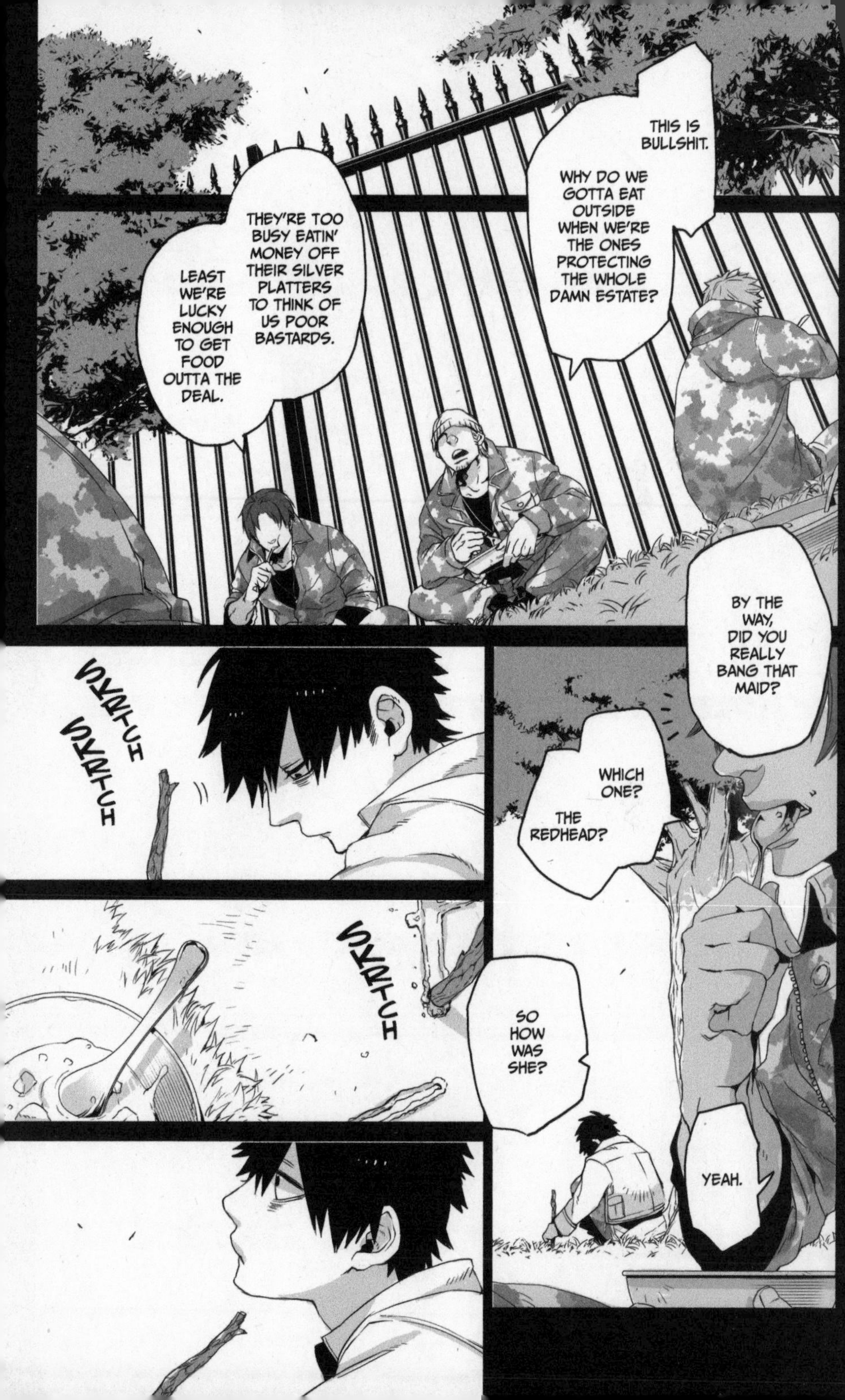
THIS IS BULLSHIT.
WHY DO WE GOTTA EAT OUTSIDE WHEN WE'RE THE ONES PROTECTING THE WHOLE DAMN ESTATE?
THEY'RE TOO BUSY EATIN' MONEY OFF THEIR SILVER PLATTERS TO THINK OF US POOR BASTARDS.
LEAST WE'RE LUCKY ENOUGH TO GET FOOD OUTTA THE DEAL.
BY THE WAY, DID YOU REALLY BANG THAT MAID?
WHICH ONE? THE REDHEAD?
SO HOW WAS SHE?
YEAH.
SKRTCH SKRTCH
SKRTCH

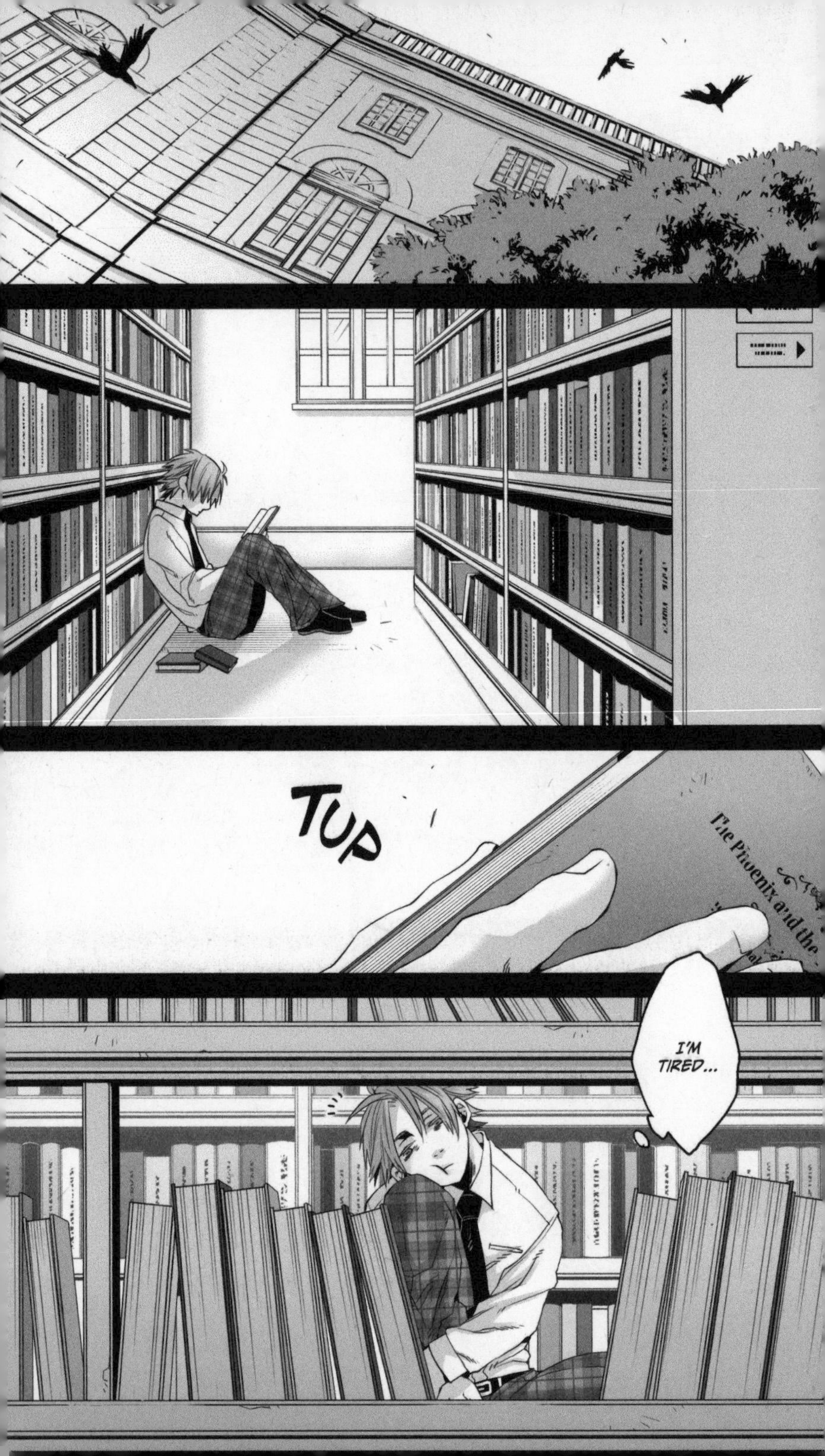
TUP
I'M TIRED...

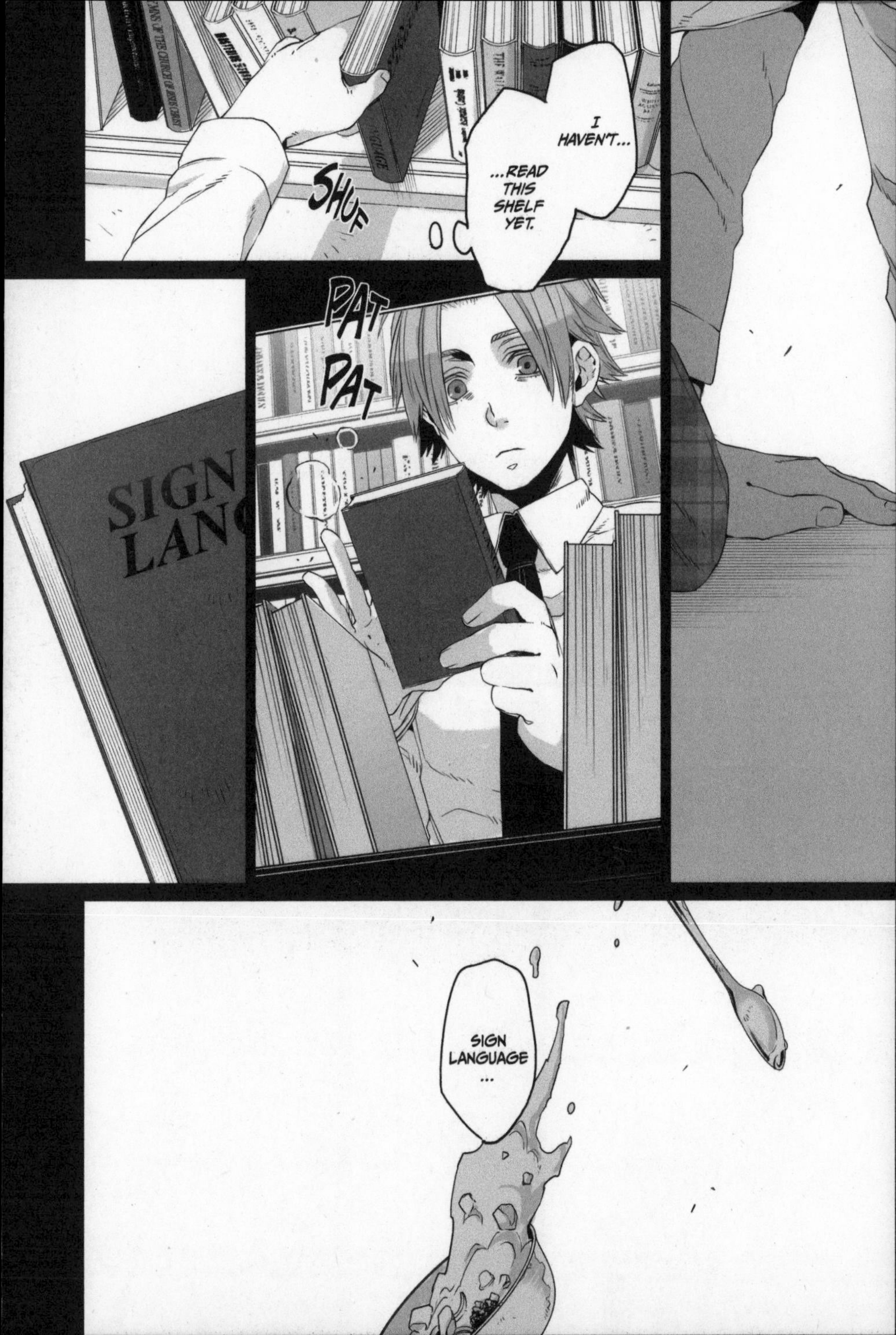
I HAVEN'T...
...READ THIS SHELF YET.
SHUF
PAT PAT
SIGN LANGUAGE ...

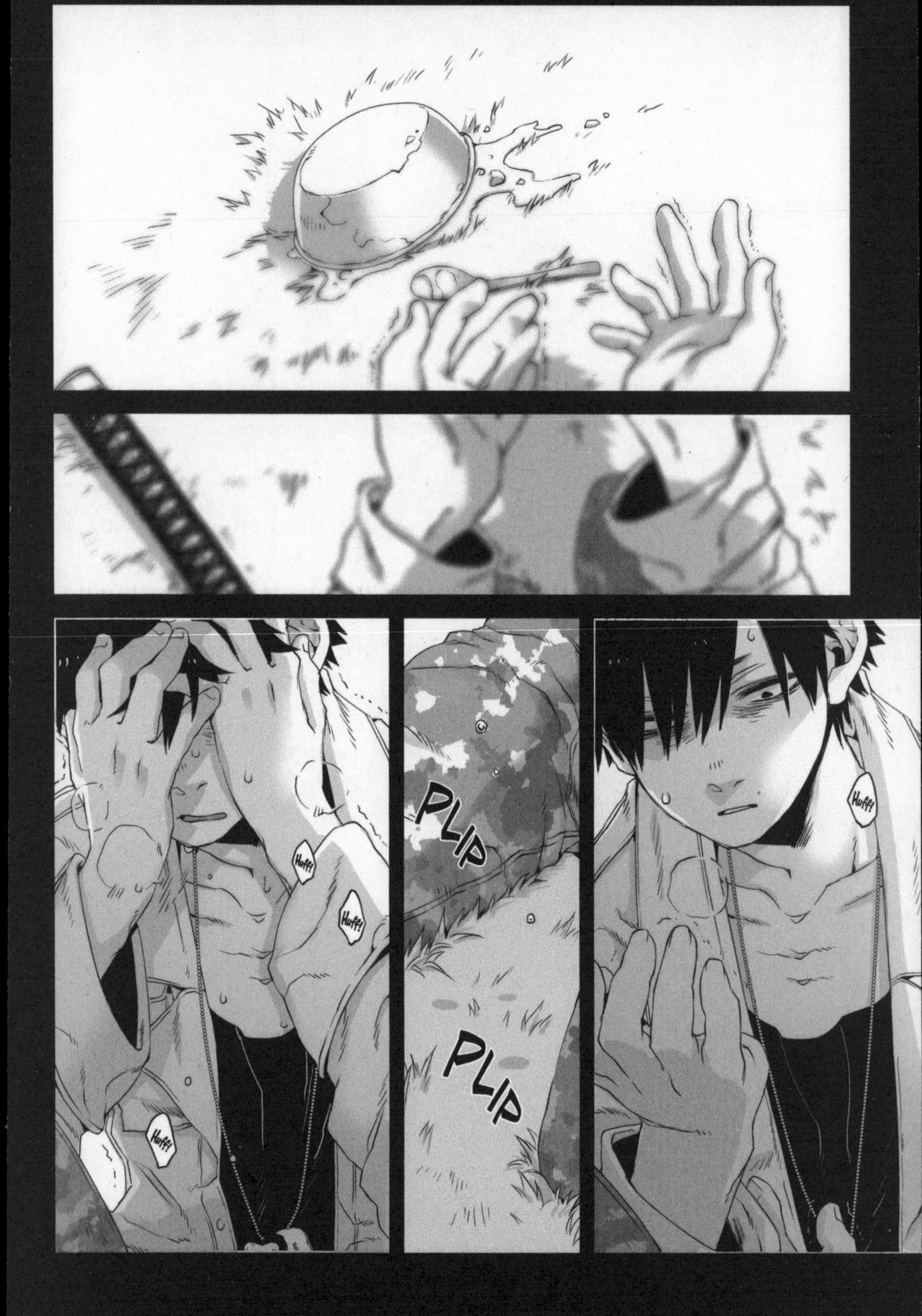
Huff!
PLIP
PLIP
Huff!
Huff!
Huff!

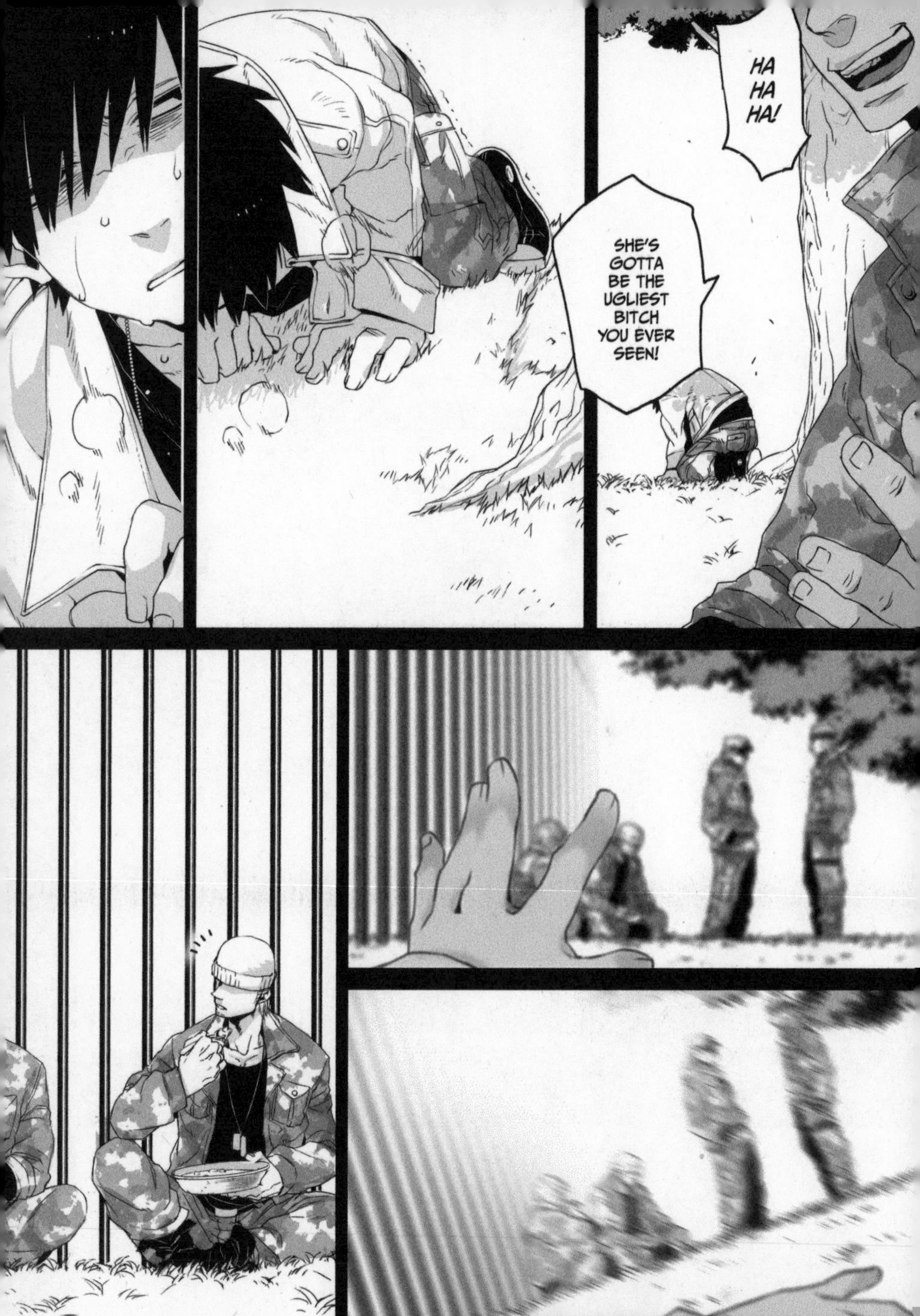
HA HA HA!
SHE'S GOTTA BE THE UGLIEST BITCH YOU EVER SEEN!

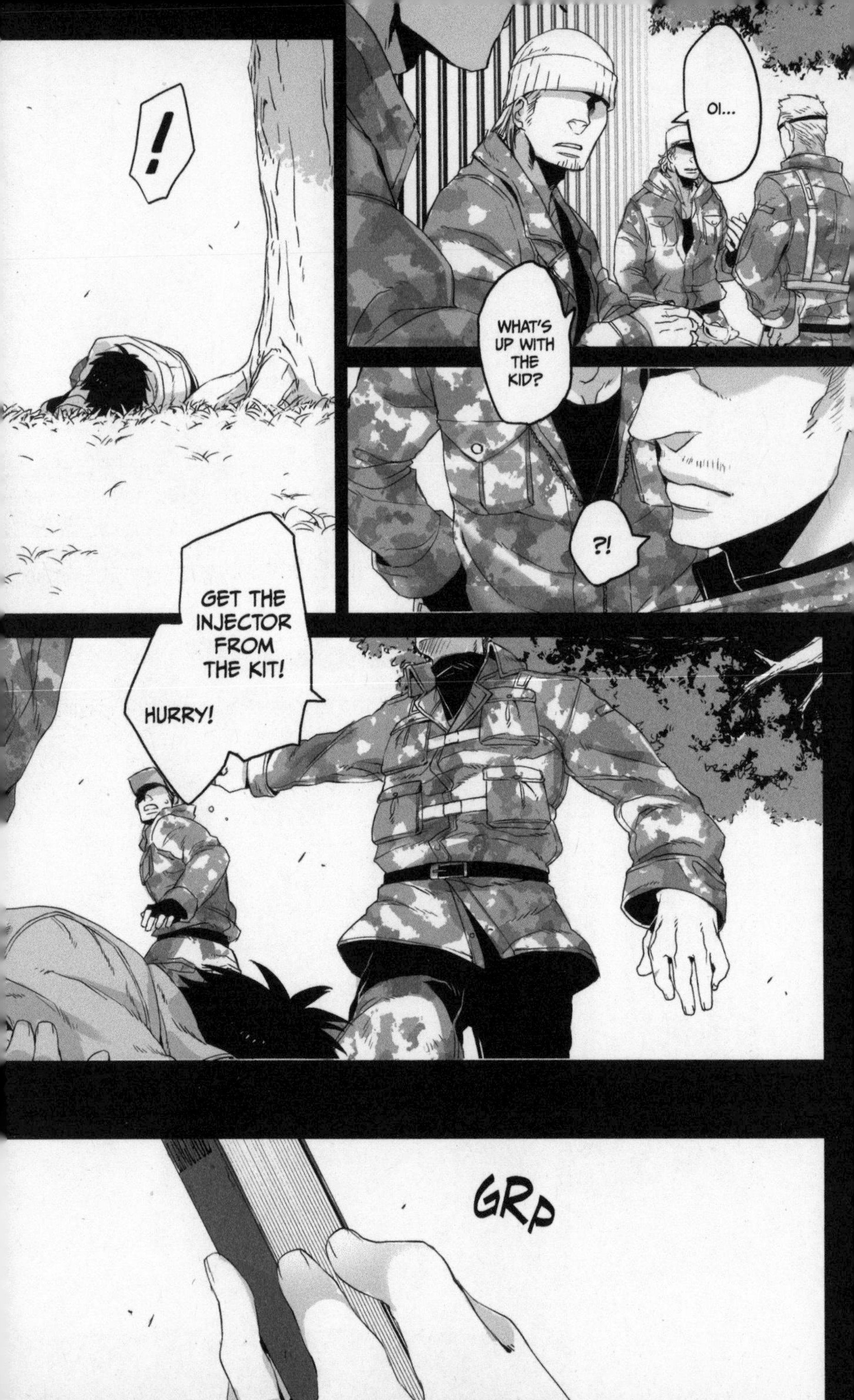
OI...
WHAT'S UP WITH THE KID?
?!
!
GET THE INJECTOR FROM THE KIT!
HURRY!
GRP

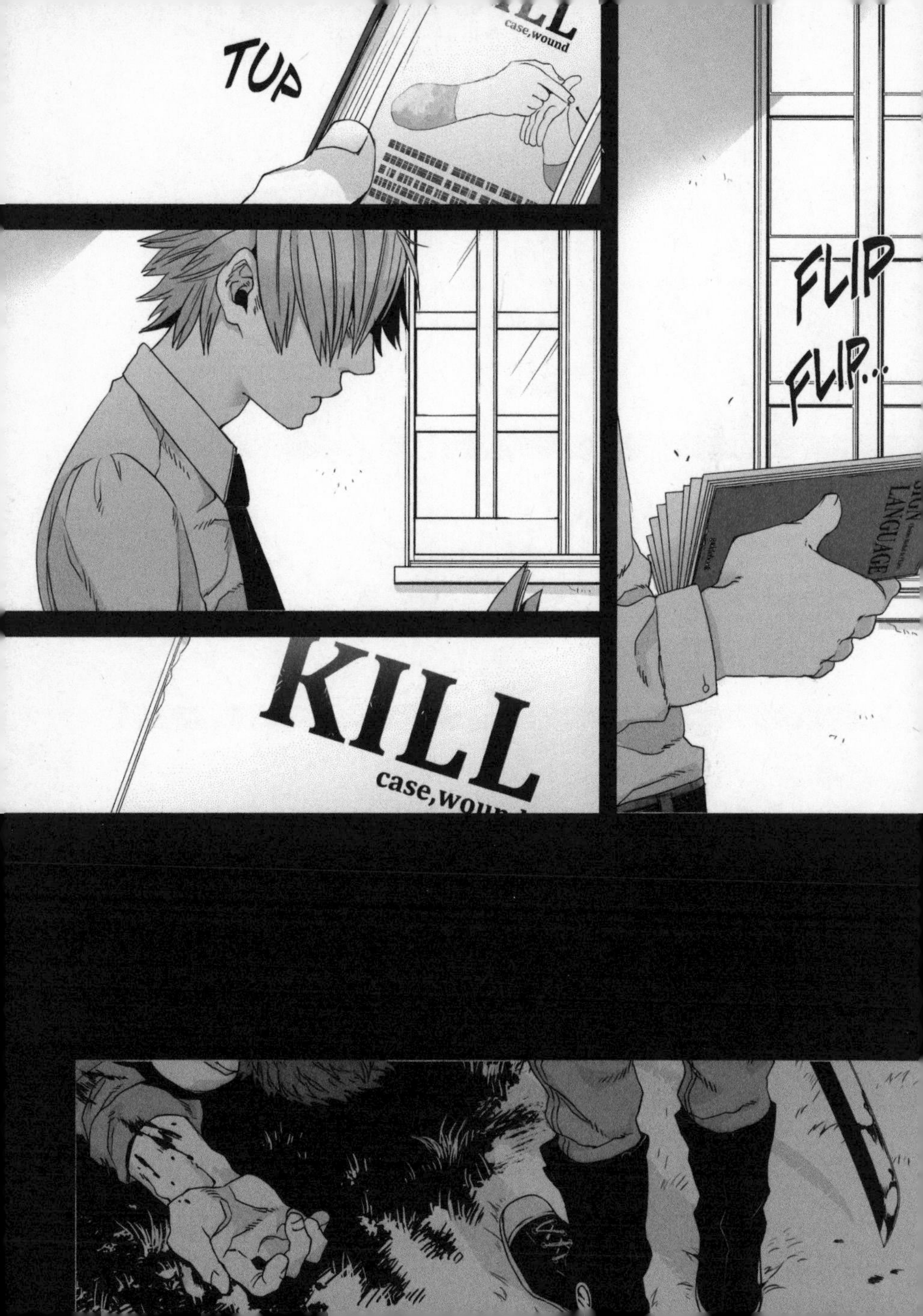
FLIP
FLIP...
LANGUAGE
TUP
case,wound
KILL

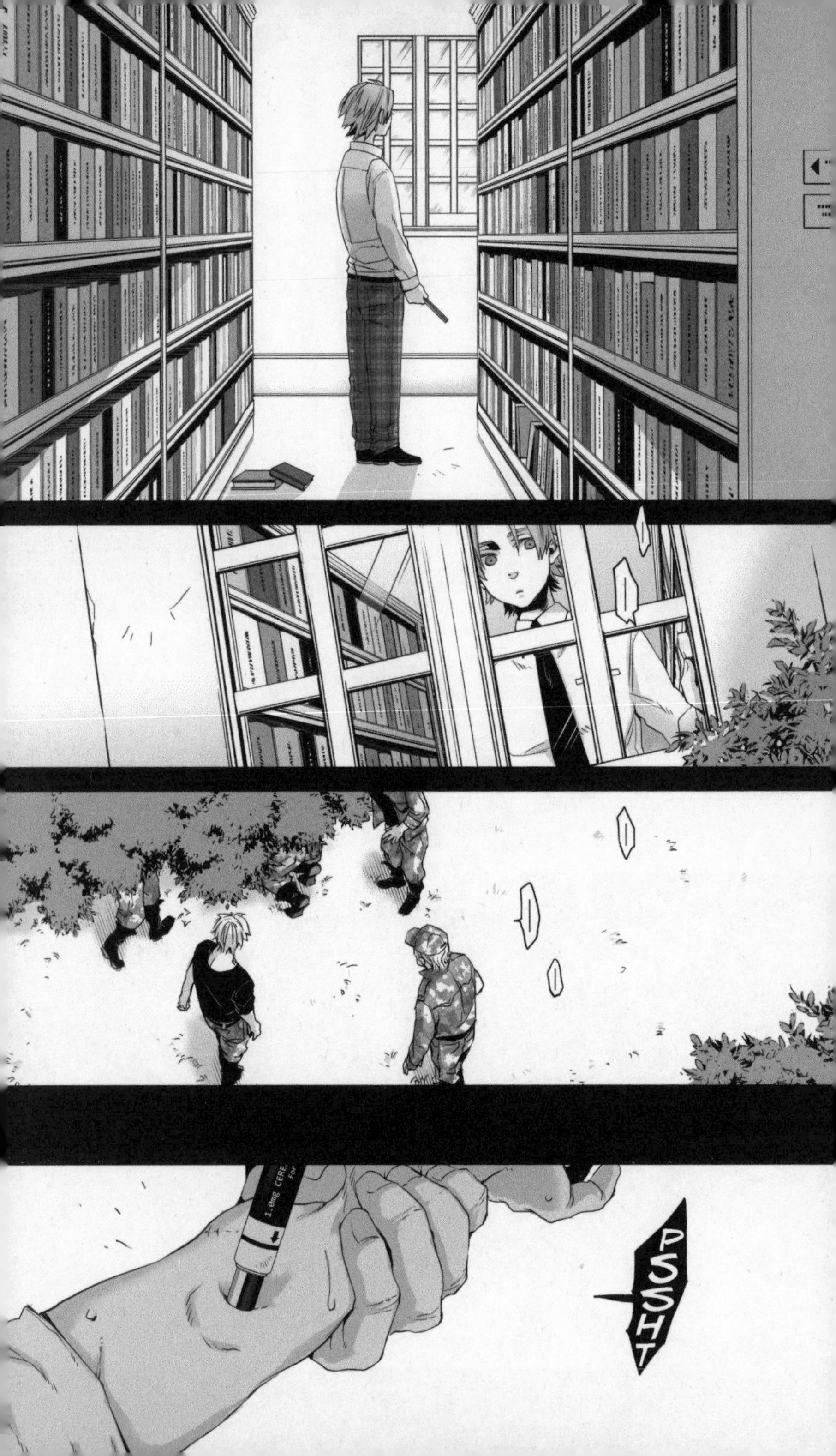
PSSHT

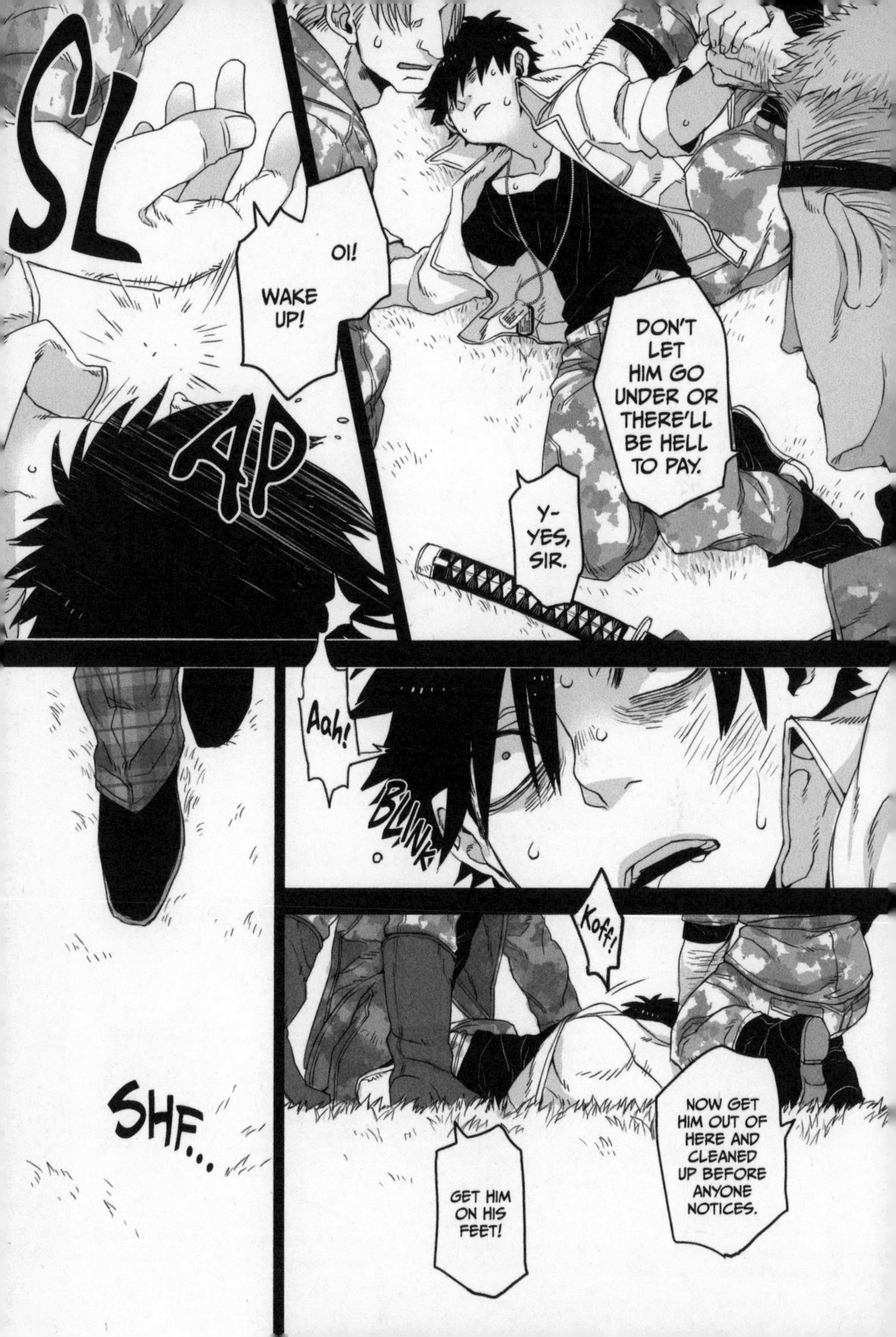
DON'T LET HIM GO UNDER OR THERE'LL BE HELL TO PAY.
Y-YES, SIR.
OI!
WAKE UP!
SLAP
Aah!
BLINK
Koff!
NOW GET HIM OUT OF HERE AND CLEANED UP BEFORE ANYONE NOTICES.
GET HIM ON HIS FEET!
SHF...

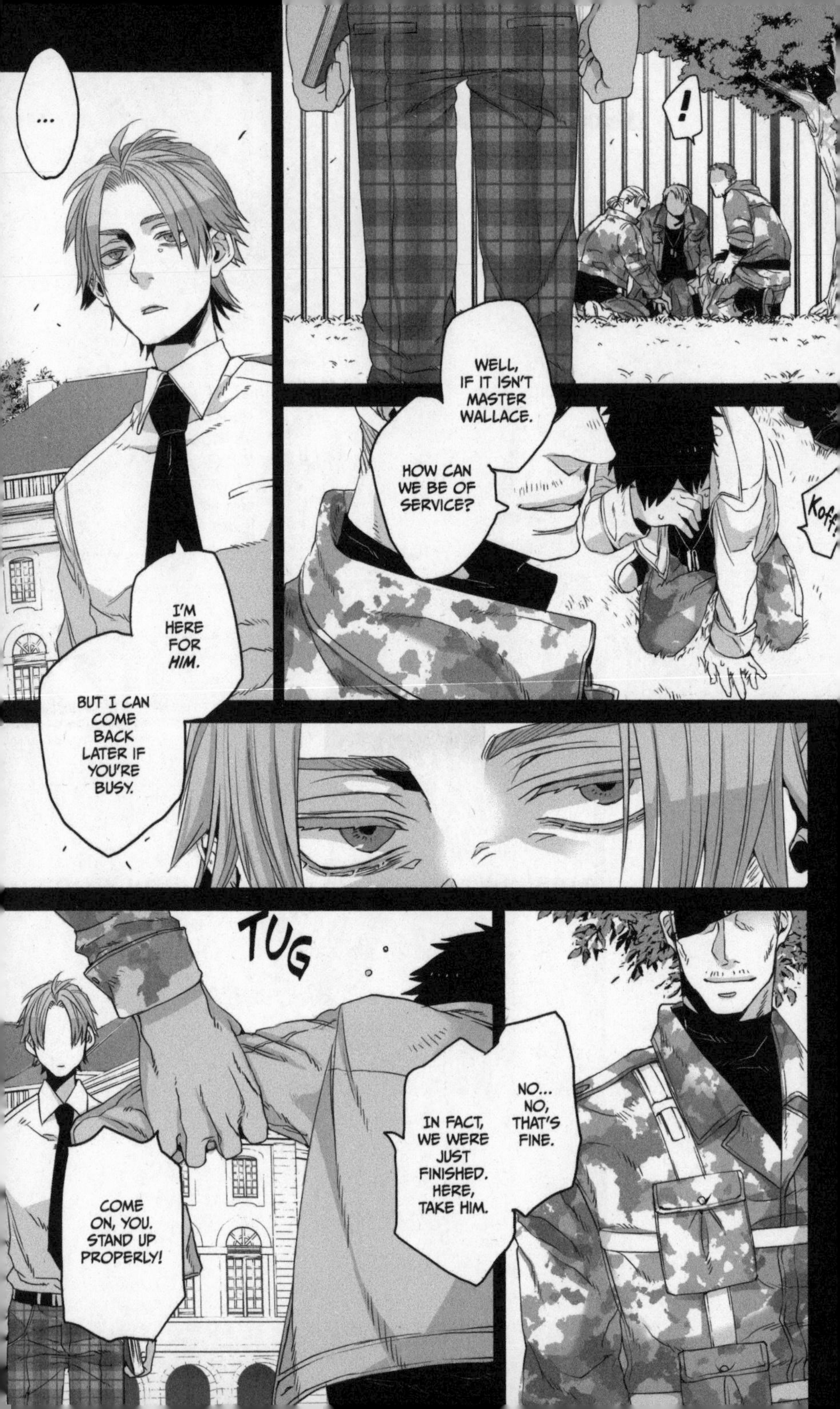
!
WELL, IF IT ISN'T MASTER WALLACE.
HOW CAN WE BE OF SERVICE?
Koff!
...
I'M HERE FOR *HIM*.
BUT I CAN COME BACK LATER IF YOU'RE BUSY.
NO... NO, THAT'S FINE.
IN FACT, WE WERE JUST FINISHED. HERE, TAKE HIM.
TUG
COME ON, YOU. STAND UP PROPERLY!

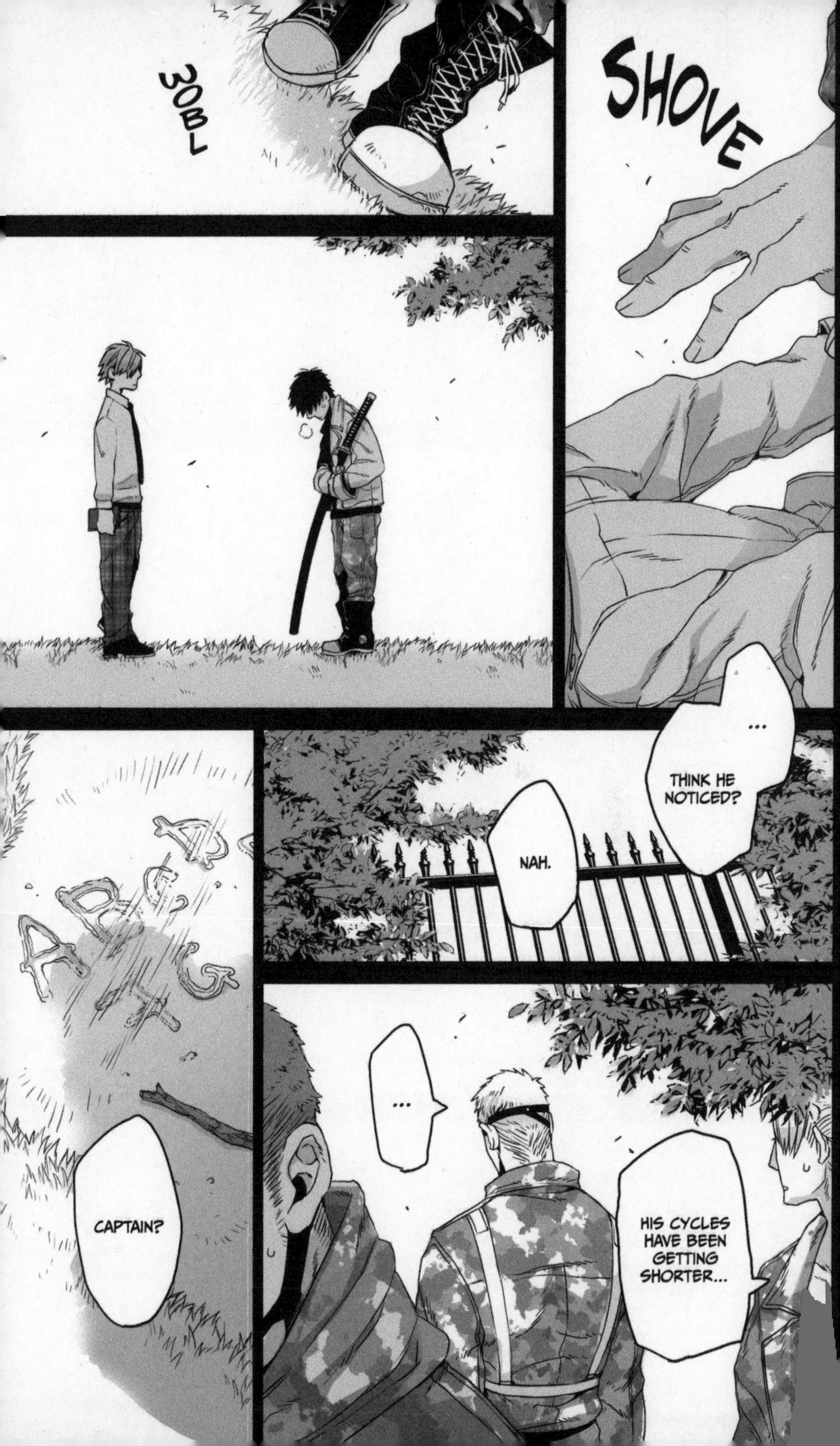
SHOVE
WOBL
...
THINK HE NOTICED?
NAH.
HIS CYCLES HAVE BEEN GETTING SHORTER...
...
CAPTAIN?

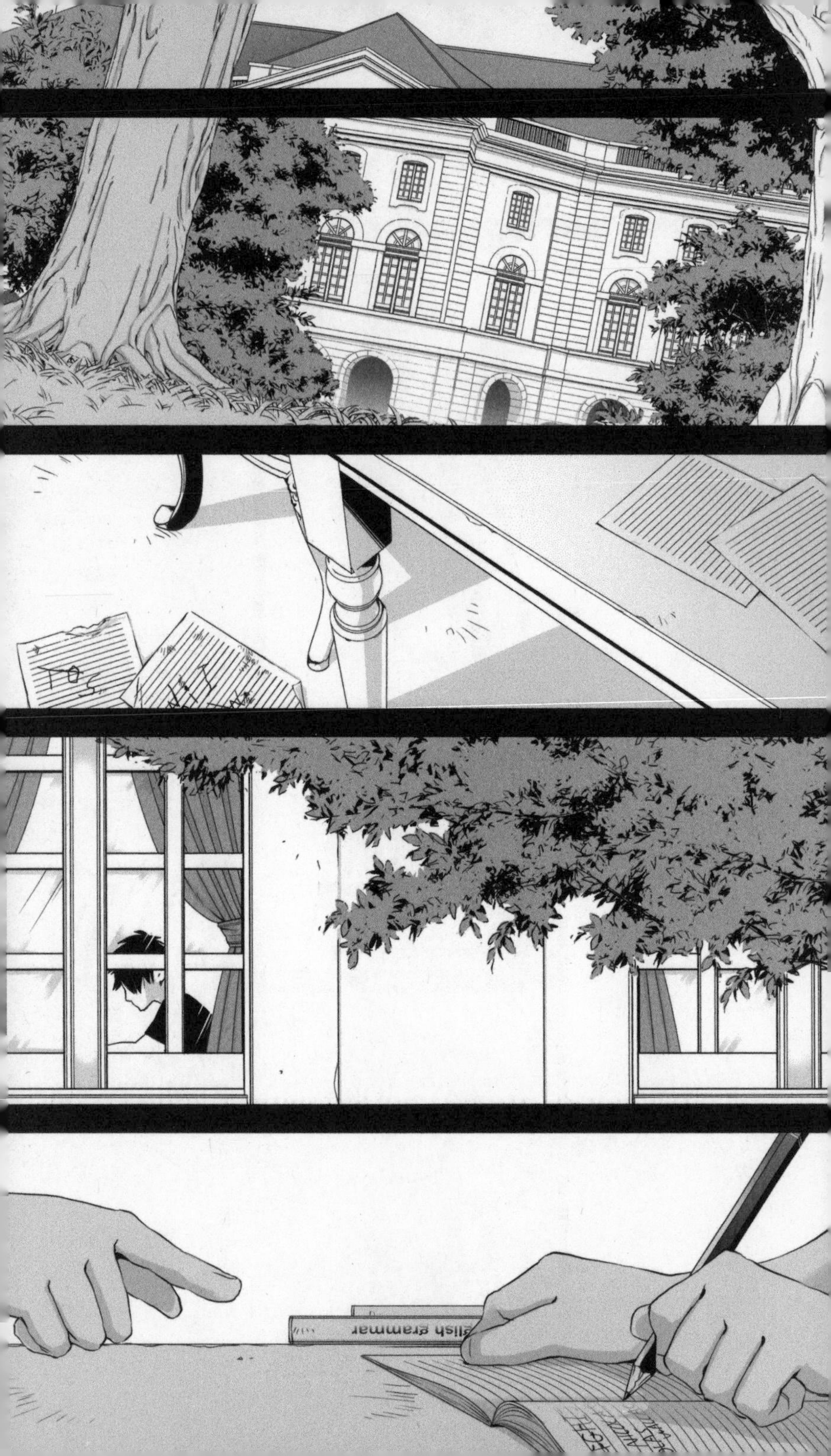
glish grammar

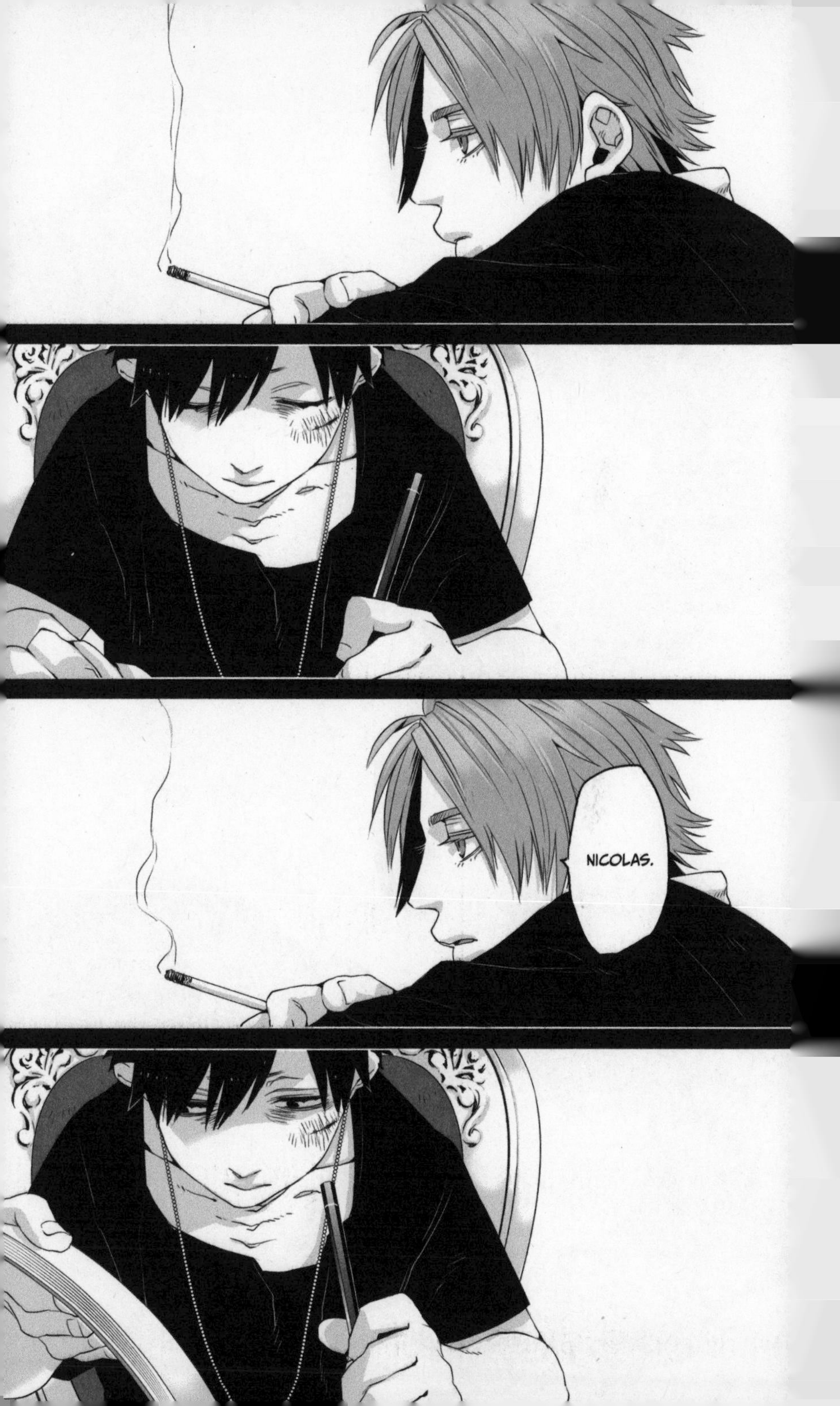
NICOLAS.

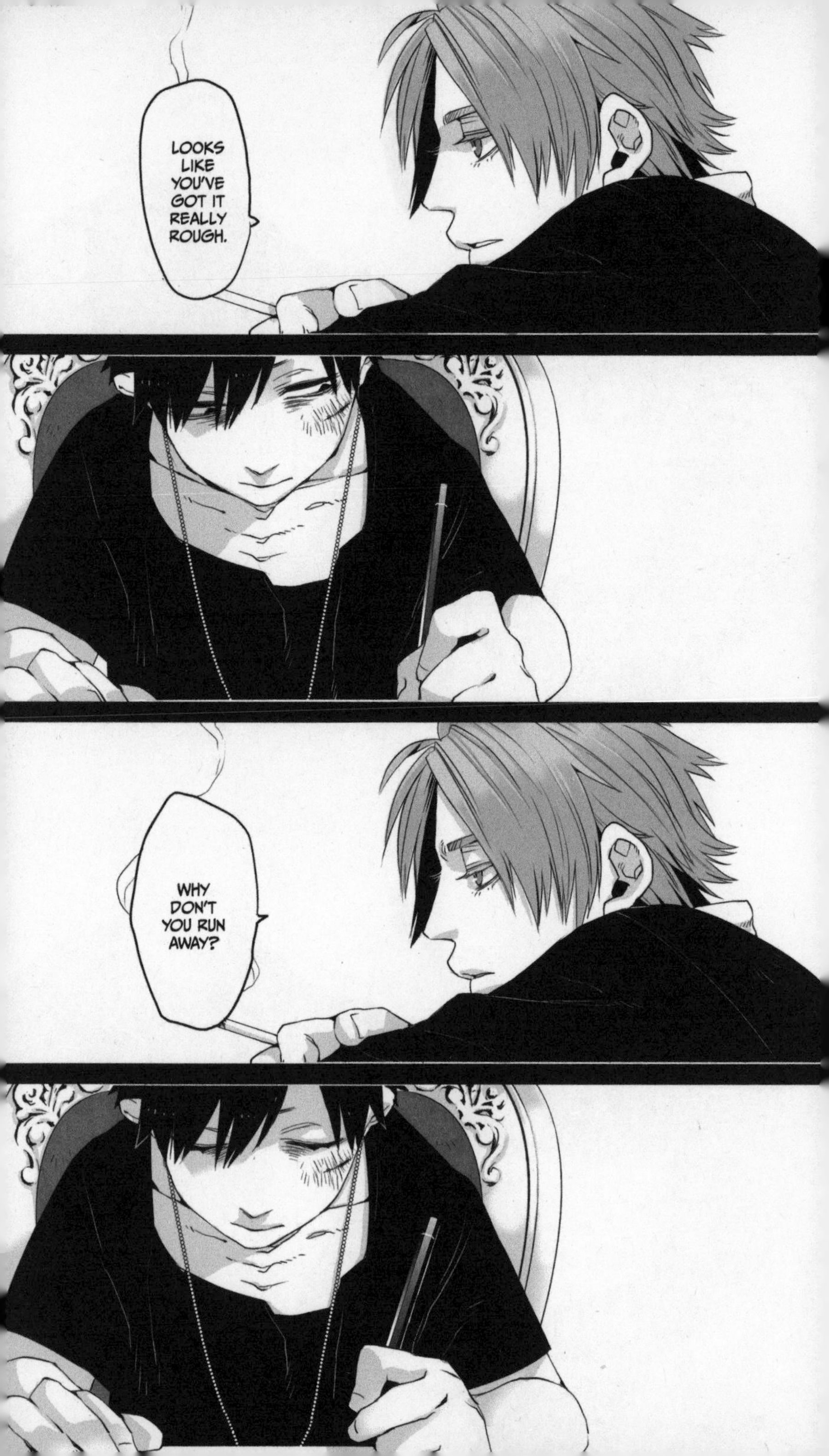
LOOKS LIKE YOU'VE GOT IT REALLY ROUGH.
WHY DON'T YOU RUN AWAY?

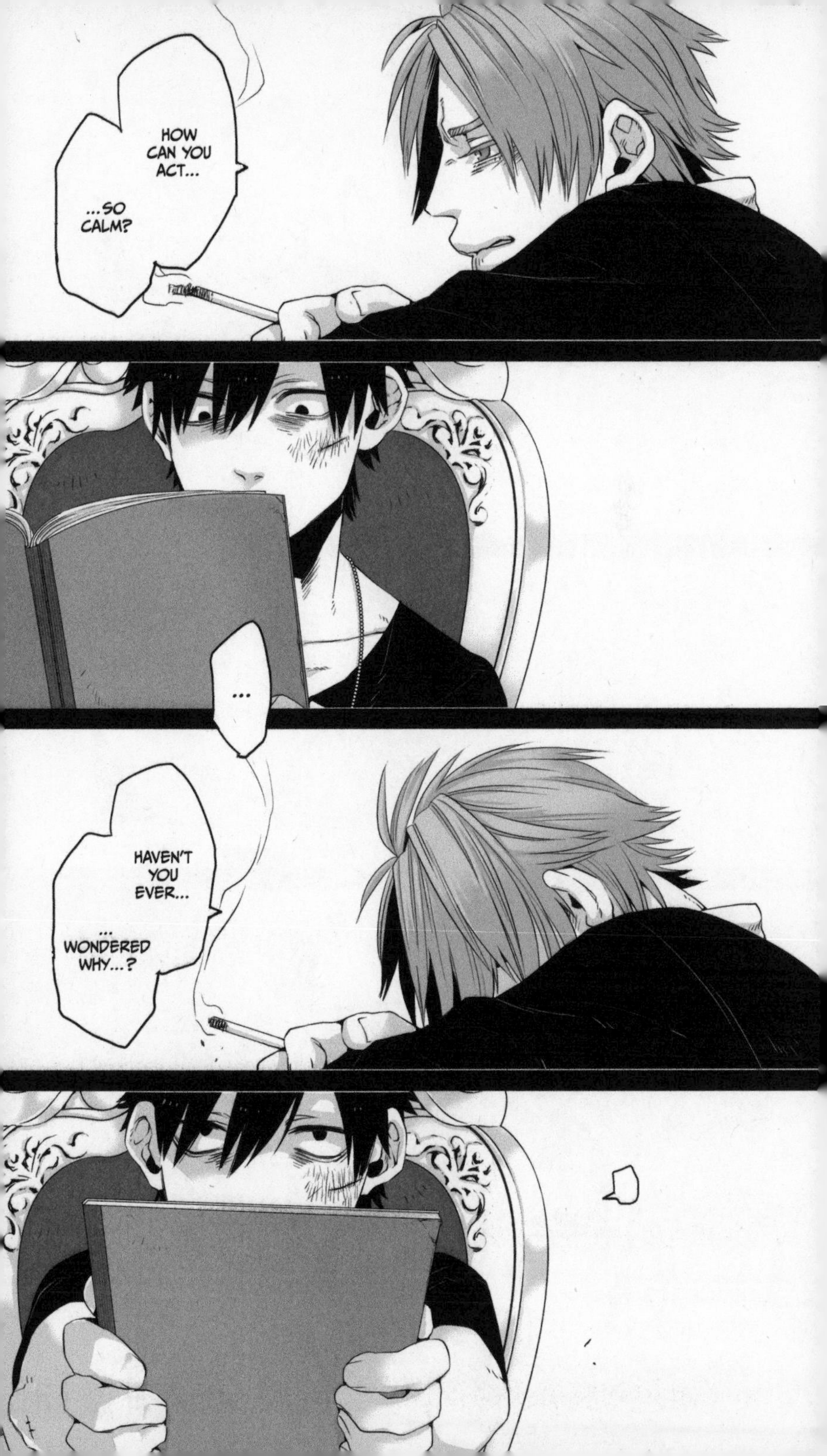
HOW CAN YOU ACT... ...SO CALM?
...
HAVEN'T YOU EVER... ...WONDERED WHY...?

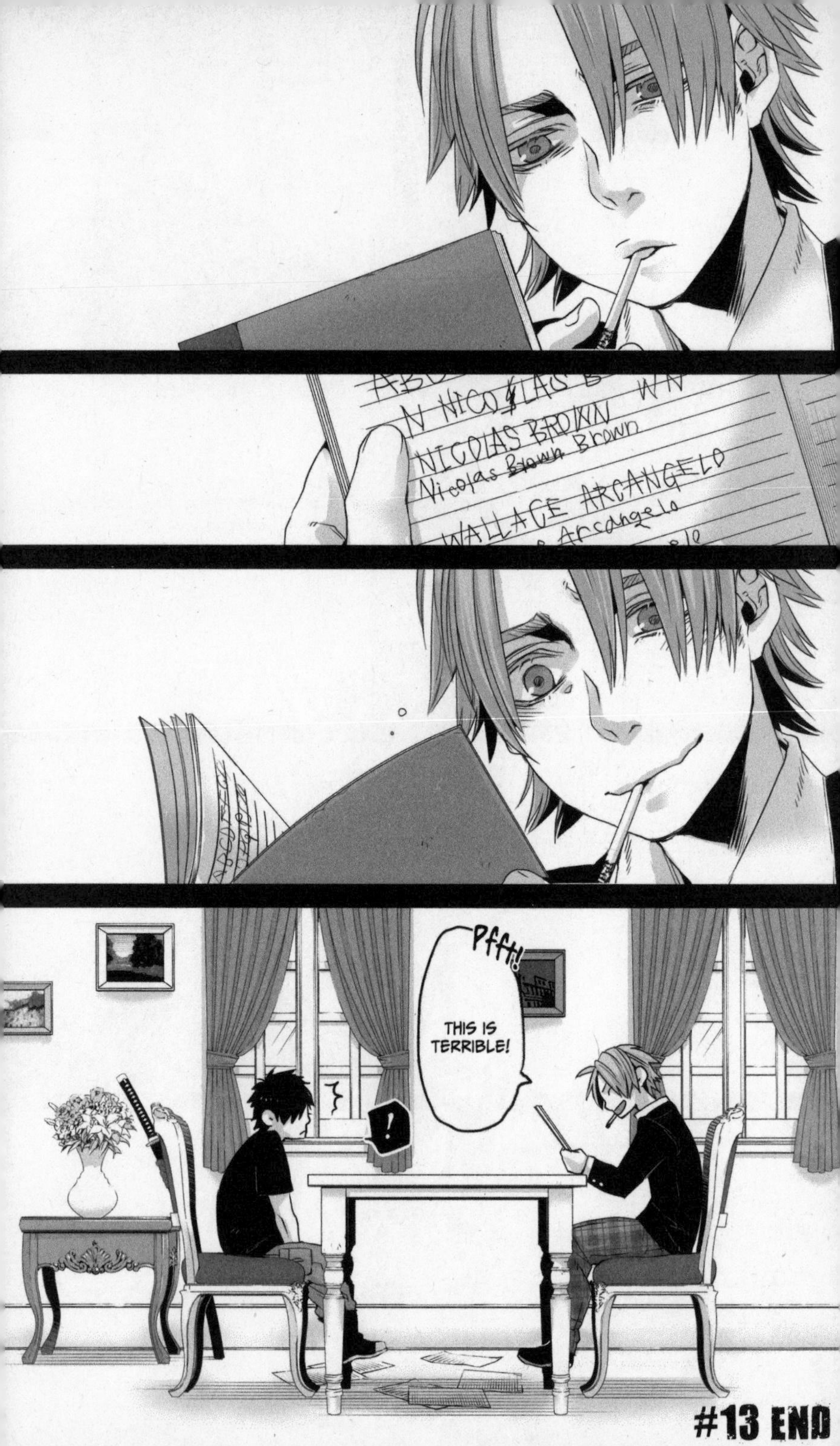

NICOLAS BROWN
Nicolas Brown Brown
WALLACE ARCANGELO
Pfft!
THIS IS TERRIBLE!
!
#13 END

GANGST

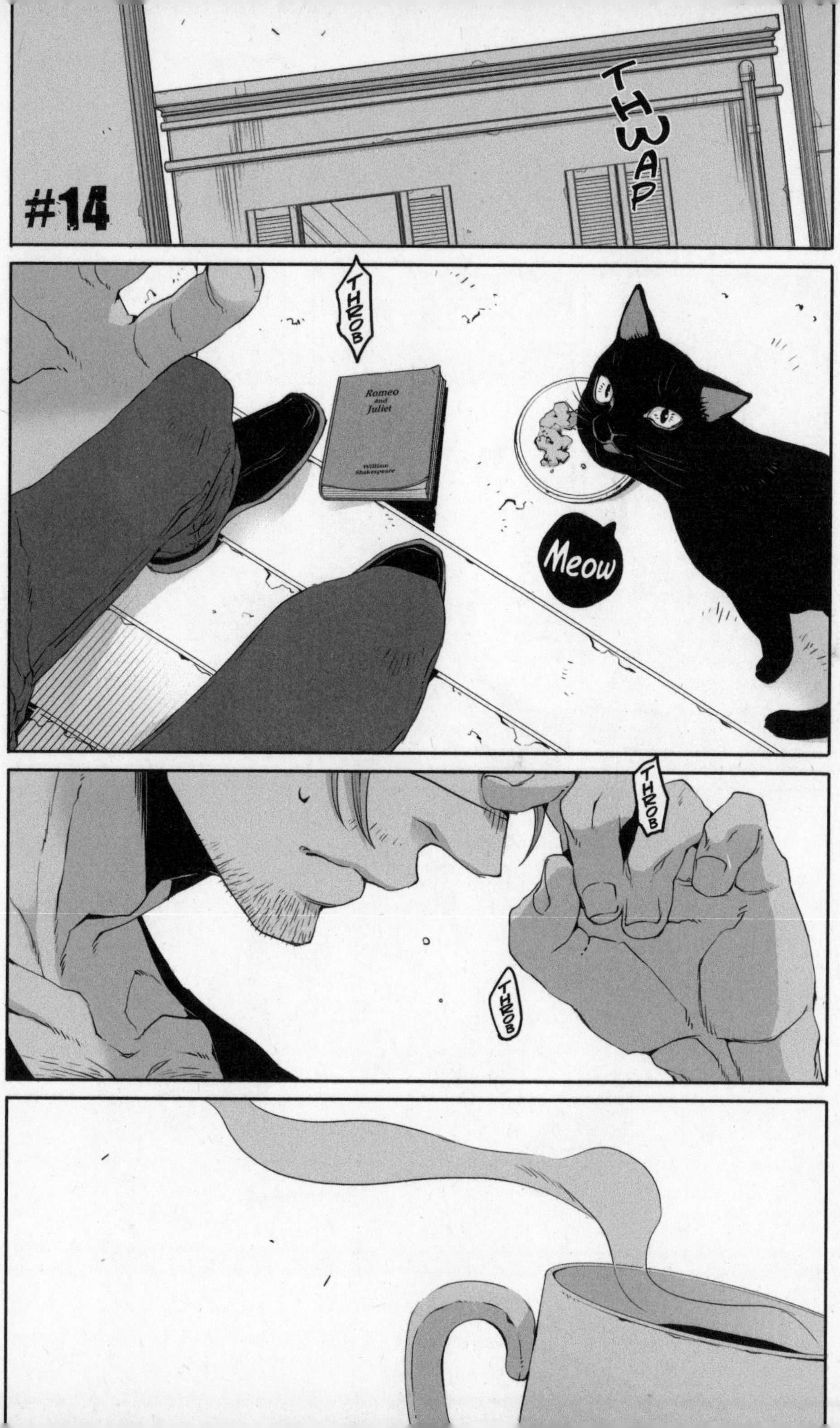

THWAP
#14
Meow
Romeo and Juliet
William Shakespeare
THROB
THROB
THROB

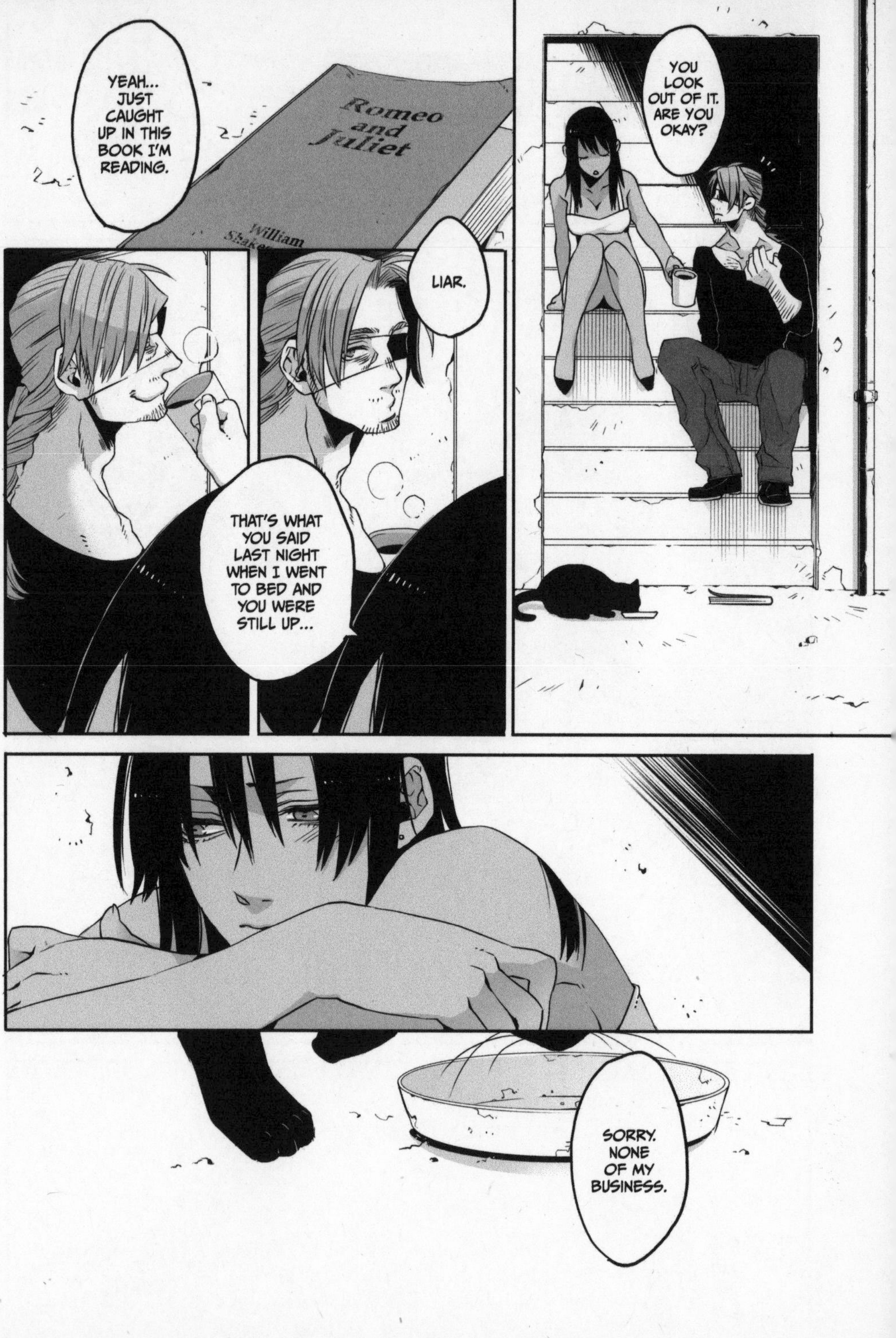
YOU LOOK OUT OF IT. ARE YOU OKAY?
YEAH... JUST CAUGHT UP IN THIS BOOK I'M READING.
Romeo and Juliet
William
LIAR.
THAT'S WHAT YOU SAID LAST NIGHT WHEN I WENT TO BED AND YOU WERE STILL UP...
SORRY. NONE OF MY BUSINESS.

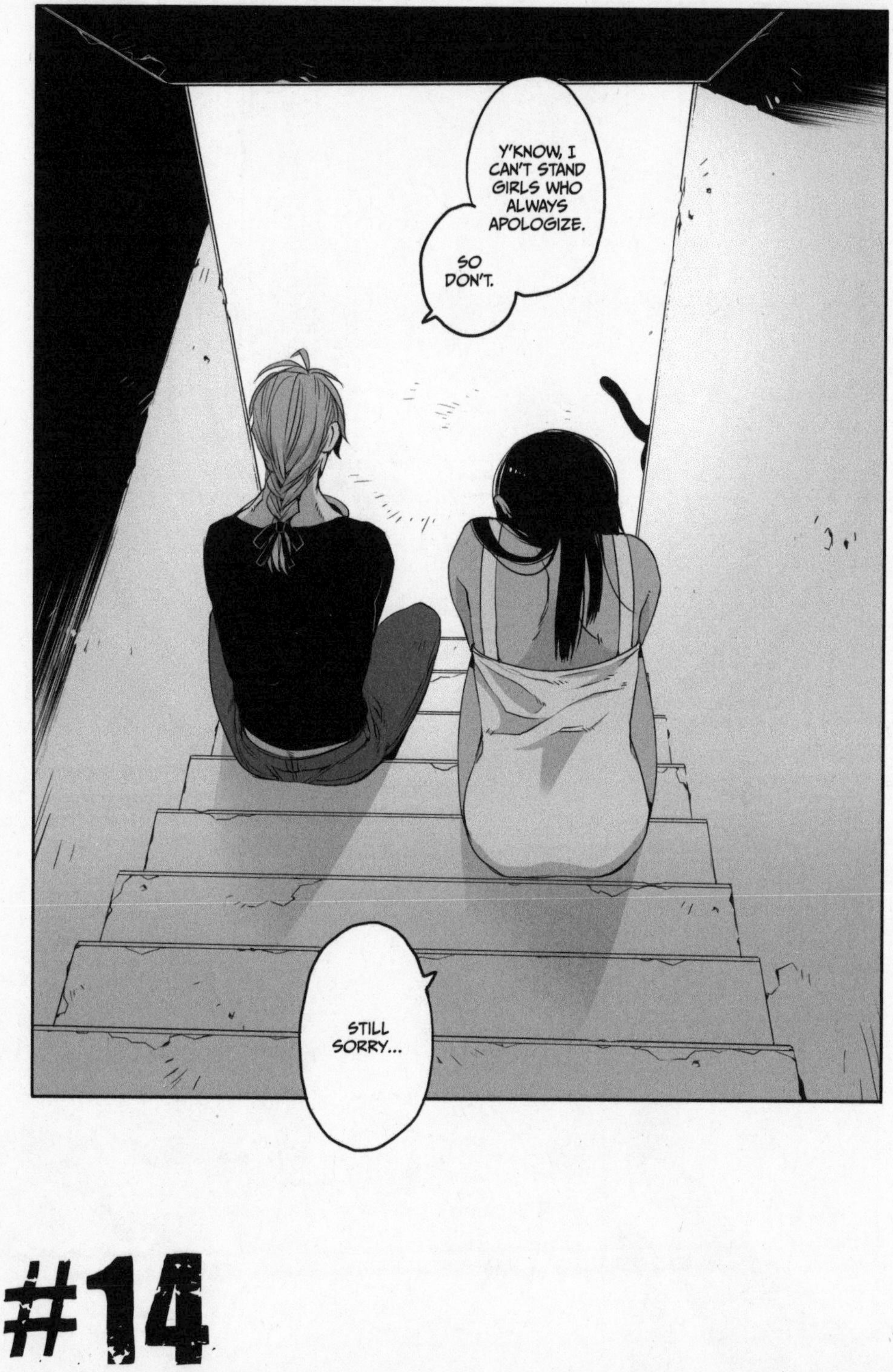
Y'KNOW, I CAN'T STAND GIRLS WHO ALWAYS APOLOGIZE.
SO DON'T.
STILL SORRY...

#14

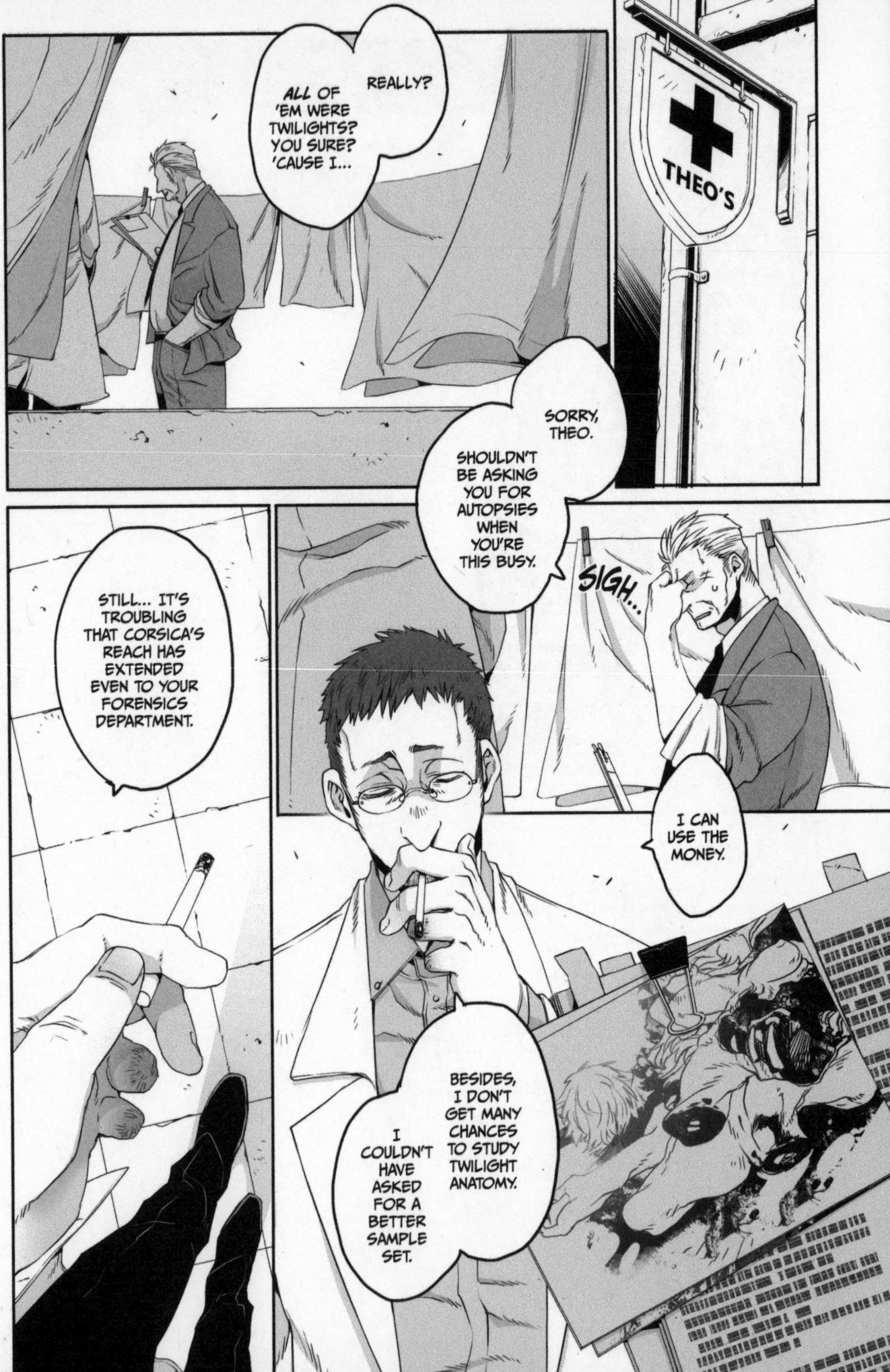
THEO'S
REALLY?
ALL OF 'EM WERE TWILIGHTS? YOU SURE? 'CAUSE I...
SORRY, THEO.
SHOULDN'T BE ASKING YOU FOR AUTOPSIES WHEN YOU'RE THIS BUSY.
SIGH...
I CAN USE THE MONEY.
STILL... IT'S TROUBLING THAT CORSICA'S REACH HAS EXTENDED EVEN TO YOUR FORENSICS DEPARTMENT.
BESIDES, I DON'T GET MANY CHANCES TO STUDY TWILIGHT ANATOMY.
I COULDN'T HAVE ASKED FOR A BETTER SAMPLE SET.

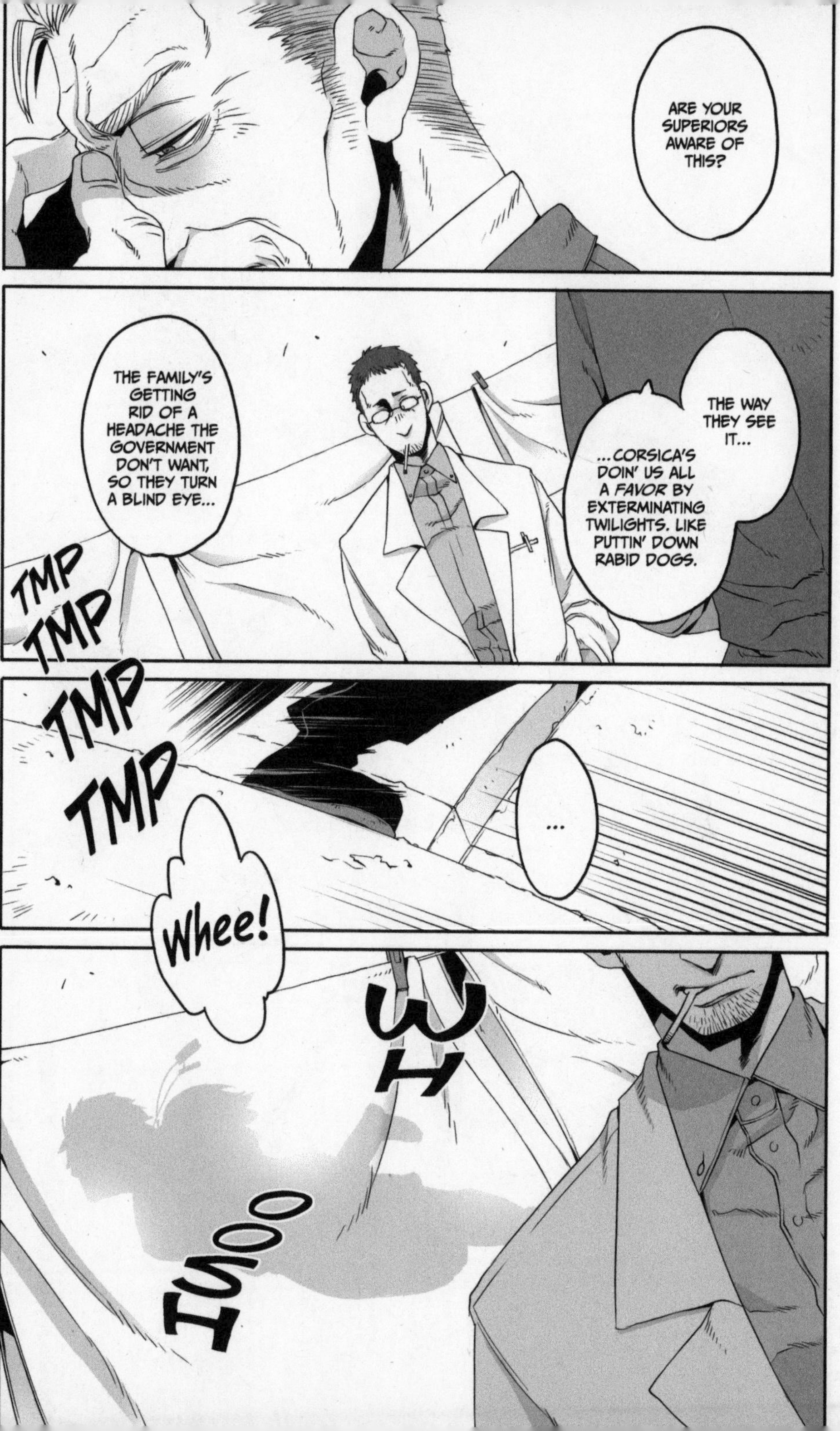
ARE YOUR SUPERIORS AWARE OF THIS?
THE WAY THEY SEE IT...
...CORSICA'S DOIN' US ALL A *FAVOR* BY EXTERMINATING TWILIGHTS. LIKE PUTTIN' DOWN RABID DOGS.
THE FAMILY'S GETTING RID OF A HEADACHE THE GOVERNMENT DON'T WANT, SO THEY TURN A BLIND EYE...
TMP TMP
TMP TMP
...
Whee!
WHOOOSH

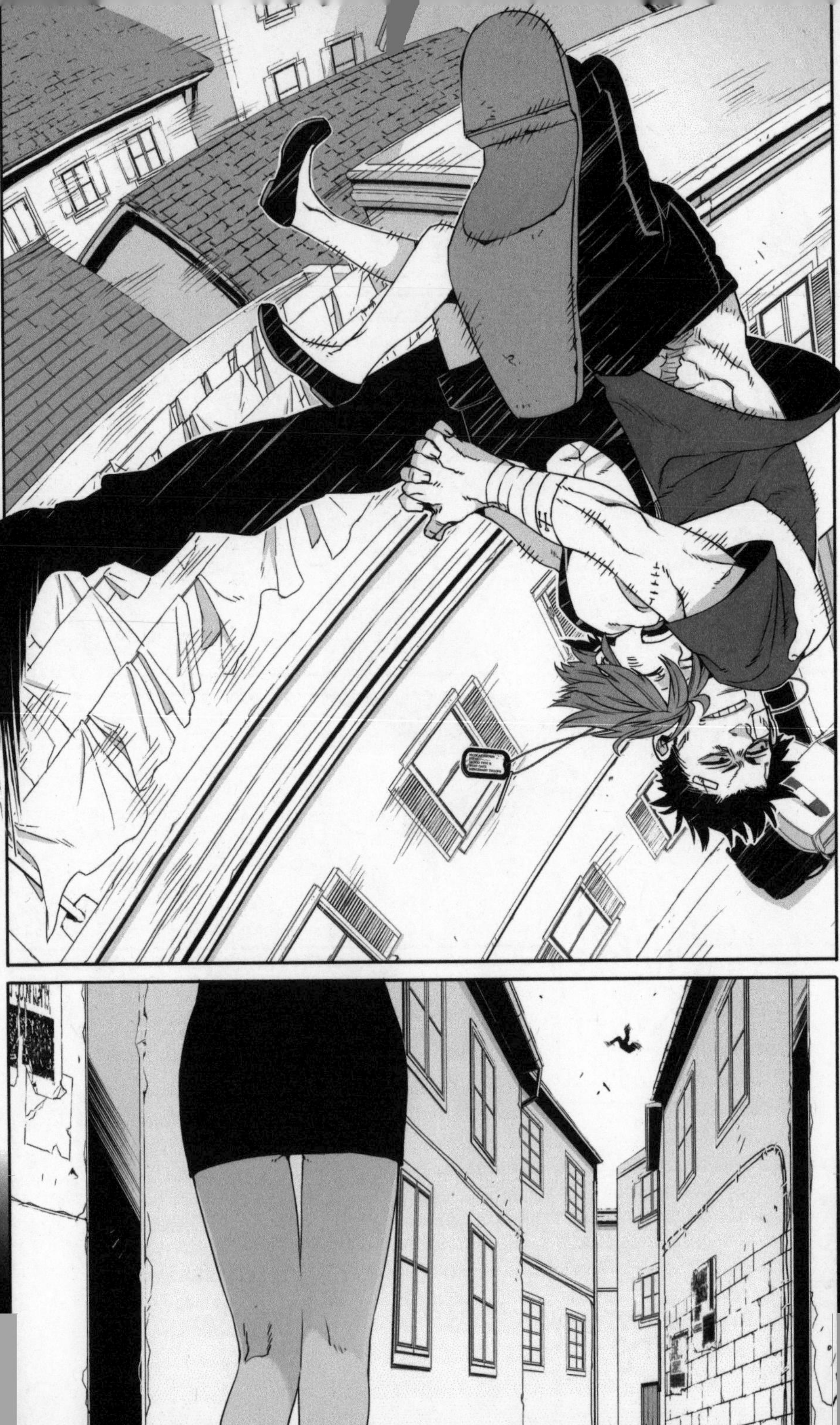

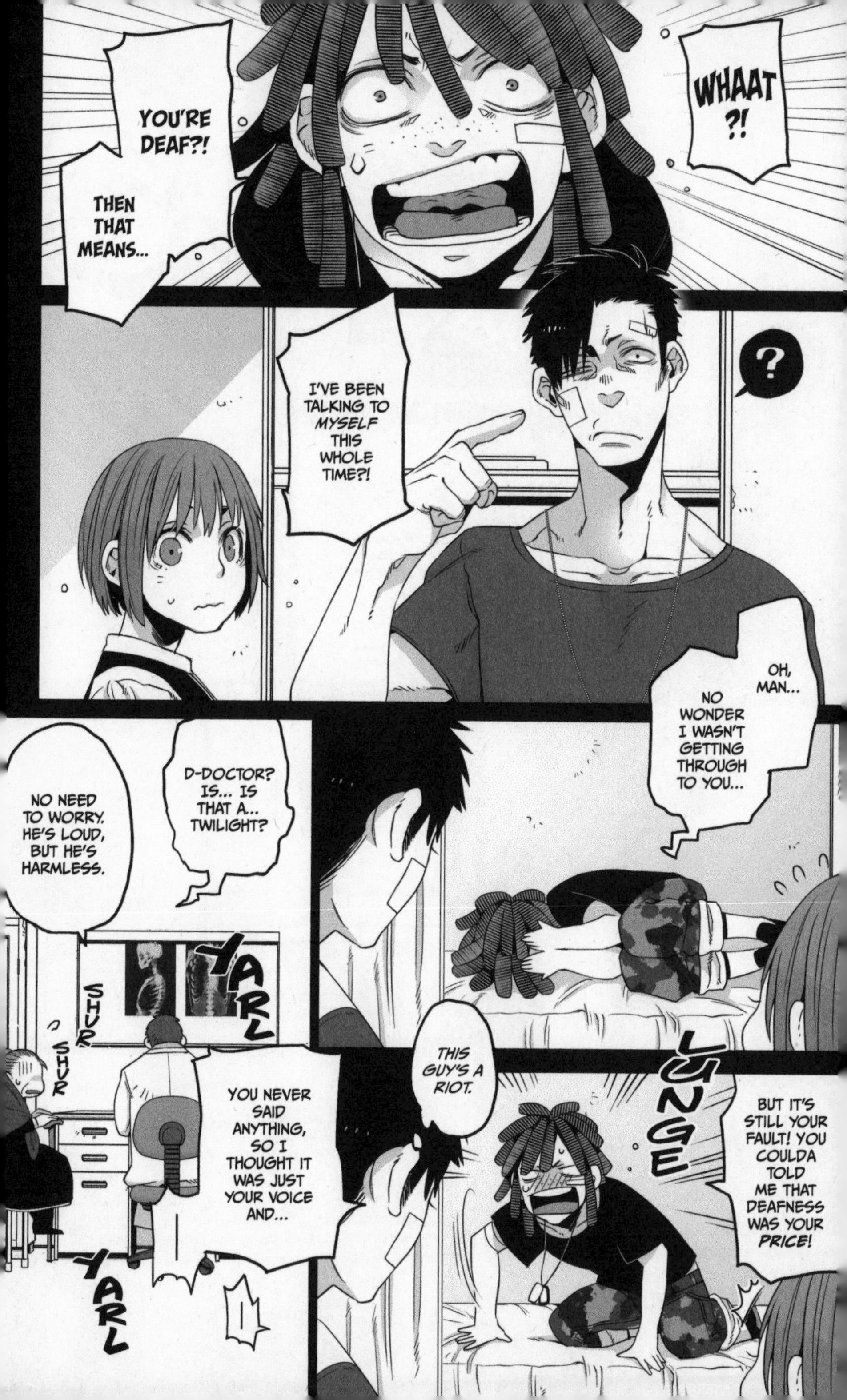
WHAAT ?!
YOU'RE DEAF?!
THEN THAT MEANS...
?
I'VE BEEN TALKING TO *MYSELF* THIS WHOLE TIME?!
OH, MAN... NO WONDER I WASN'T GETTING THROUGH TO YOU...
D-DOCTOR? IS... IS THAT A... TWILIGHT?
NO NEED TO WORRY. HE'S LOUD, BUT HE'S HARMLESS.
YARL
SHUR SHUR
LUNGE
BUT IT'S STILL YOUR FAULT! YOU COULDA TOLD ME THAT DEAFNESS WAS YOUR *PRICE*!
THIS GUY'S A RIOT.
YOU NEVER SAID ANYTHING, SO I THOUGHT IT WAS JUST YOUR VOICE AND...
!
YARL

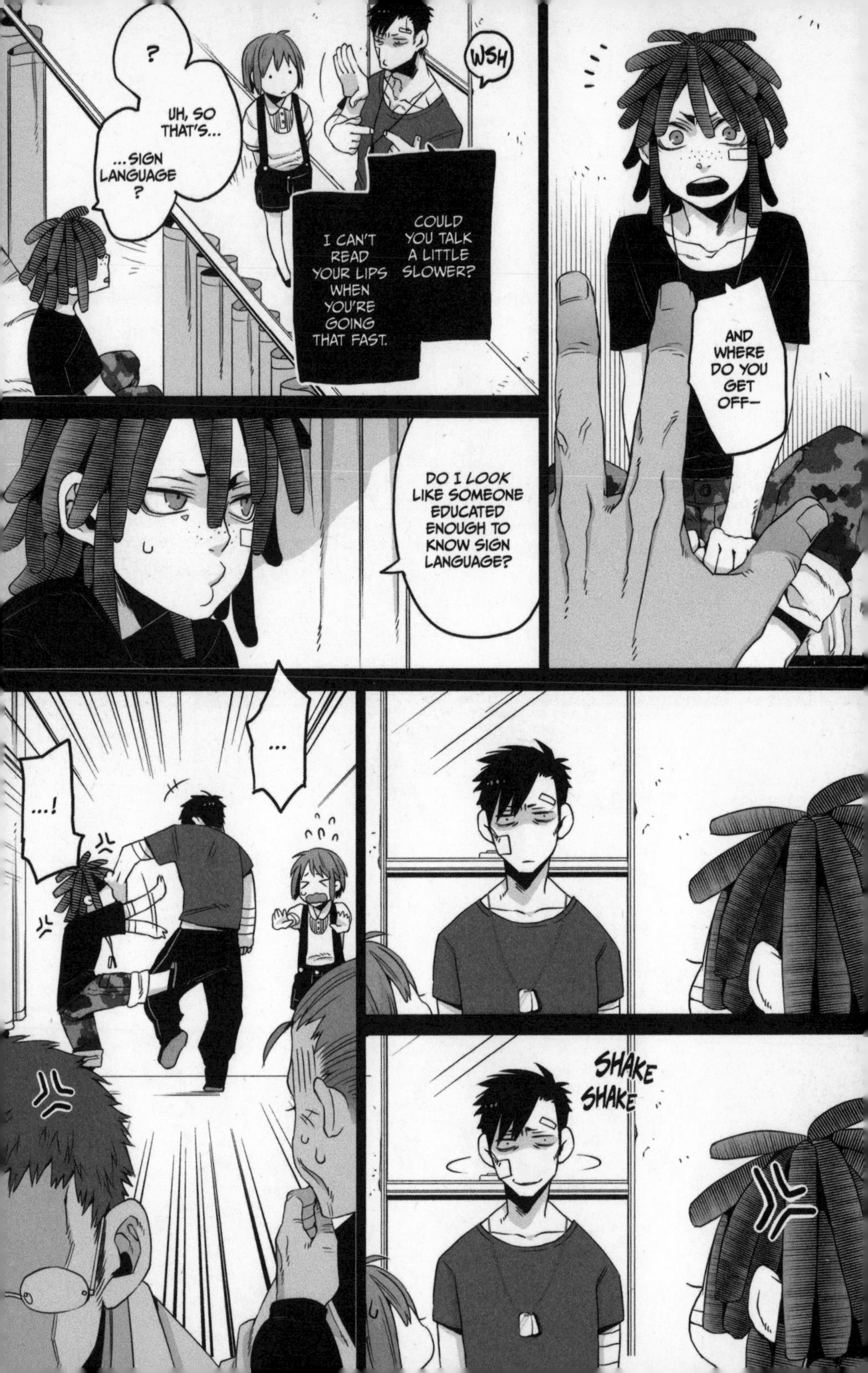
?
UH, SO THAT'S...
...SIGN LANGUAGE?
WSH
COULD YOU TALK A LITTLE SLOWER?
I CAN'T READ YOUR LIPS WHEN YOU'RE GOING THAT FAST.
AND WHERE DO YOU GET OFF—
DO I LOOK LIKE SOMEONE EDUCATED ENOUGH TO KNOW SIGN LANGUAGE?
...
...!
SHAKE
SHAKE

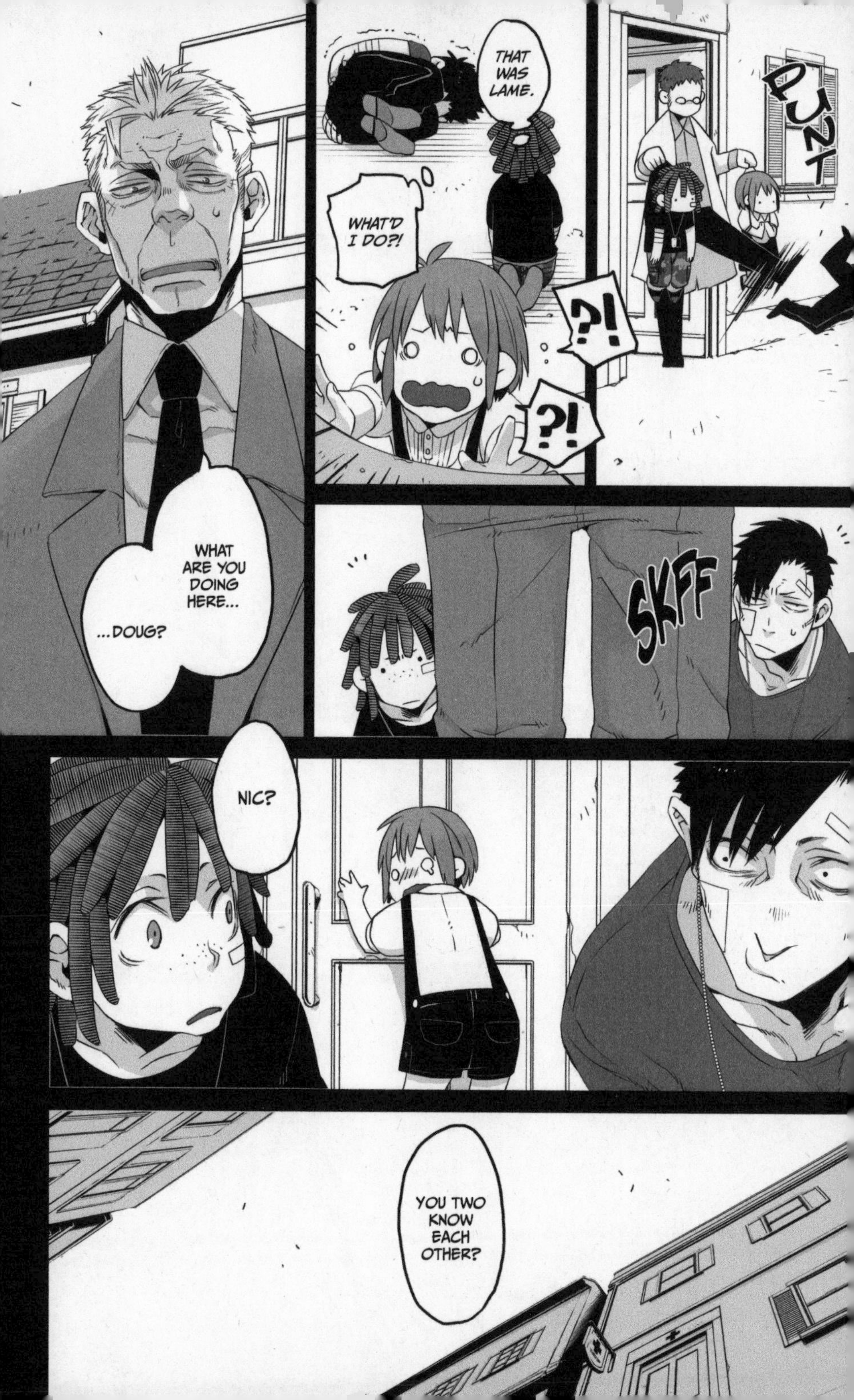
PUNT
THAT WAS LAME.
WHAT'D I DO?!
?!
?!
SKFF
WHAT ARE YOU DOING HERE...
...DOUG?
NIC?
YOU TWO KNOW EACH OTHER?

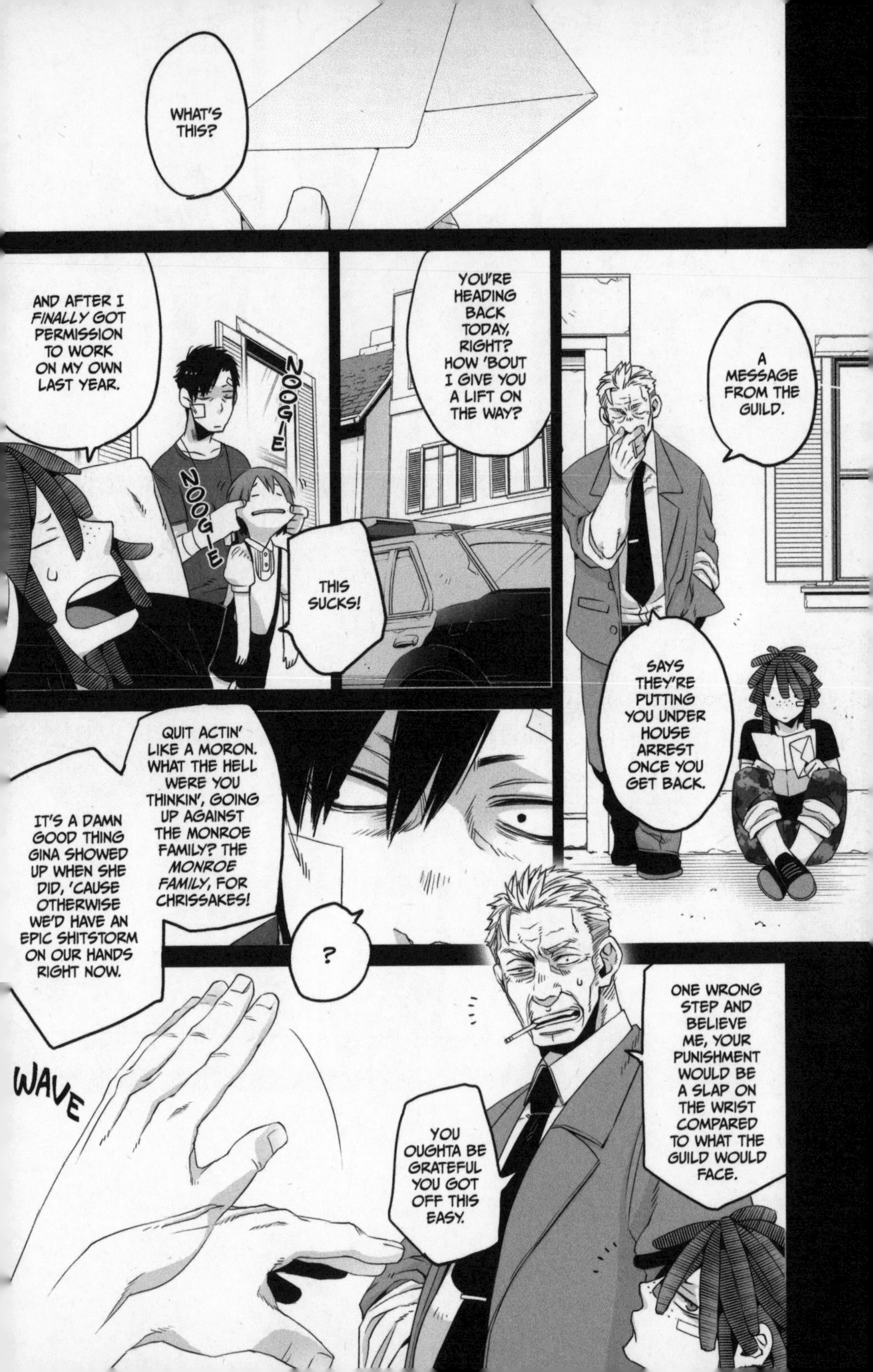
WHAT'S THIS?
A MESSAGE FROM THE GUILD.
SAYS THEY'RE PUTTING YOU UNDER HOUSE ARREST ONCE YOU GET BACK.
YOU'RE HEADING BACK TODAY, RIGHT? HOW 'BOUT I GIVE YOU A LIFT ON THE WAY?
THIS SUCKS!
NOOGIE
NOOGIE
AND AFTER I *FINALLY* GOT PERMISSION TO WORK ON MY OWN LAST YEAR.
QUIT ACTIN' LIKE A MORON. WHAT THE HELL WERE YOU THINKIN', GOING UP AGAINST THE MONROE FAMILY? THE *MONROE FAMILY*, FOR CHRISSAKES!
IT'S A DAMN GOOD THING GINA SHOWED UP WHEN SHE DID, 'CAUSE OTHERWISE WE'D HAVE AN EPIC SHITSTORM ON OUR HANDS RIGHT NOW.
?
ONE WRONG STEP AND BELIEVE ME, YOUR PUNISHMENT WOULD BE A SLAP ON THE WRIST COMPARED TO WHAT THE GUILD WOULD FACE.
YOU OUGHTA BE GRATEFUL YOU GOT OFF THIS EASY.
WAVE

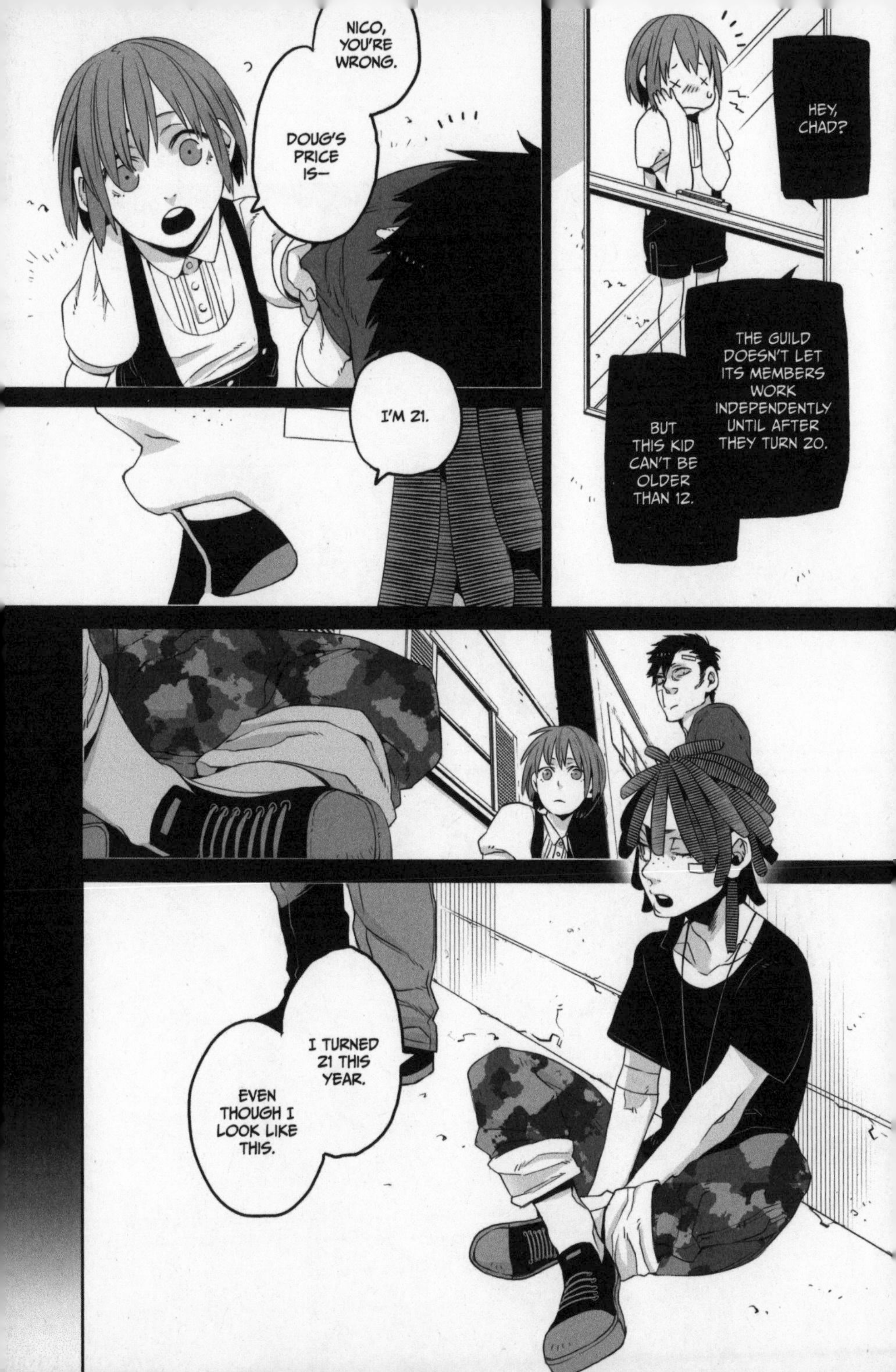
HEY, CHAD?
THE GUILD DOESN'T LET ITS MEMBERS WORK INDEPENDENTLY UNTIL AFTER THEY TURN 20.
BUT THIS KID CAN'T BE OLDER THAN 12.
NICO, YOU'RE WRONG.
DOUG'S PRICE IS—
I'M 21.
I TURNED 21 THIS YEAR.
EVEN THOUGH I LOOK LIKE THIS.

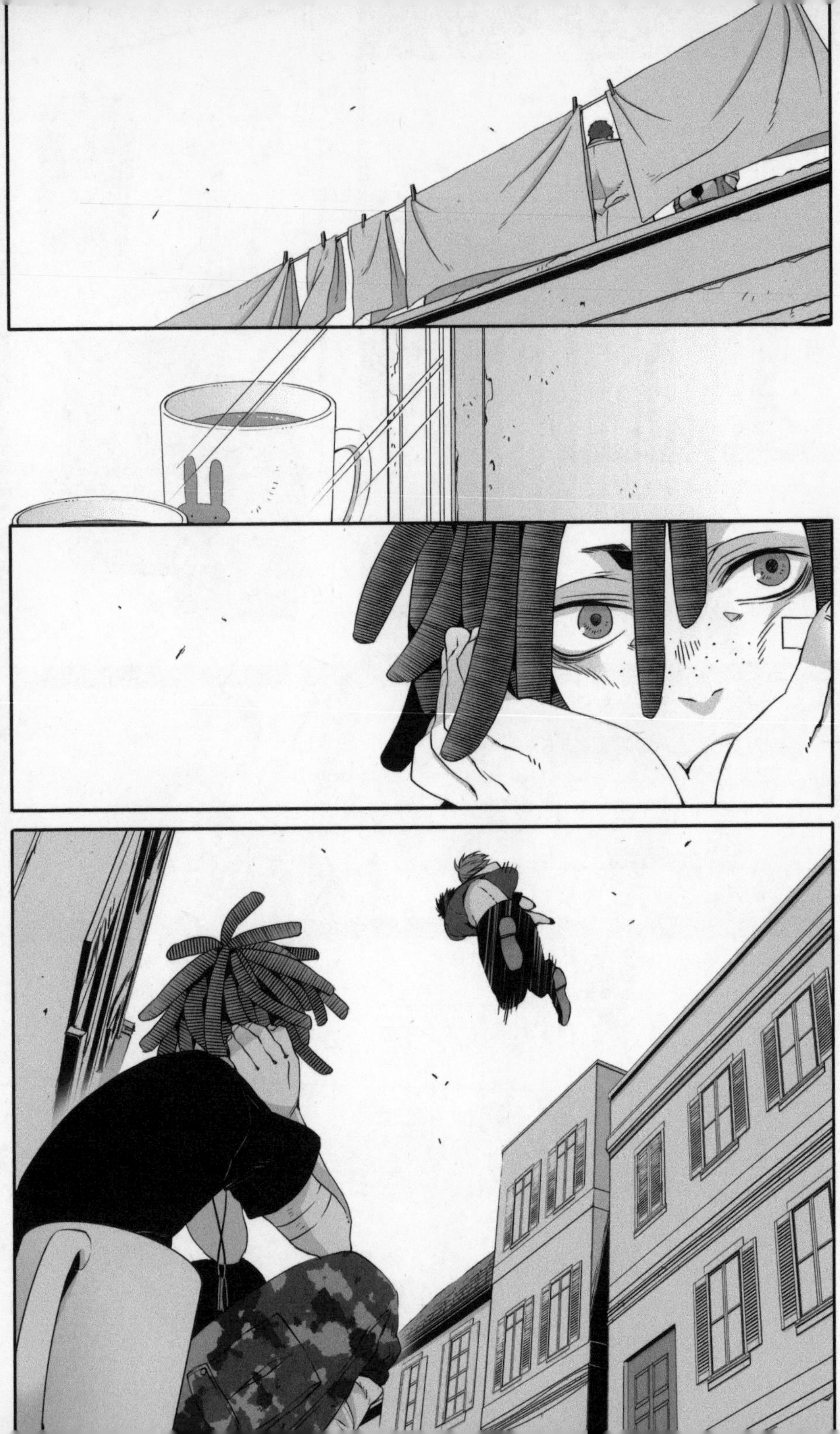

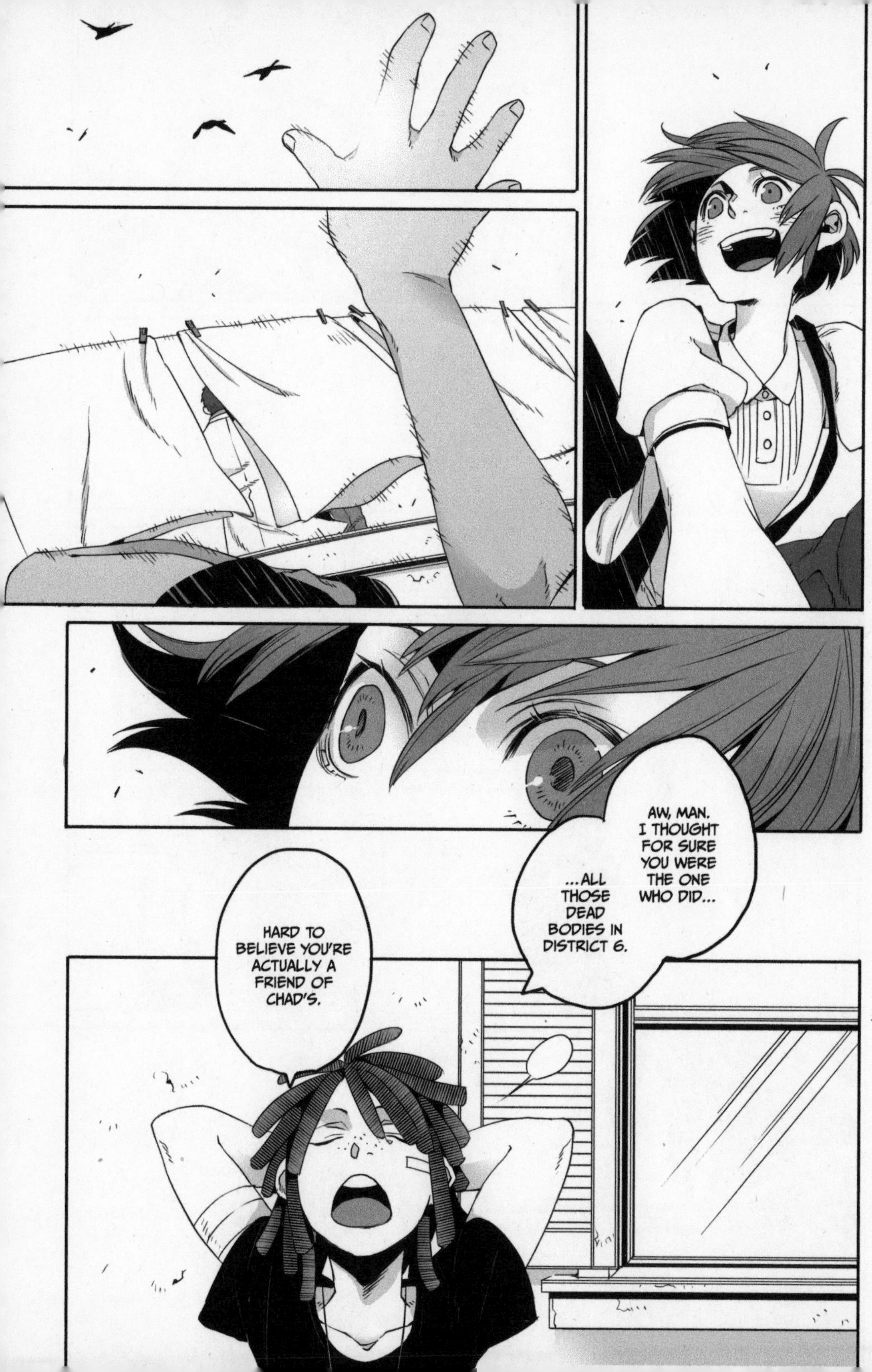
AW, MAN. I THOUGHT FOR SURE YOU WERE THE ONE WHO DID...
...ALL THOSE DEAD BODIES IN DISTRICT 6.
HARD TO BELIEVE YOU'RE ACTUALLY A FRIEND OF CHAD'S.

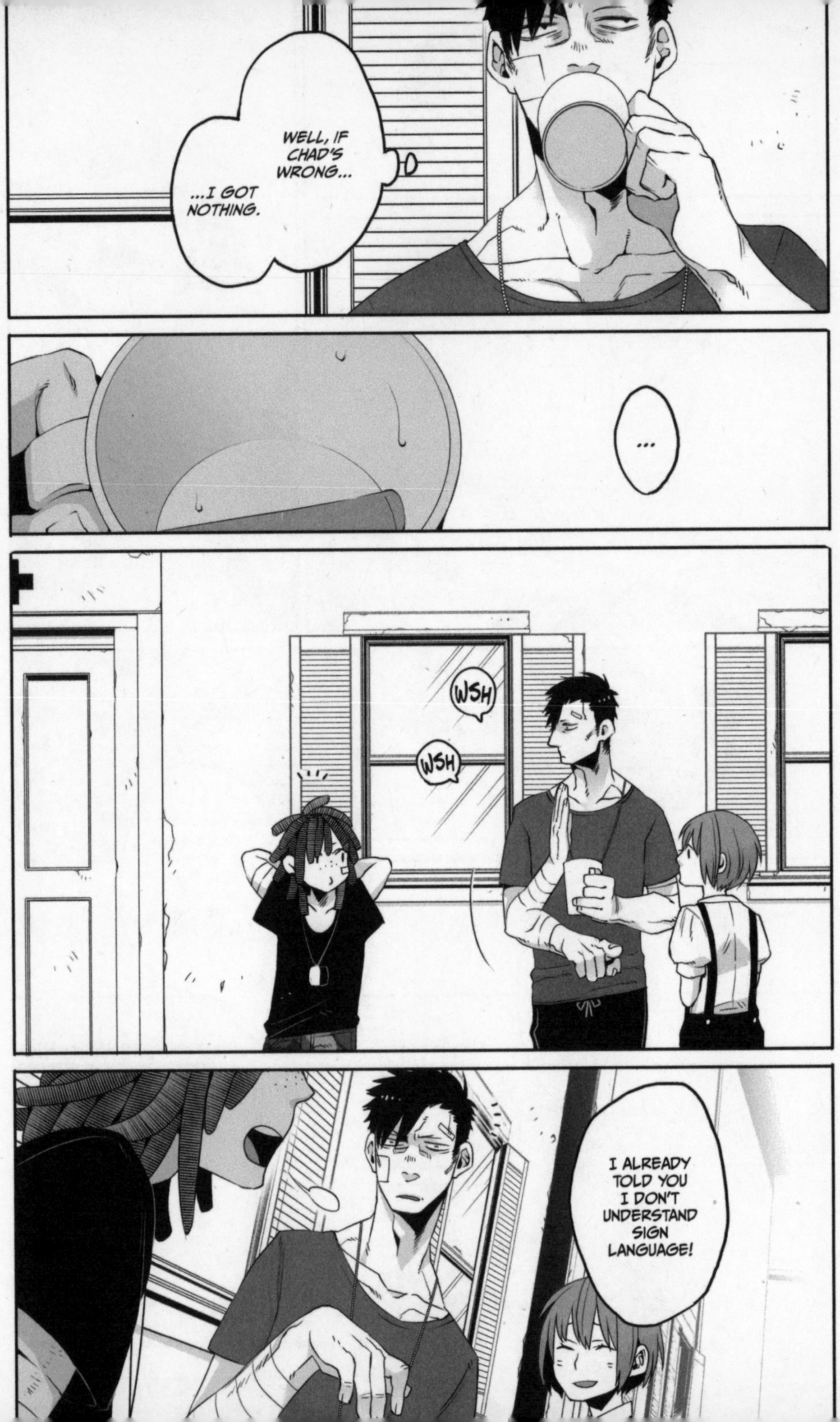
WELL, IF CHAD'S WRONG...
...I GOT NOTHING.
...
WSH
WSH
I ALREADY TOLD YOU I DON'T UNDERSTAND SIGN LANGUAGE!

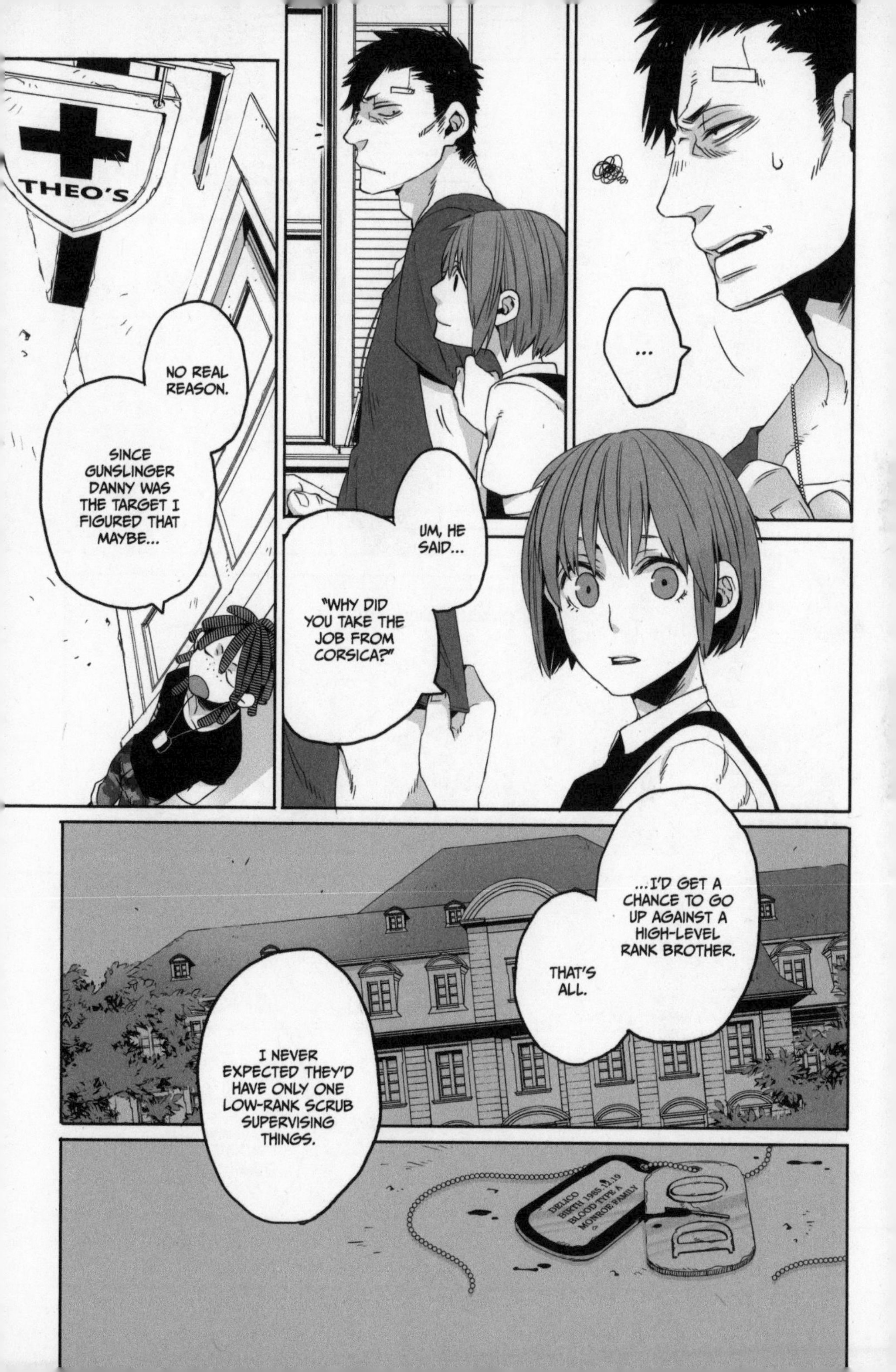
...
UM, HE SAID...
"WHY DID YOU TAKE THE JOB FROM CORSICA?"
THEO'S
NO REAL REASON.
SINCE GUNSLINGER DANNY WAS THE TARGET I FIGURED THAT MAYBE...
...I'D GET A CHANCE TO GO UP AGAINST A HIGH-LEVEL RANK BROTHER.
THAT'S ALL.
I NEVER EXPECTED THEY'D HAVE ONLY ONE LOW-RANK SCRUB SUPERVISING THINGS.
DELICO BIRTH 1985.12.19 BLOOD TYPE A MONROE FAMILY

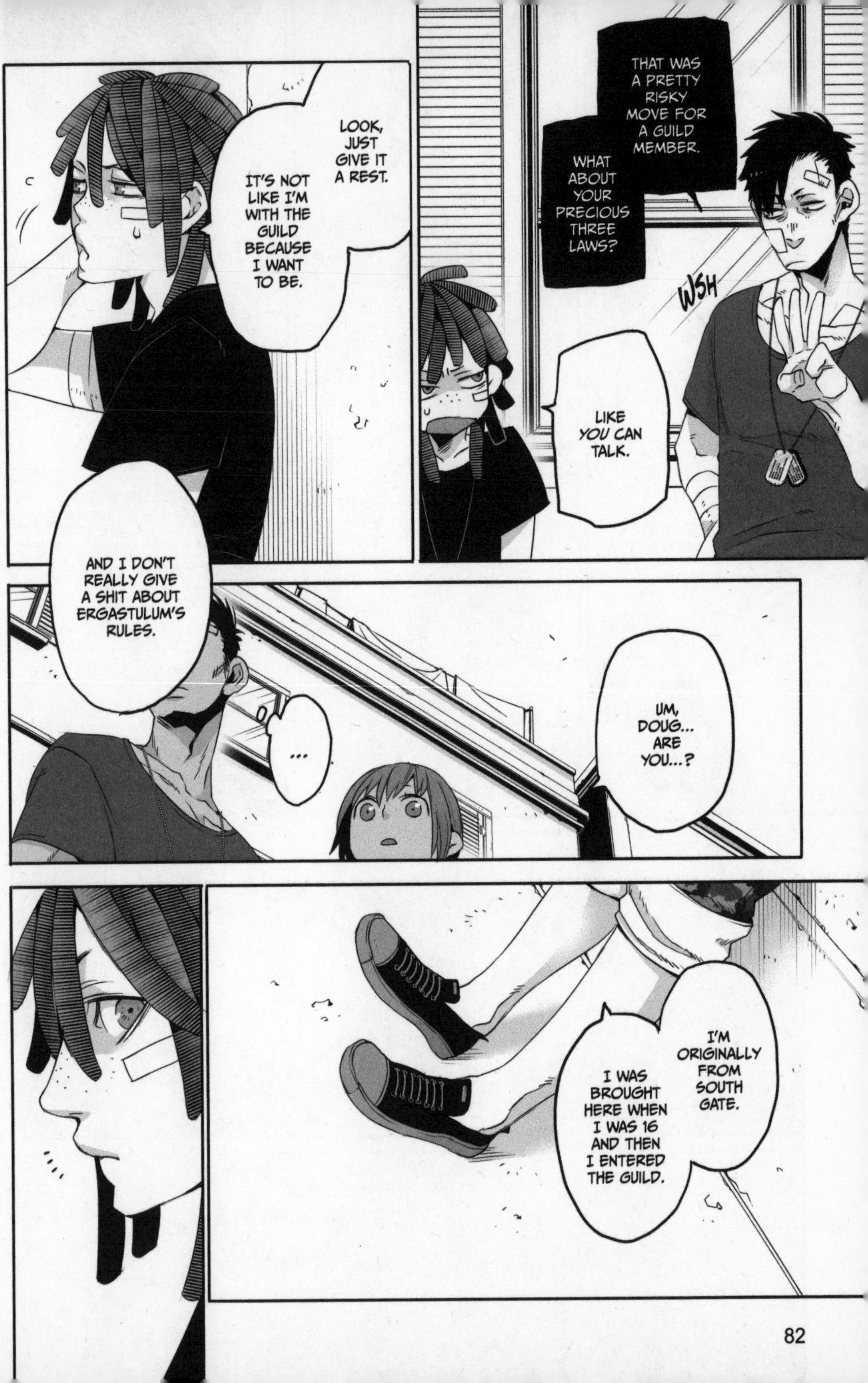
THAT WAS A PRETTY RISKY MOVE FOR A GUILD MEMBER.
WHAT ABOUT YOUR PRECIOUS THREE LAWS?
WSH
LIKE *YOU* CAN TALK.
LOOK, JUST GIVE IT A REST.
IT'S NOT LIKE I'M WITH THE GUILD BECAUSE I WANT TO BE.
AND I DON'T REALLY GIVE A SHIT ABOUT ERGASTULUM'S RULES.
UM, DOUG... ARE YOU...?
...
I'M ORIGINALLY FROM SOUTH GATE.
I WAS BROUGHT HERE WHEN I WAS 16 AND THEN I ENTERED THE GUILD.

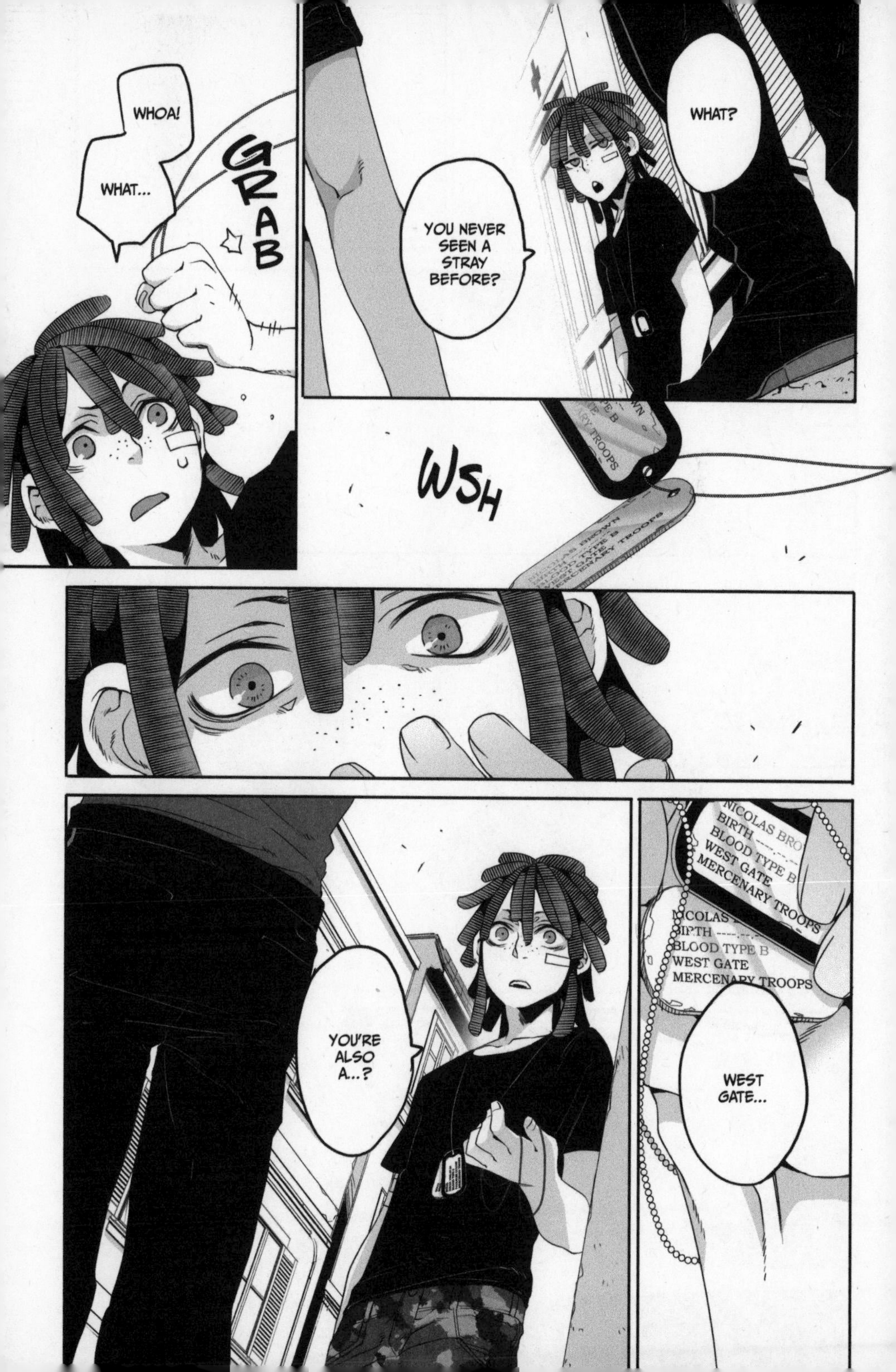
WHAT?
YOU NEVER SEEN A STRAY BEFORE?
WHOA!
WHAT...
GRAB
WSH
NICOLAS BROWN
BLOOD TYPE B
WEST GATE
MERCENARY TROOPS
NICOLAS BRO
BIRTH
BLOOD TYPE B
WEST GATE
MERCENARY TROOPS
BIRTH
BLOOD TYPE B
WEST GATE
MERCENARY TROOPS
WEST GATE...
YOU'RE ALSO A...?

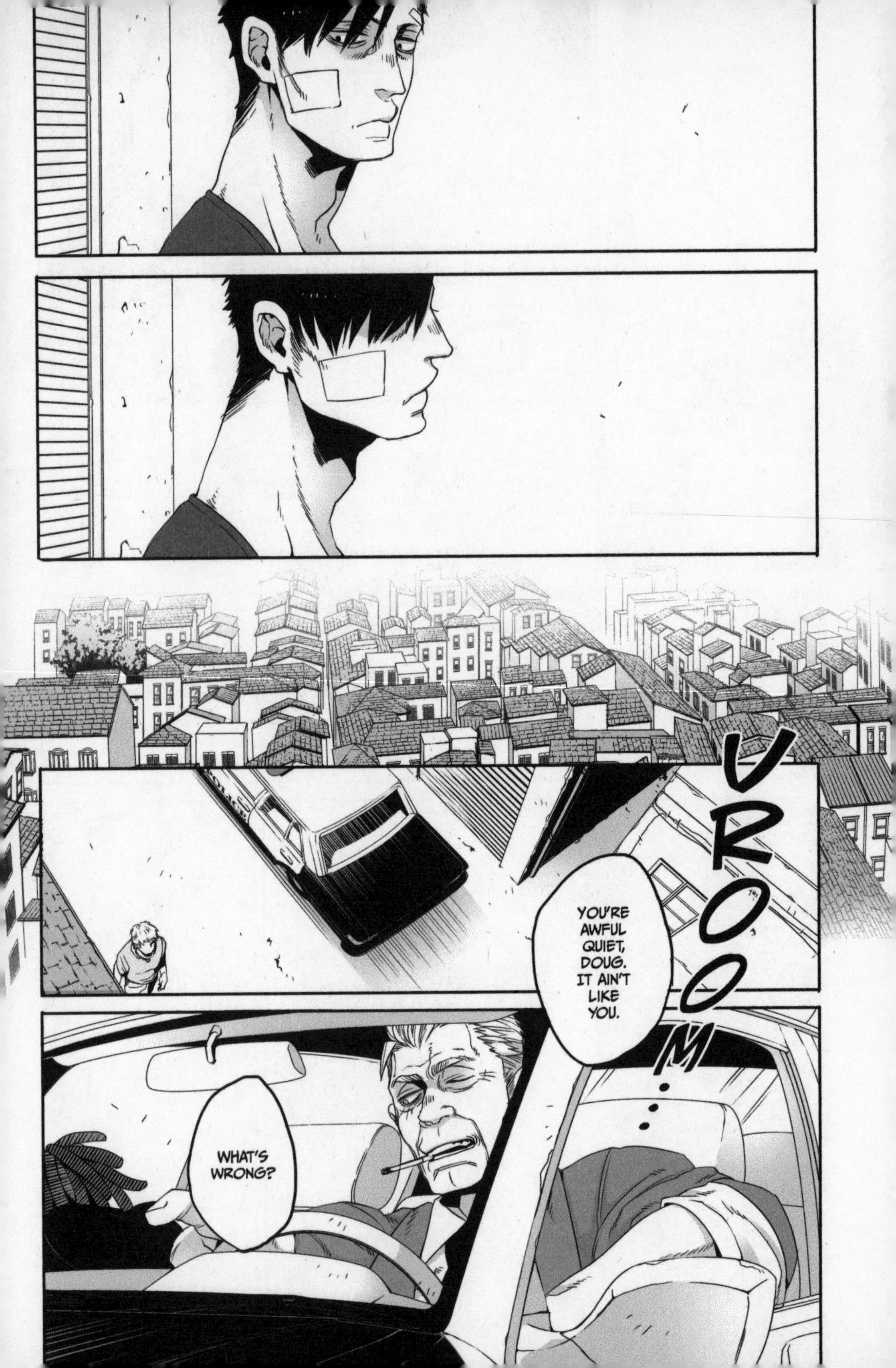
VROOOM...
YOU'RE AWFUL QUIET, DOUG. IT AIN'T LIKE YOU.
WHAT'S WRONG?

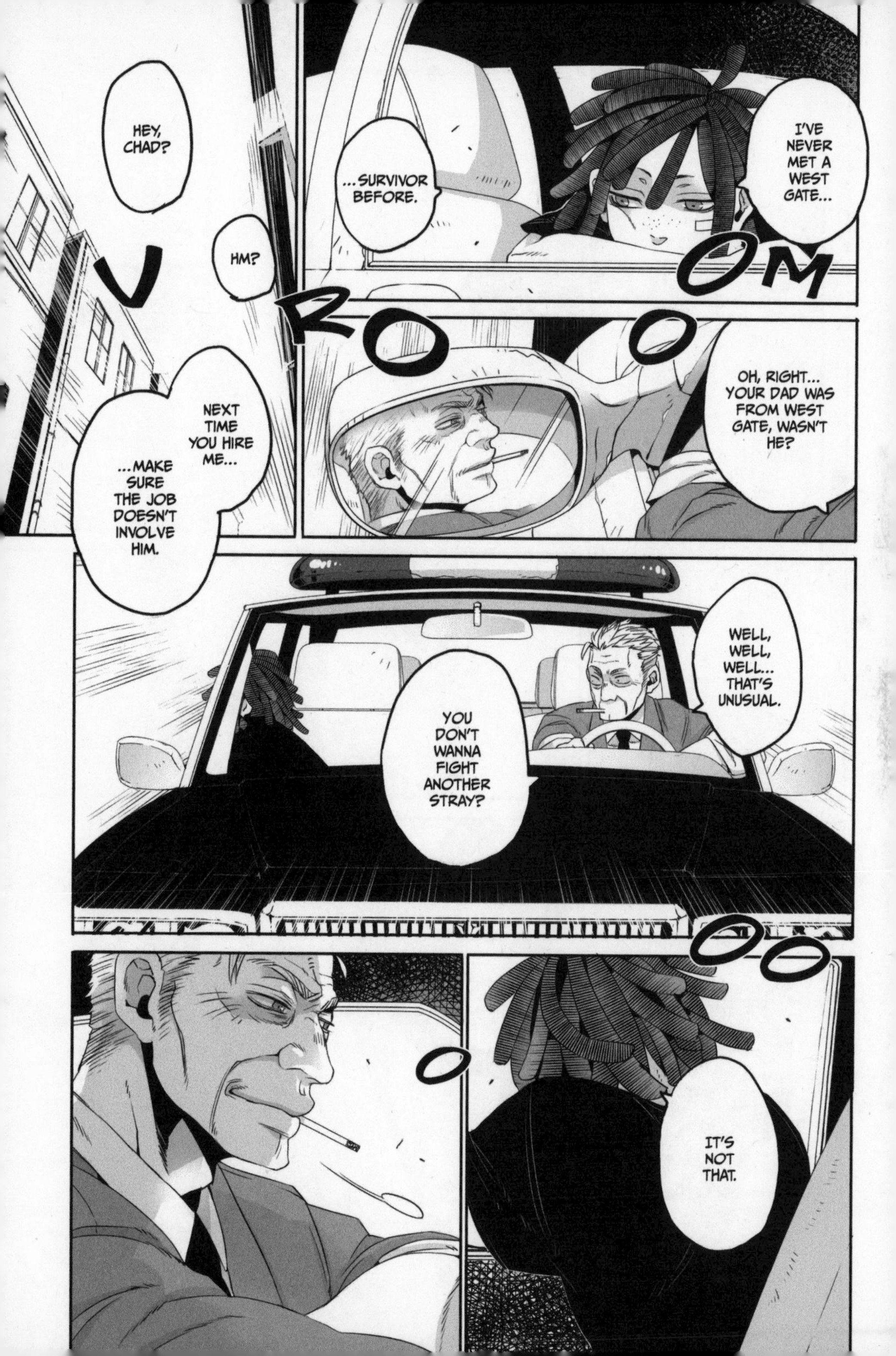
I'VE NEVER MET A WEST GATE...
...SURVIVOR BEFORE.
VROOOOM
OH, RIGHT... YOUR DAD WAS FROM WEST GATE, WASN'T HE?
HEY, CHAD?
HM?
NEXT TIME YOU HIRE ME...
...MAKE SURE THE JOB DOESN'T INVOLVE HIM.
WELL, WELL, WELL... THAT'S UNUSUAL.
YOU DON'T WANNA FIGHT ANOTHER STRAY?
OOO
IT'S NOT THAT.

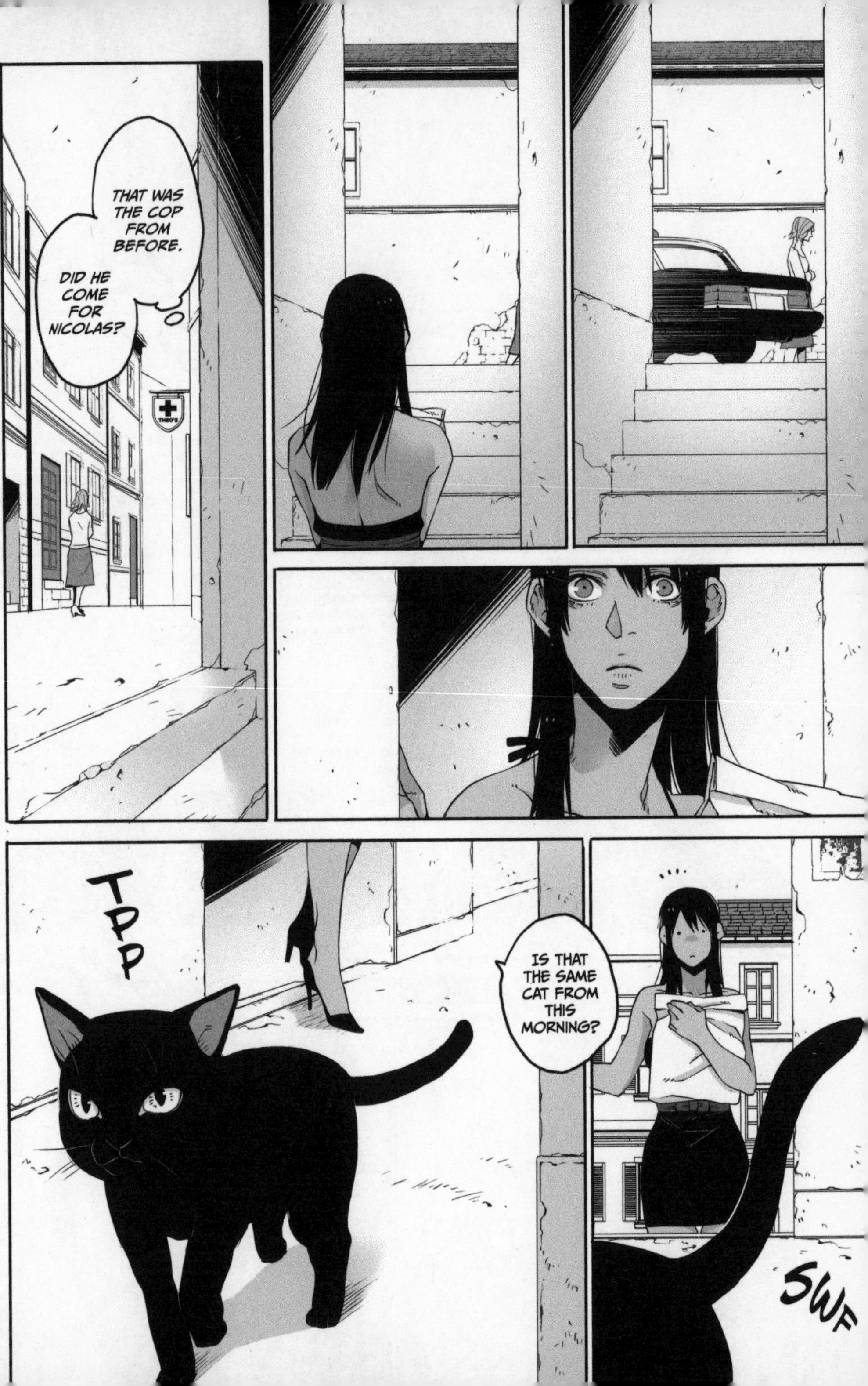
THAT WAS THE COP FROM BEFORE.
DID HE COME FOR NICOLAS?
THEO'S
IS THAT THE SAME CAT FROM THIS MORNING?
SWF
TPP

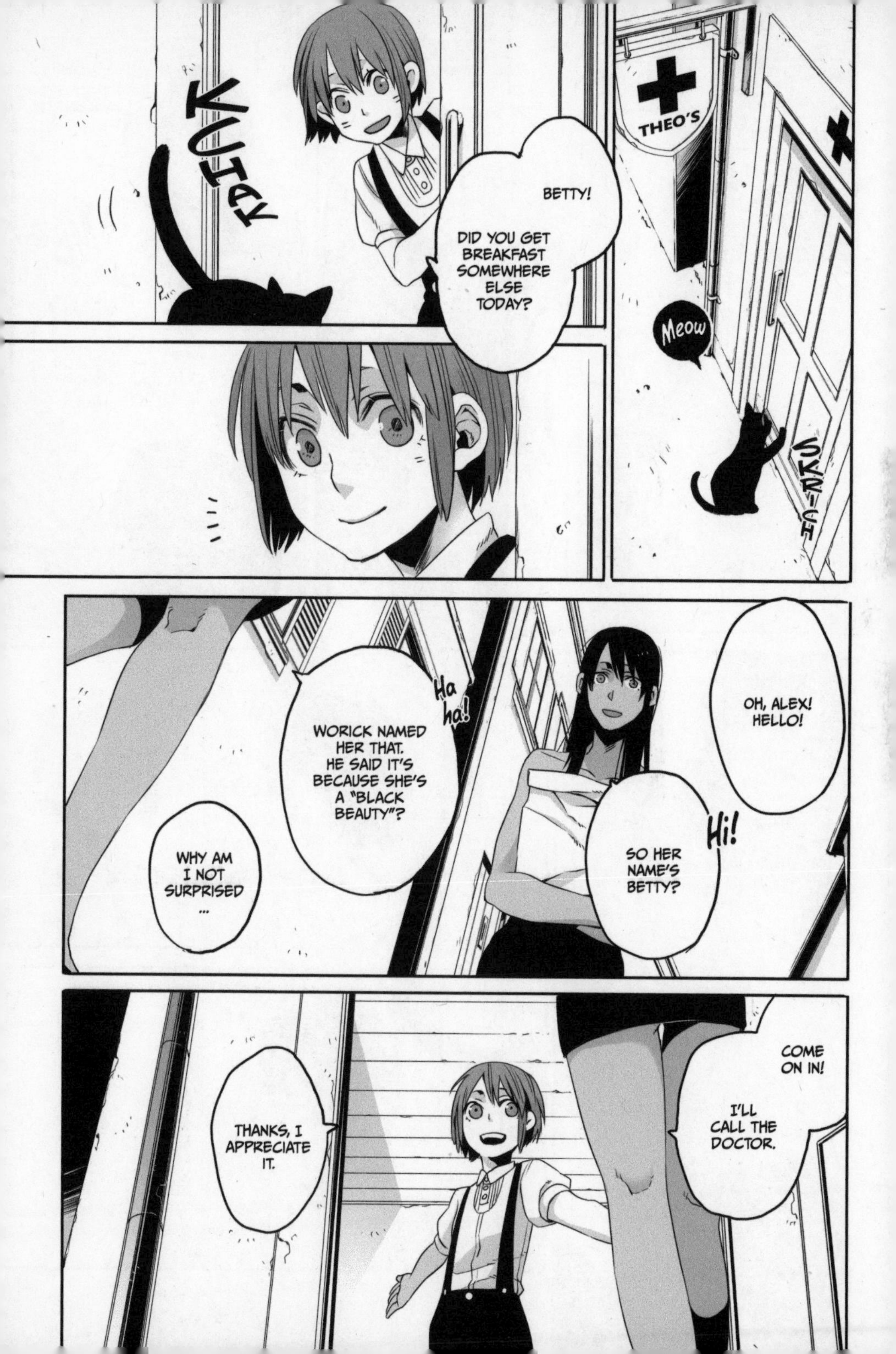

THEO'S
Meow
SKRICH
KACHAK
BETTY!
DID YOU GET BREAKFAST SOMEWHERE ELSE TODAY?
OH, ALEX! HELLO!
Hi!
SO HER NAME'S BETTY?
Ha ha!
WORICK NAMED HER THAT. HE SAID IT'S BECAUSE SHE'S A "BLACK BEAUTY"?
WHY AM I NOT SURPRISED...
COME ON IN!
I'LL CALL THE DOCTOR.
THANKS, I APPRECIATE IT.

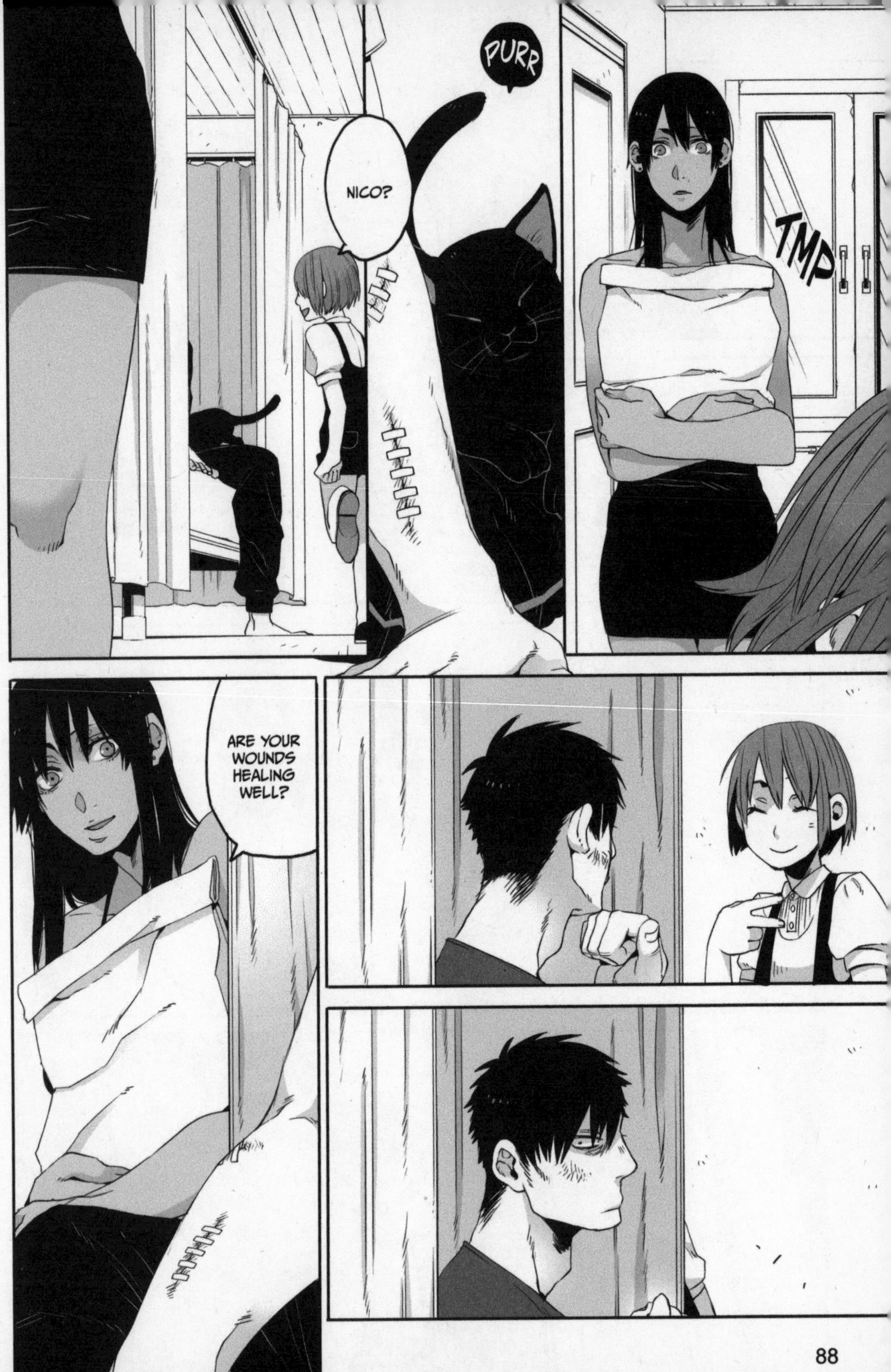
TMP
PURR
NICO?
ARE YOUR WOUNDS HEALING WELL?

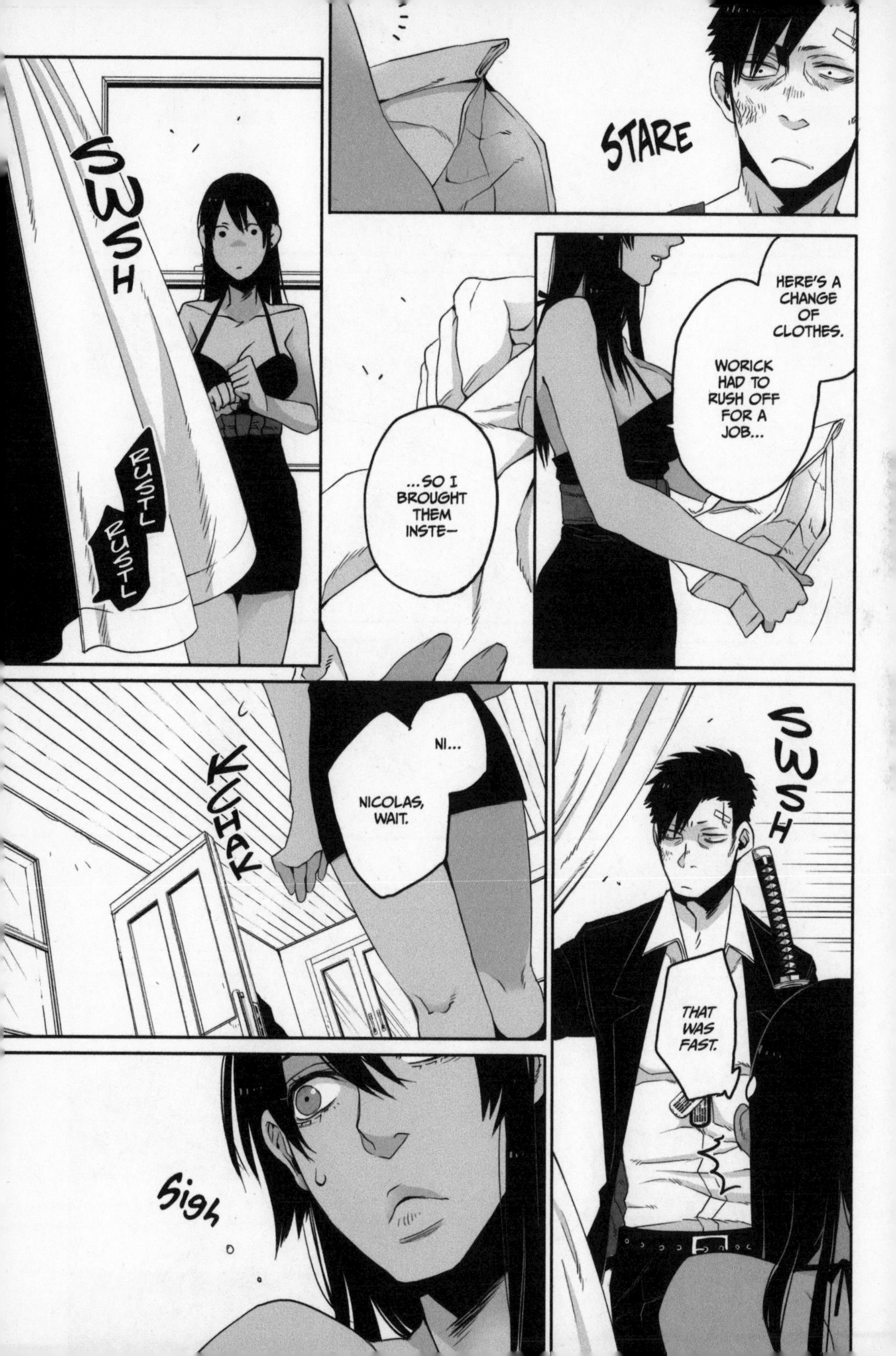
STARE
HERE'S A CHANGE OF CLOTHES.
WORICK HAD TO RUSH OFF FOR A JOB...
...SO I BROUGHT THEM INSTE—
SWSH
RUSTL
RUSTL
SWSH
THAT WAS FAST.
NI...
NICOLAS, WAIT.
KCHAK
Sigh

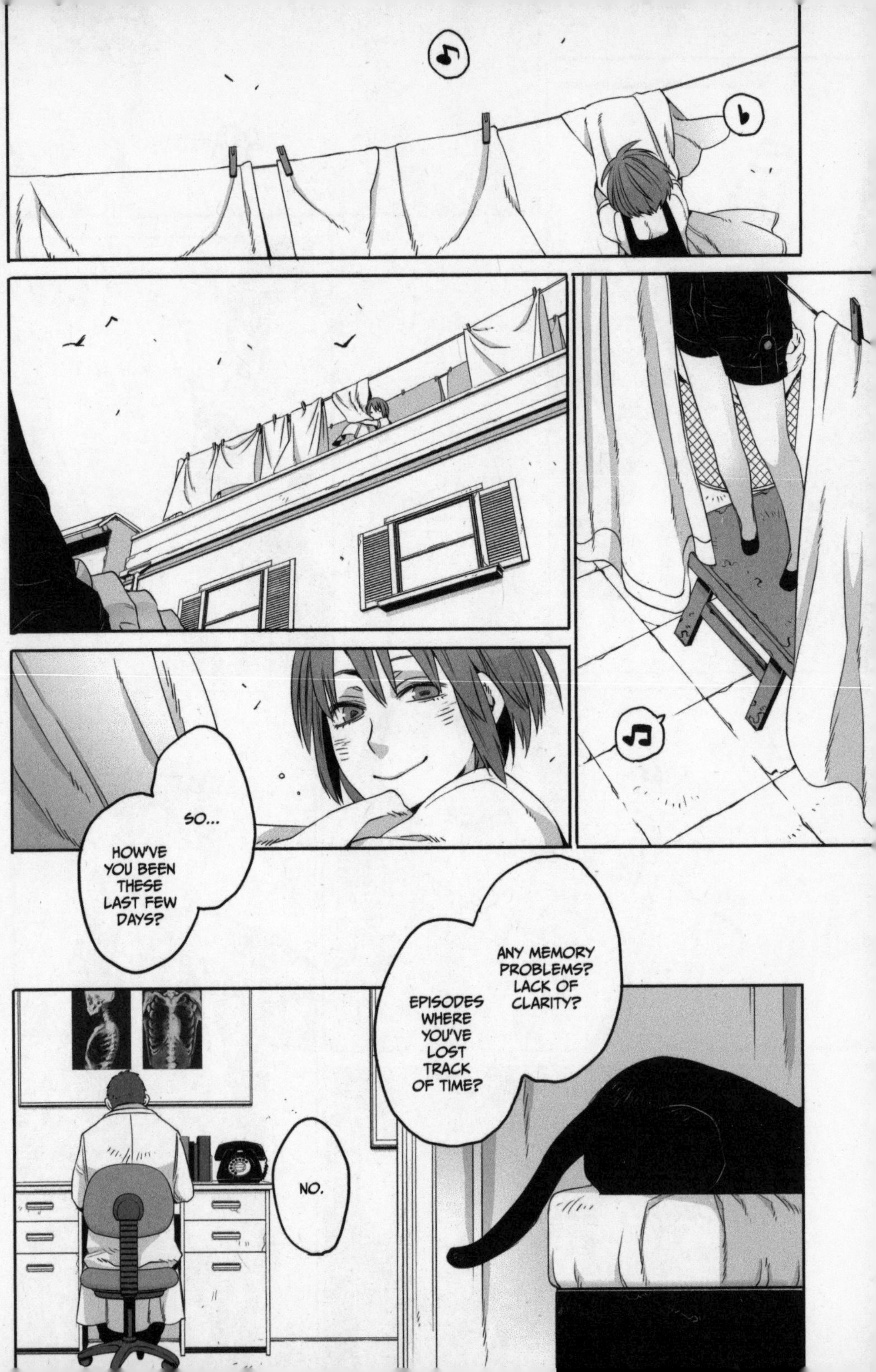
SO...
HOW'VE YOU BEEN THESE LAST FEW DAYS?
ANY MEMORY PROBLEMS? LACK OF CLARITY?
EPISODES WHERE YOU'VE LOST TRACK OF TIME?
NO.

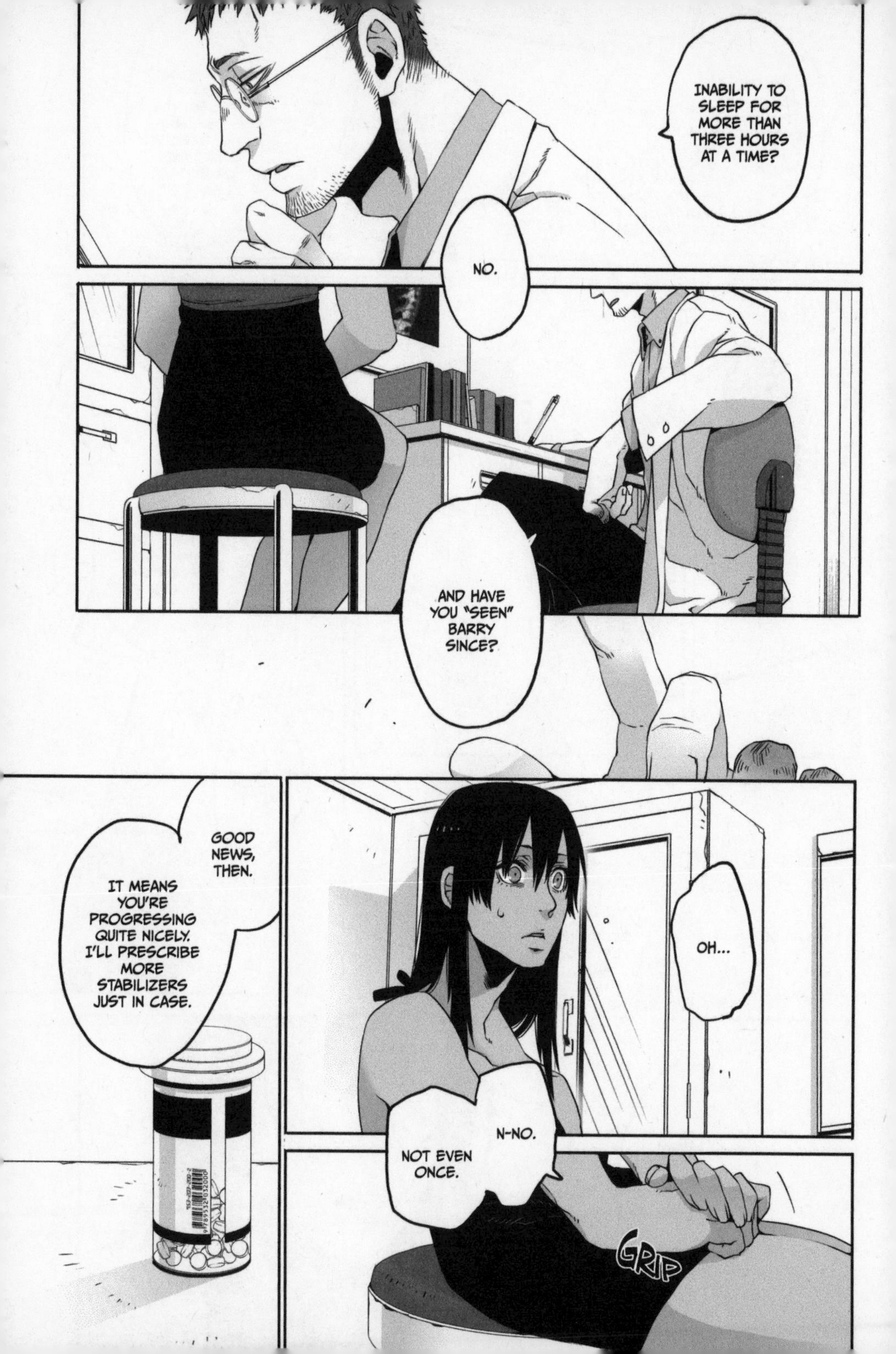
INABILITY TO SLEEP FOR MORE THAN THREE HOURS AT A TIME?
NO.
AND HAVE YOU "SEEN" BARRY SINCE?
OH...
N-NO.
NOT EVEN ONCE.
GRIP
GOOD NEWS, THEN.
IT MEANS YOU'RE PROGRESSING QUITE NICELY. I'LL PRESCRIBE MORE STABILIZERS JUST IN CASE.

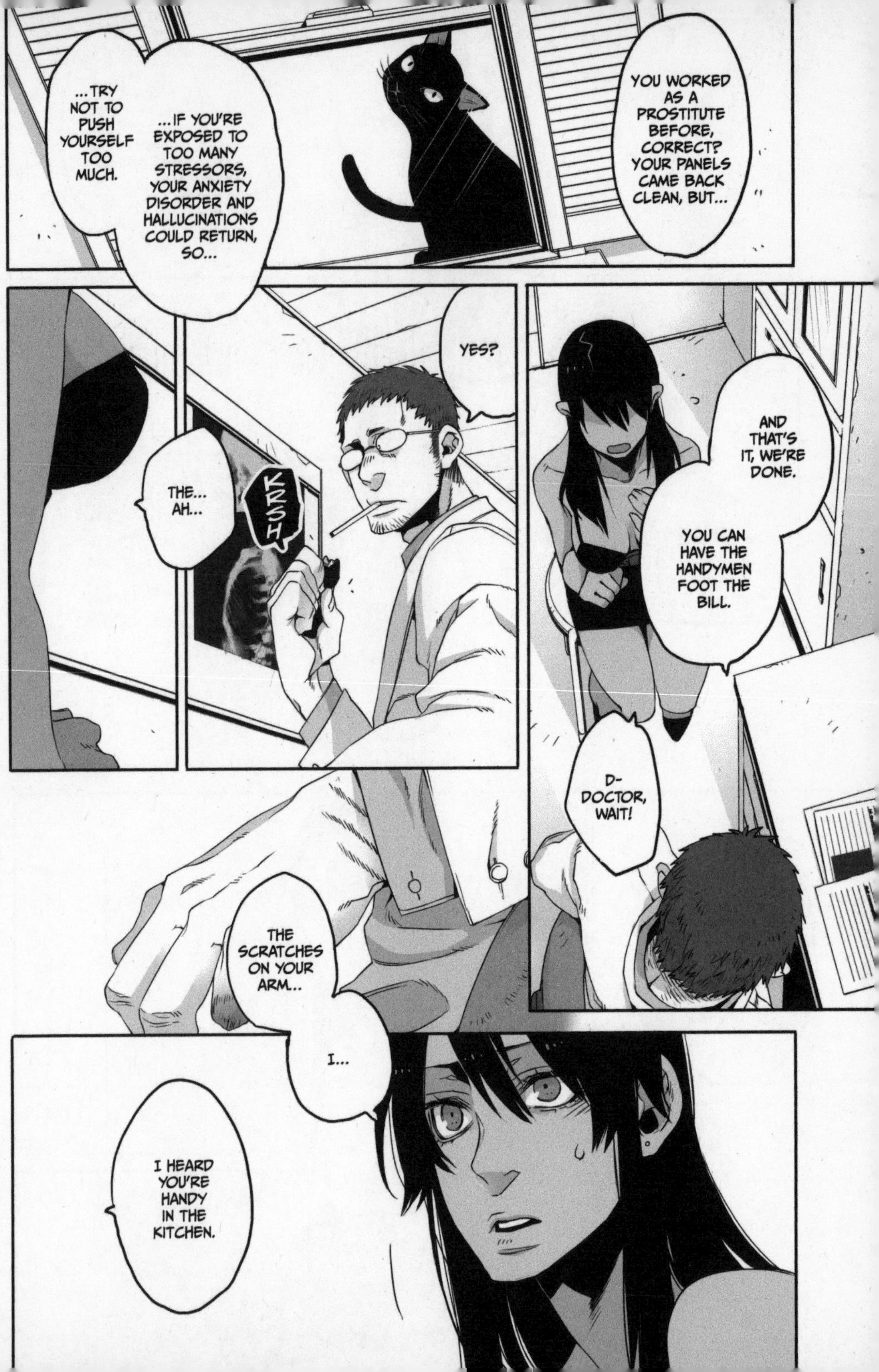
YOU WORKED AS A PROSTITUTE BEFORE, CORRECT? YOUR PANELS CAME BACK CLEAN, BUT...
...IF YOU'RE EXPOSED TO TOO MANY STRESSORS, YOUR ANXIETY DISORDER AND HALLUCINATIONS COULD RETURN, SO...
...TRY NOT TO PUSH YOURSELF TOO MUCH.
AND THAT'S IT, WE'RE DONE.
YOU CAN HAVE THE HANDYMEN FOOT THE BILL.
D-DOCTOR, WAIT!
YES?
KRSH
THE... AH...
THE SCRATCHES ON YOUR ARM...
I...
I HEARD YOU'RE HANDY IN THE KITCHEN.

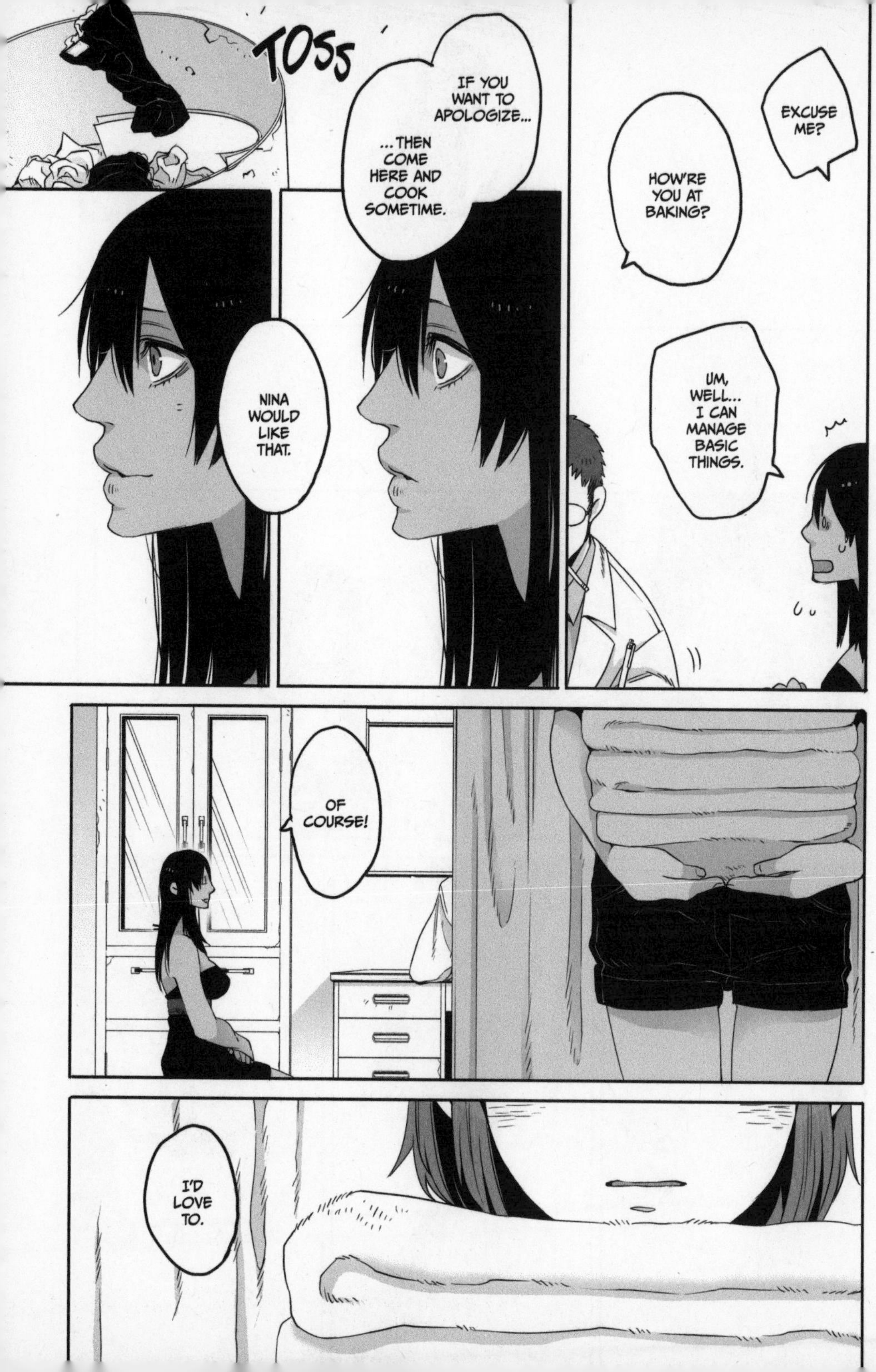
EXCUSE ME?
HOW'RE YOU AT BAKING?
UM, WELL... I CAN MANAGE BASIC THINGS.
TOSS
IF YOU WANT TO APOLOGIZE...
...THEN COME HERE AND COOK SOMETIME.
NINA WOULD LIKE THAT.
OF COURSE!
I'D LOVE TO.

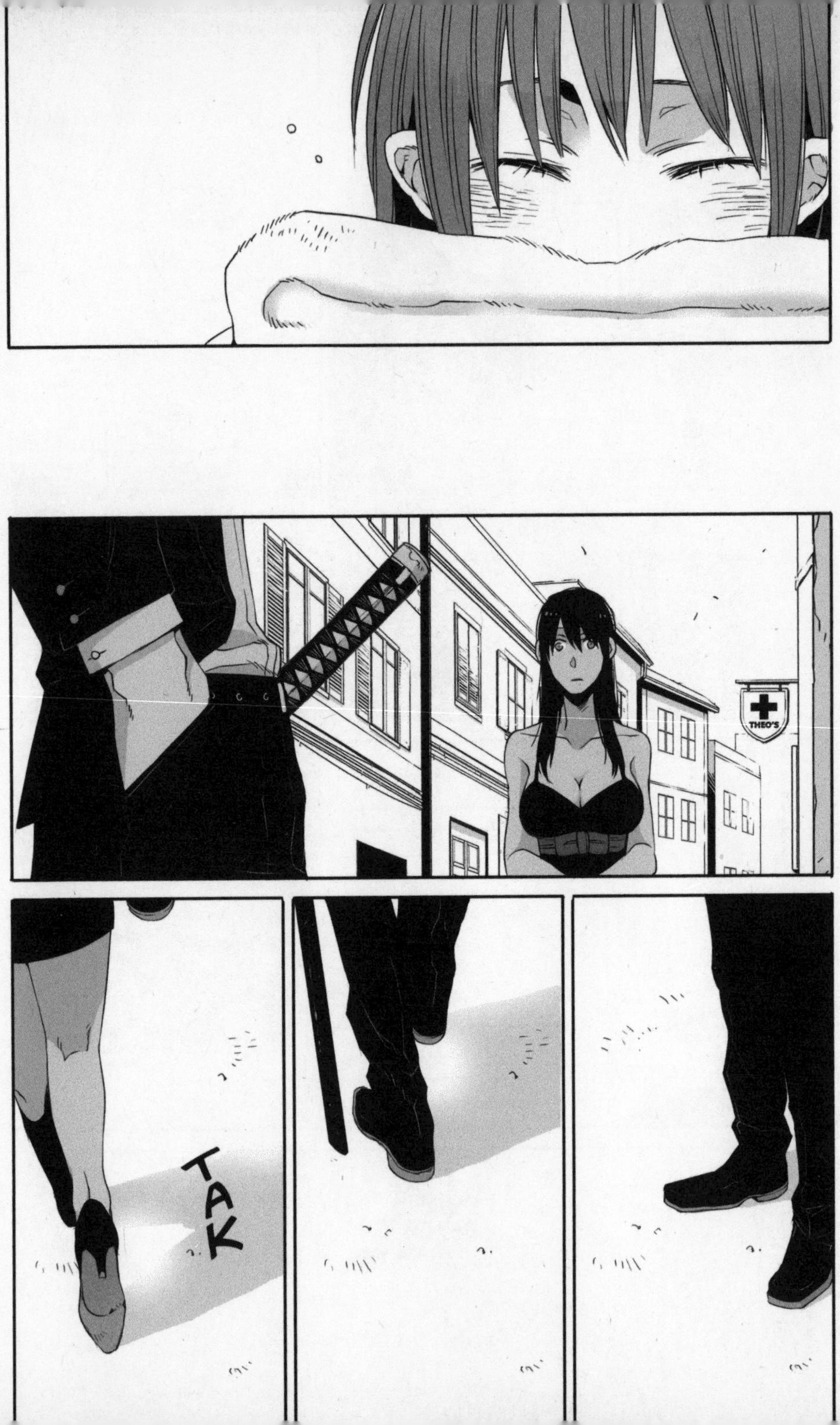
THEO'S
TAK

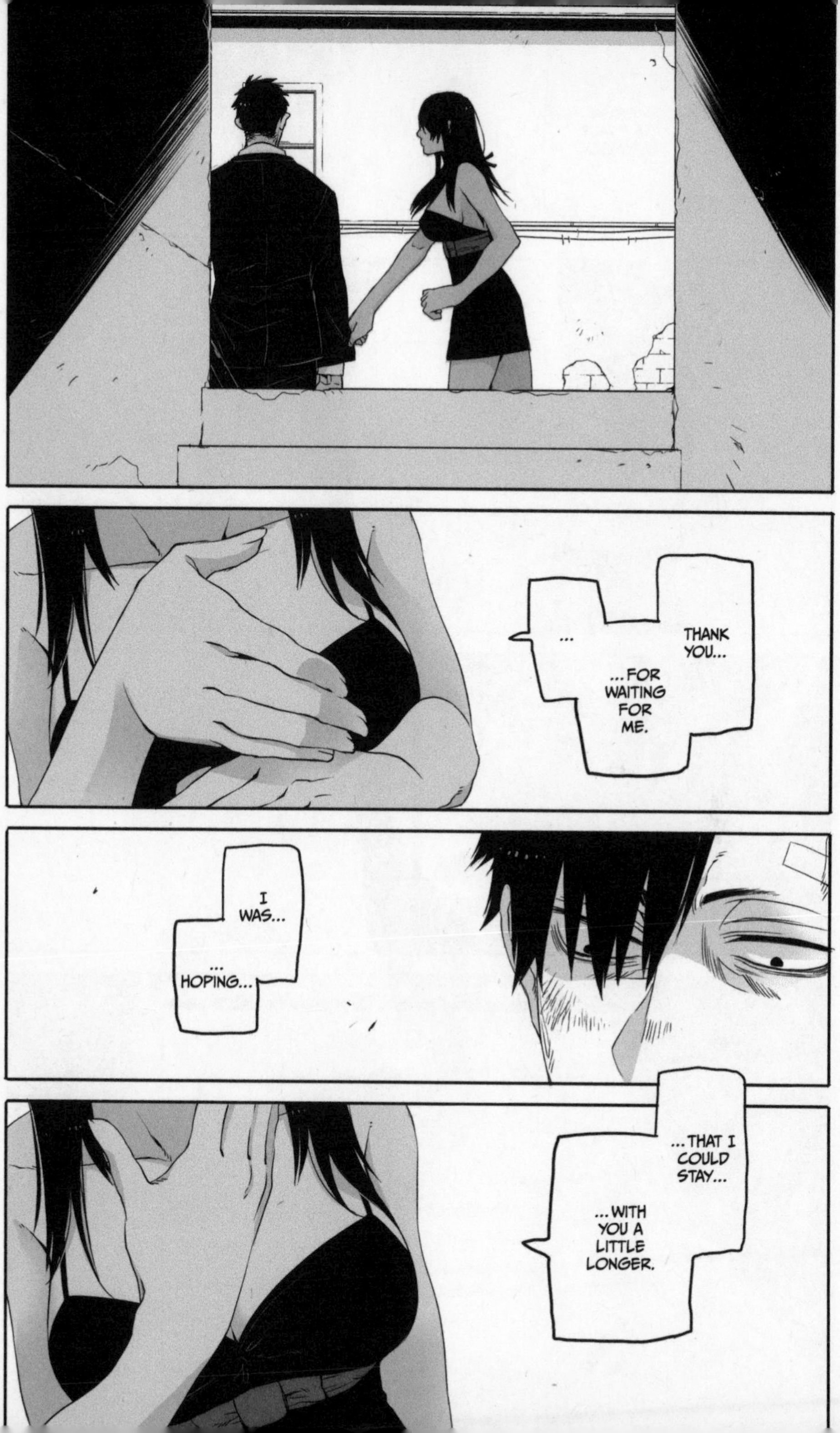
... THANK YOU... ...FOR WAITING FOR ME.
I WAS... ...HOPING...
...THAT I COULD STAY... ...WITH YOU A LITTLE LONGER.

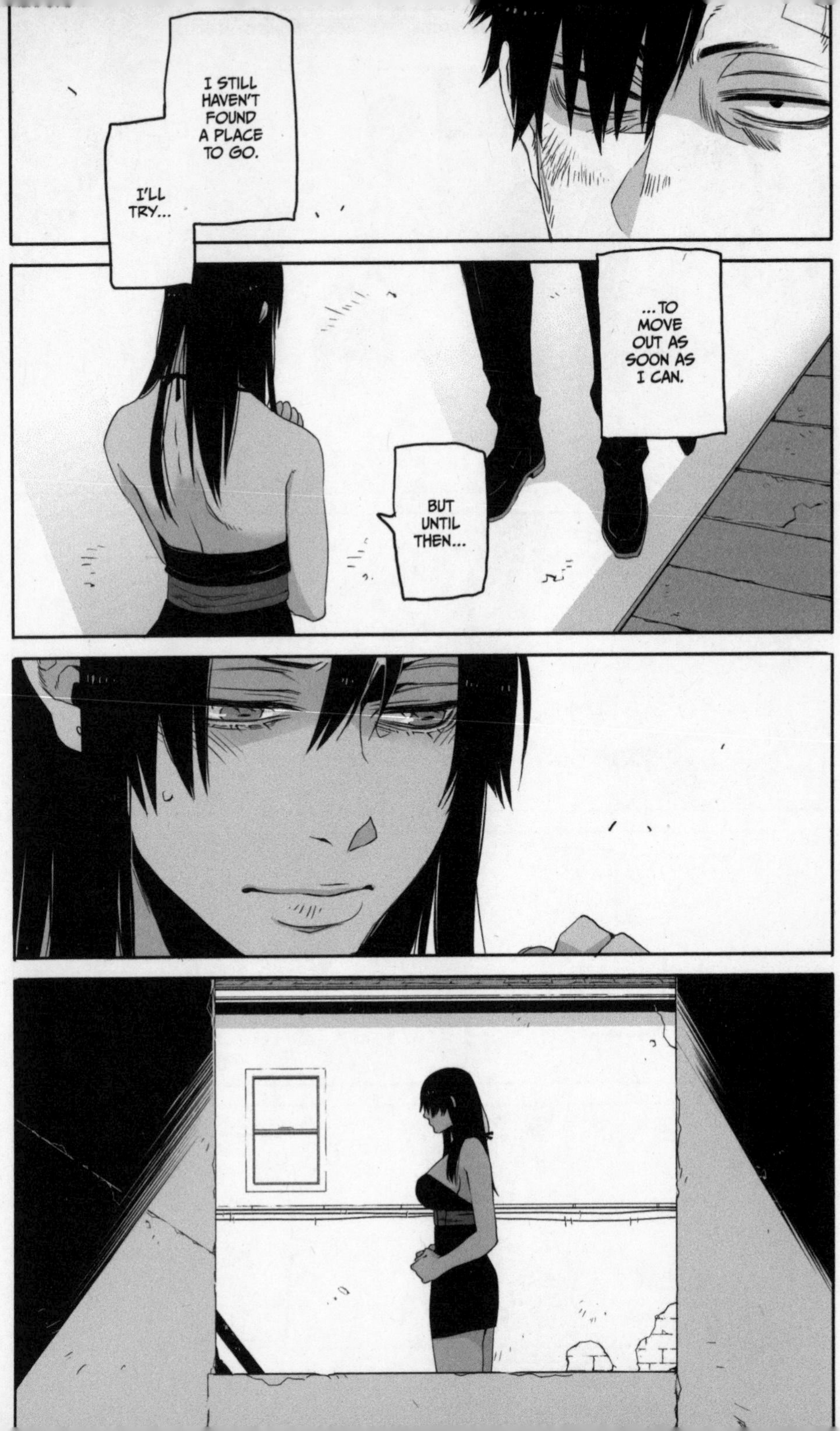
I STILL HAVEN'T FOUND A PLACE TO GO.
I'LL TRY...
...TO MOVE OUT AS SOON AS I CAN.
BUT UNTIL THEN...

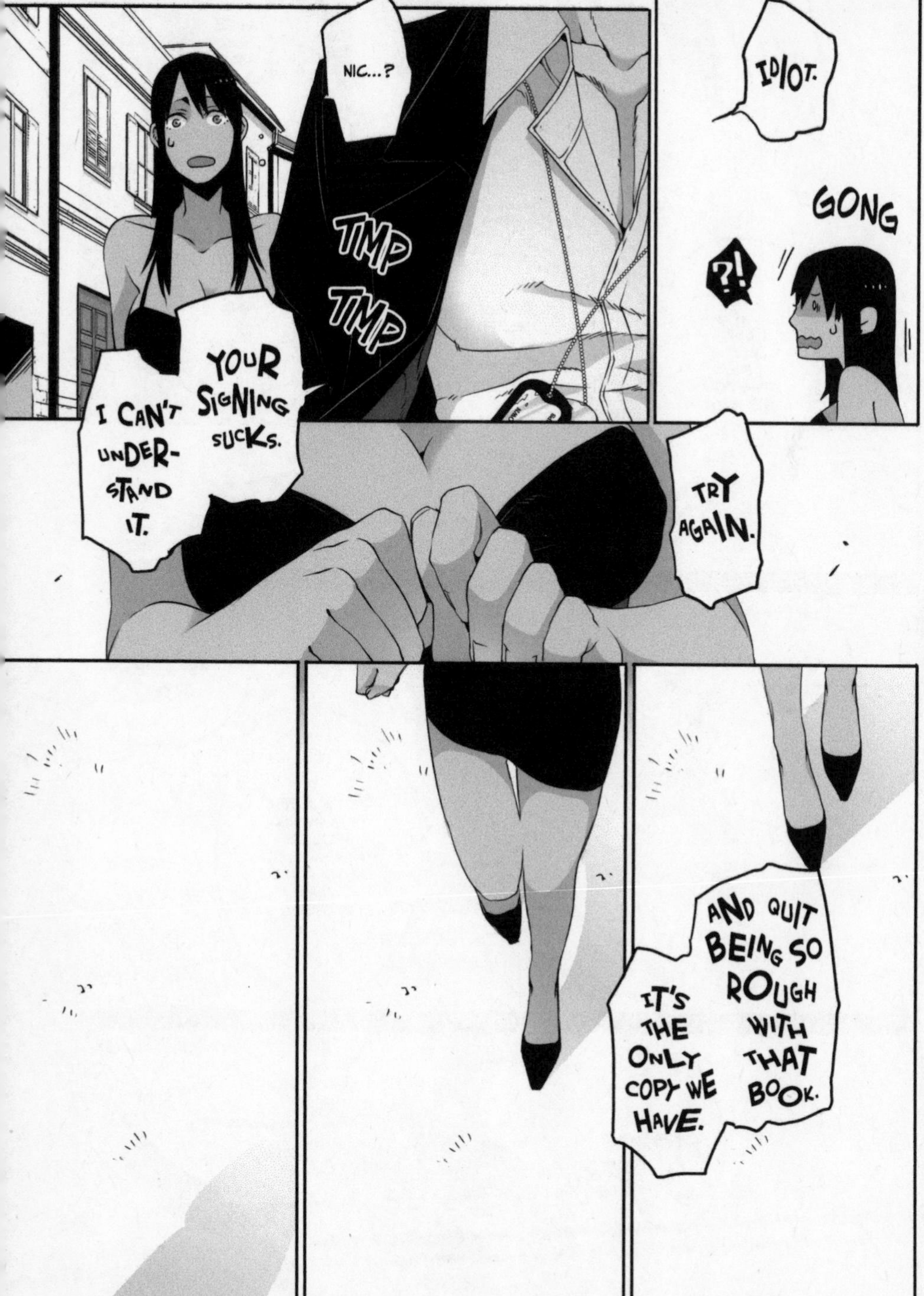
IDIOT.
GONG
?!
NIC...?
TMP
TMP
YOUR SIGNING SUCKS. I CAN'T UNDER-STAND IT.
TRY AGAIN.
AND QUIT BEING SO ROUGH WITH THAT BOOK. IT'S THE ONLY COPY WE HAVE.

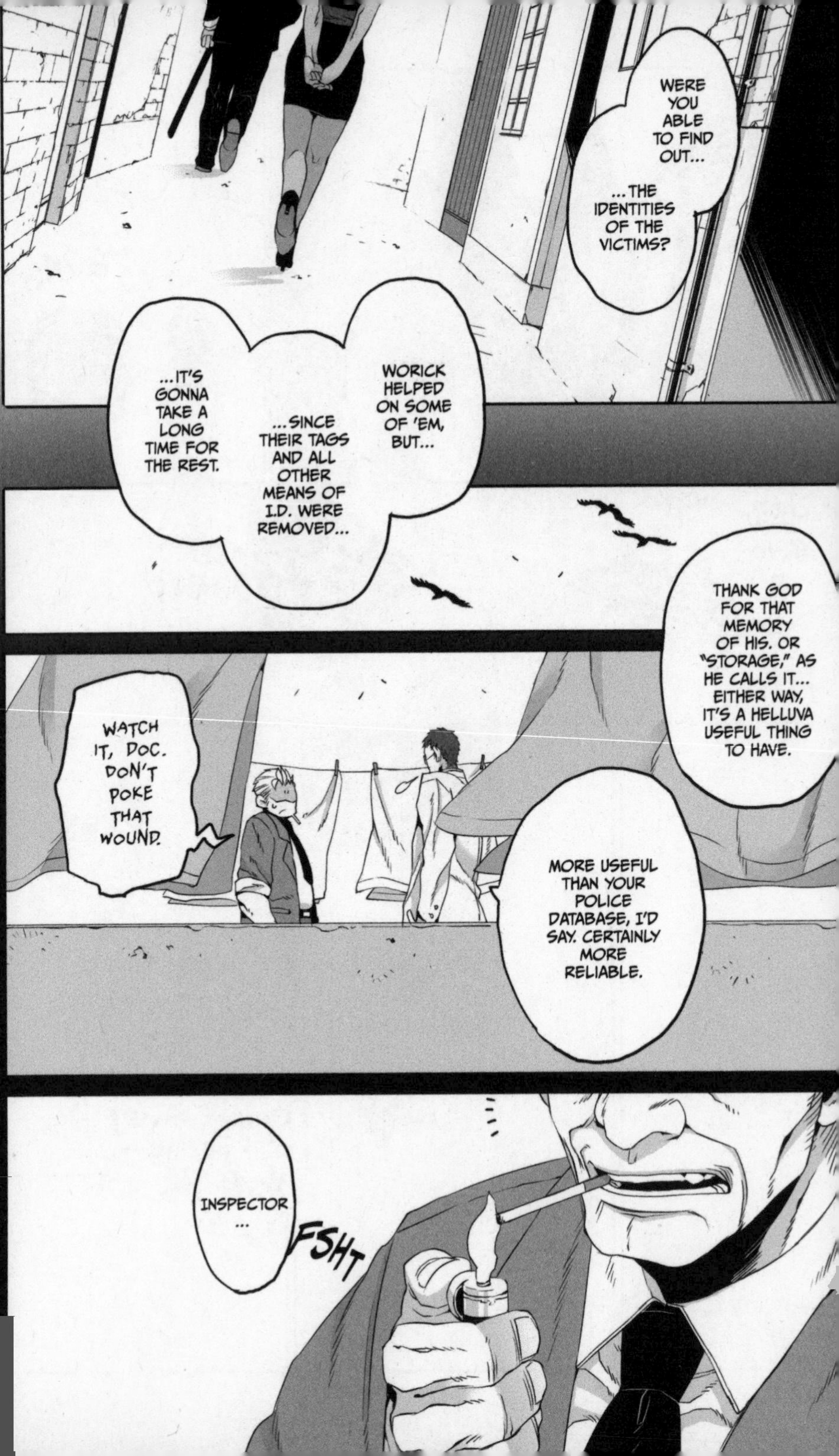
WERE YOU ABLE TO FIND OUT...
...THE IDENTITIES OF THE VICTIMS?
WORICK HELPED ON SOME OF 'EM, BUT...
...SINCE THEIR TAGS AND ALL OTHER MEANS OF I.D. WERE REMOVED...
...IT'S GONNA TAKE A LONG TIME FOR THE REST.
THANK GOD FOR THAT MEMORY OF HIS. OR "STORAGE," AS HE CALLS IT... EITHER WAY, IT'S A HELLUVA USEFUL THING TO HAVE.
MORE USEFUL THAN YOUR POLICE DATABASE, I'D SAY. CERTAINLY MORE RELIABLE.
WATCH IT, DOC. DON'T POKE THAT WOUND.
INSPECTOR...
FSHT

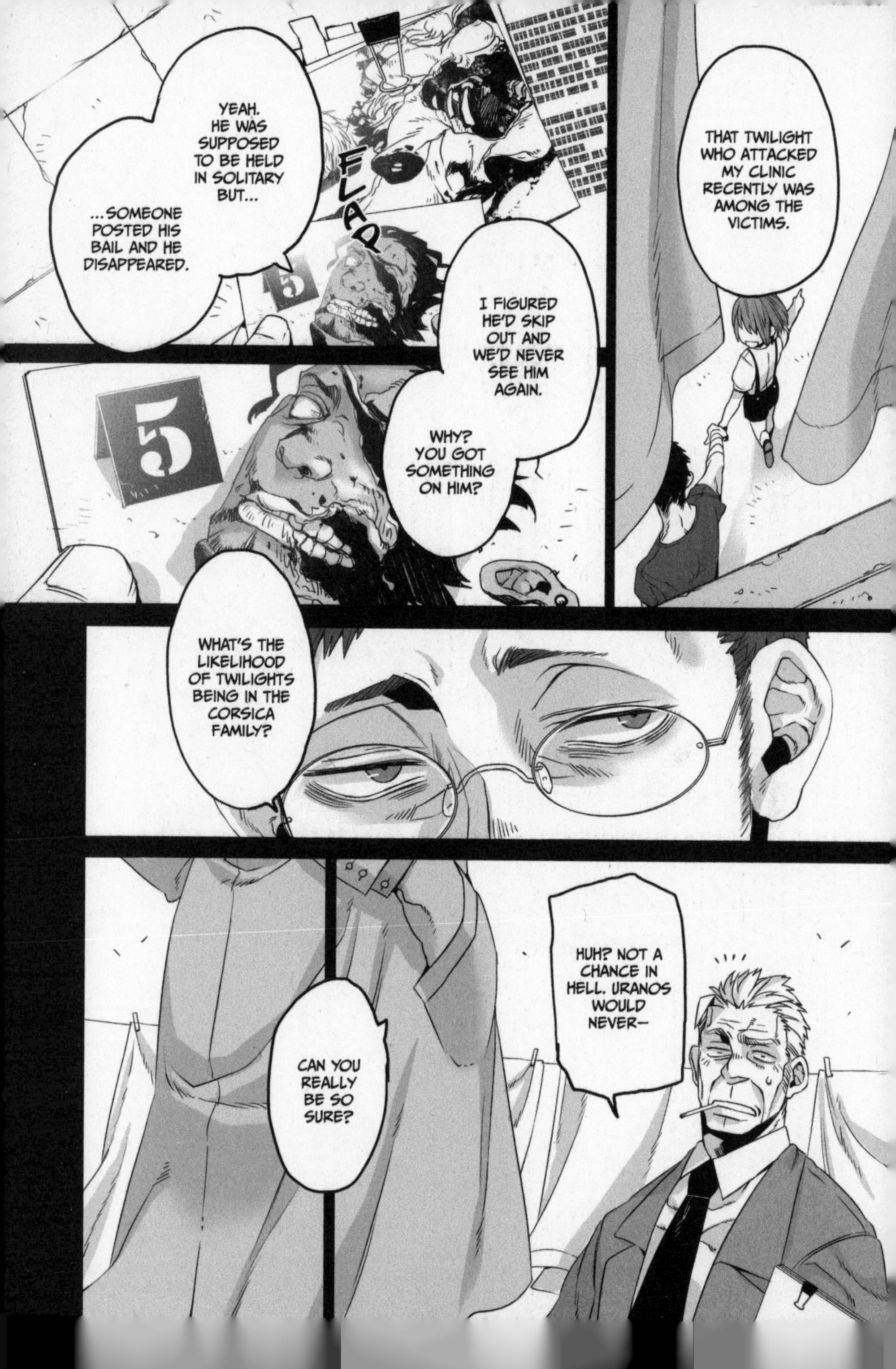

THAT TWILIGHT WHO ATTACKED MY CLINIC RECENTLY WAS AMONG THE VICTIMS.
YEAH. HE WAS SUPPOSED TO BE HELD IN SOLITARY BUT...
...SOMEONE POSTED HIS BAIL AND HE DISAPPEARED.
FLAP
I FIGURED HE'D SKIP OUT AND WE'D NEVER SEE HIM AGAIN.
WHY? YOU GOT SOMETHING ON HIM?
WHAT'S THE LIKELIHOOD OF TWILIGHTS BEING IN THE CORSICA FAMILY?
HUH? NOT A CHANCE IN HELL. URANOS WOULD NEVER—
CAN YOU REALLY BE SO SURE?

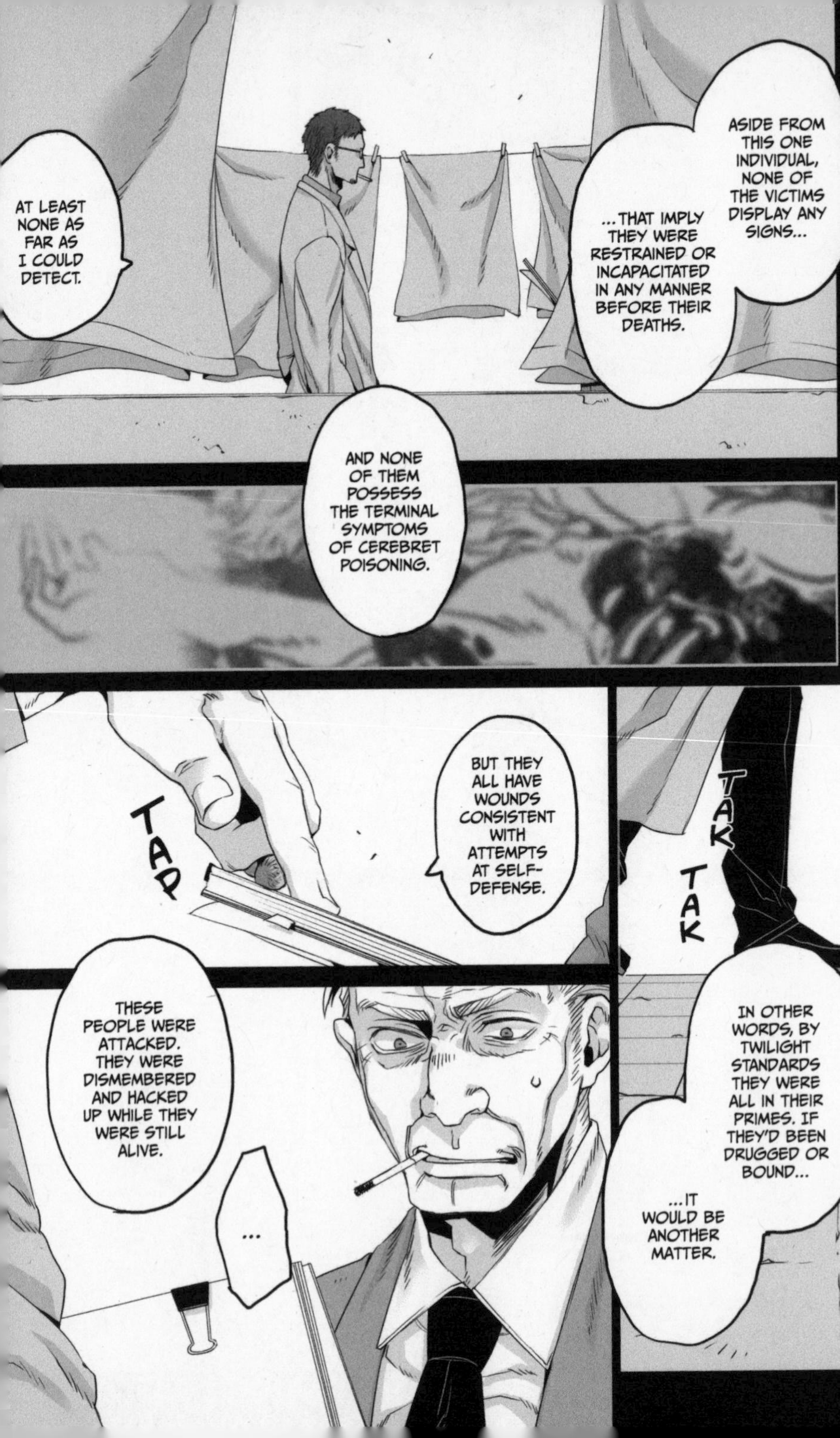
ASIDE FROM THIS ONE INDIVIDUAL, NONE OF THE VICTIMS DISPLAY ANY SIGNS...
...THAT IMPLY THEY WERE RESTRAINED OR INCAPACITATED IN ANY MANNER BEFORE THEIR DEATHS.
AT LEAST NONE AS FAR AS I COULD DETECT.
AND NONE OF THEM POSSESS THE TERMINAL SYMPTOMS OF CEREBRET POISONING.
TAK
TAK
BUT THEY ALL HAVE WOUNDS CONSISTENT WITH ATTEMPTS AT SELF-DEFENSE.
TAP
IN OTHER WORDS, BY TWILIGHT STANDARDS THEY WERE ALL IN THEIR PRIMES. IF THEY'D BEEN DRUGGED OR BOUND...
...IT WOULD BE ANOTHER MATTER.
THESE PEOPLE WERE ATTACKED. THEY WERE DISMEMBERED AND HACKED UP WHILE THEY WERE STILL ALIVE.
...

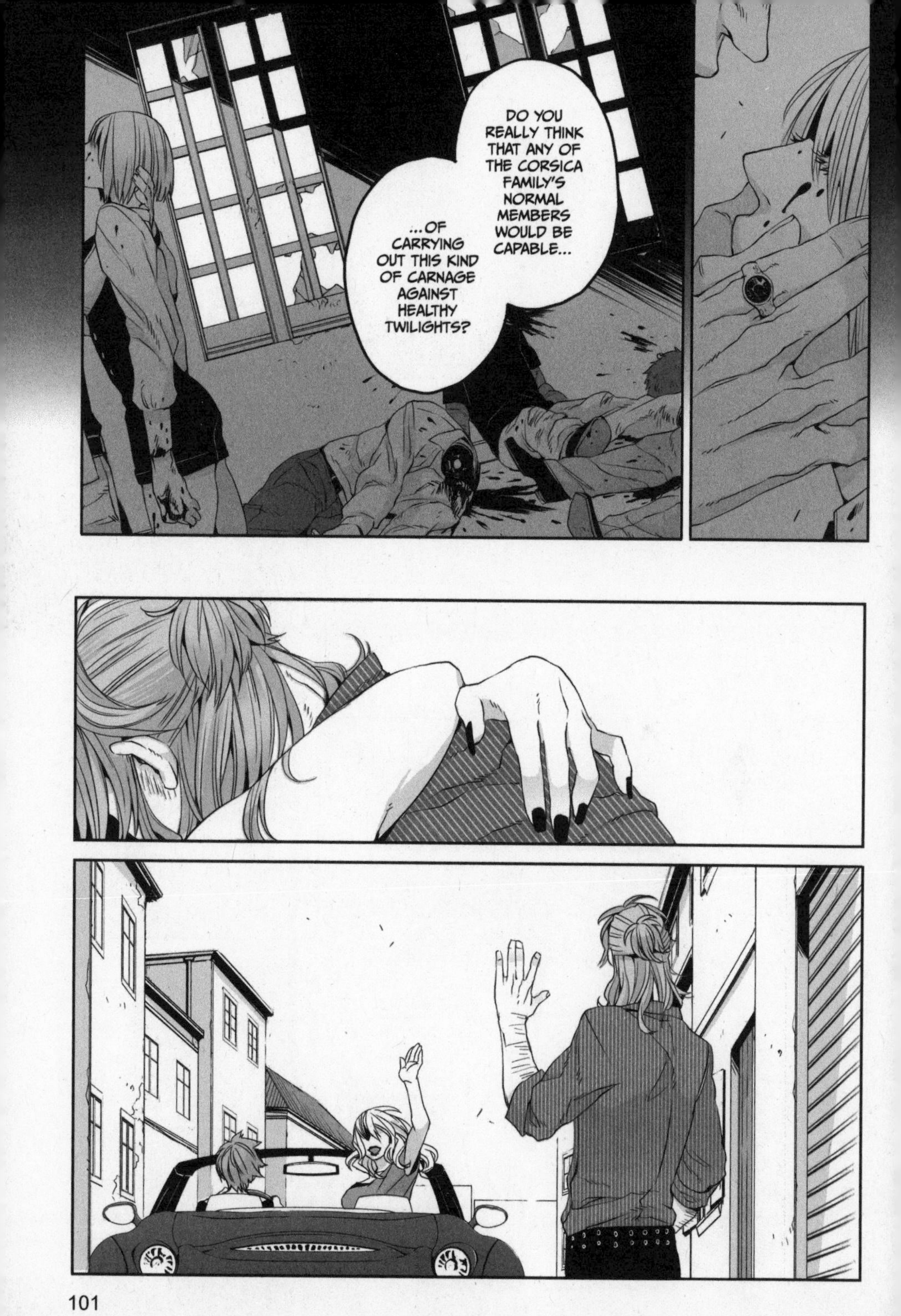
DO YOU REALLY THINK THAT ANY OF THE CORSICA FAMILY'S NORMAL MEMBERS WOULD BE CAPABLE...
...OF CARRYING OUT THIS KIND OF CARNAGE AGAINST HEALTHY TWILIGHTS?

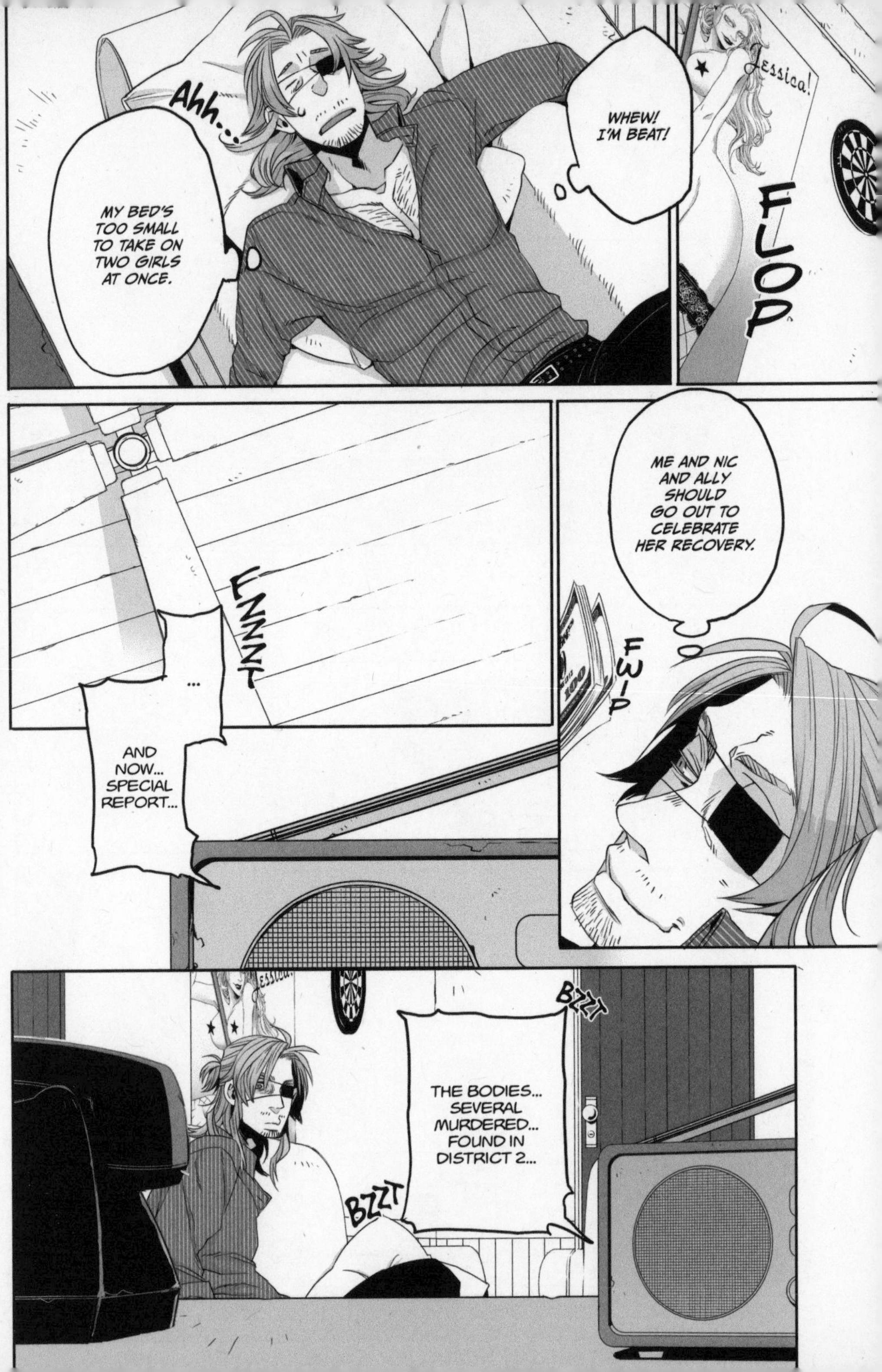
Jessica!
FLOP
WHEW! I'M BEAT!
Ahh...
MY BED'S TOO SMALL TO TAKE ON TWO GIRLS AT ONCE.
ME AND NIC AND ALLY SHOULD GO OUT TO CELEBRATE HER RECOVERY.
FWIP
FZZZT
...
AND NOW... SPECIAL REPORT...
BZZZT
THE BODIES... SEVERAL MURDERED... FOUND IN DISTRICT 2...
BZZT

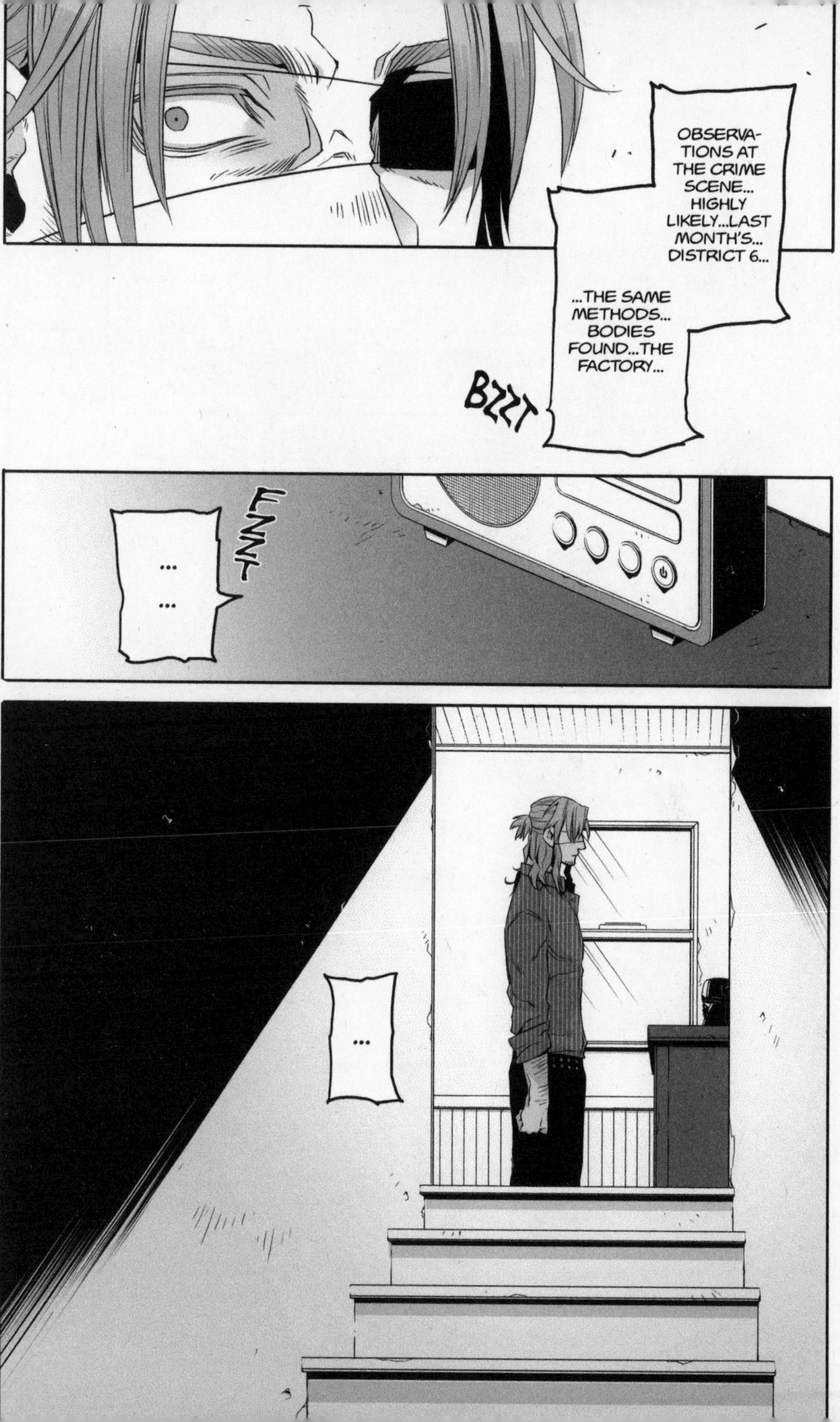
OBSERVATIONS AT THE CRIME SCENE... HIGHLY LIKELY...LAST MONTH'S... DISTRICT 6...
...THE SAME METHODS... BODIES FOUND...THE FACTORY...
BZZT
FZZT
...
...
...

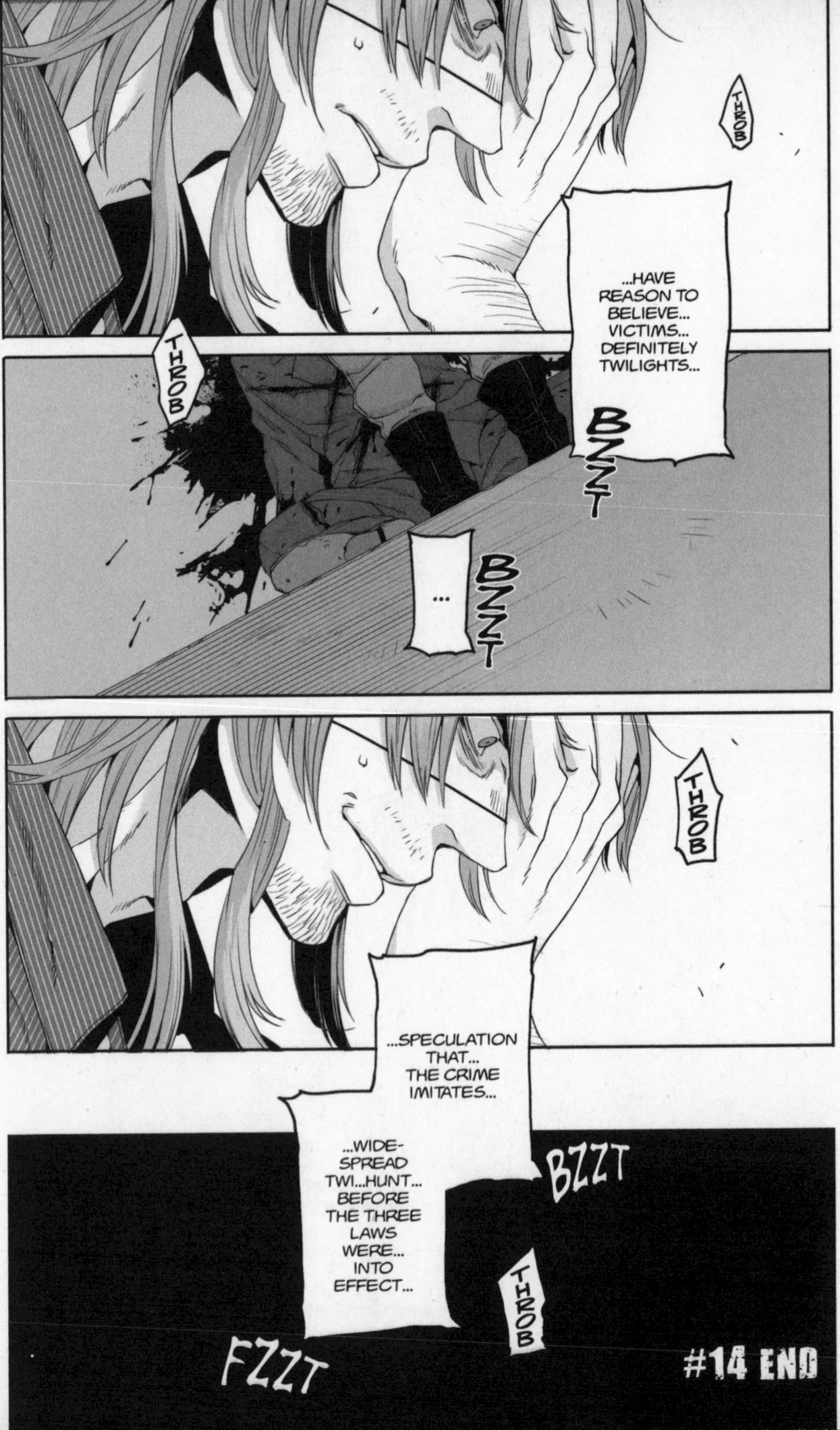
THROB
...HAVE REASON TO BELIEVE... VICTIMS... DEFINITELY TWILIGHTS...
THROB
BZZZT
...
BZZZT
THROB
...SPECULATION THAT... THE CRIME IMITATES...
...WIDE-SPREAD TWI...HUNT... BEFORE THE THREE LAWS WERE... INTO EFFECT...
BZZT
THROB
FZZT
#14 END

GANGST

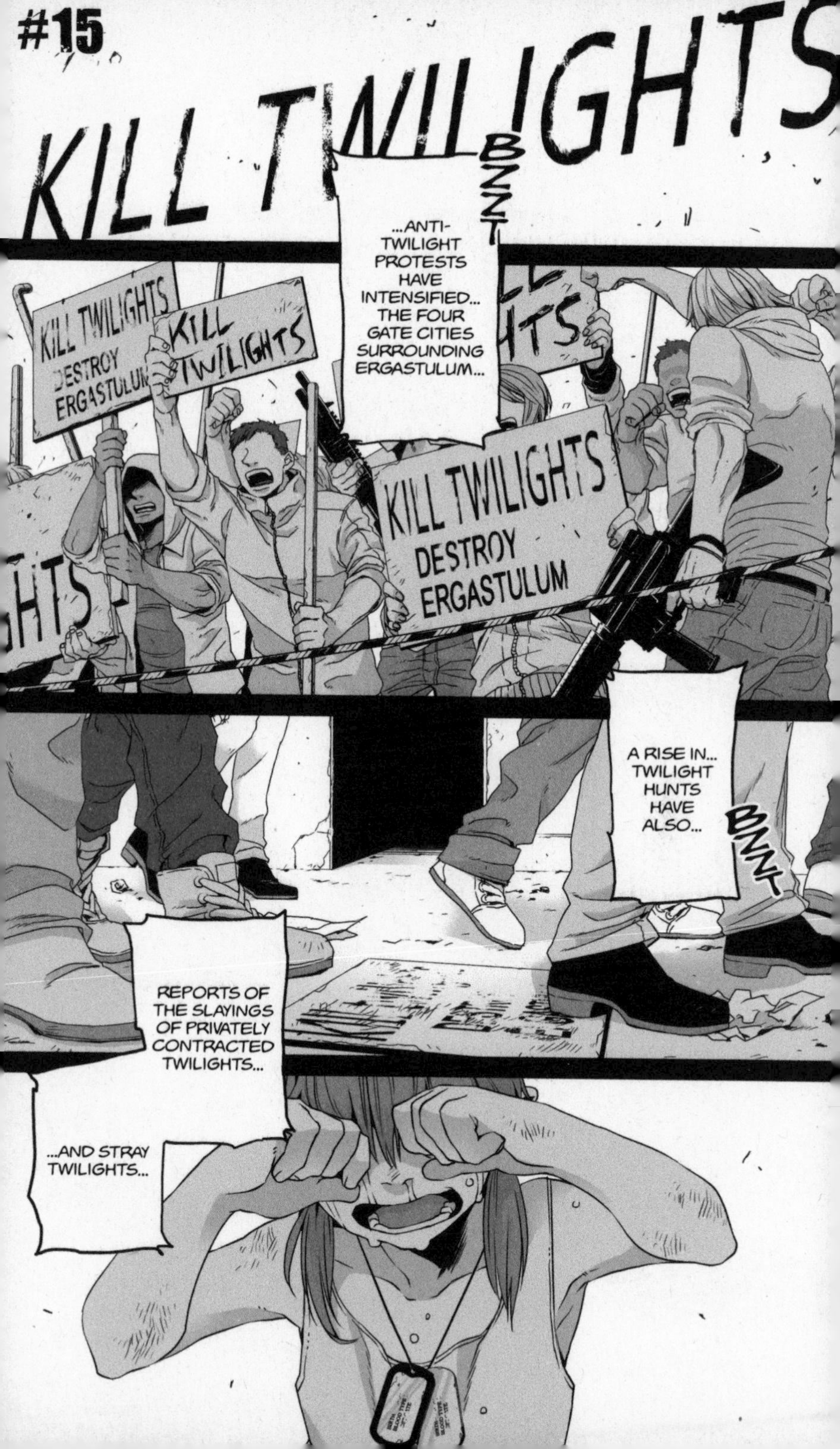
#15
KILL TWILIGHTS
BZZT
...ANTI-TWILIGHT PROTESTS HAVE INTENSIFIED... THE FOUR GATE CITIES SURROUNDING ERGASTULUM...
KILL TWILIGHTS DESTROY ERGASTULUM
KILL TWILIGHTS DESTROY ERGASTULUM
KILL TWILIGHTS
A RISE IN... TWILIGHT HUNTS HAVE ALSO...
BZZT
REPORTS OF THE SLAYINGS OF PRIVATELY CONTRACTED TWILIGHTS...
...AND STRAY TWILIGHTS...

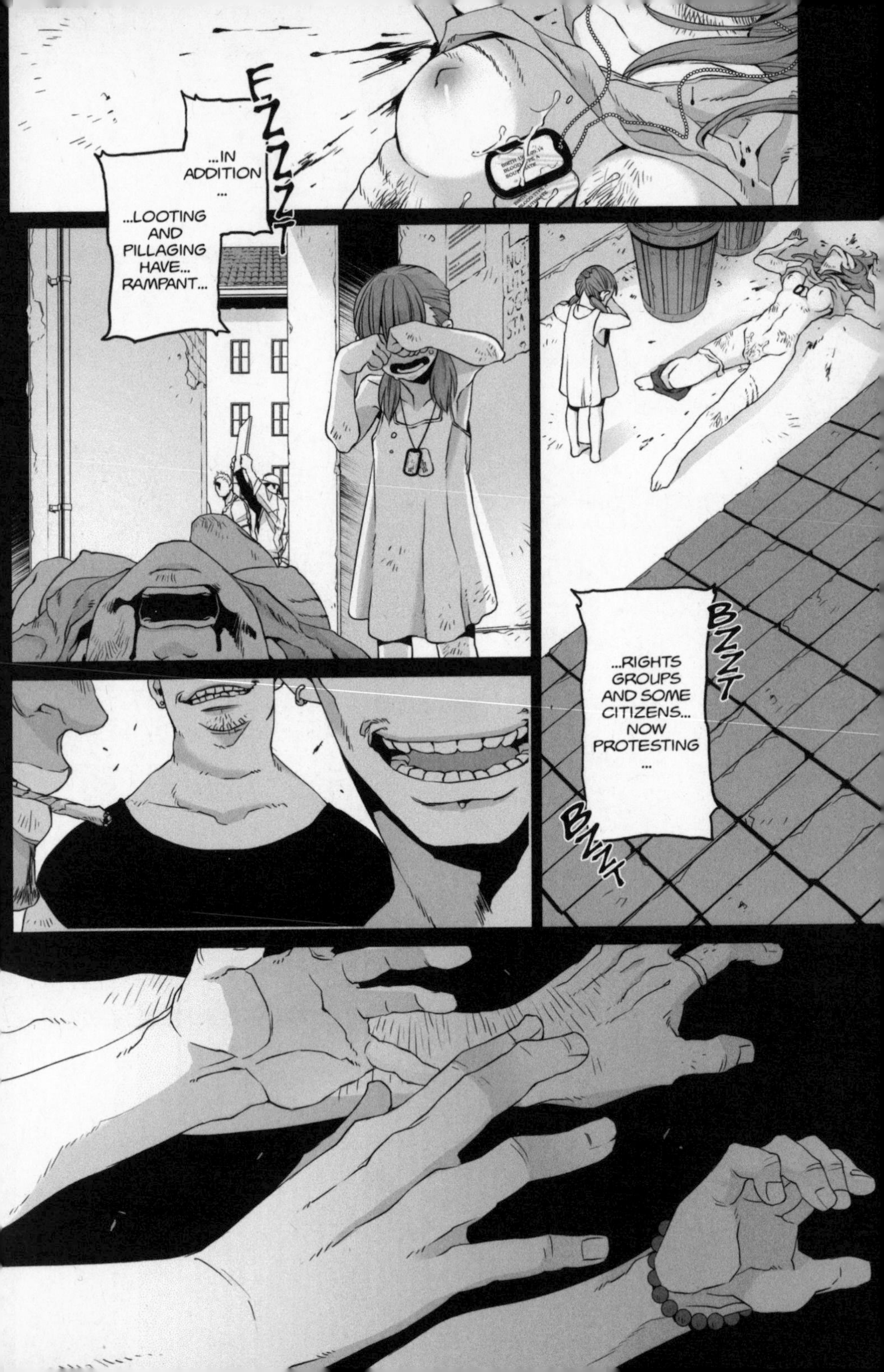

FZZZT
...IN ADDITION ... ...LOOTING AND PILLAGING HAVE... RAMPANT...
BZZZT
...RIGHTS GROUPS AND SOME CITIZENS... NOW PROTESTING ...
BWWWT

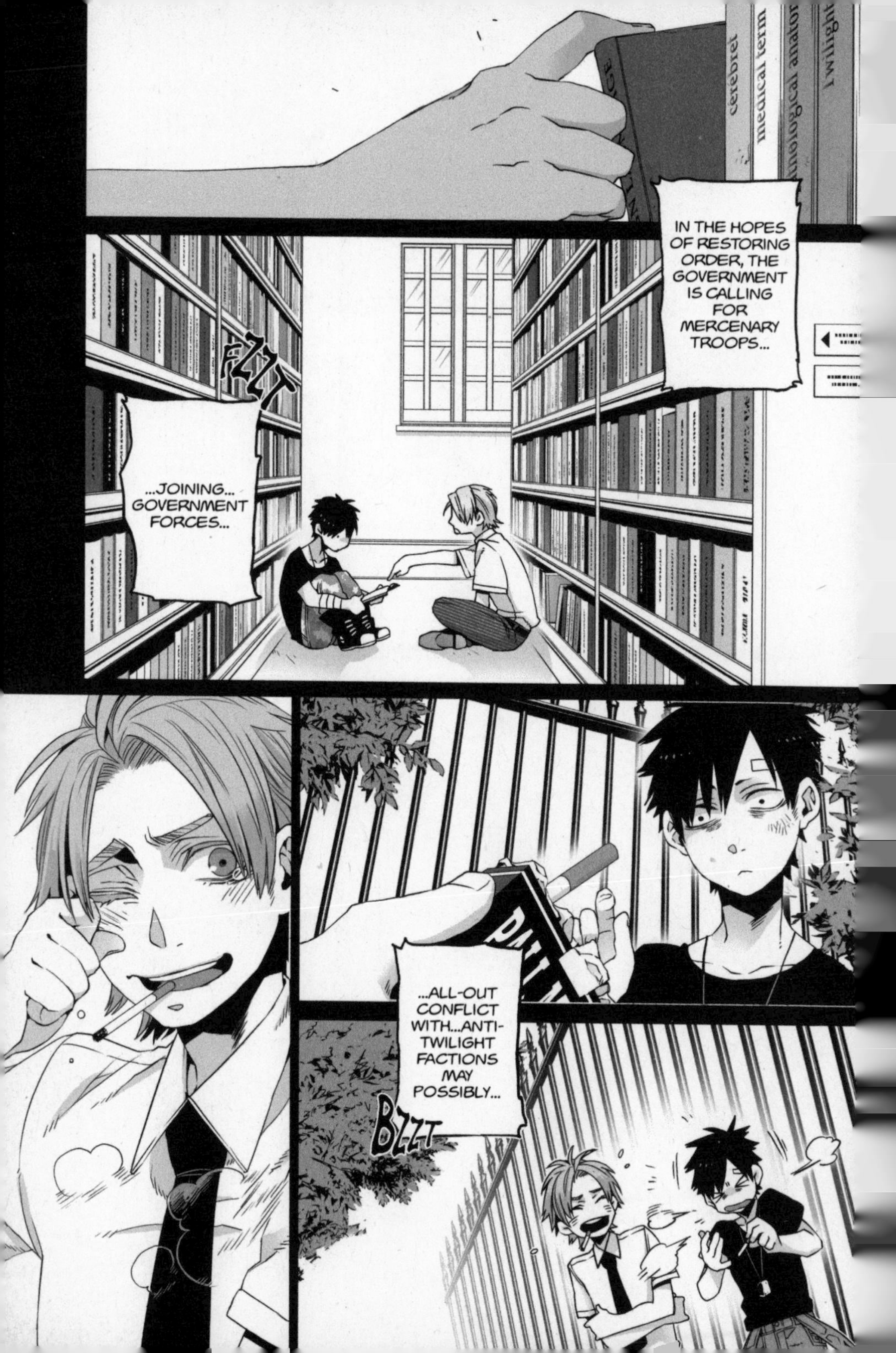
Twilight
medical term
IN THE HOPES OF RESTORING ORDER, THE GOVERNMENT IS CALLING FOR MERCENARY TROOPS...
FZZT
...JOINING... GOVERNMENT FORCES...
...ALL-OUT CONFLICT WITH...ANTI-TWILIGHT FACTIONS MAY POSSIBLY...
BZZT

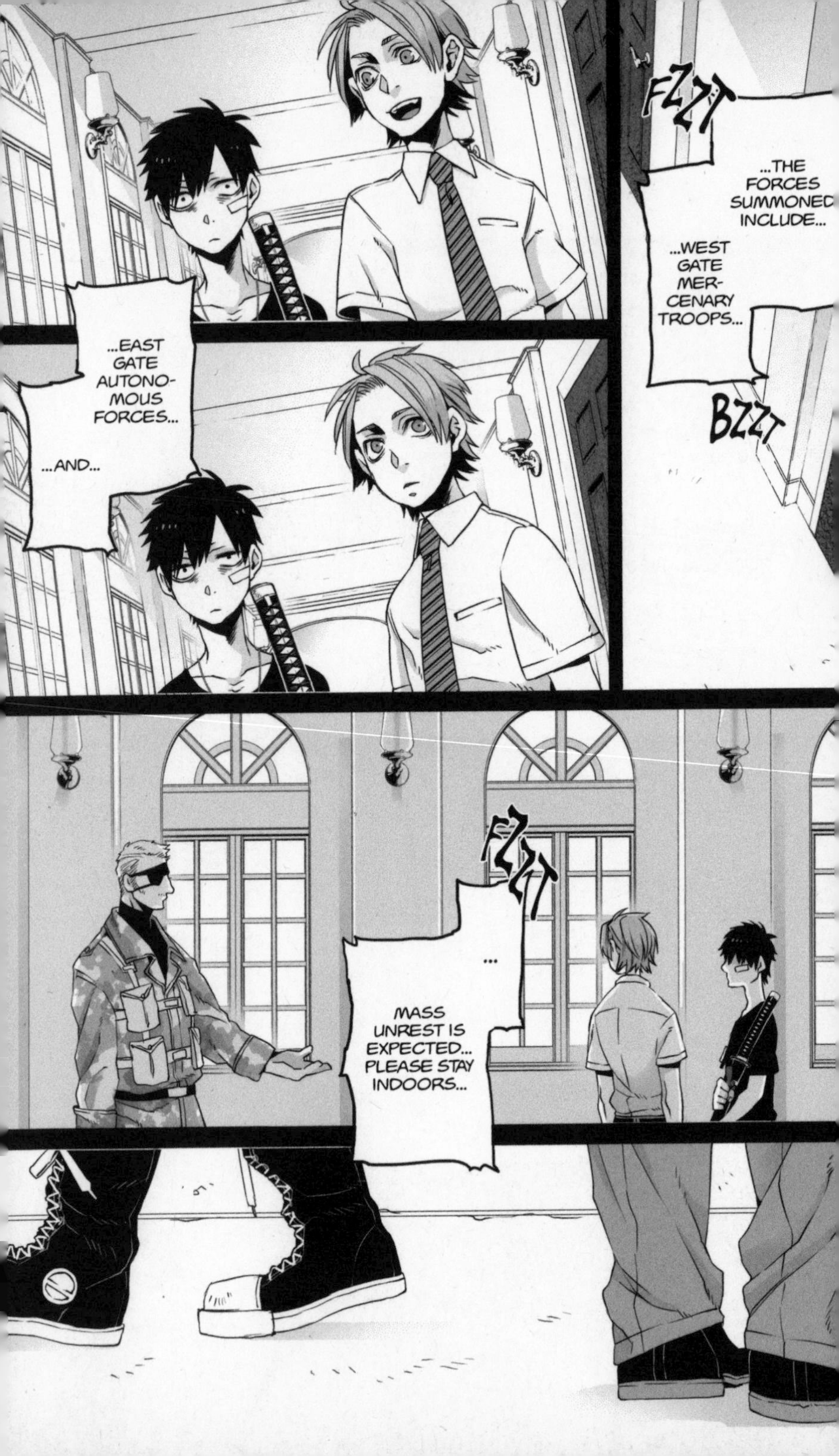
FZZT
...THE FORCES SUMMONED INCLUDE...
...WEST GATE MERCENARY TROOPS...
BZZT
...EAST GATE AUTONOMOUS FORCES...
...AND...
FZZT
...
MASS UNREST IS EXPECTED... PLEASE STAY INDOORS...

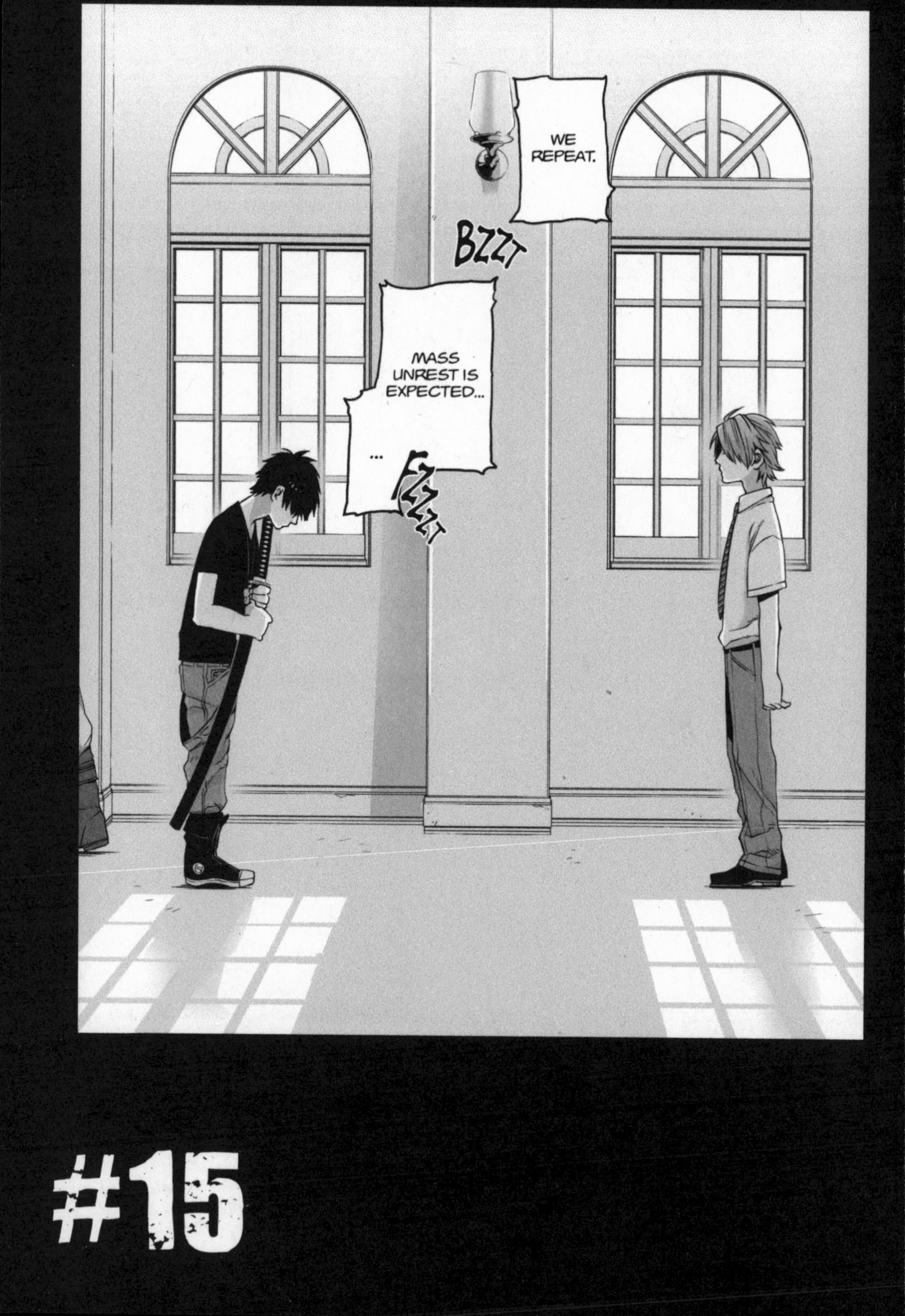
WE REPEAT.
BZZT
MASS UNREST IS EXPECTED...
...
FZZZT

#15

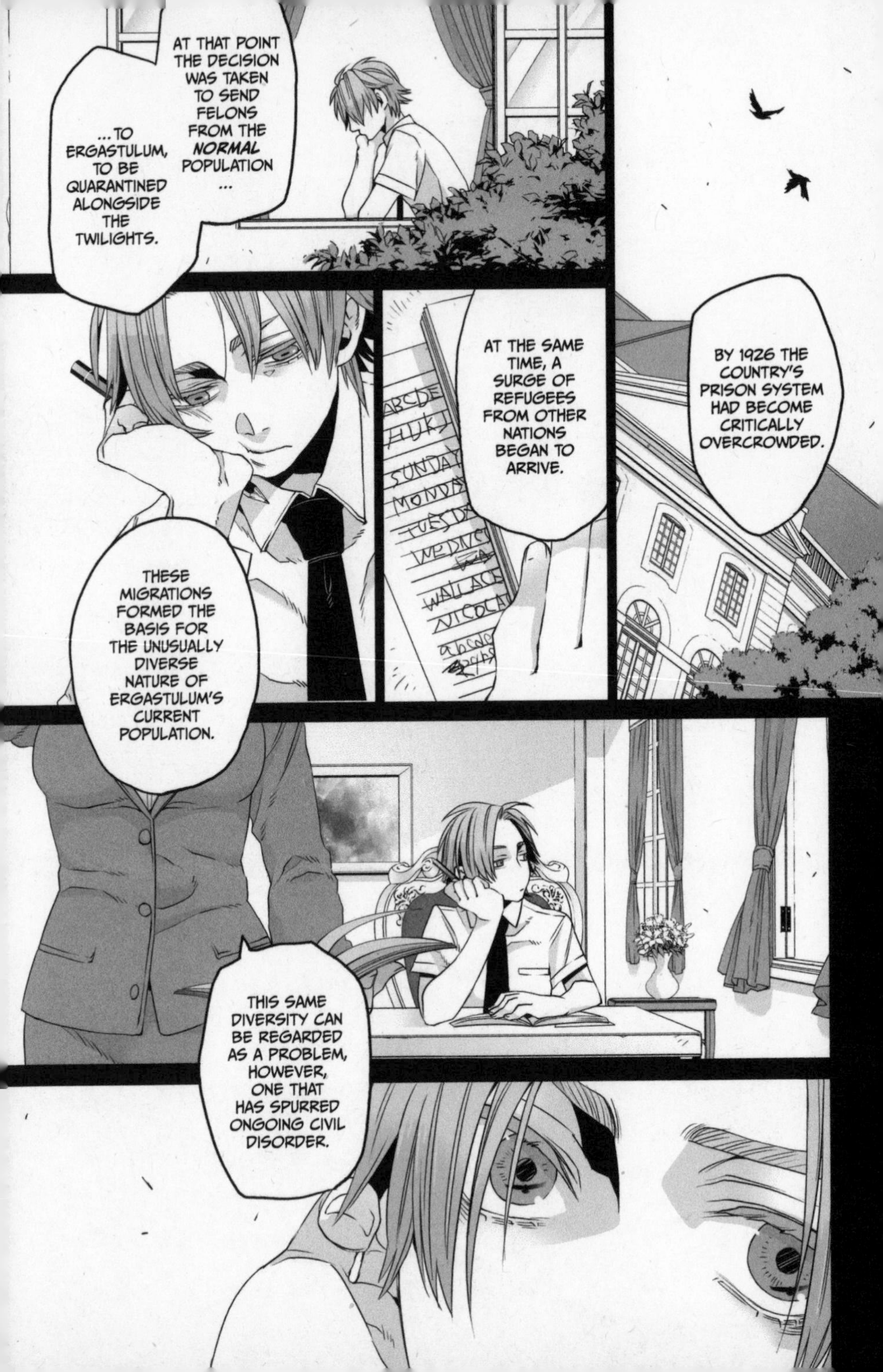
AT THAT POINT THE DECISION WAS TAKEN TO SEND FELONS FROM THE *NORMAL* POPULATION ...
...TO ERGASTULUM, TO BE QUARANTINED ALONGSIDE THE TWILIGHTS.
BY 1926 THE COUNTRY'S PRISON SYSTEM HAD BECOME CRITICALLY OVERCROWDED.
AT THE SAME TIME, A SURGE OF REFUGEES FROM OTHER NATIONS BEGAN TO ARRIVE.
THESE MIGRATIONS FORMED THE BASIS FOR THE UNUSUALLY DIVERSE NATURE OF ERGASTULUM'S CURRENT POPULATION.
THIS SAME DIVERSITY CAN BE REGARDED AS A PROBLEM, HOWEVER, ONE THAT HAS SPURRED ONGOING CIVIL DISORDER.

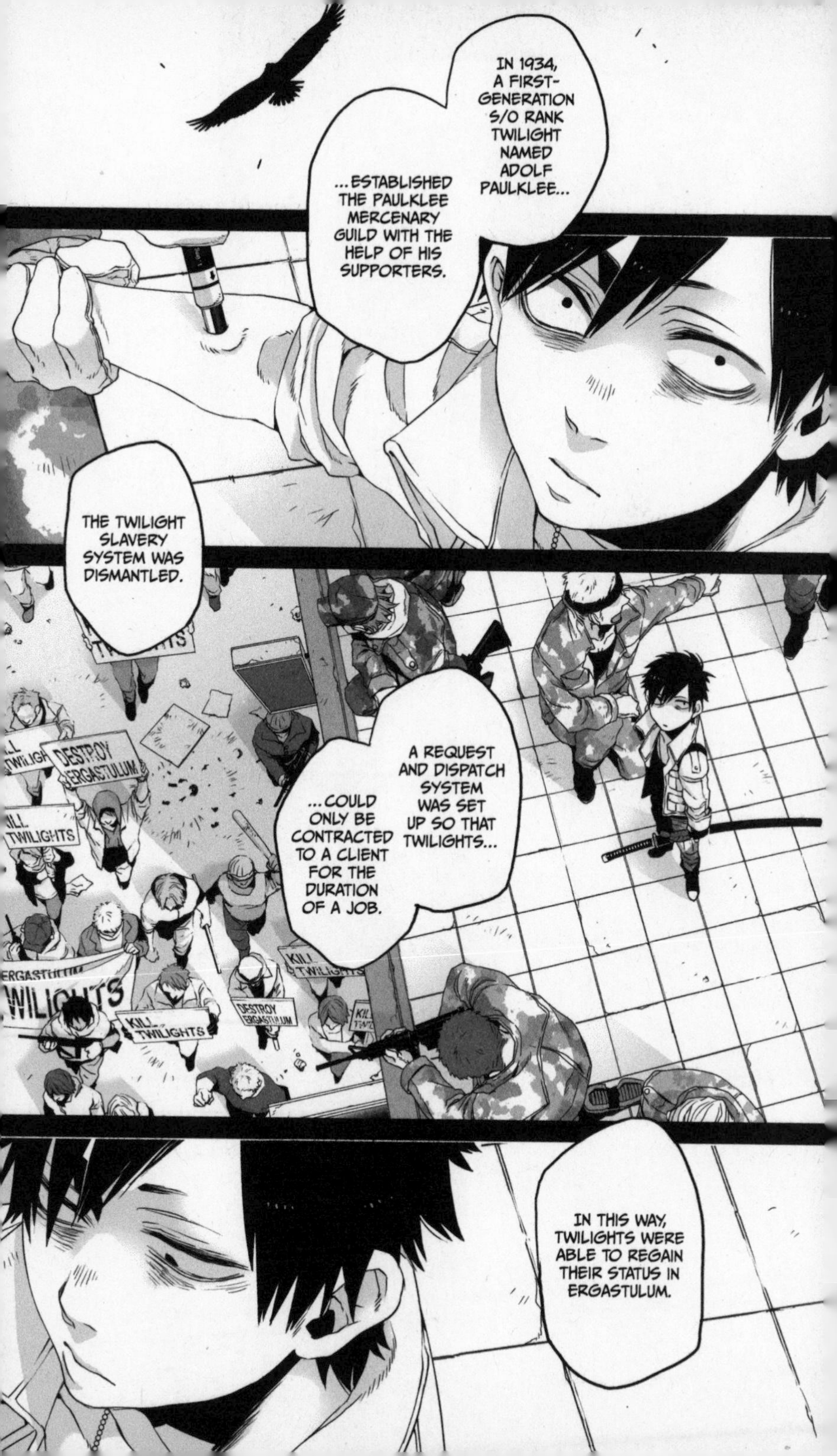
IN 1934, A FIRST-GENERATION S/O RANK TWILIGHT NAMED ADOLF PAULKLEE...
...ESTABLISHED THE PAULKLEE MERCENARY GUILD WITH THE HELP OF HIS SUPPORTERS.
THE TWILIGHT SLAVERY SYSTEM WAS DISMANTLED.
A REQUEST AND DISPATCH SYSTEM WAS SET UP SO THAT TWILIGHTS...
...COULD ONLY BE CONTRACTED TO A CLIENT FOR THE DURATION OF A JOB.
DESTROY ERGASTULUM
KILL TWILIGHTS
KILL TWILIGHTS
DESTROY ERGASTULUM
KILL TWILIGHTS
IN THIS WAY, TWILIGHTS WERE ABLE TO REGAIN THEIR STATUS IN ERGASTULUM.

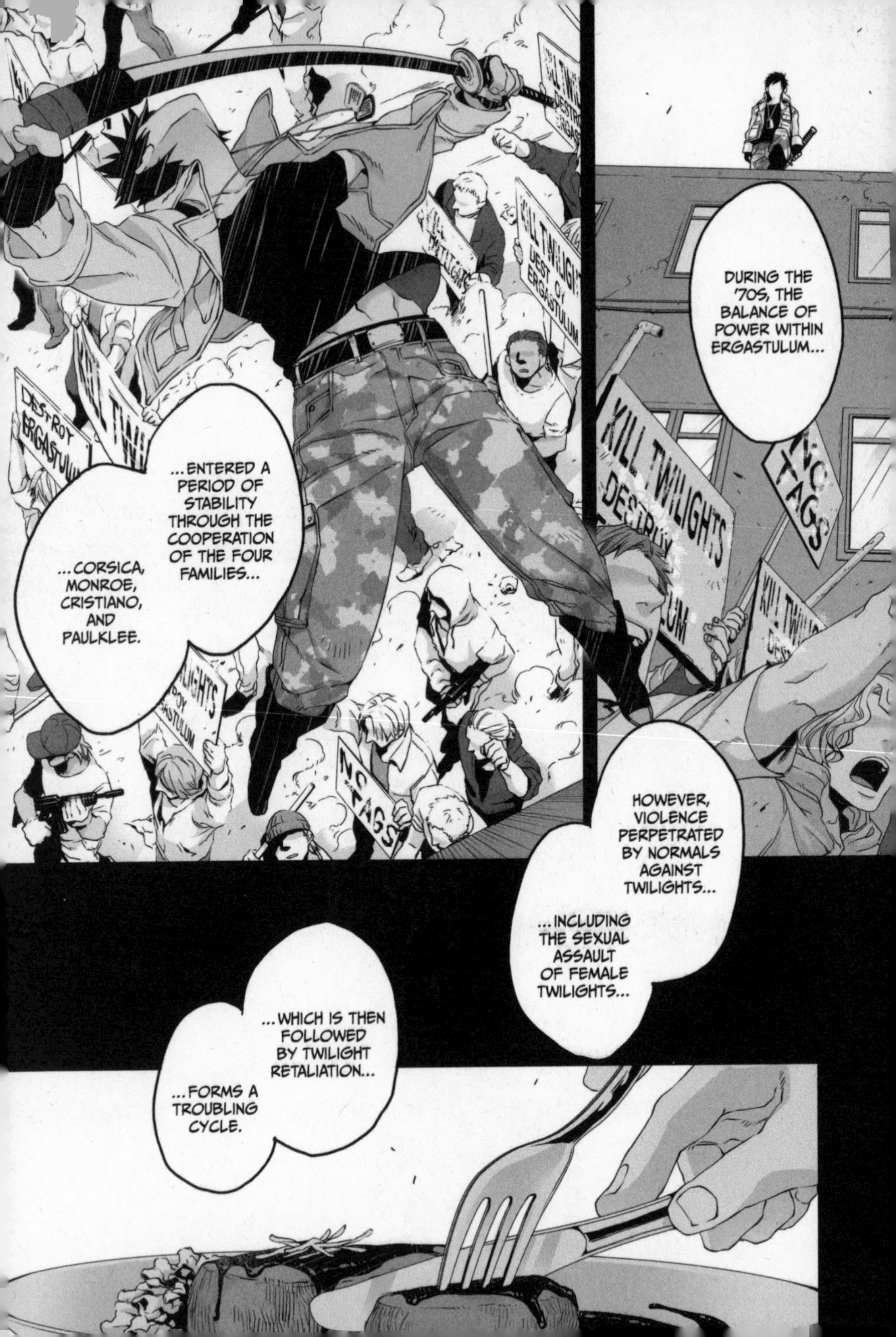
DURING THE '70S, THE BALANCE OF POWER WITHIN ERGASTULUM...
KILL TWILIGHTS
NO TAGS
...ENTERED A PERIOD OF STABILITY THROUGH THE COOPERATION OF THE FOUR FAMILIES...
...CORSICA, MONROE, CRISTIANO, AND PAULKLEE.
HOWEVER, VIOLENCE PERPETRATED BY NORMALS AGAINST TWILIGHTS...
...INCLUDING THE SEXUAL ASSAULT OF FEMALE TWILIGHTS...
...WHICH IS THEN FOLLOWED BY TWILIGHT RETALIATION...
...FORMS A TROUBLING CYCLE.

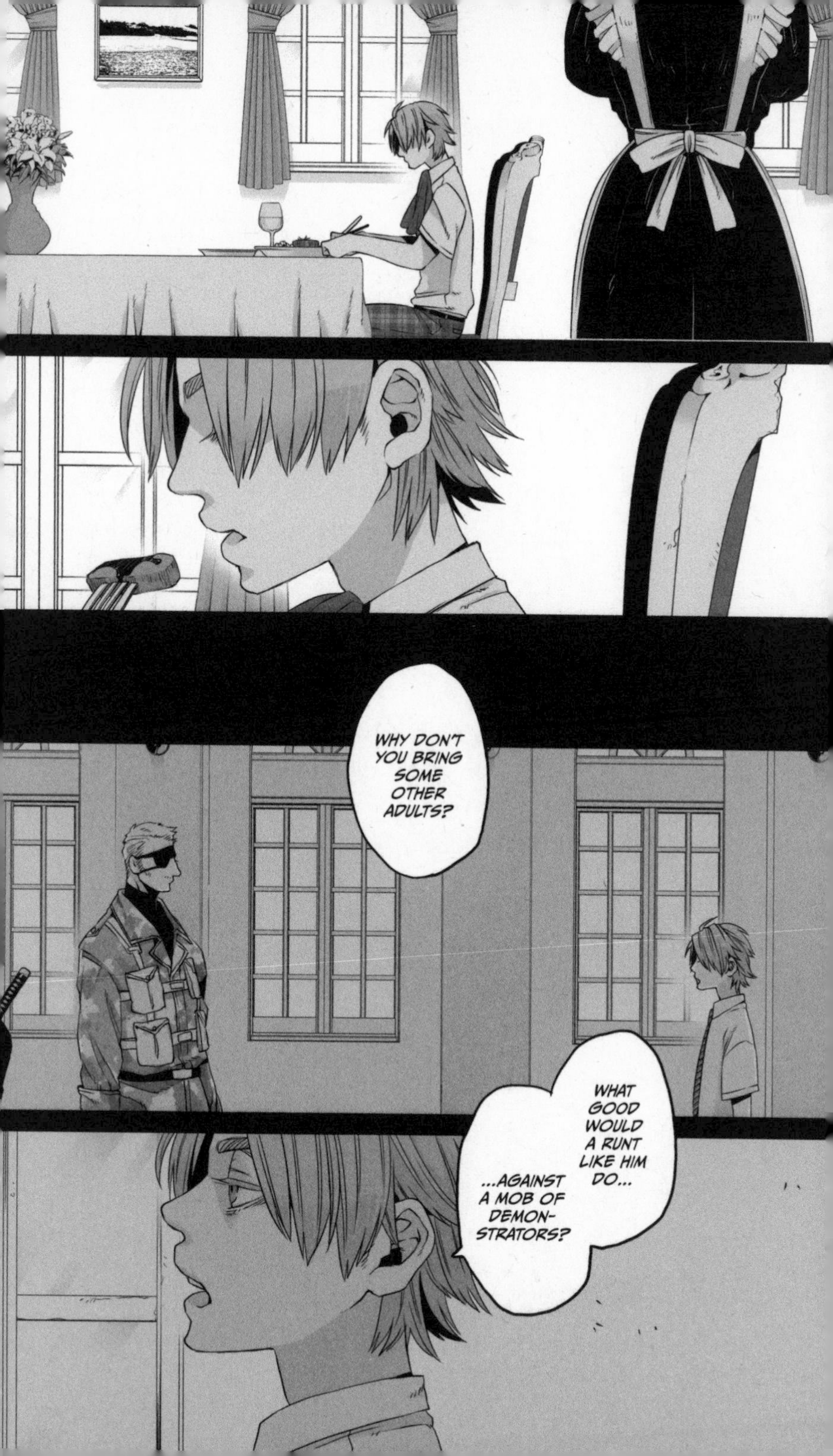

WHY DON'T YOU BRING SOME OTHER ADULTS?
WHAT GOOD WOULD A RUNT LIKE HIM DO...
...AGAINST A MOB OF DEMON-STRATORS?

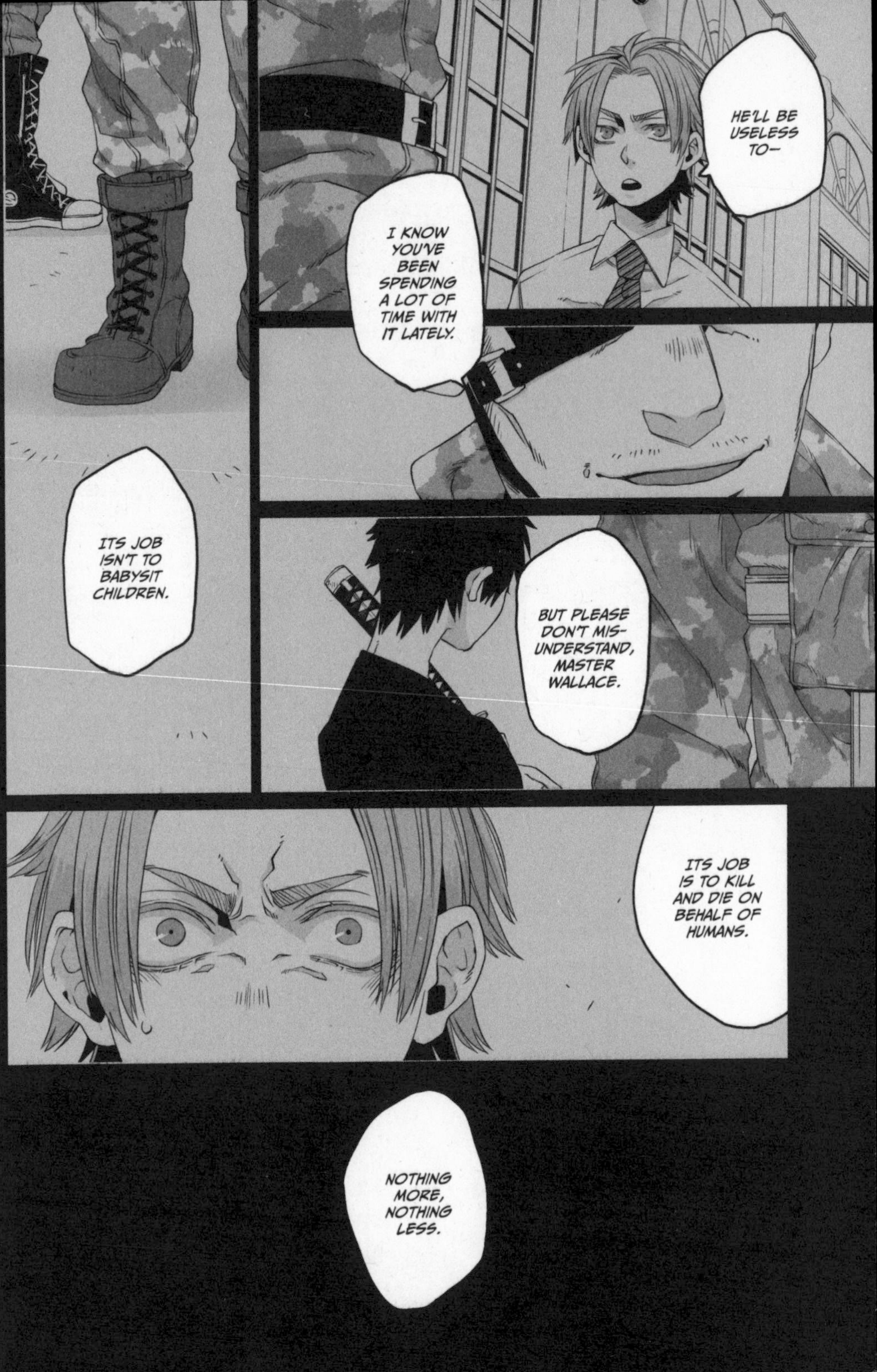
HE'LL BE USELESS TO—
I KNOW YOU'VE BEEN SPENDING A LOT OF TIME WITH IT LATELY.
BUT PLEASE DON'T MIS-UNDERSTAND, MASTER WALLACE.
ITS JOB ISN'T TO BABYSIT CHILDREN.
ITS JOB IS TO KILL AND DIE ON BEHALF OF HUMANS.
NOTHING MORE, NOTHING LESS.

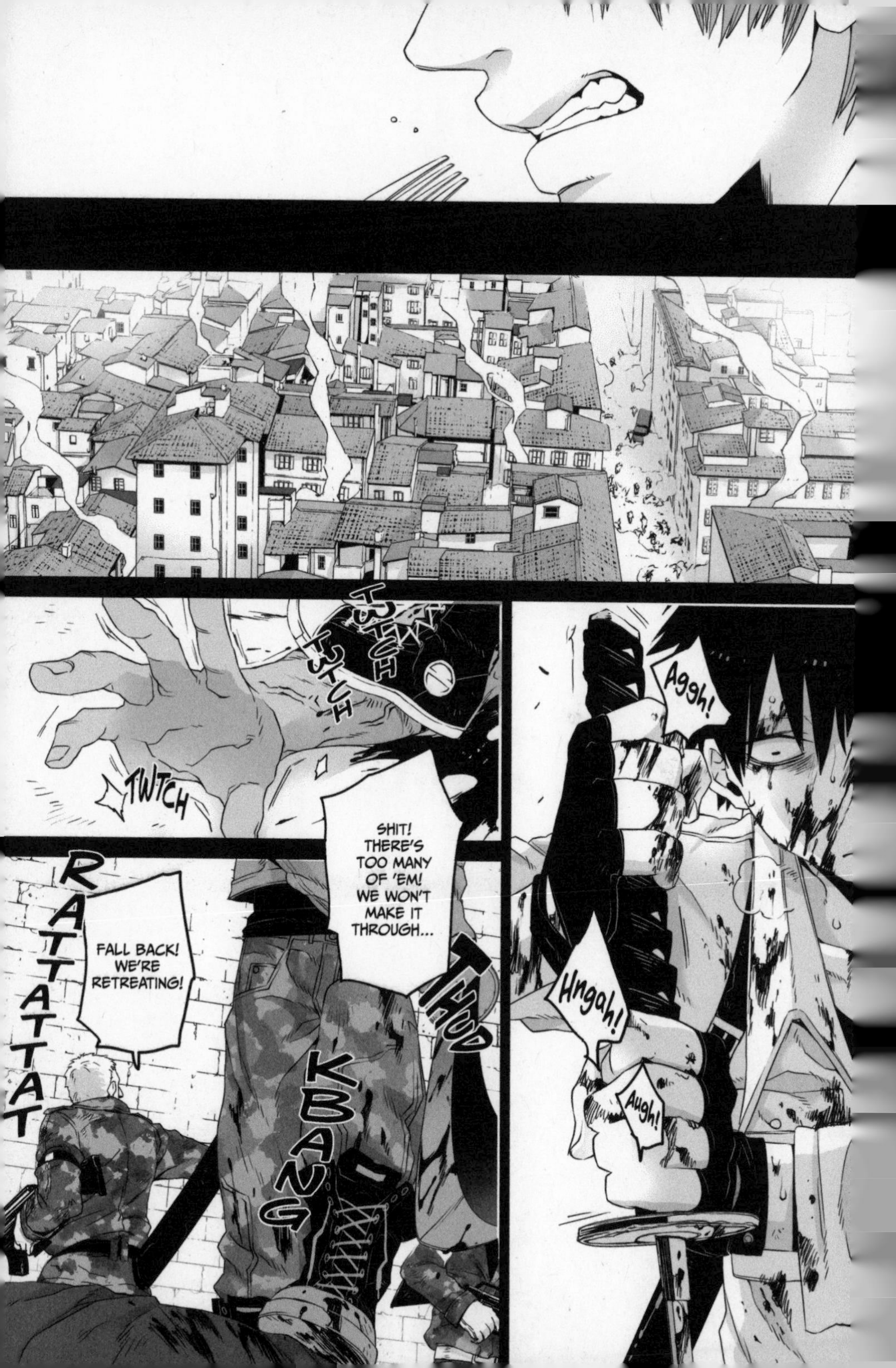
Agggh!
Hngah!
Augh!
TWITCH
TWITCH
TWITCH
SHIT! THERE'S TOO MANY OF 'EM! WE WON'T MAKE IT THROUGH...
THUD
KBANG
FALL BACK! WE'RE RETREATING!
RATTATTAT

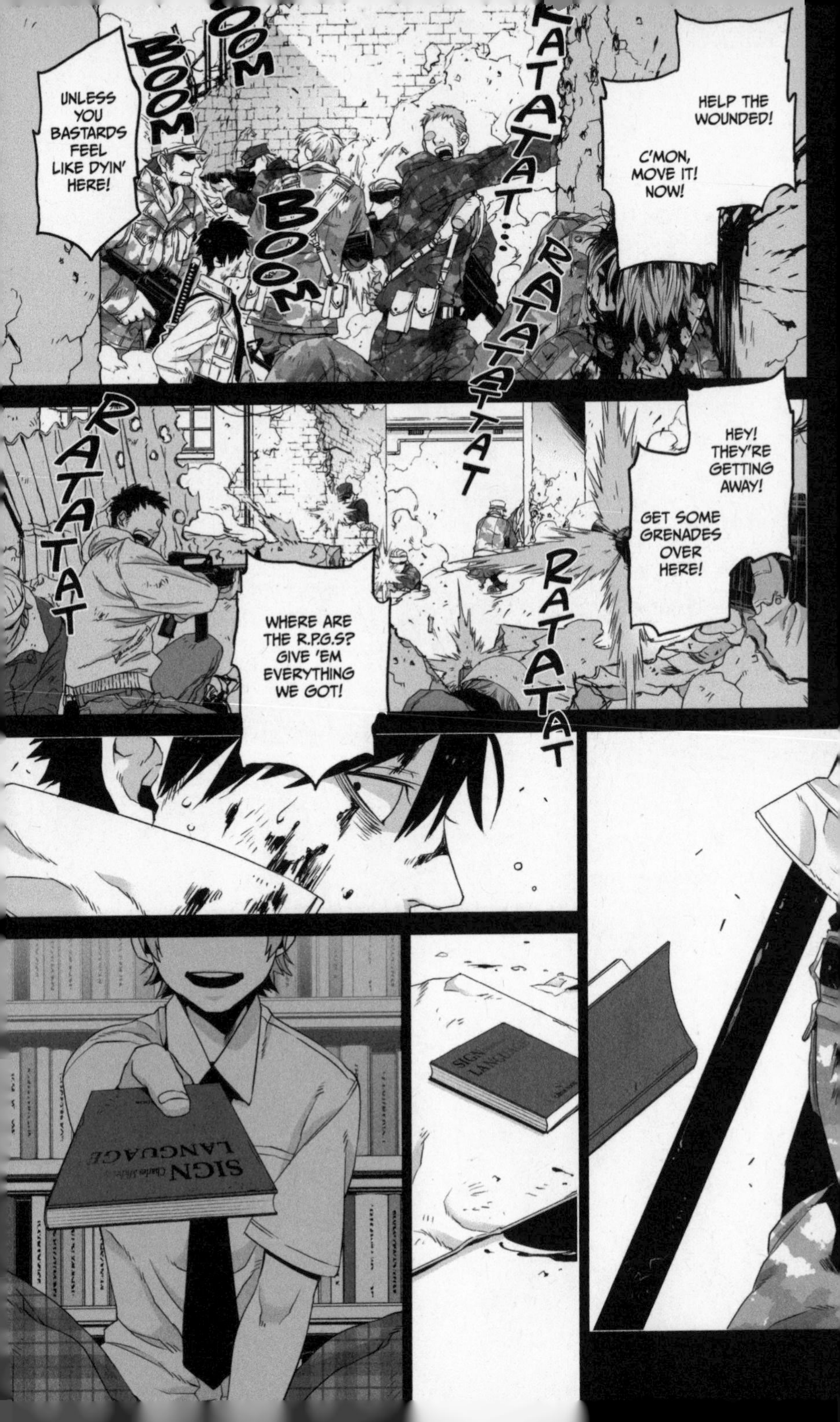

RATATAT...
HELP THE WOUNDED!
C'MON, MOVE IT! NOW!
RATATATATAT
BOOM
BOOM
BOOM
OOM
UNLESS YOU BASTARDS FEEL LIKE DYIN' HERE!
HEY! THEY'RE GETTING AWAY!
GET SOME GRENADES OVER HERE!
RATATAT
WHERE ARE THE R.P.G.S? GIVE 'EM EVERYTHING WE GOT!
RATATAT
SIGN LANGUAGE

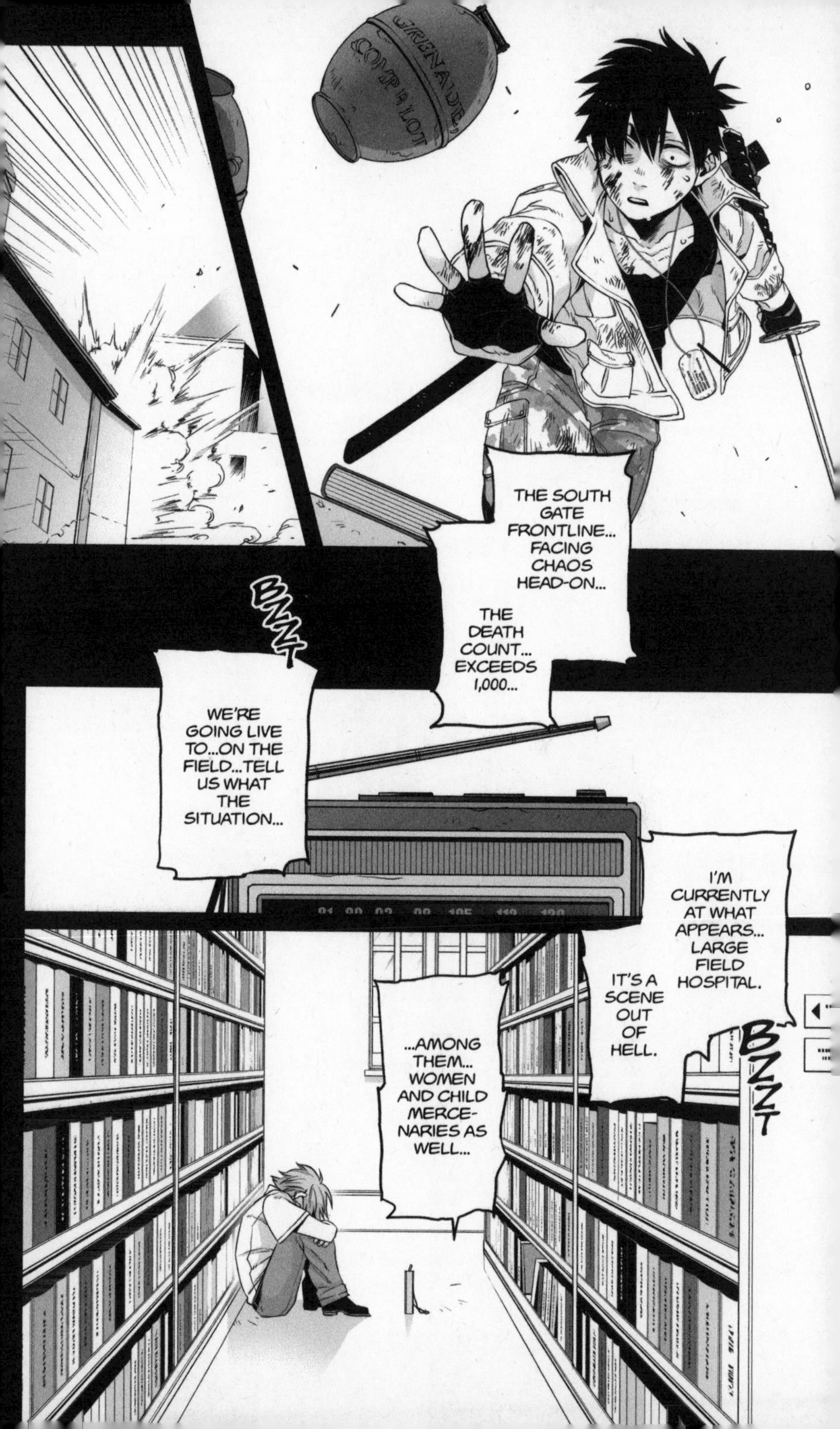
THE SOUTH GATE FRONTLINE... FACING CHAOS HEAD-ON...
THE DEATH COUNT... EXCEEDS 1,000...
BZZZ
WE'RE GOING LIVE TO...ON THE FIELD...TELL US WHAT THE SITUATION...
I'M CURRENTLY AT WHAT APPEARS... LARGE FIELD HOSPITAL.
IT'S A SCENE OUT OF HELL.
BZZZT
...AMONG THEM... WOMEN AND CHILD MERCENARIES AS WELL...

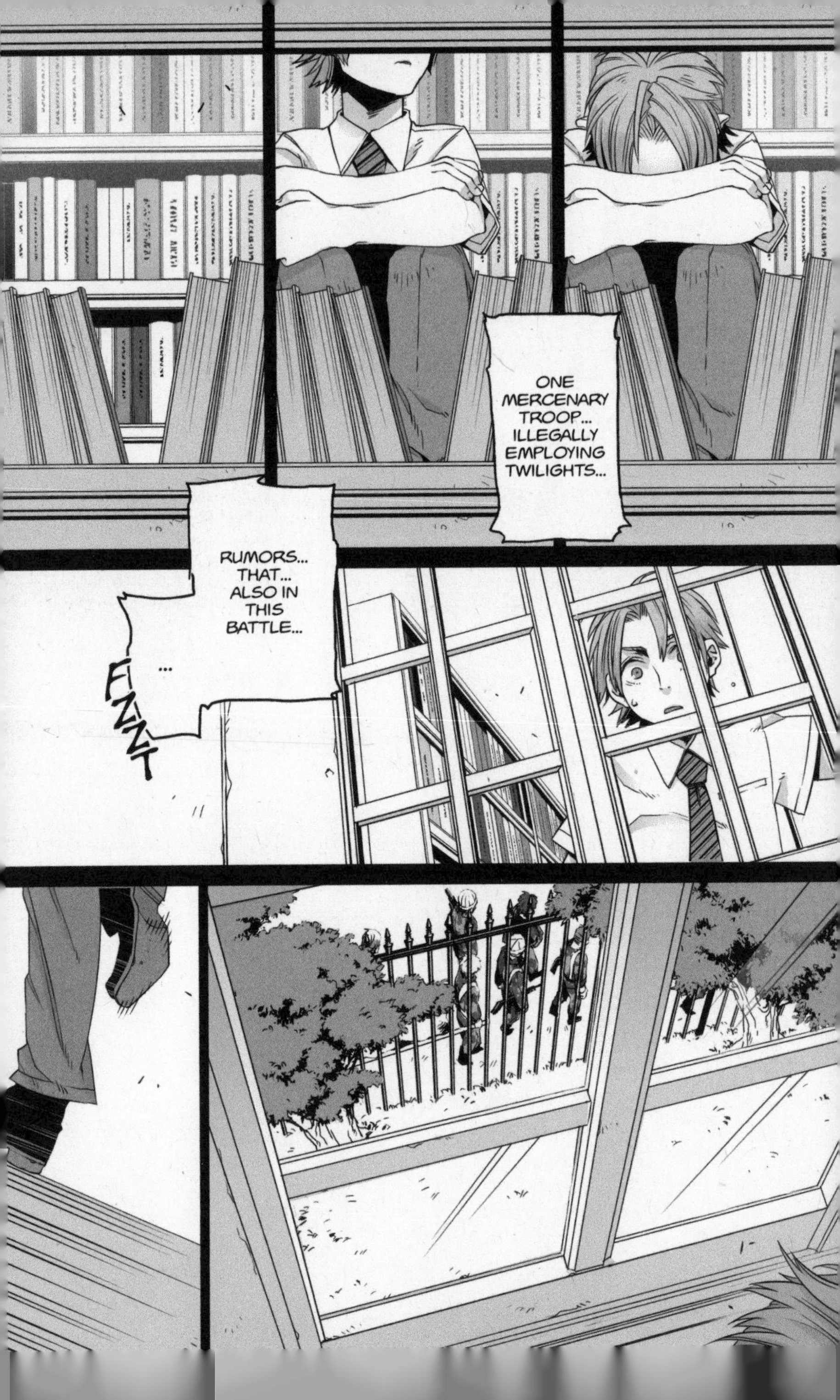
ONE MERCENARY TROOP... ILLEGALLY EMPLOYING TWILIGHTS...
RUMORS... THAT... ALSO IN THIS BATTLE...
...
FIZZT

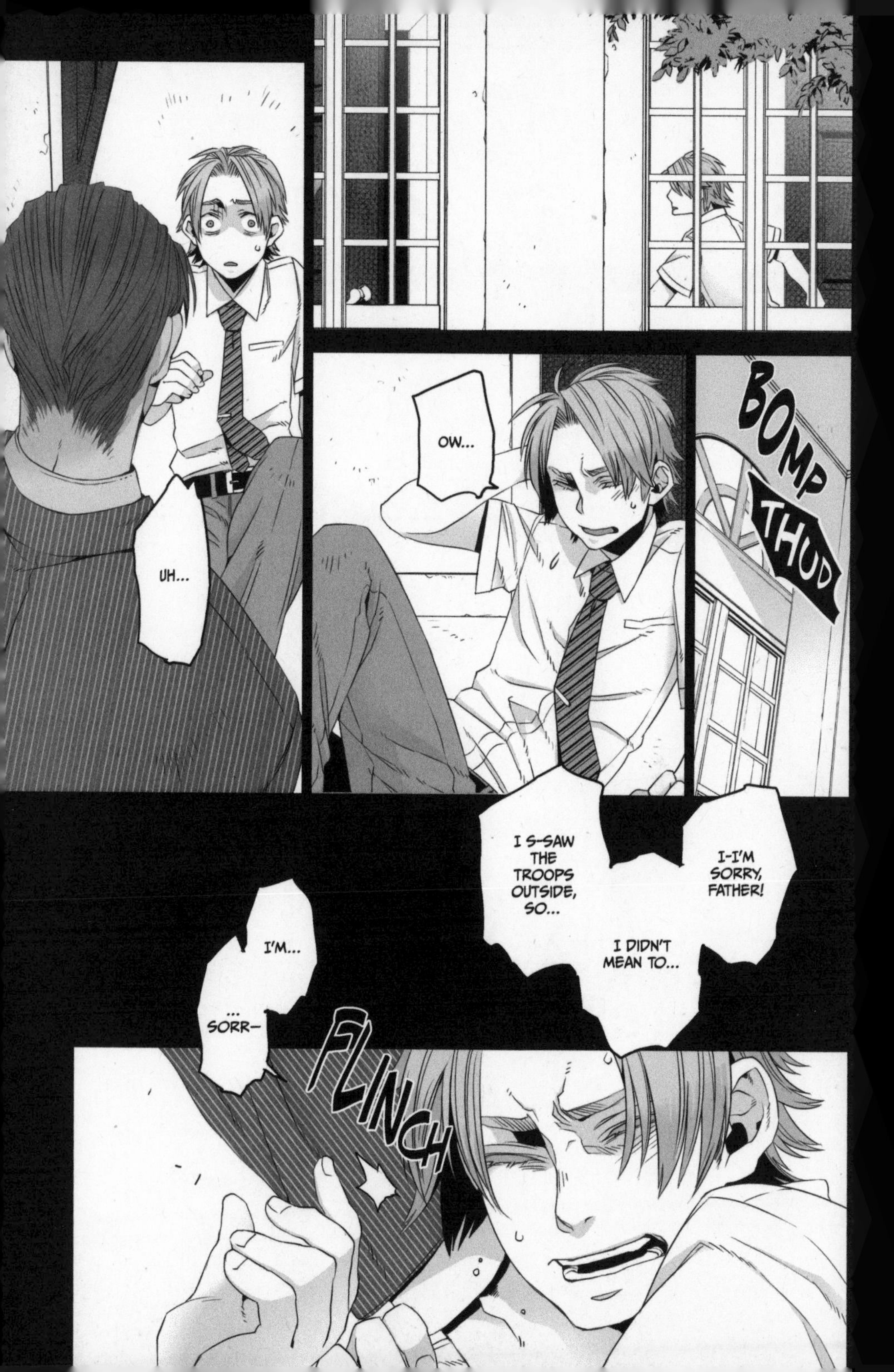
BOMP
THUD
OW...
UH...
I-I'M SORRY, FATHER!
I S-SAW THE TROOPS OUTSIDE, SO...
I DIDN'T MEAN TO...
I'M...
... SORR-
FLINCH

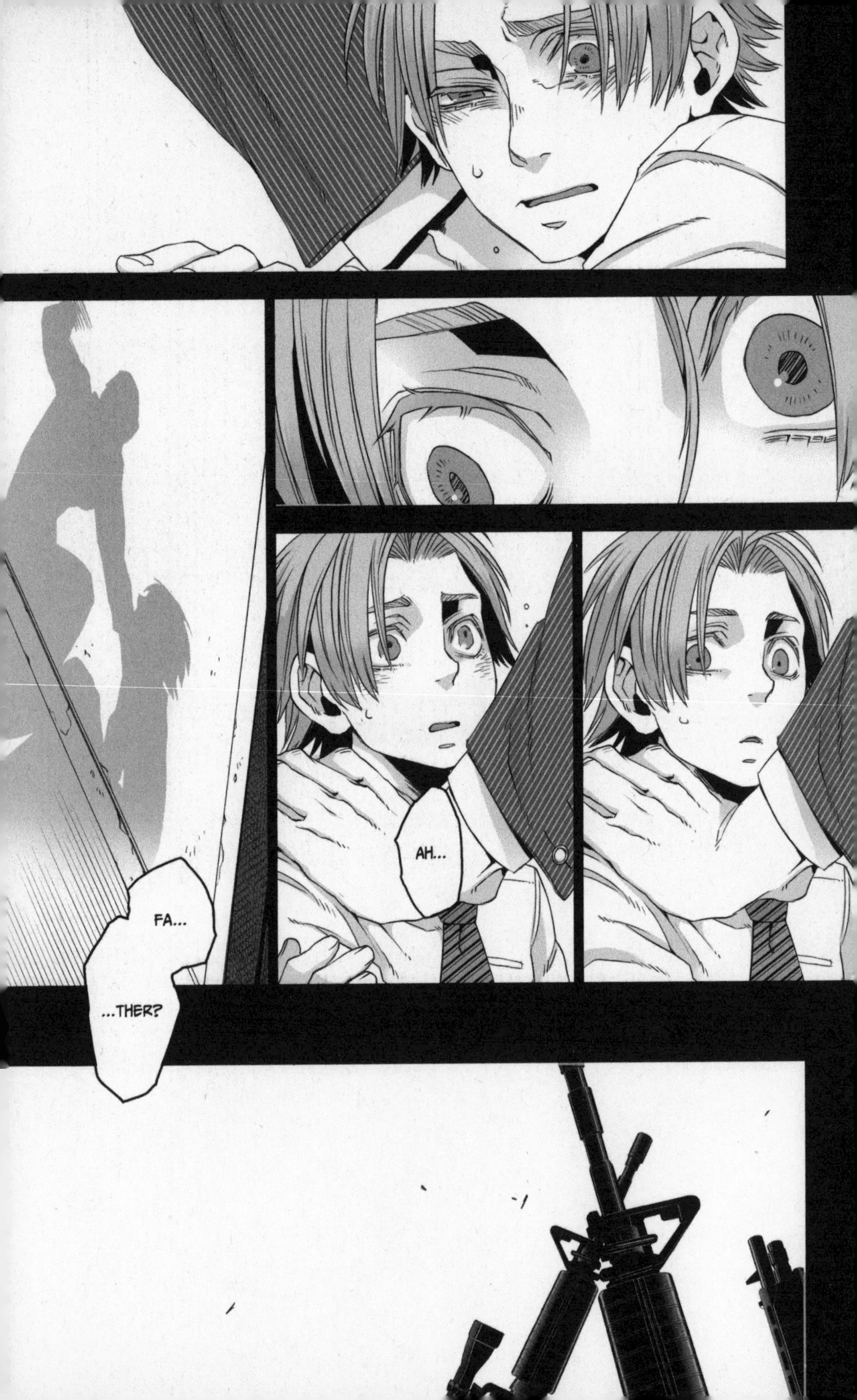
AH...
FA... ...THER?

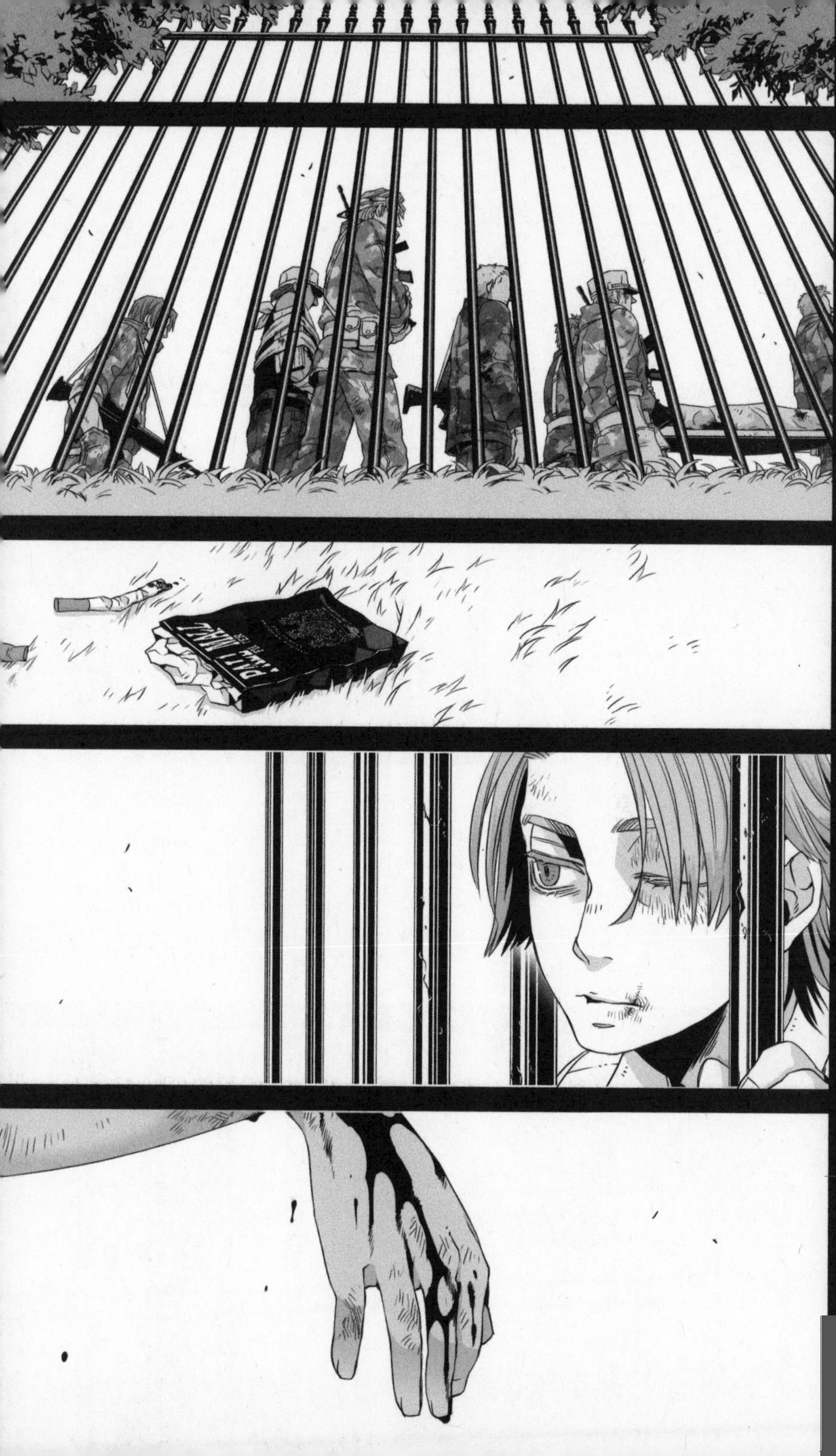

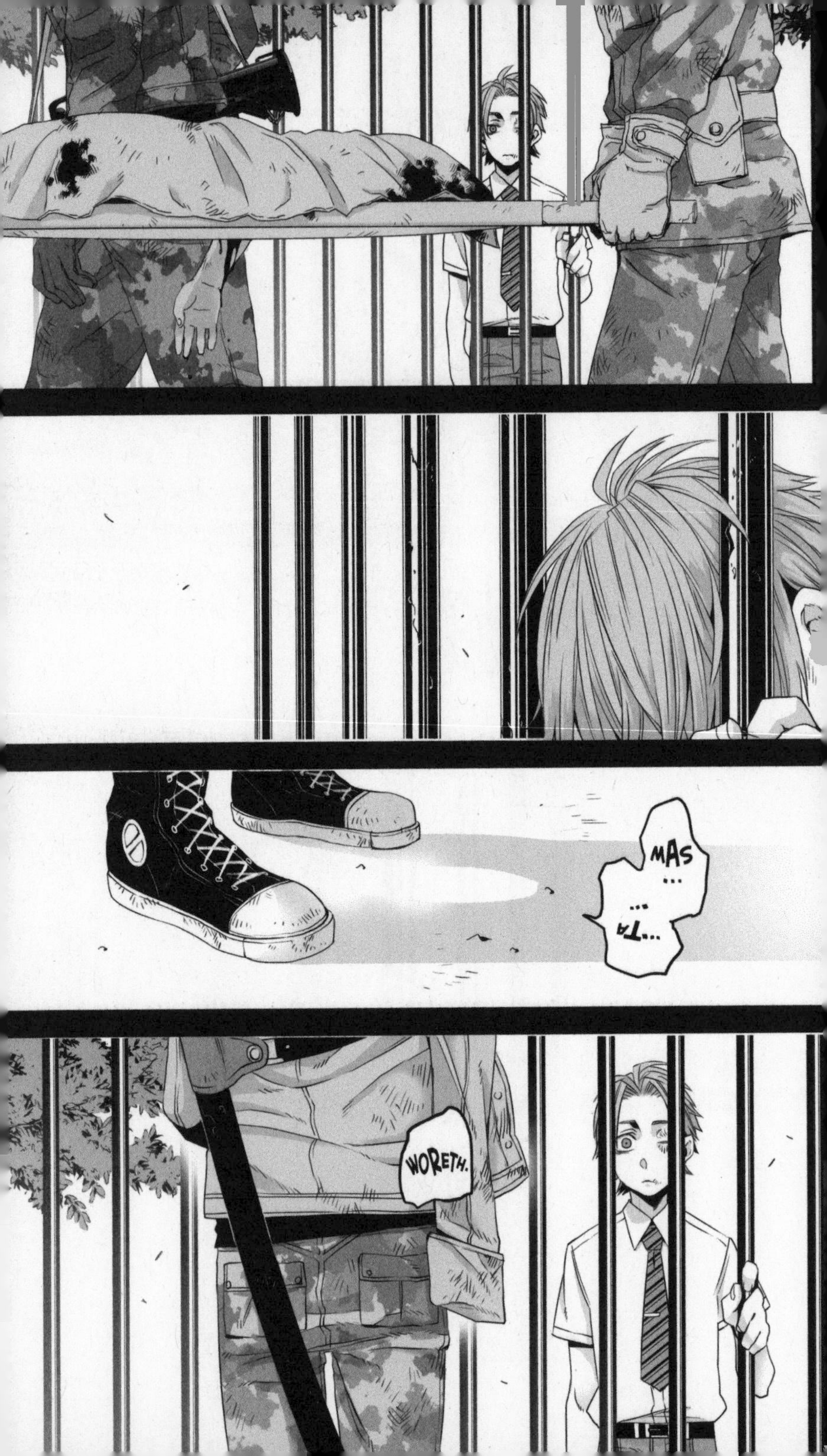
MAS... ...TA...
WORETH.

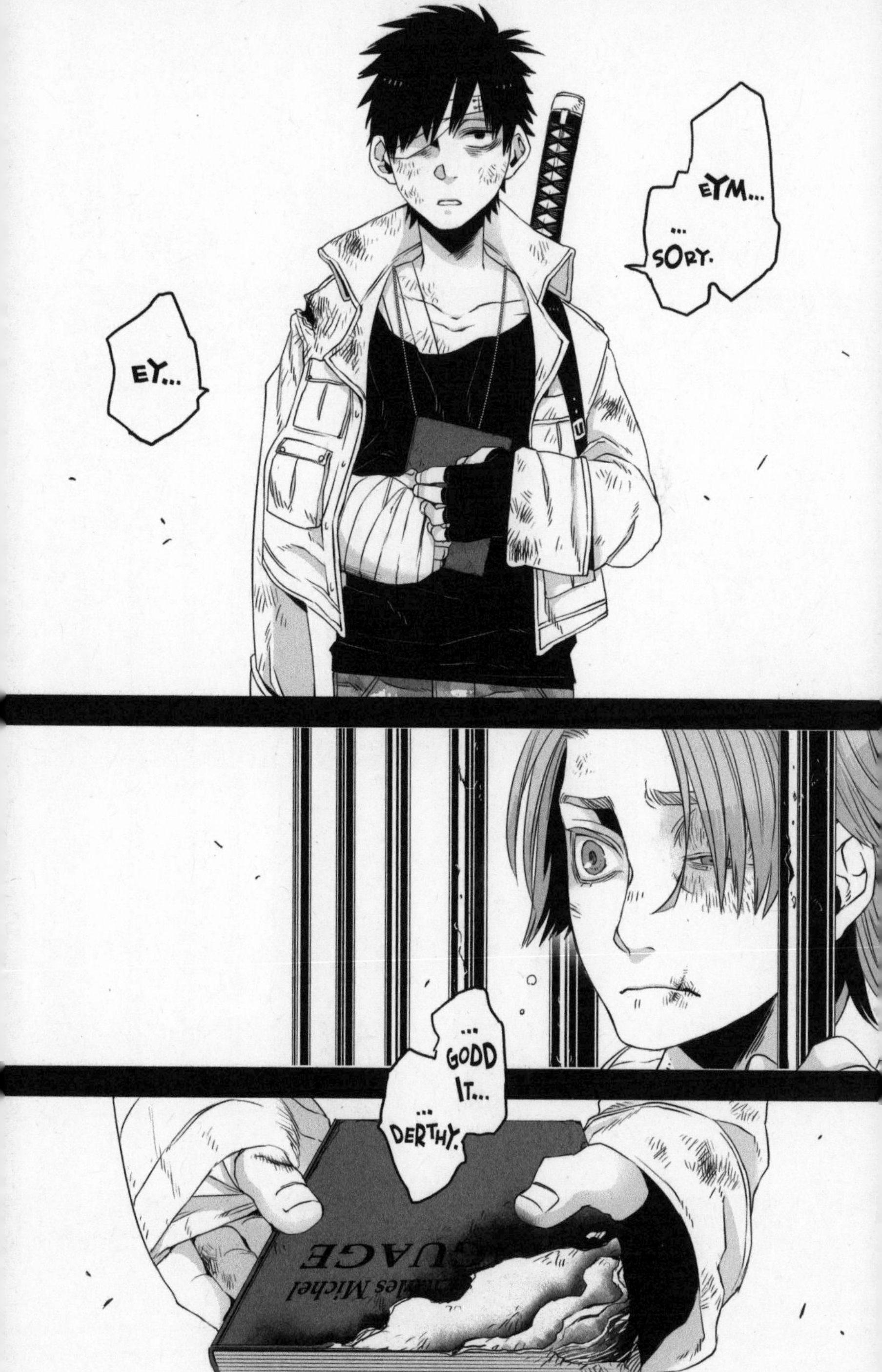
EYM... ... SORY.
EY...
... GODD IT... ... DERTHY.

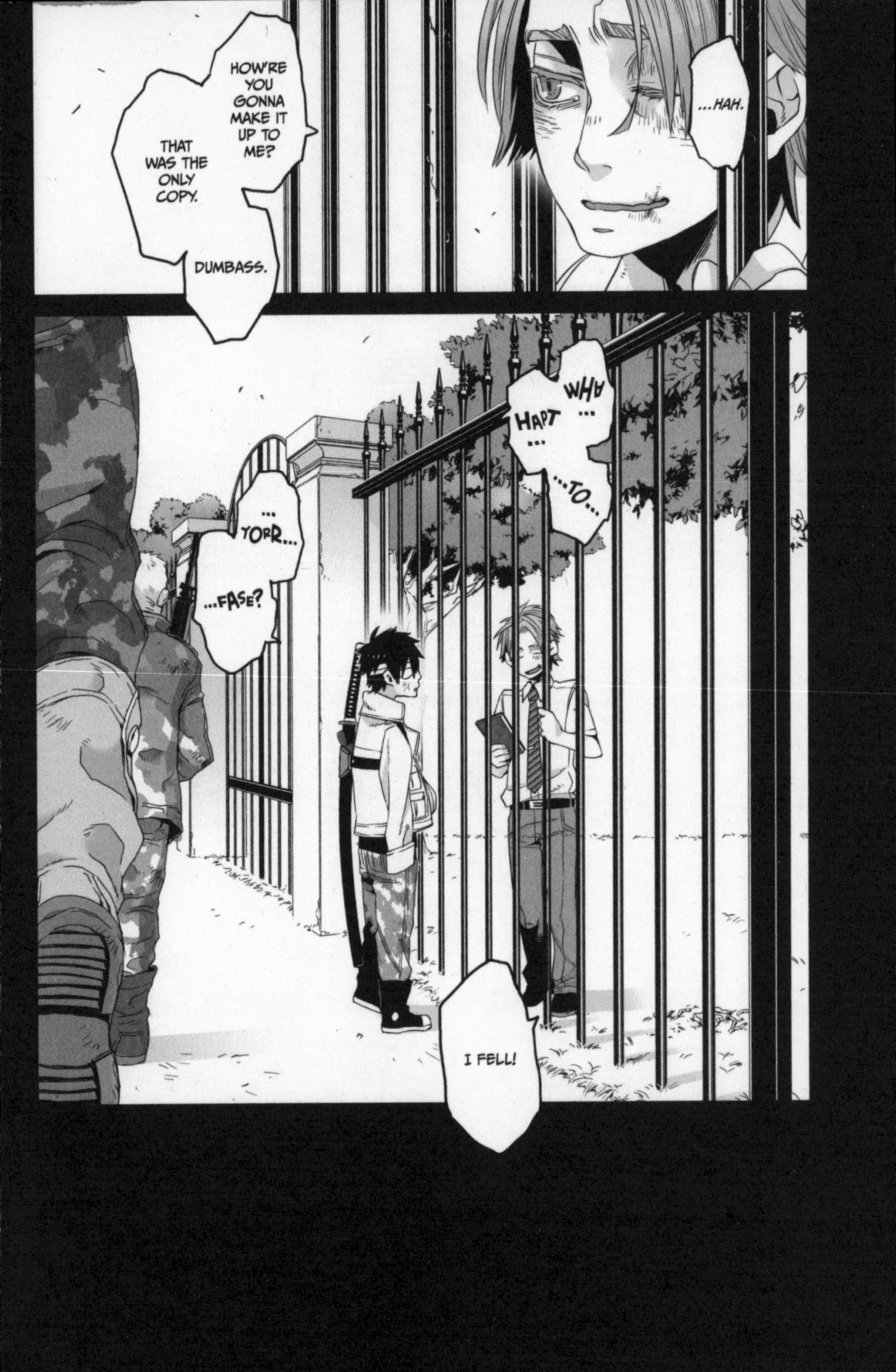
...HAH.
HOW'RE YOU GONNA MAKE IT UP TO ME?
THAT WAS THE ONLY COPY.
DUMBASS.
WHA ... HAPT ... ...TO...
... YORR... ...FASE?
I FELL!

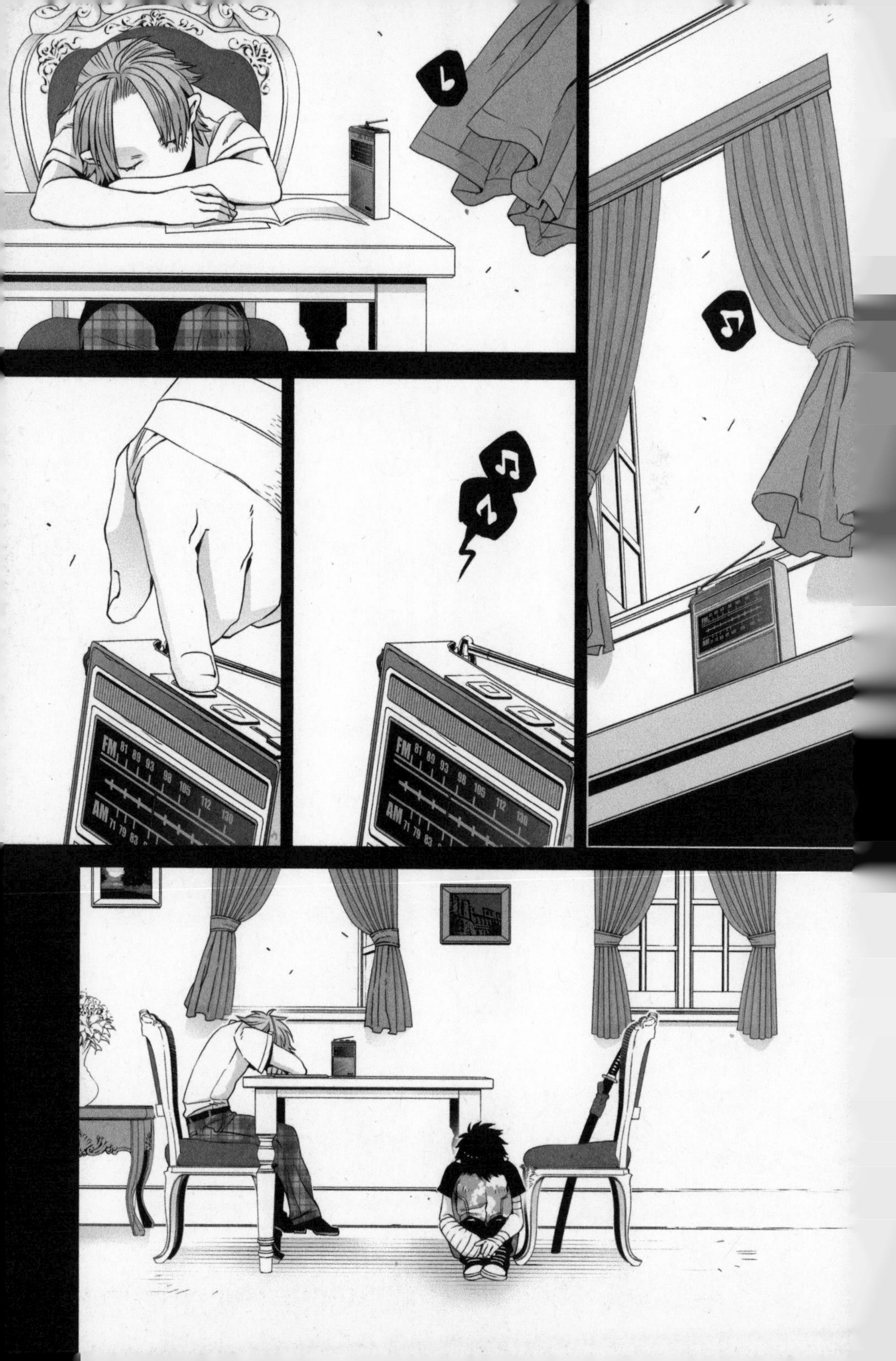
FM 81 89 93 98 105 112 130
AM 71 79 83
FM 81 89 93 98 105 112 130
AM 71 79 83

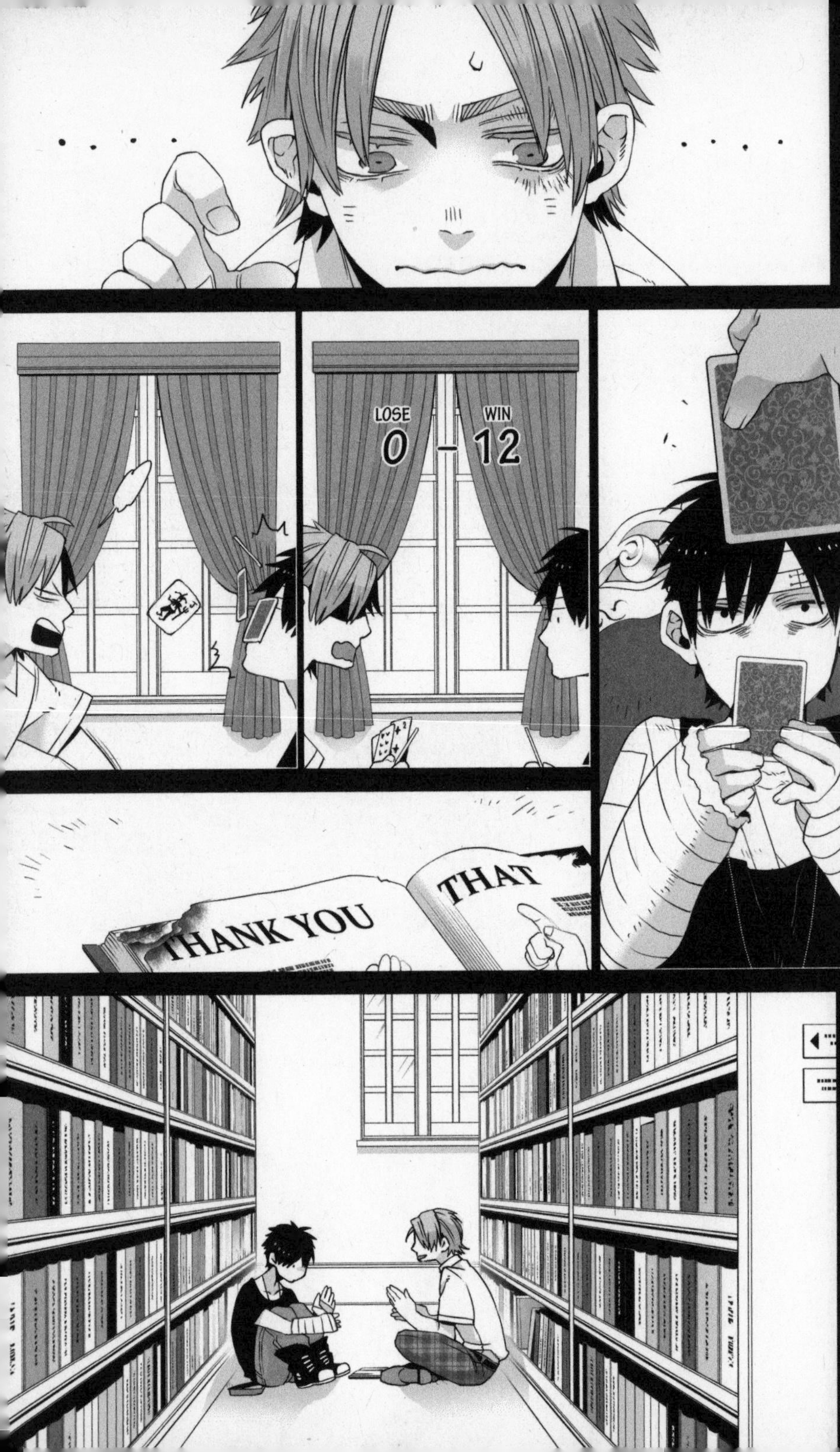
. . . .
. . . .
LOSE
WIN
0 – 12
THAT
THANK YOU

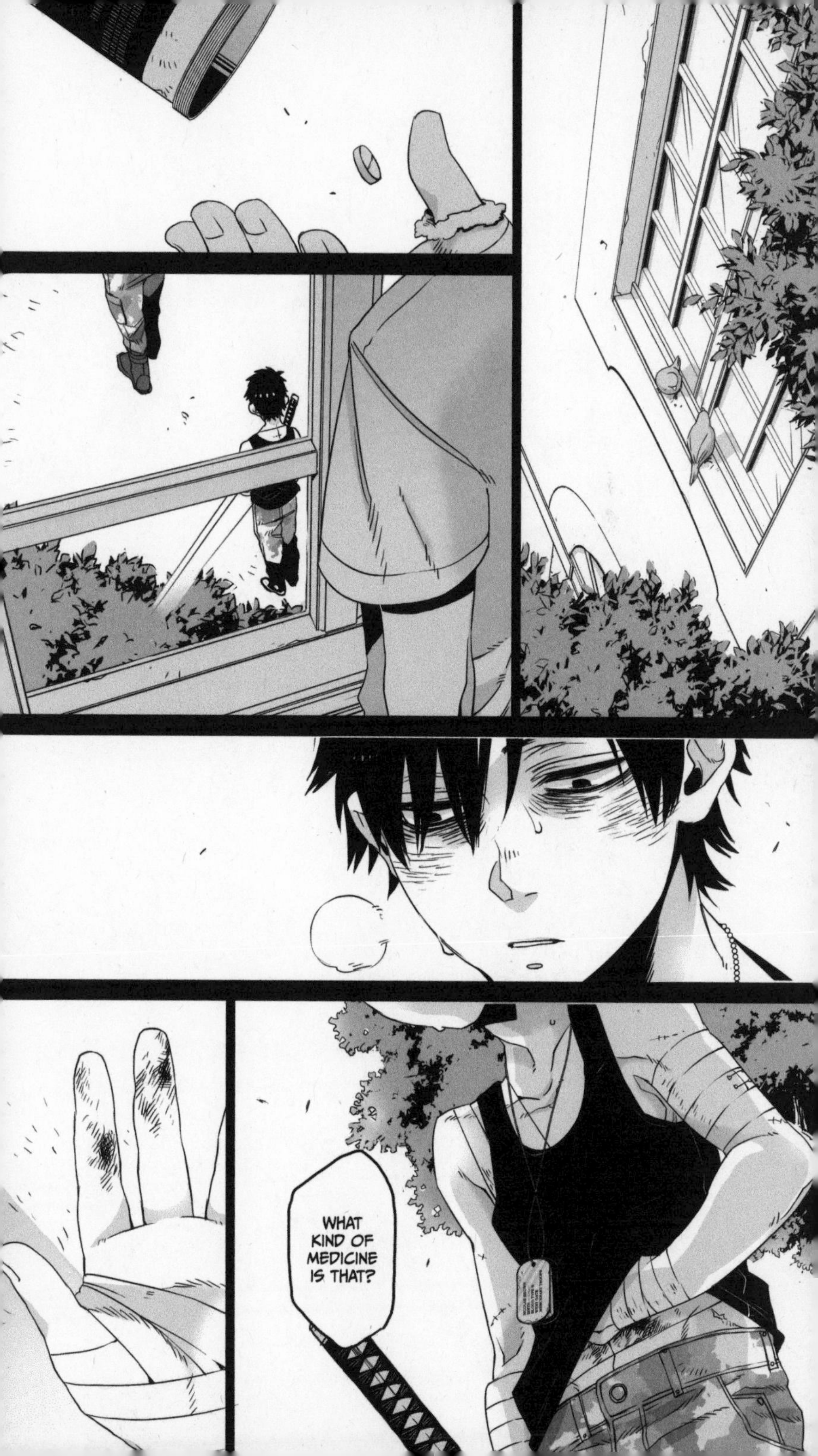
WHAT KIND OF MEDICINE IS THAT?

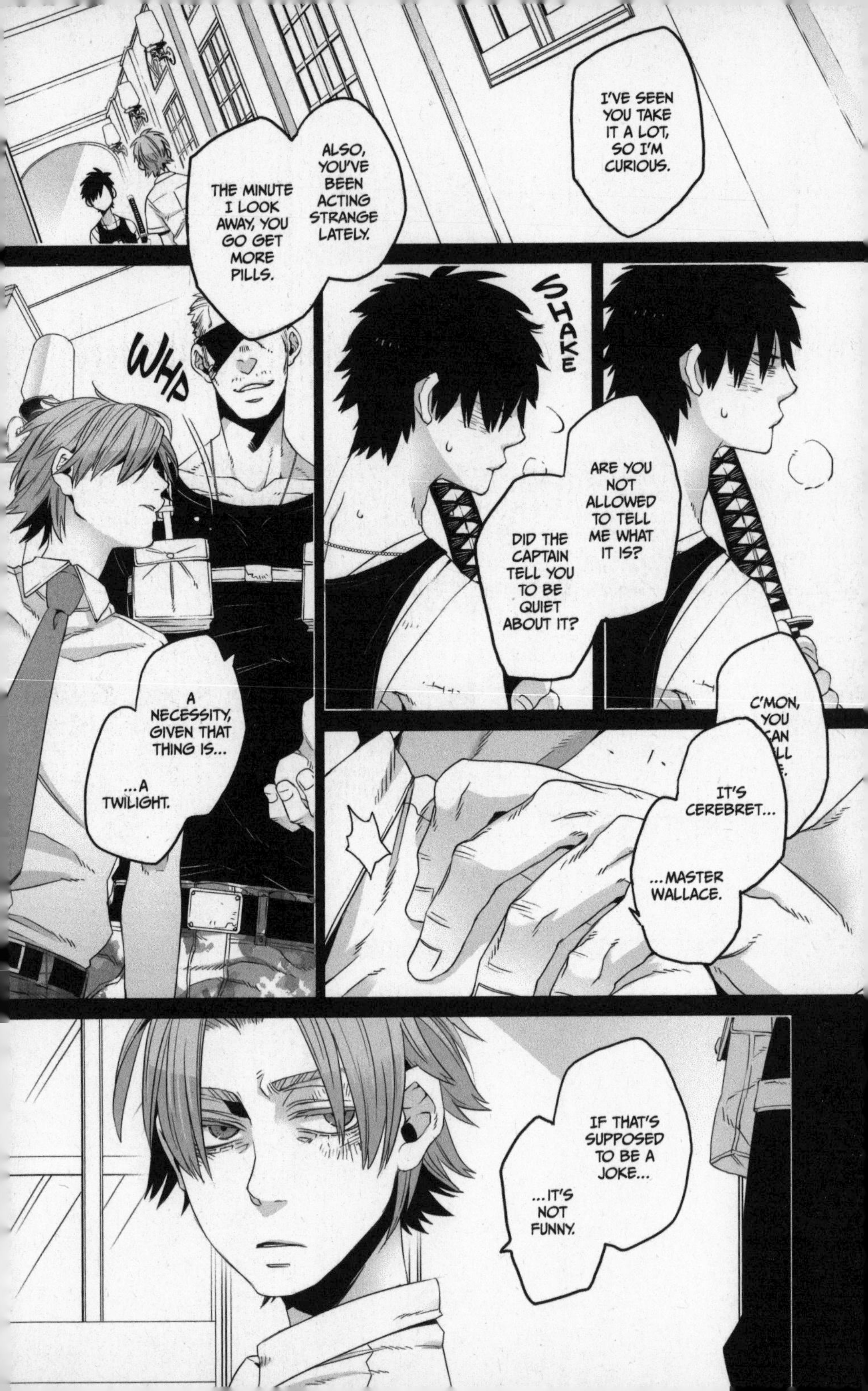
I'VE SEEN YOU TAKE IT A LOT, SO I'M CURIOUS.
ALSO, YOU'VE BEEN ACTING STRANGE LATELY.
THE MINUTE I LOOK AWAY, YOU GO GET MORE PILLS.
ARE YOU NOT ALLOWED TO TELL ME WHAT IT IS?
DID THE CAPTAIN TELL YOU TO BE QUIET ABOUT IT?
SHAKE
C'MON, YOU
IT'S CEREBRET...
...MASTER WALLACE.
WHP
A NECESSITY, GIVEN THAT THING IS...
...A TWILIGHT.
IF THAT'S SUPPOSED TO BE A JOKE...
...IT'S NOT FUNNY.

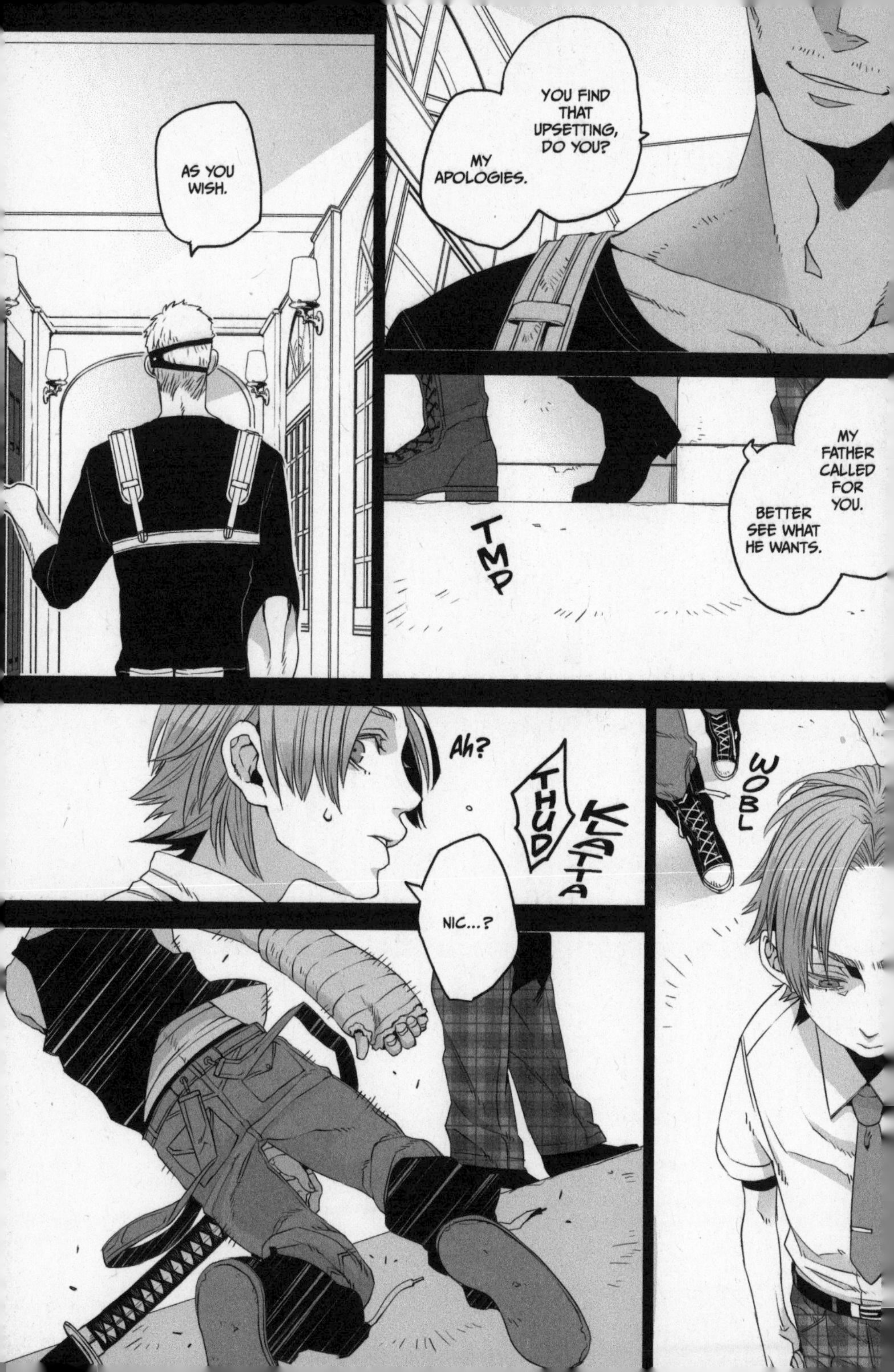
YOU FIND THAT UPSETTING, DO YOU?
MY APOLOGIES.
MY FATHER CALLED FOR YOU.
BETTER SEE WHAT HE WANTS.
TMP
AS YOU WISH.
WOBL
Ah?
KLATTA
THUD
NIC...?

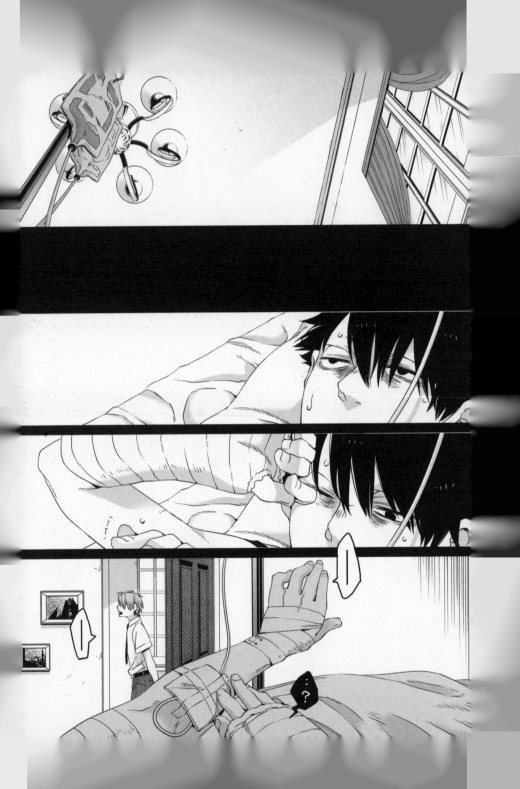

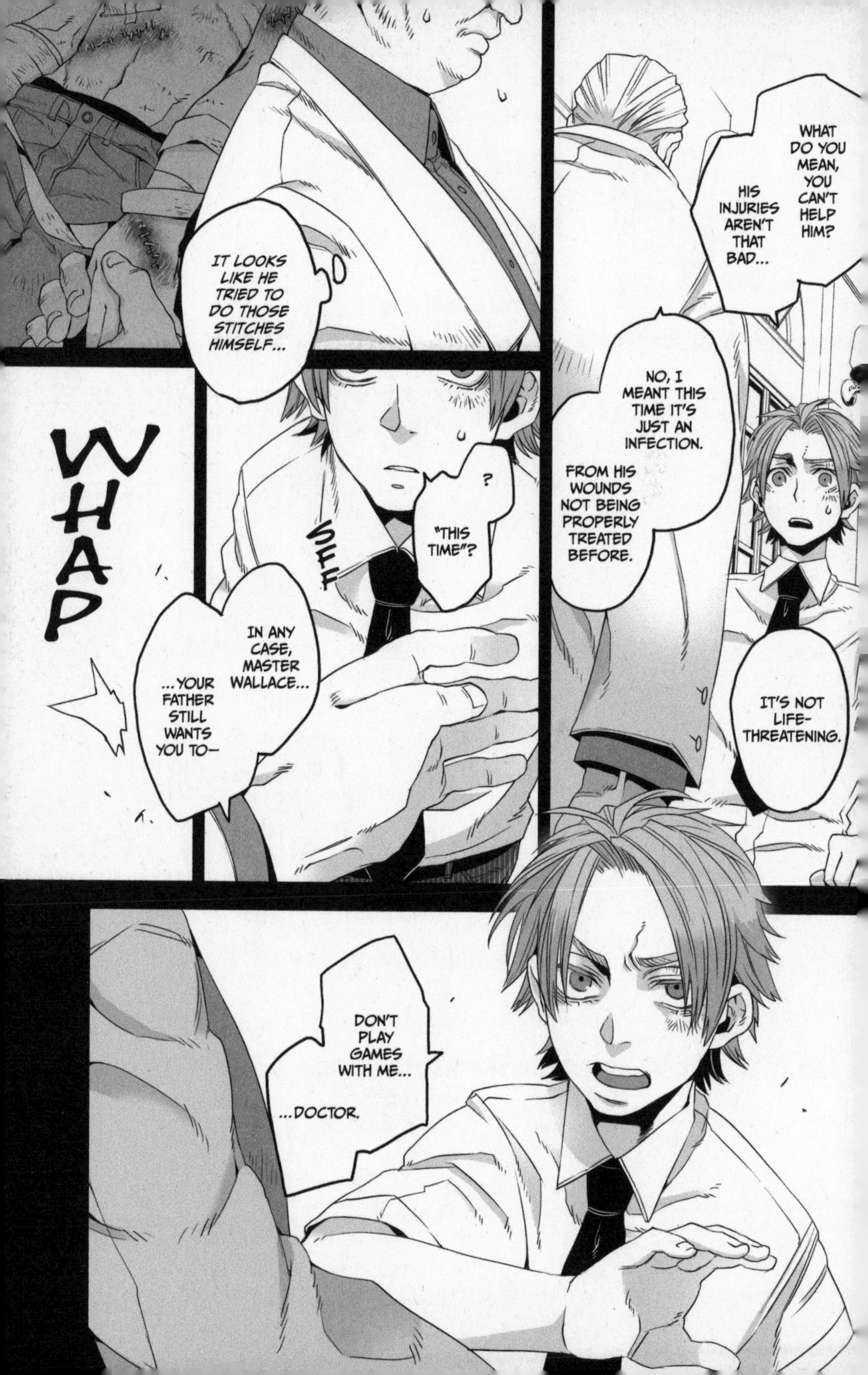
WHAT DO YOU MEAN, YOU CAN'T HELP HIM?
HIS INJURIES AREN'T THAT BAD...
NO, I MEANT THIS TIME IT'S JUST AN INFECTION.
FROM HIS WOUNDS NOT BEING PROPERLY TREATED BEFORE.
IT'S NOT LIFE-THREATENING.
IT LOOKS LIKE HE TRIED TO DO THOSE STITCHES HIMSELF...
?
"THIS TIME"?
SFF
IN ANY CASE, MASTER WALLACE...
...YOUR FATHER STILL WANTS YOU TO–
WHAP
DON'T PLAY GAMES WITH ME...
...DOCTOR.

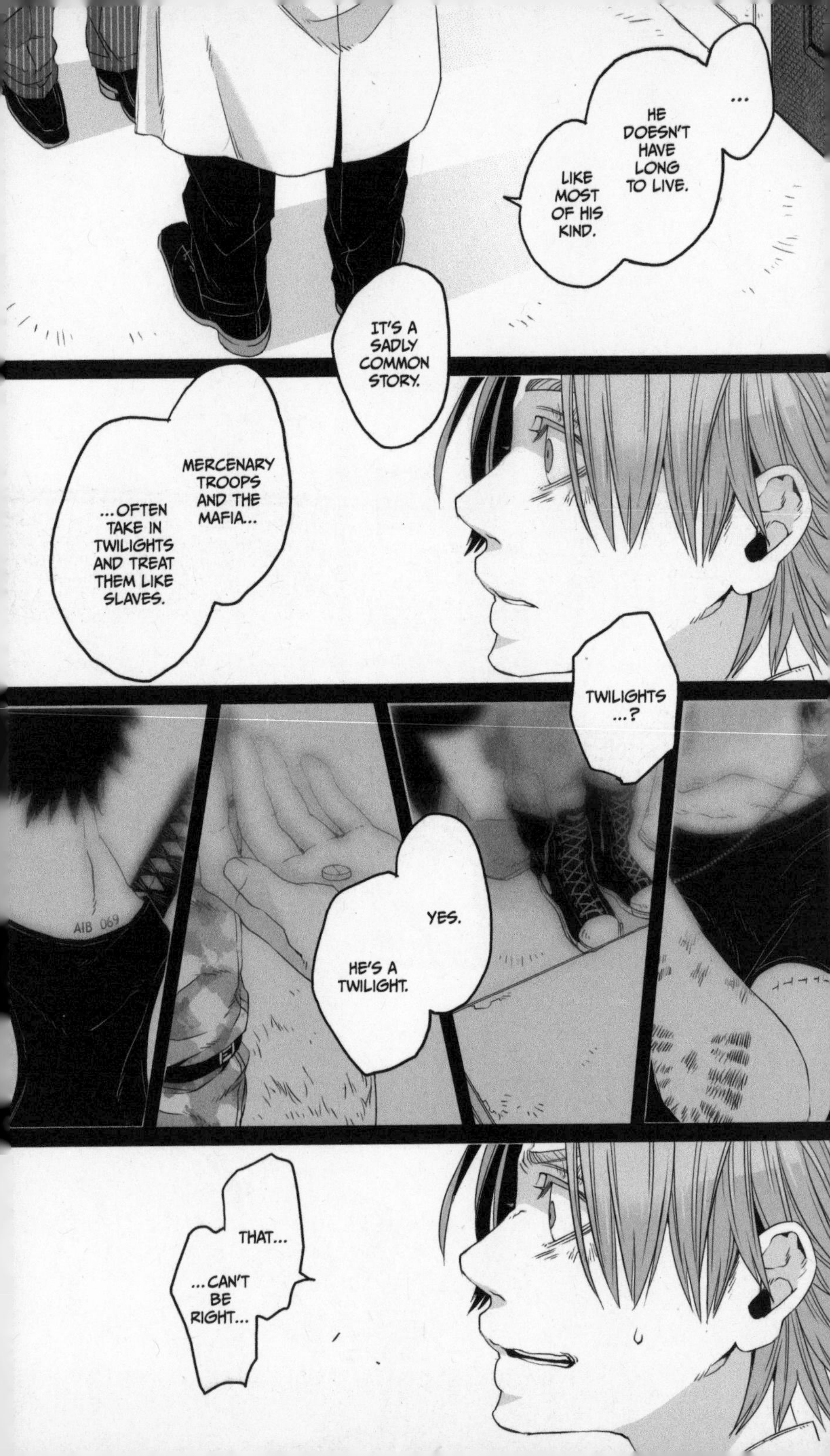
...
HE DOESN'T HAVE LONG TO LIVE.
LIKE MOST OF HIS KIND.
IT'S A SADLY COMMON STORY.
MERCENARY TROOPS AND THE MAFIA...
...OFTEN TAKE IN TWILIGHTS AND TREAT THEM LIKE SLAVES.
TWILIGHTS ...?
YES.
HE'S A TWILIGHT.
AIB 069
THAT...
...CAN'T BE RIGHT...

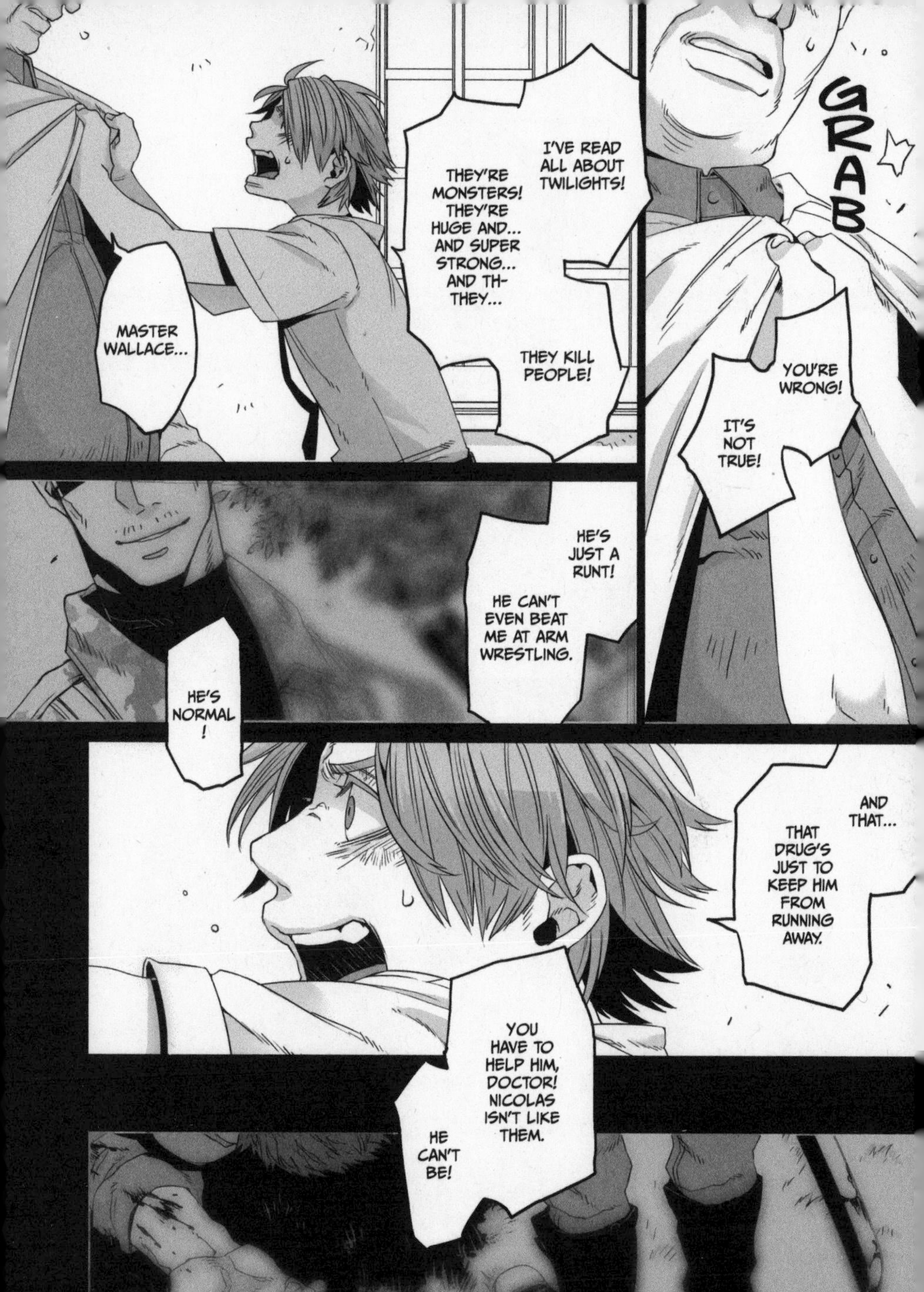
GRAB
YOU'RE WRONG!
IT'S NOT TRUE!
I'VE READ ALL ABOUT TWILIGHTS!
THEY'RE MONSTERS! THEY'RE HUGE AND... AND SUPER STRONG... AND TH-THEY...
THEY KILL PEOPLE!
MASTER WALLACE...
HE'S JUST A RUNT!
HE CAN'T EVEN BEAT ME AT ARM WRESTLING.
HE'S NORMAL!
AND THAT...
THAT DRUG'S JUST TO KEEP HIM FROM RUNNING AWAY.
YOU HAVE TO HELP HIM, DOCTOR! NICOLAS ISN'T LIKE THEM.
HE CAN'T BE!

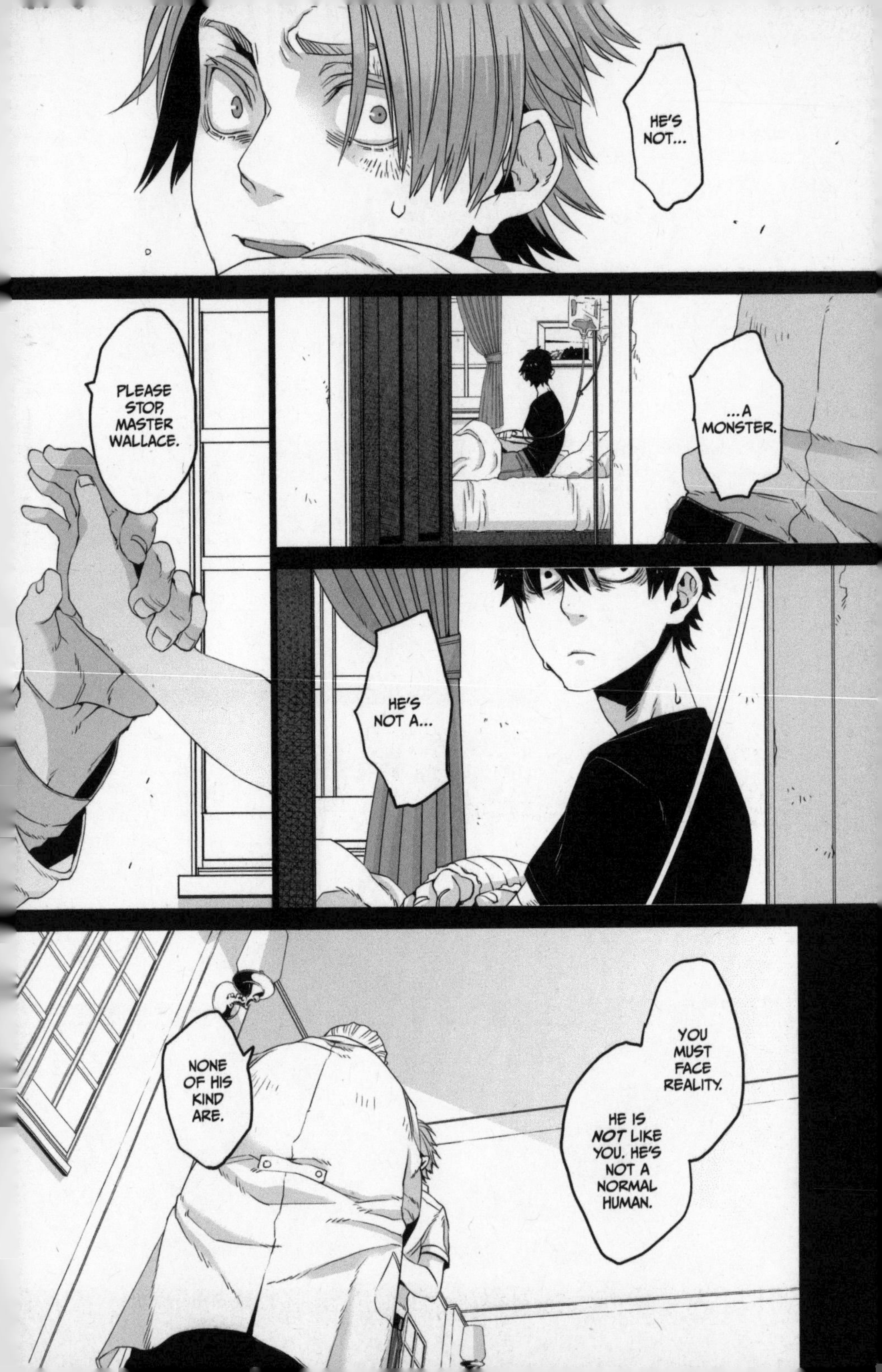
HE'S NOT...
...A MONSTER.
HE'S NOT A...
PLEASE STOP, MASTER WALLACE.
YOU MUST FACE REALITY.
HE IS *NOT* LIKE YOU. HE'S NOT A NORMAL HUMAN.
NONE OF HIS KIND ARE.

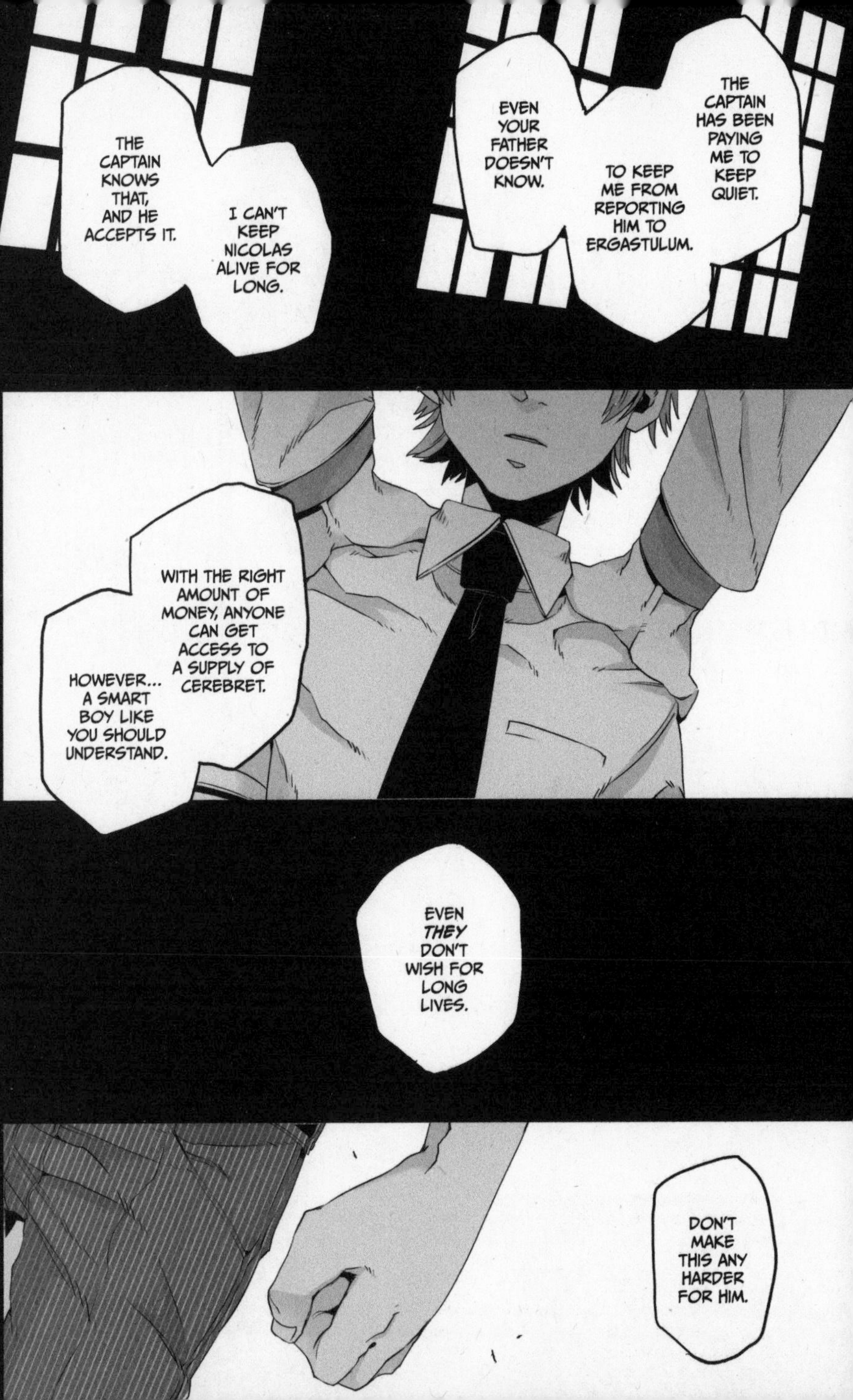
THE CAPTAIN HAS BEEN PAYING ME TO KEEP QUIET.
TO KEEP ME FROM REPORTING HIM TO ERGASTULUM.
EVEN YOUR FATHER DOESN'T KNOW.
I CAN'T KEEP NICOLAS ALIVE FOR LONG.
THE CAPTAIN KNOWS THAT, AND HE ACCEPTS IT.
WITH THE RIGHT AMOUNT OF MONEY, ANYONE CAN GET ACCESS TO A SUPPLY OF CEREBRET.
HOWEVER... A SMART BOY LIKE YOU SHOULD UNDERSTAND.
EVEN *THEY* DON'T WISH FOR LONG LIVES.
DON'T MAKE THIS ANY HARDER FOR HIM.

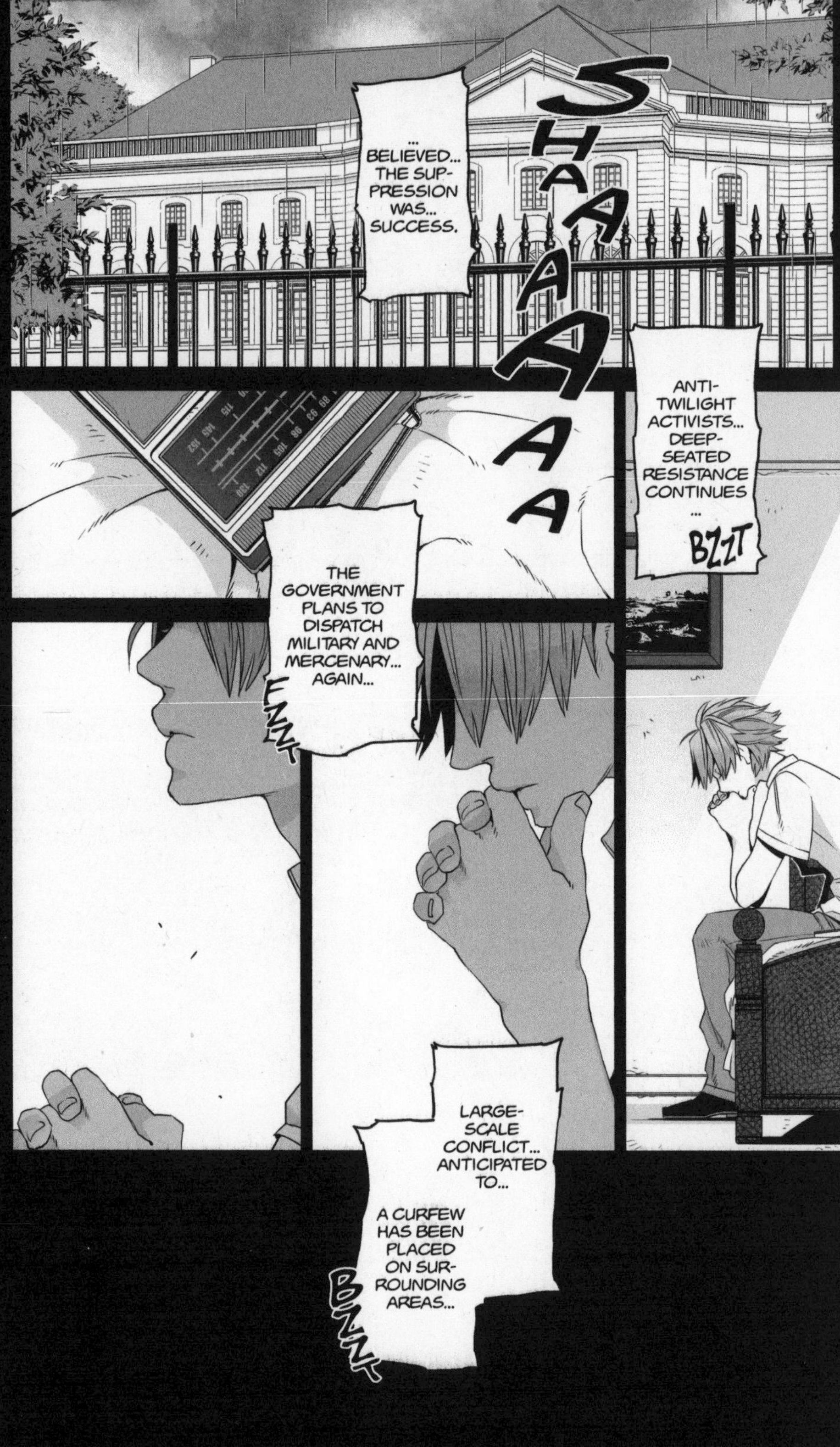
...BELIEVED... THE SUPPRESSION WAS... SUCCESS.
SHAAAAAAA
ANTI-TWILIGHT ACTIVISTS... DEEP-SEATED RESISTANCE CONTINUES ...
BZZT
THE GOVERNMENT PLANS TO DISPATCH MILITARY AND MERCENARY... AGAIN...
FZZZT
LARGE-SCALE CONFLICT... ANTICIPATED TO...
A CURFEW HAS BEEN PLACED ON SURROUNDING AREAS...
BZZZT

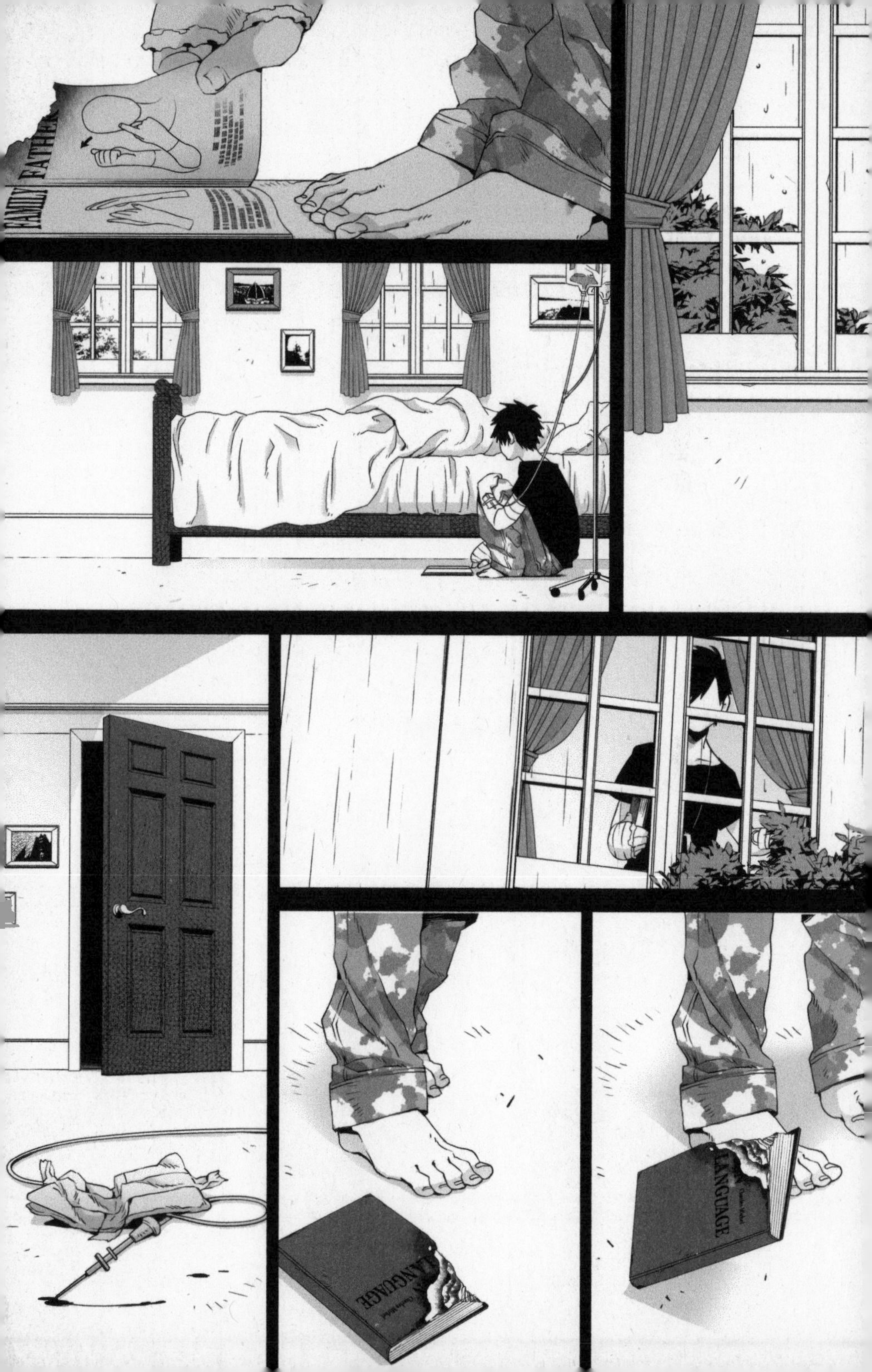
FAMILY FATHER
LANGUAGE
LANGUAGE

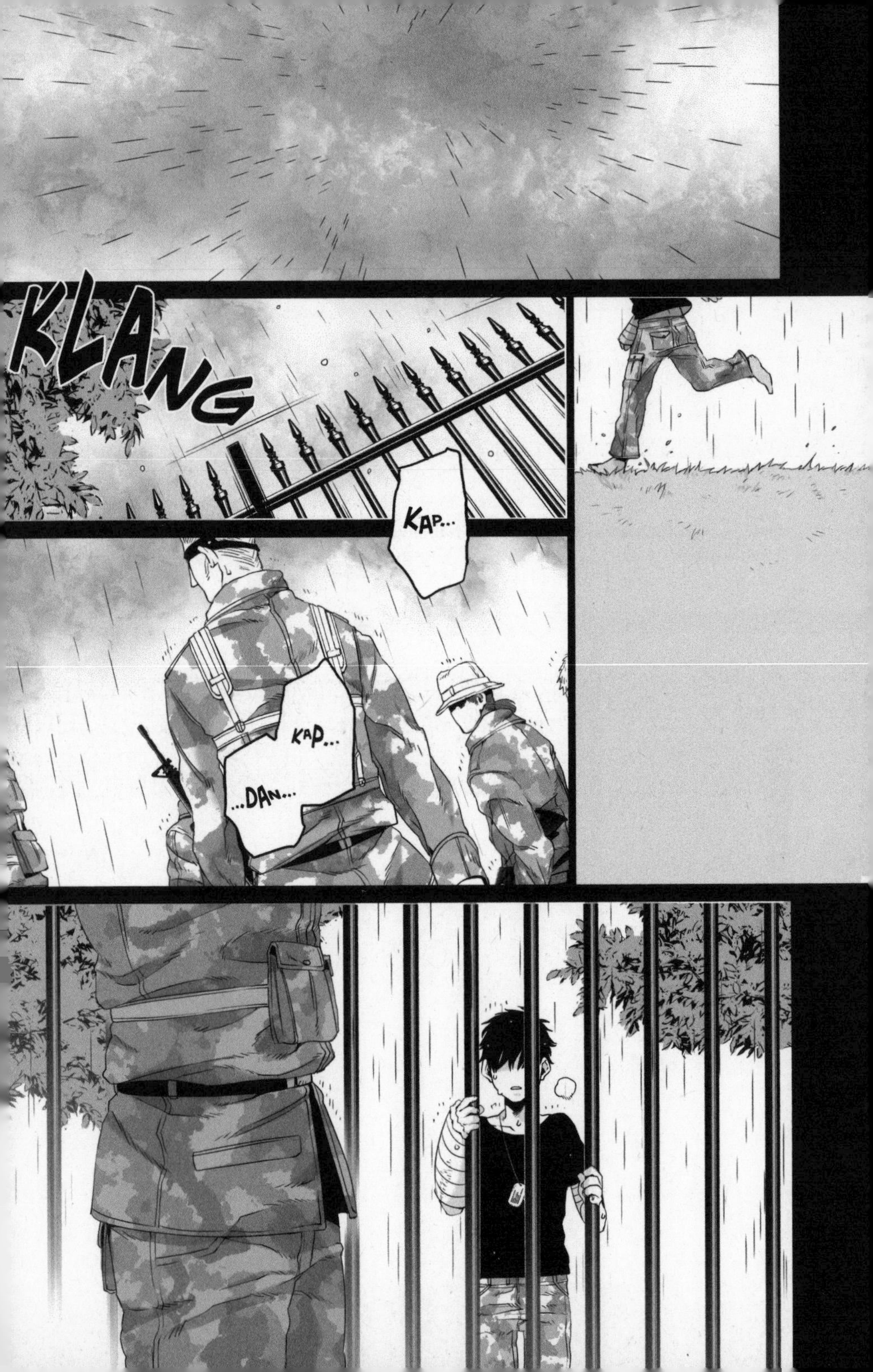
KLANG
KAP...
KAP...
...DAN...

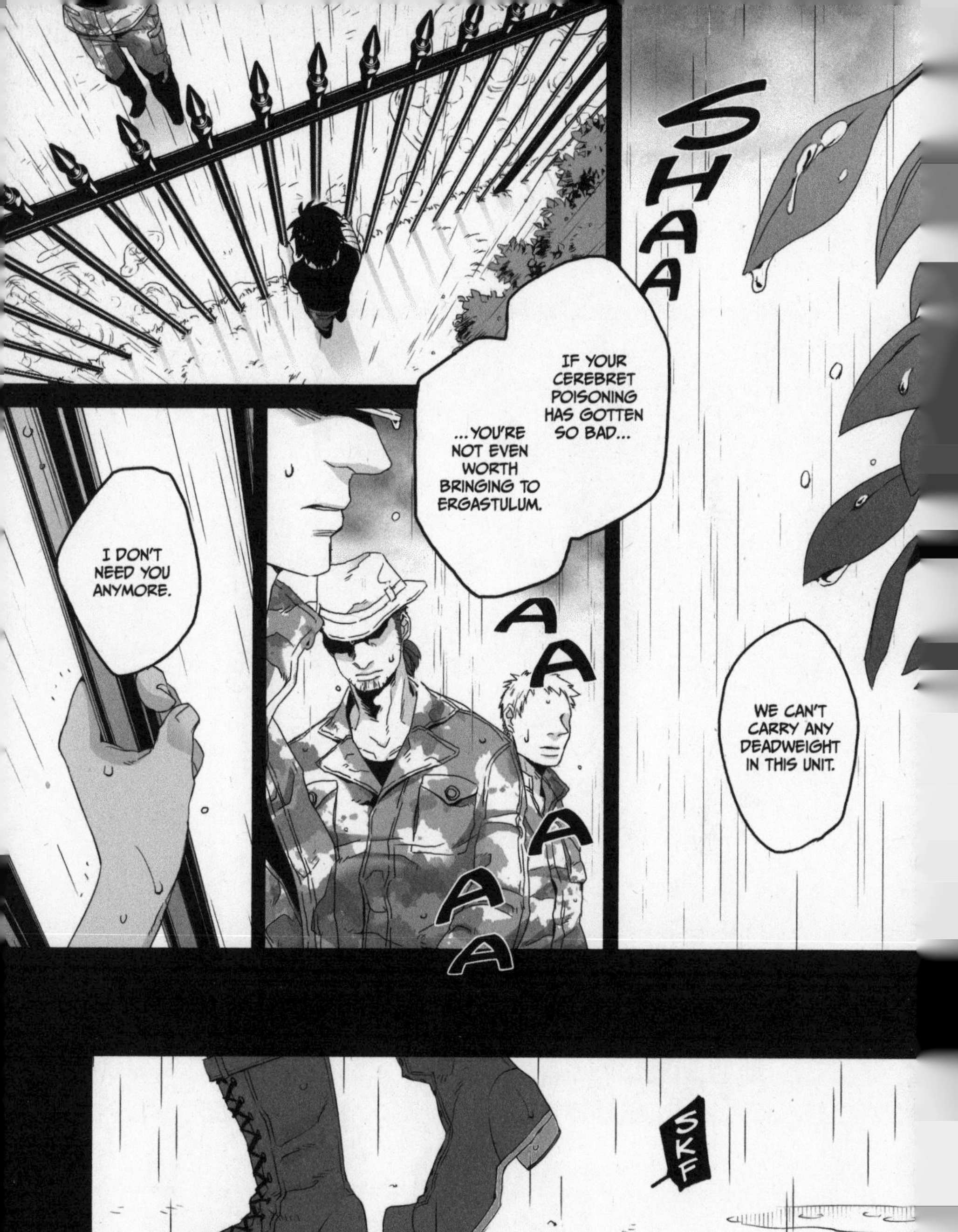
SHAAAAAAA
WE CAN'T CARRY ANY DEADWEIGHT IN THIS UNIT.
IF YOUR CEREBRET POISONING HAS GOTTEN SO BAD...
...YOU'RE NOT EVEN WORTH BRINGING TO ERGASTULUM.
I DON'T NEED YOU ANYMORE.
SKF

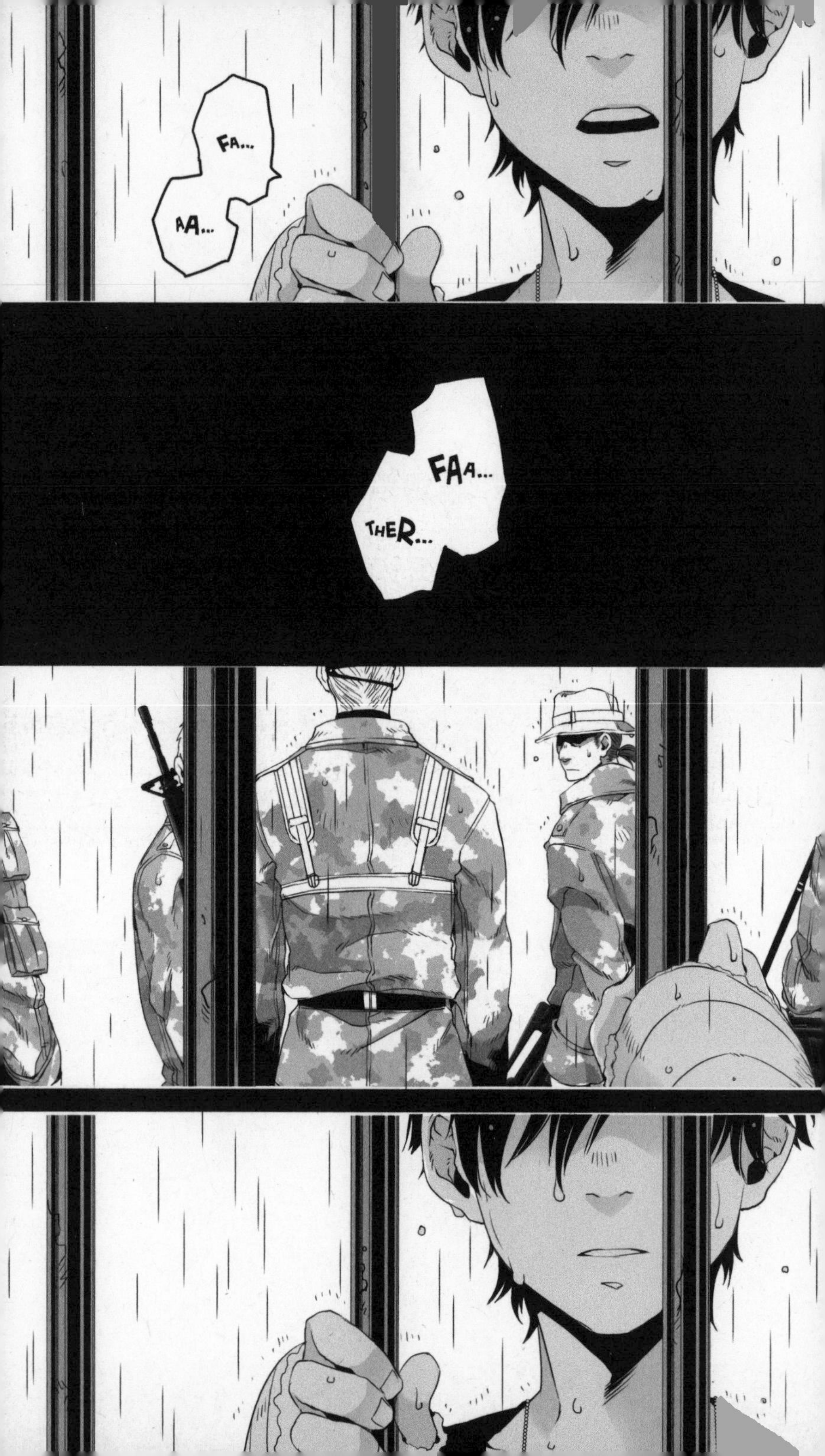
FA...
AA...
FAA...
THER...

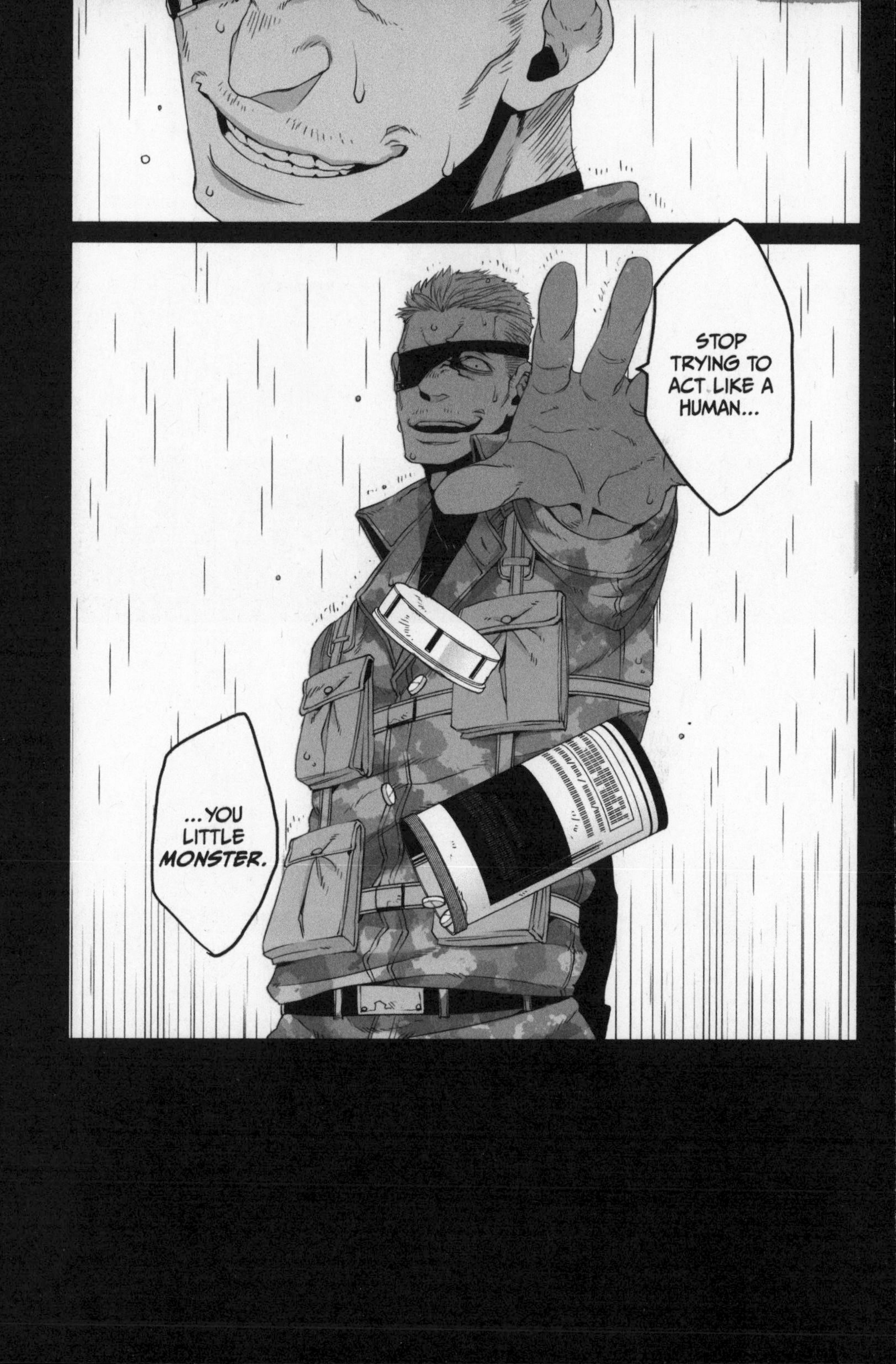
STOP TRYING TO ACT LIKE A HUMAN...
...YOU LITTLE MONSTER.

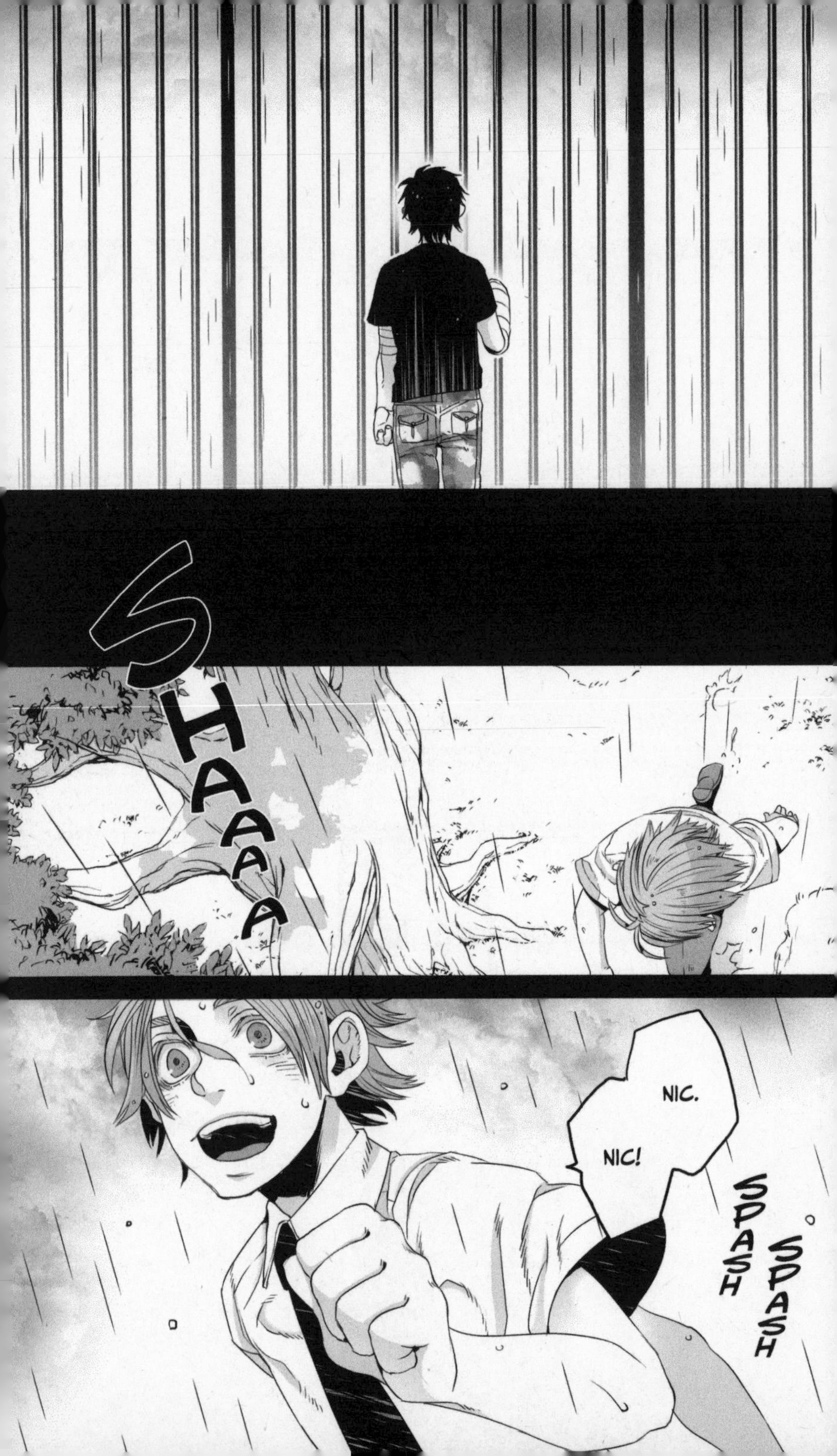
SHAAAA
NIC.
NIC!
SPASH
SPASH

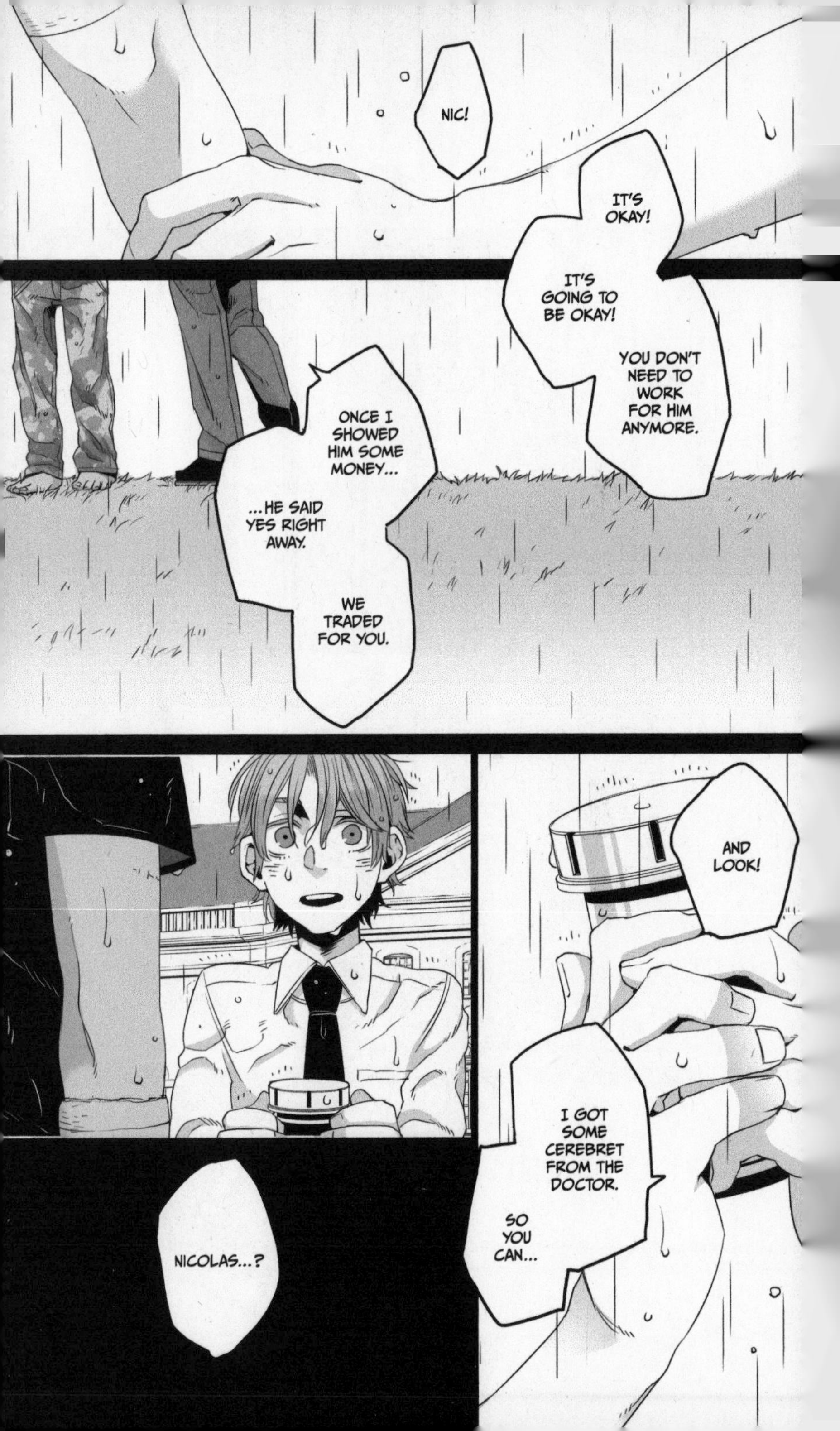
NIC!
IT'S OKAY!
IT'S GOING TO BE OKAY!
YOU DON'T NEED TO WORK FOR HIM ANYMORE.
ONCE I SHOWED HIM SOME MONEY...
...HE SAID YES RIGHT AWAY.
WE TRADED FOR YOU.
AND LOOK!
I GOT SOME CEREBRET FROM THE DOCTOR.
SO YOU CAN...
NICOLAS...?

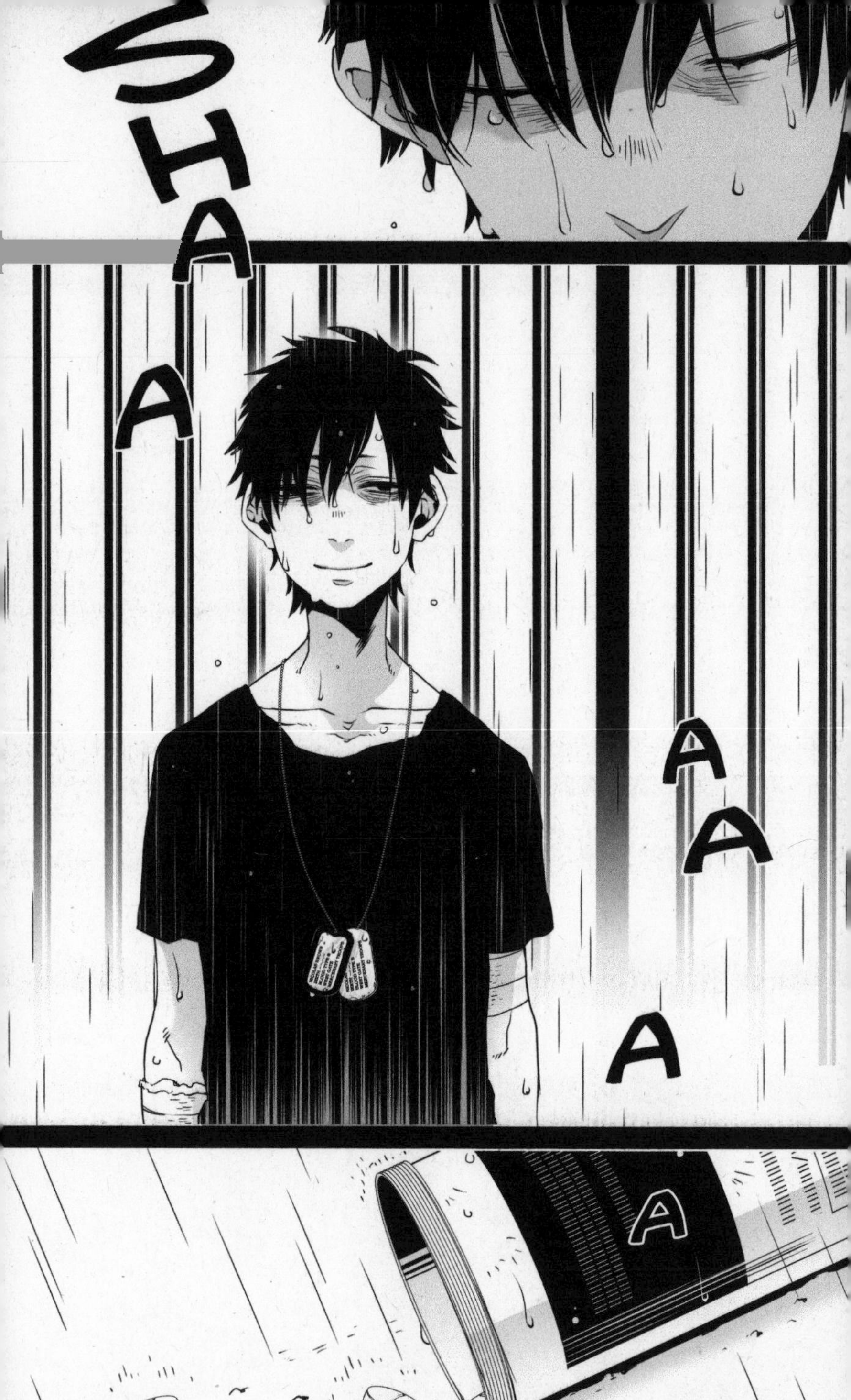
SHAAAAAA

#15 END

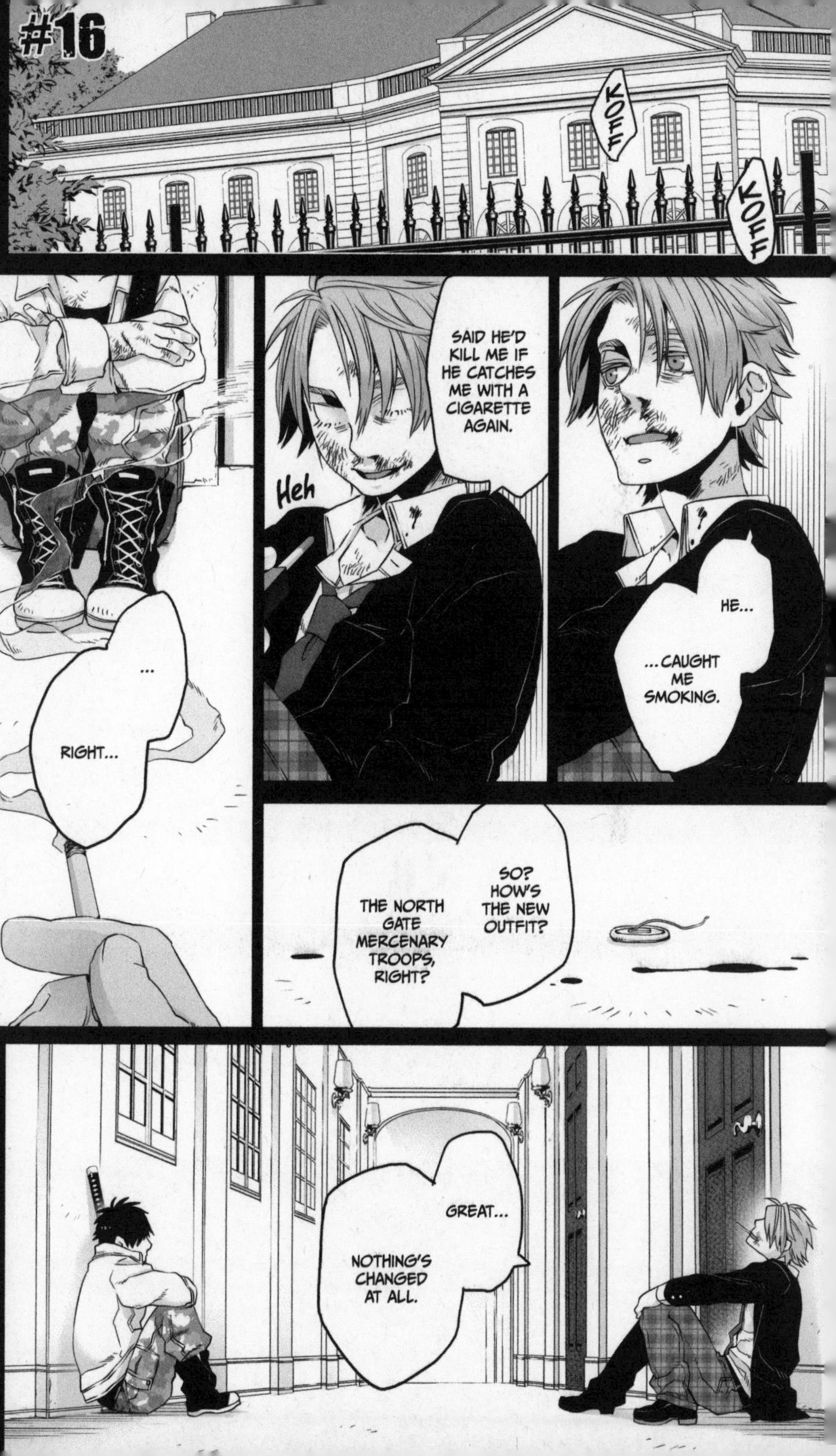
#16
KOFF
KOFF
HE...
...CAUGHT ME SMOKING.
SAID HE'D KILL ME IF HE CATCHES ME WITH A CIGARETTE AGAIN.
Heh
SO? HOW'S THE NEW OUTFIT?
THE NORTH GATE MERCENARY TROOPS, RIGHT?
...
RIGHT...
GREAT...
NOTHING'S CHANGED AT ALL.

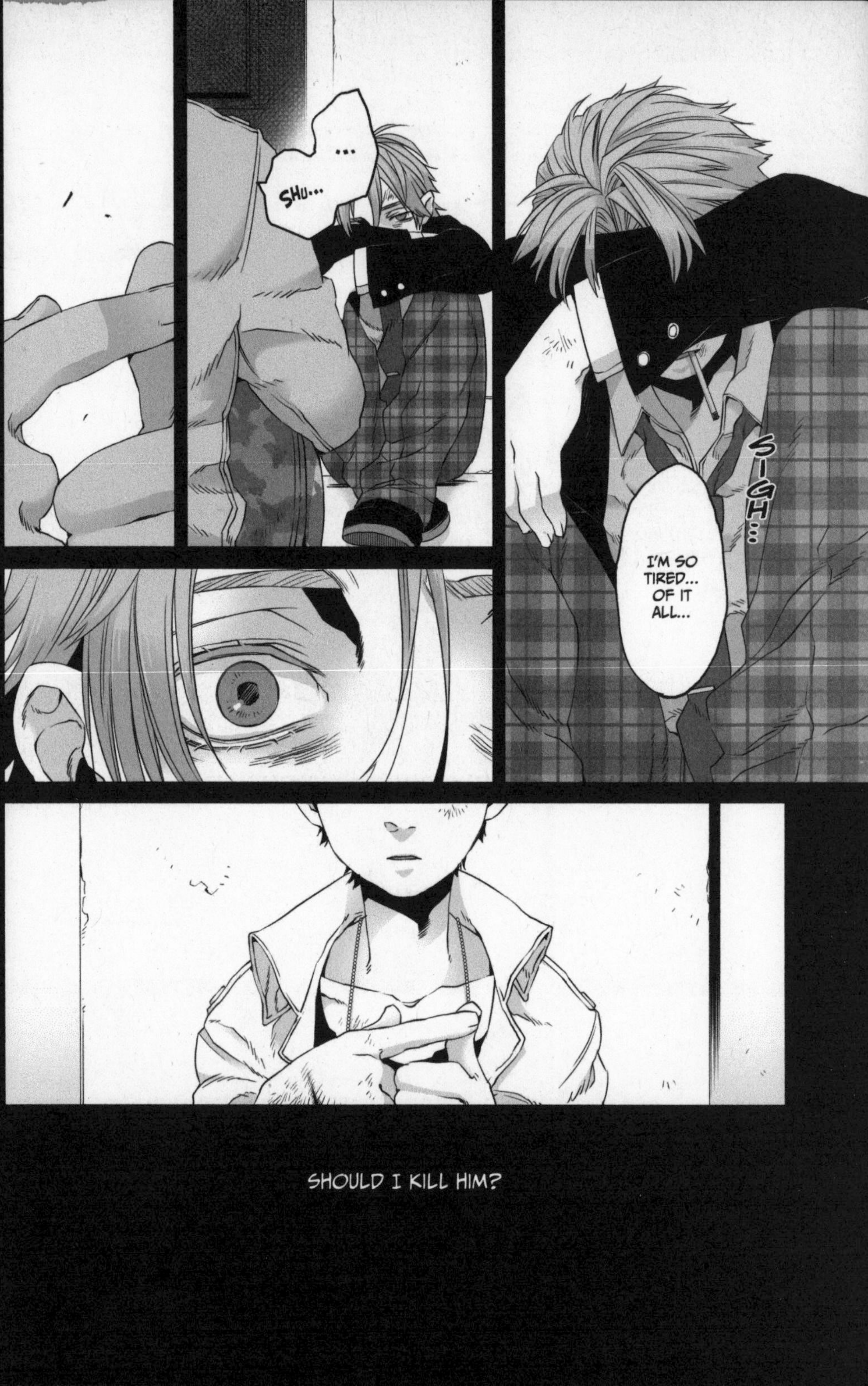
SIGH...
I'M SO TIRED... OF IT ALL...
... SHU...
SHOULD I KILL HIM?

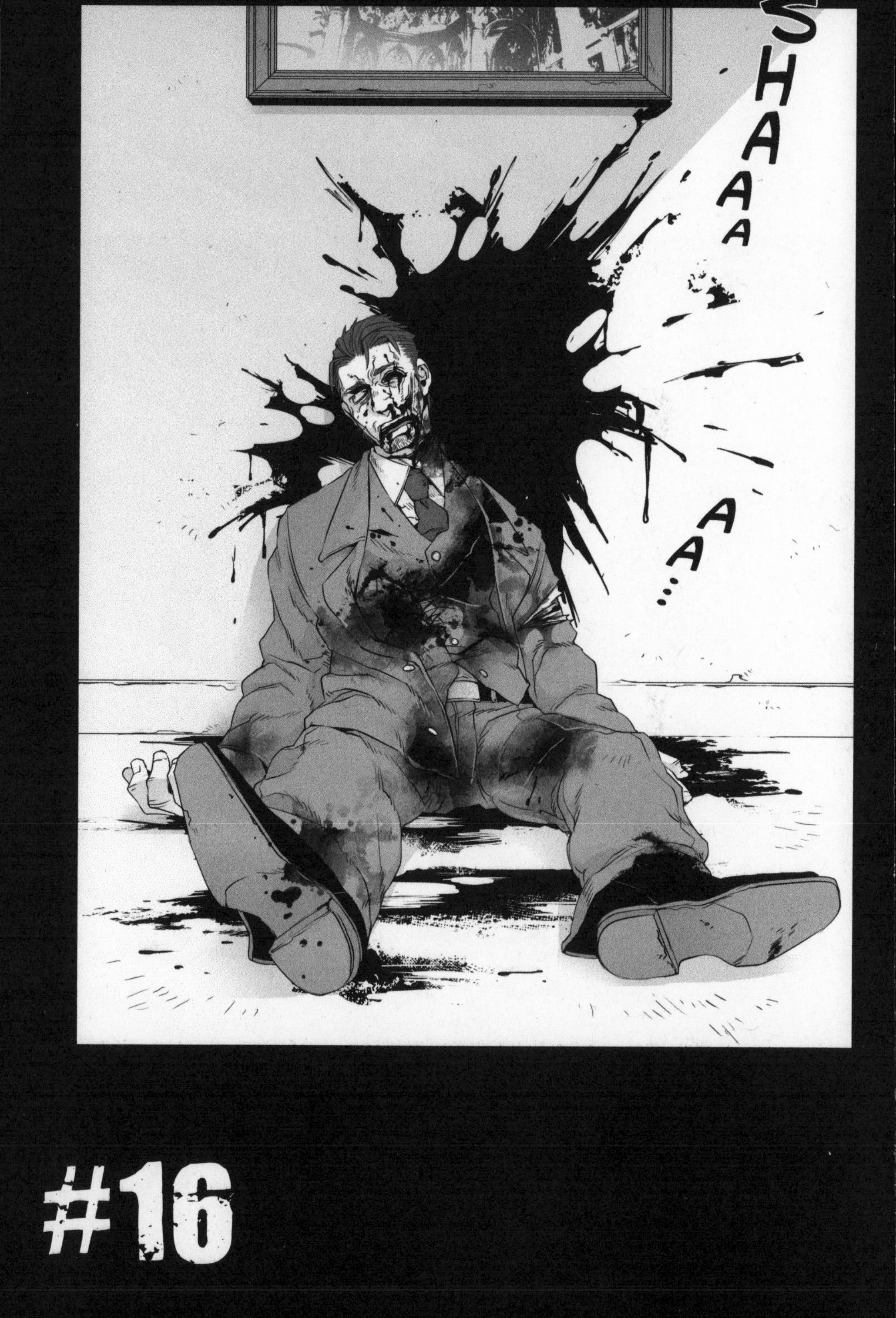
SHAAAA
AA...

#16

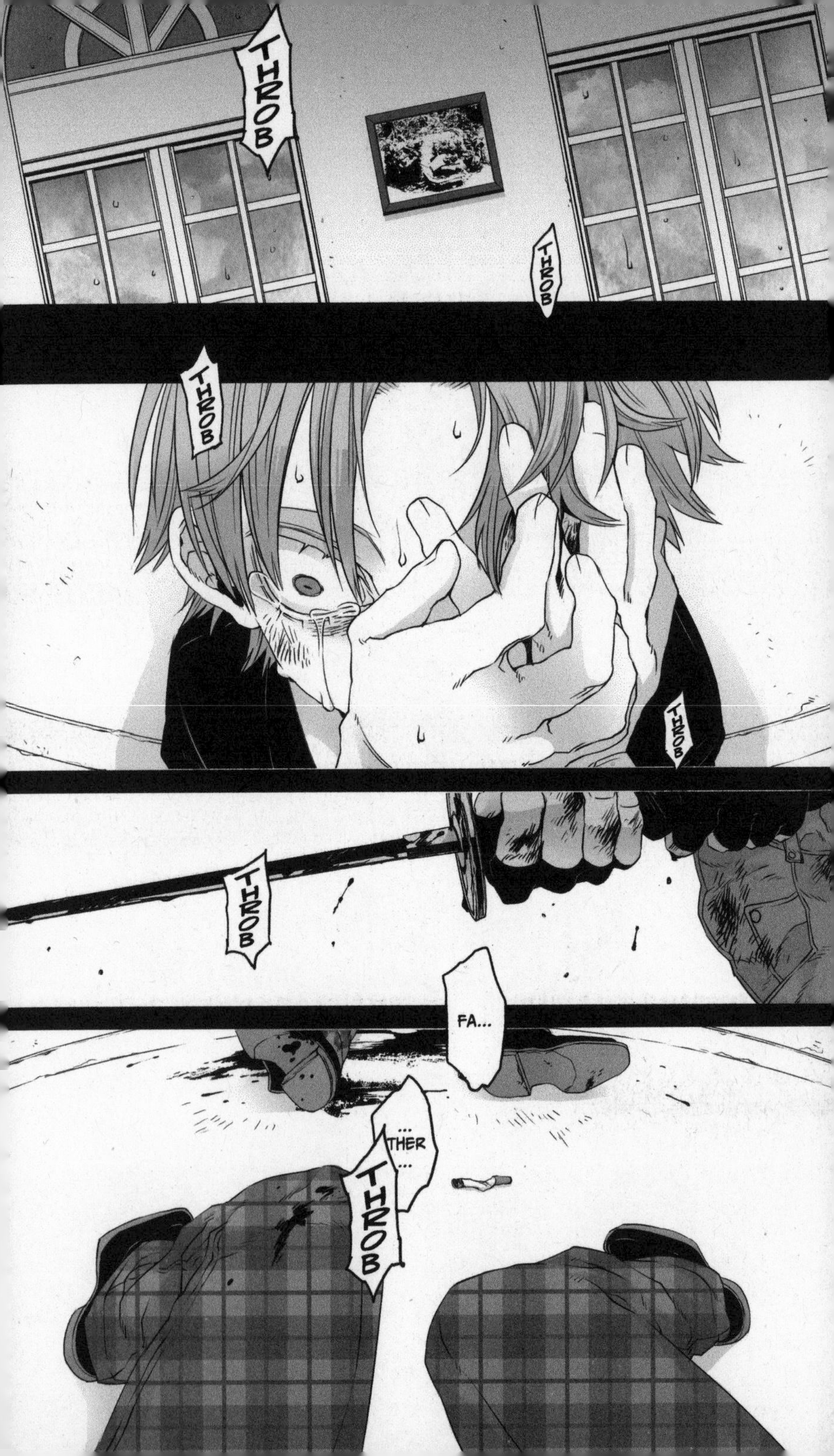
THROB
THROB
THROB
THROB
THROB
FA...
...THER...
THROB

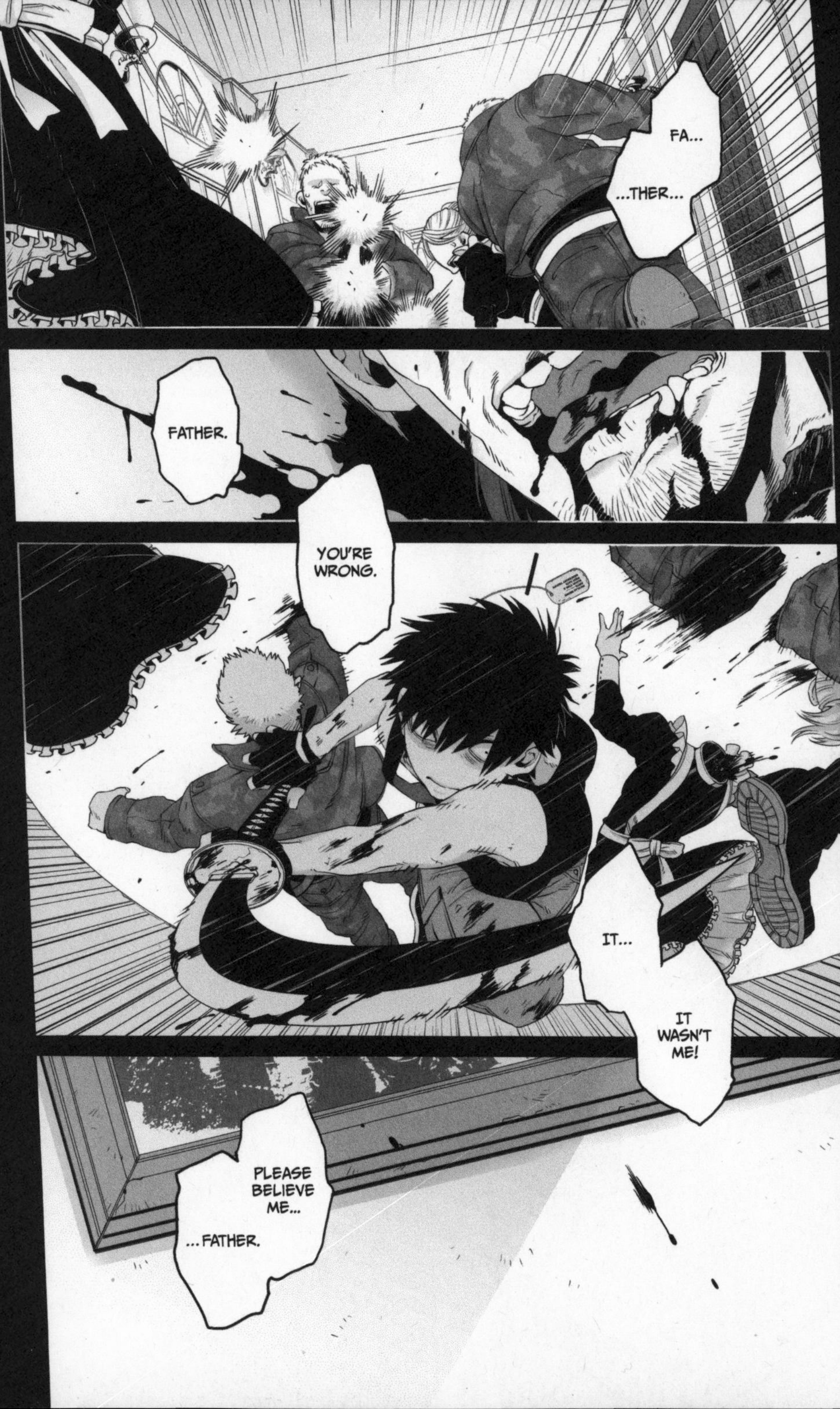
FA...
...THER...
FATHER.
YOU'RE WRONG.
IT...
IT WASN'T ME!
PLEASE BELIEVE ME...
...FATHER.

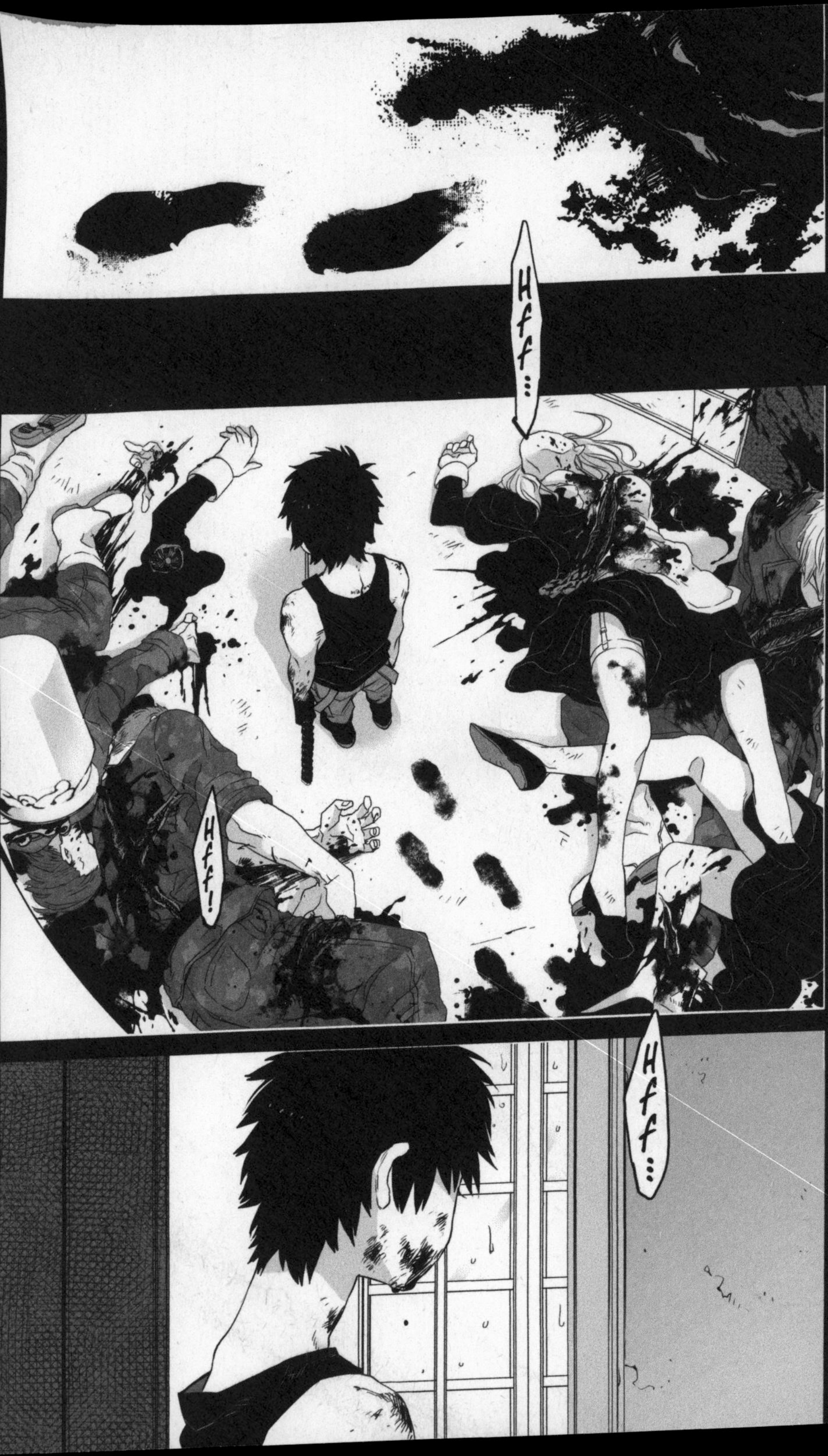
Hff...
Hff!
Hff...

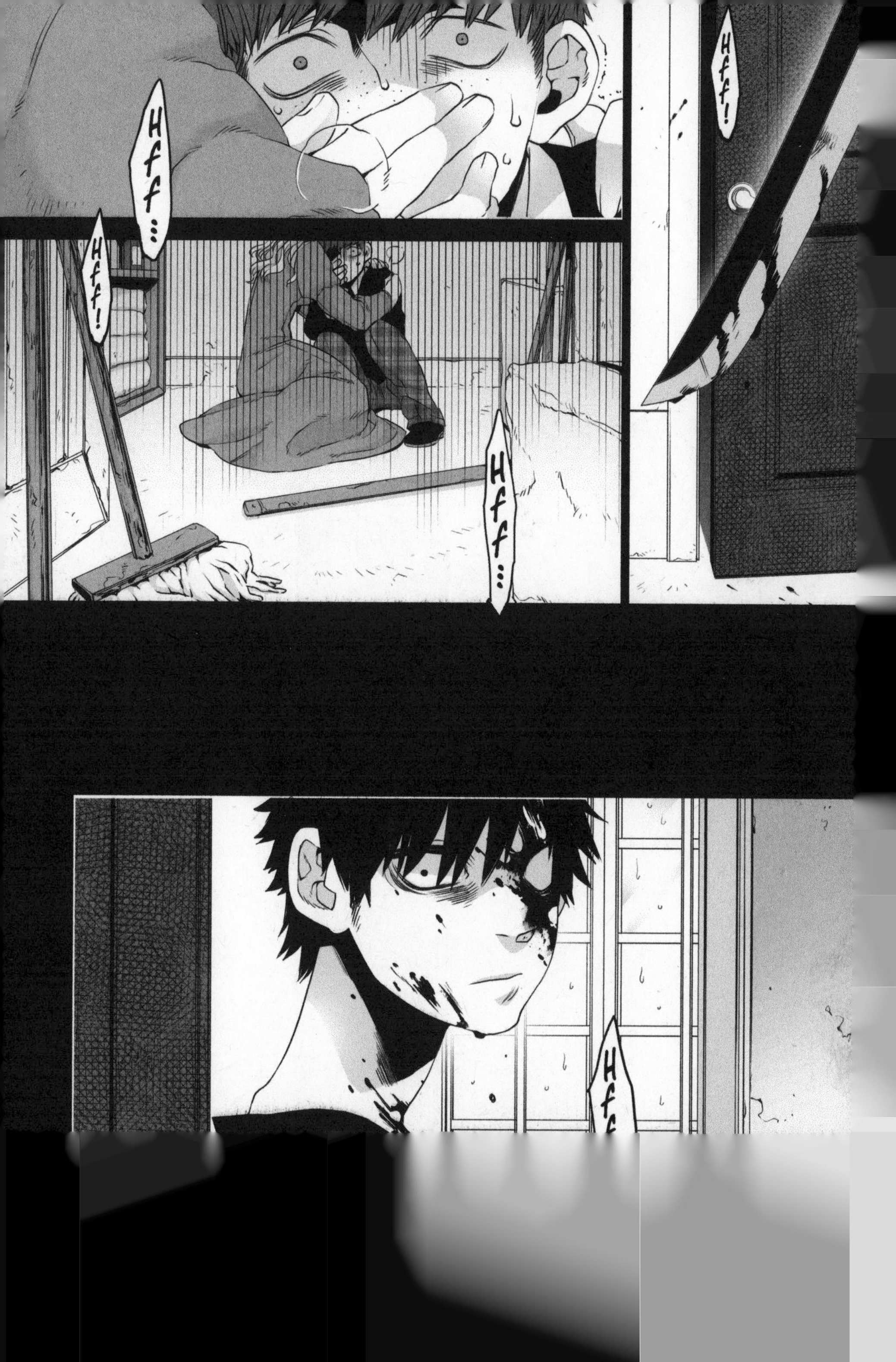
Hff!
Hff...
Hff!
Hff...

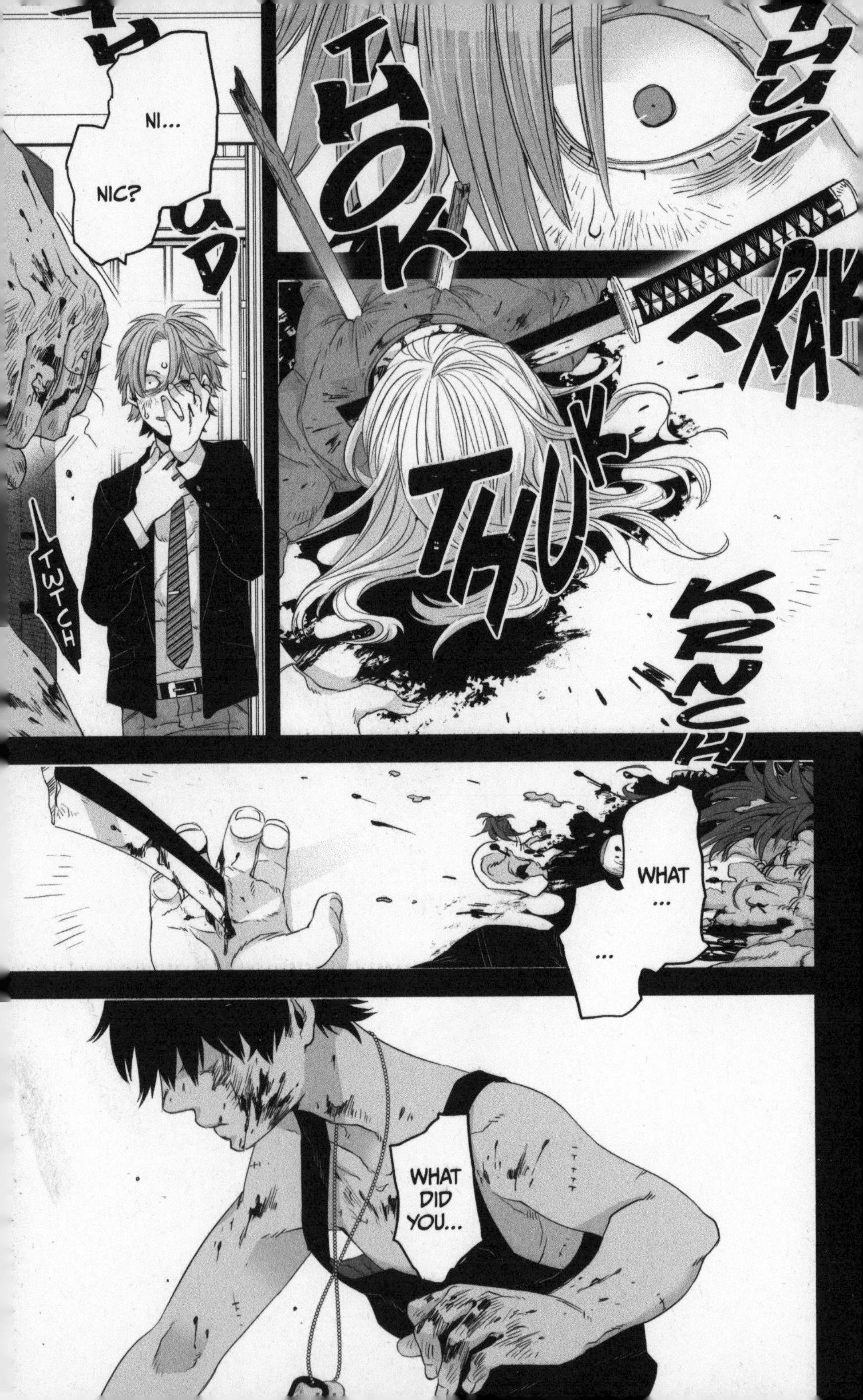

THUD
THOK
KRAK
THUK
KRNCH
NI...
NIC?
THUD
TWITCH
WHAT
...
...
WHAT DID YOU...

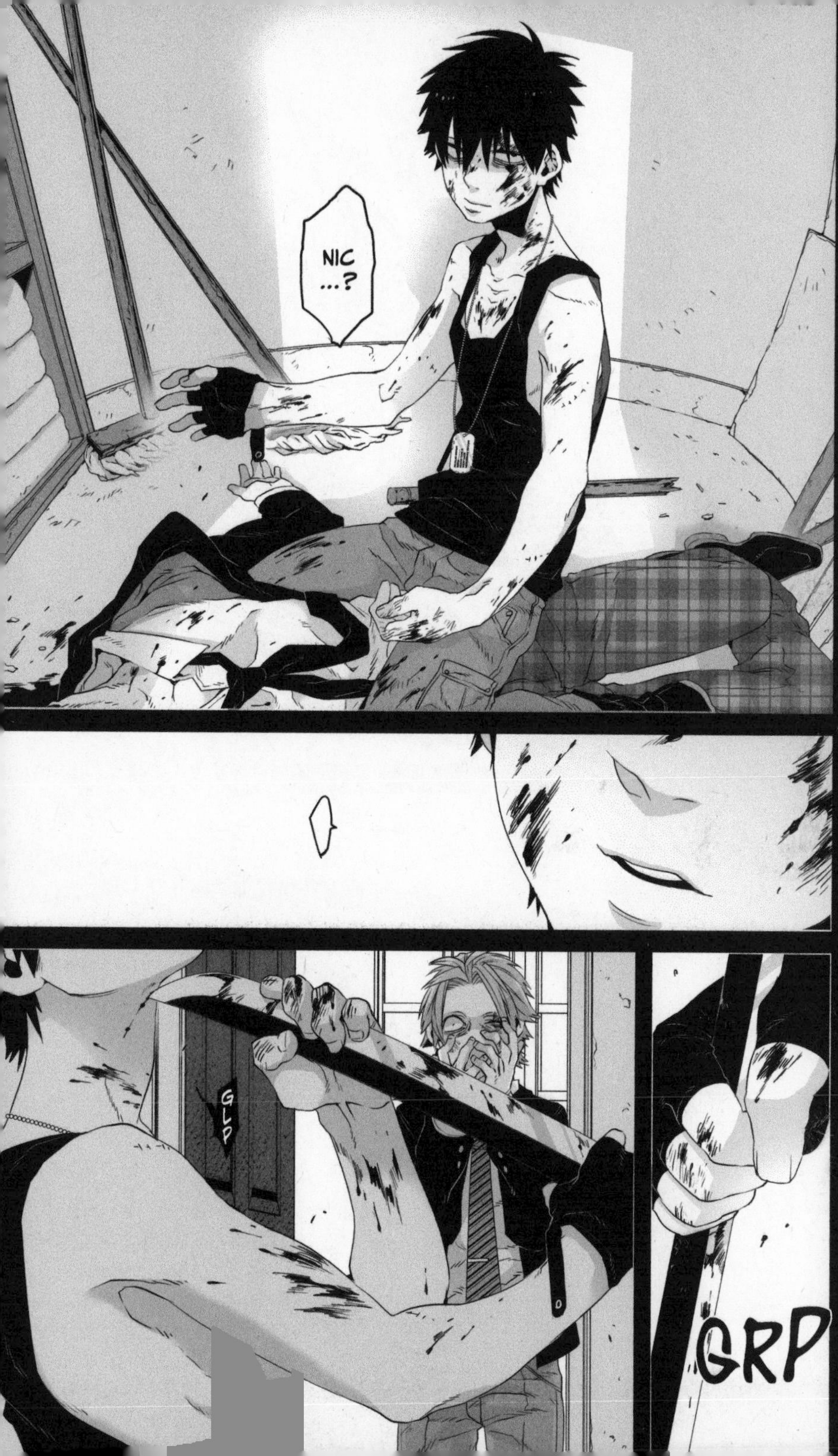
NIC ...?
GRP
GLP

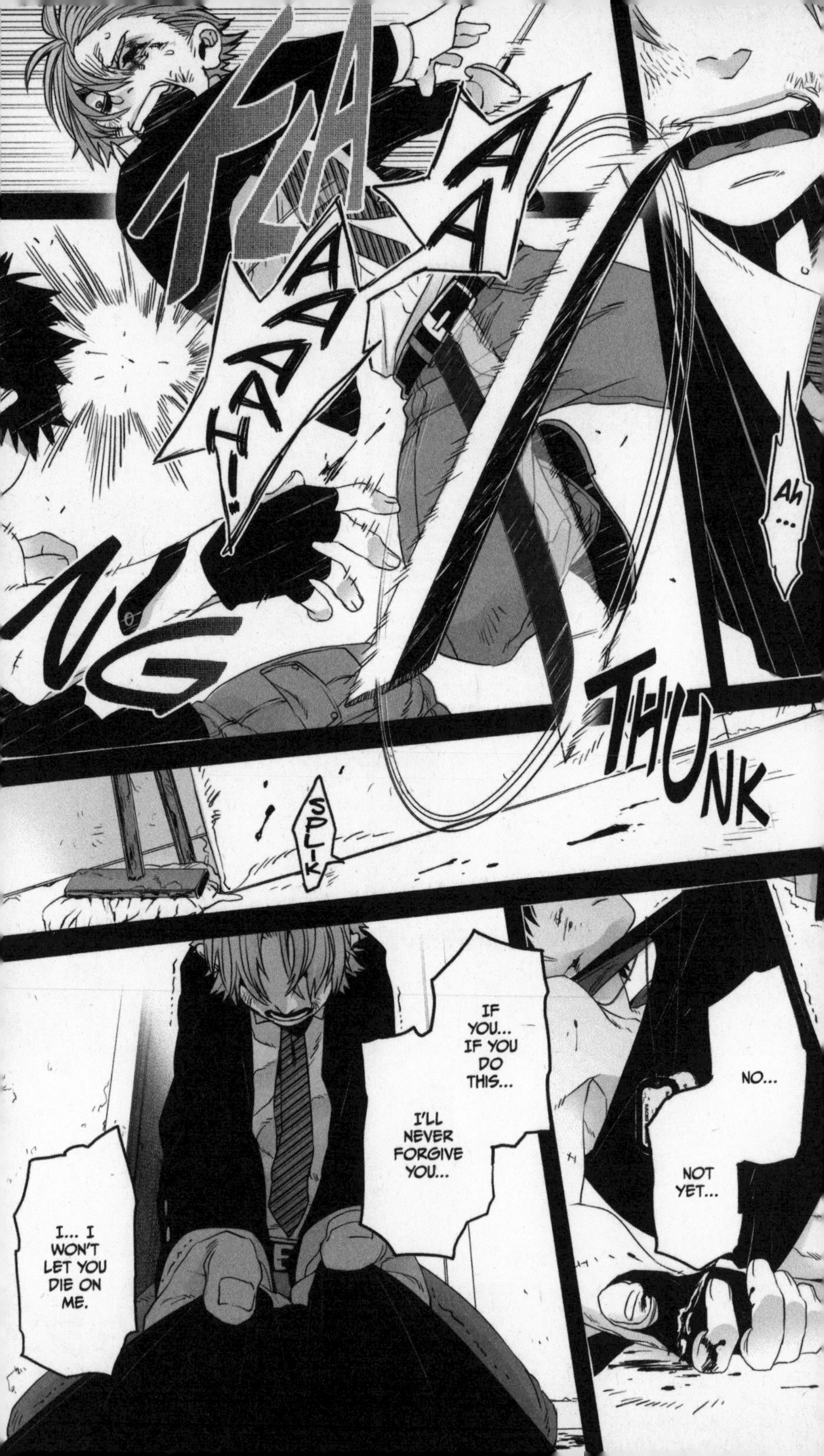
Ah...
AAAAAAH!!
NG
THUNK
SPLIK
NO...
NOT YET...
IF YOU... IF YOU DO THIS...
I'LL NEVER FORGIVE YOU...
I... I WON'T LET YOU DIE ON ME.

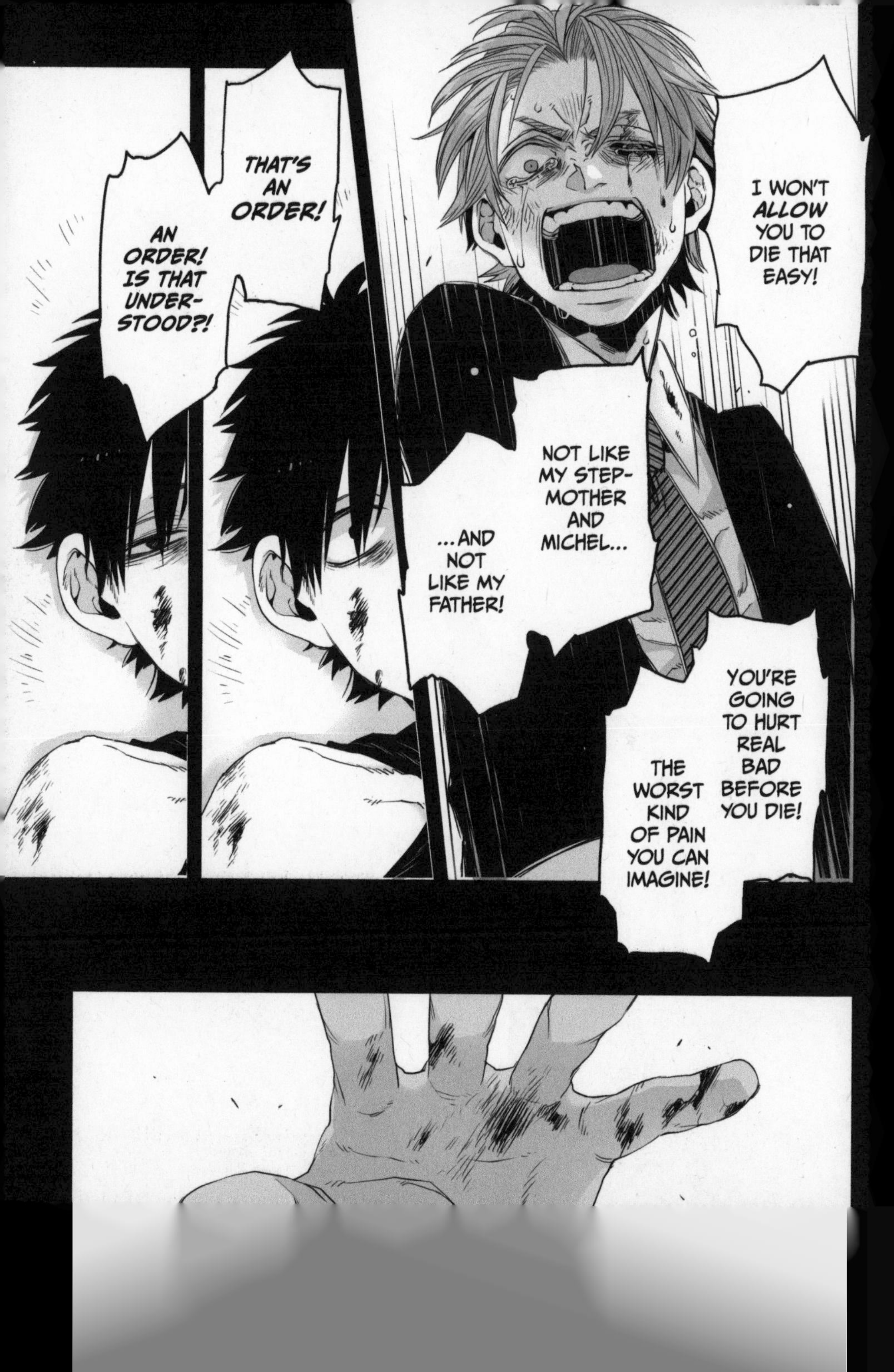
I WON'T ALLOW YOU TO DIE THAT EASY!
NOT LIKE MY STEP-MOTHER AND MICHEL...
...AND NOT LIKE MY FATHER!
YOU'RE GOING TO HURT REAL BAD BEFORE YOU DIE!
THE WORST KIND OF PAIN YOU CAN IMAGINE!
THAT'S AN ORDER!
AN ORDER! IS THAT UNDER-STOOD?!

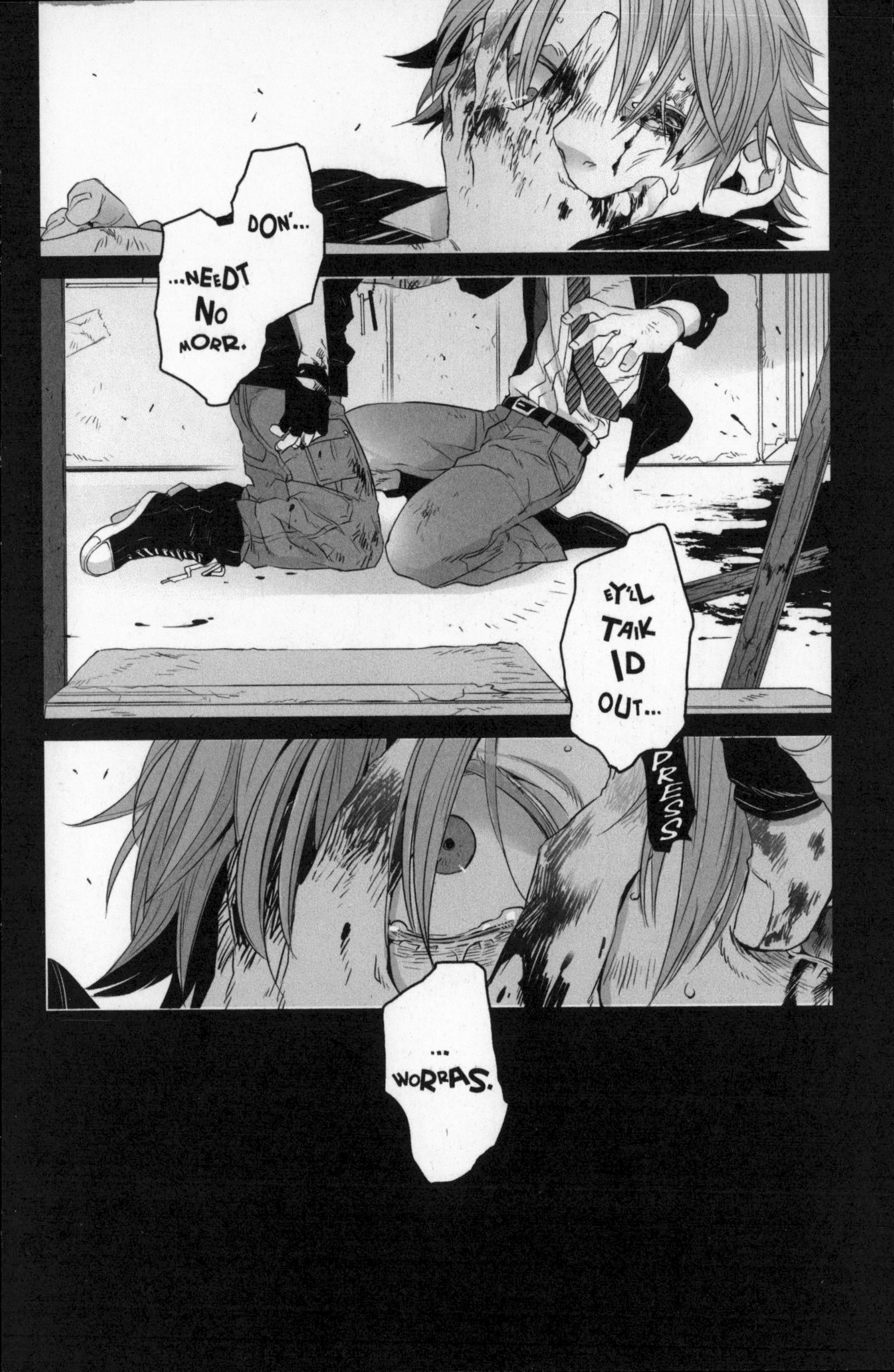
DON'...
...NEEDT NO MORR.
EY'LL TAIK ID OUT...
PRESS
... WORRAS.

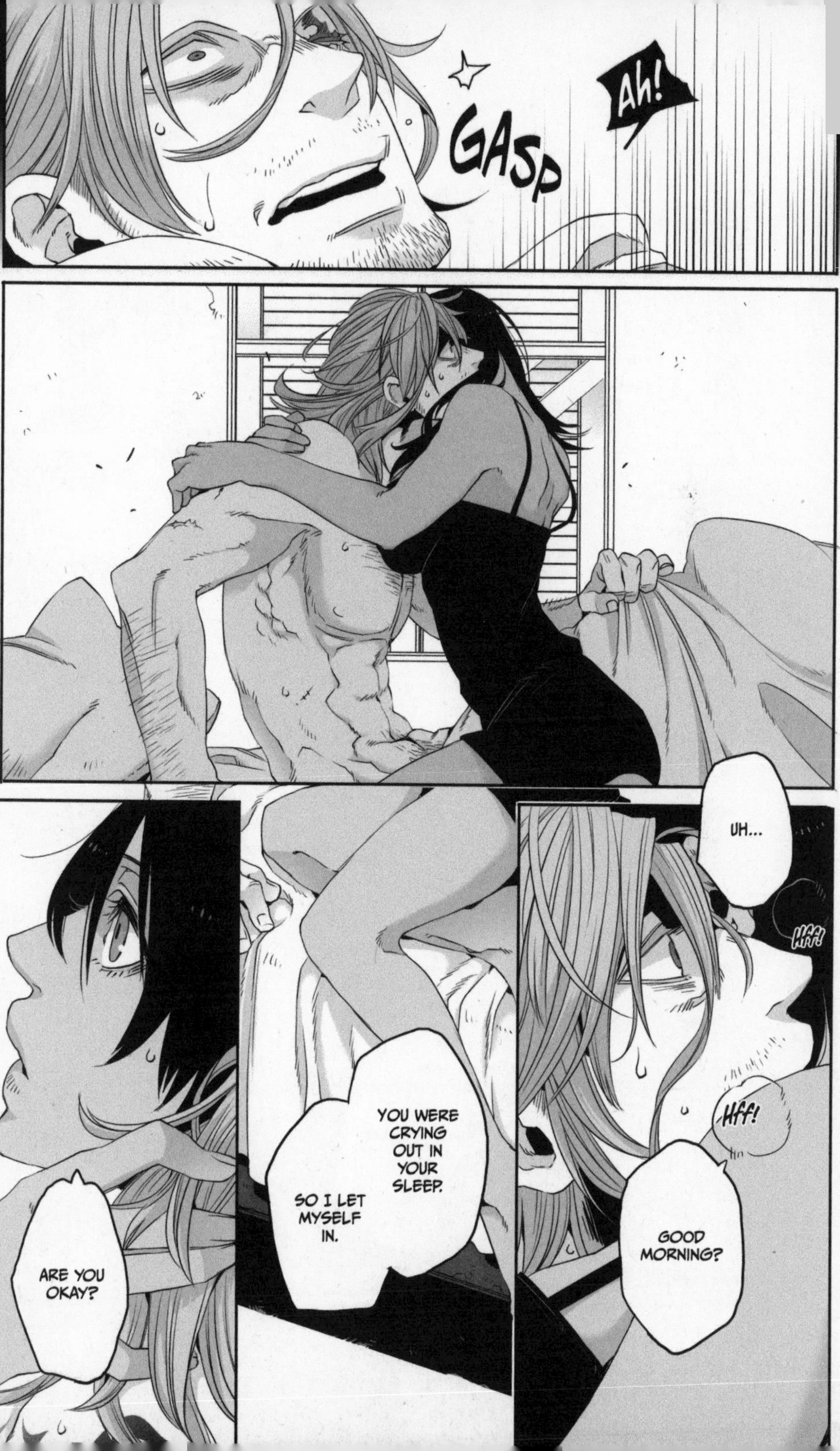
Ah!
GASP
UH...
Hff!
Hff!
GOOD MORNING?
YOU WERE CRYING OUT IN YOUR SLEEP.
SO I LET MYSELF IN.
ARE YOU OKAY?

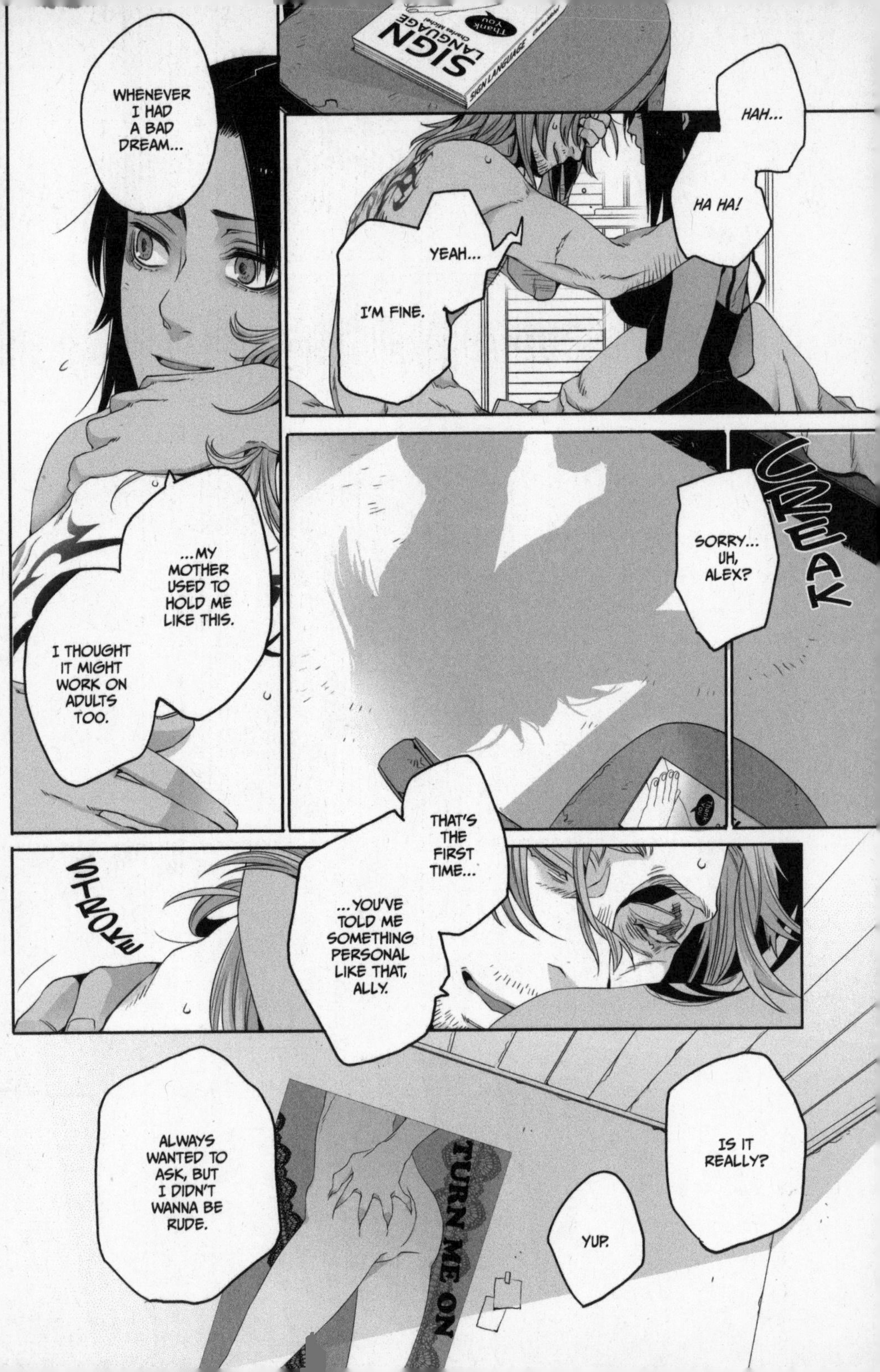
SIGN LANGUAGE
Thank you
HAH...
HA HA!
YEAH...
I'M FINE.
CREAK
SORRY... UH, ALEX?
WHENEVER I HAD A BAD DREAM...
...MY MOTHER USED TO HOLD ME LIKE THIS.
I THOUGHT IT MIGHT WORK ON ADULTS TOO.
STROKE
THAT'S THE FIRST TIME...
...YOU'VE TOLD ME SOMETHING PERSONAL LIKE THAT, ALLY.
IS IT REALLY?
YUP.
ALWAYS WANTED TO ASK, BUT I DIDN'T WANNA BE RUDE.
TURN ME ON

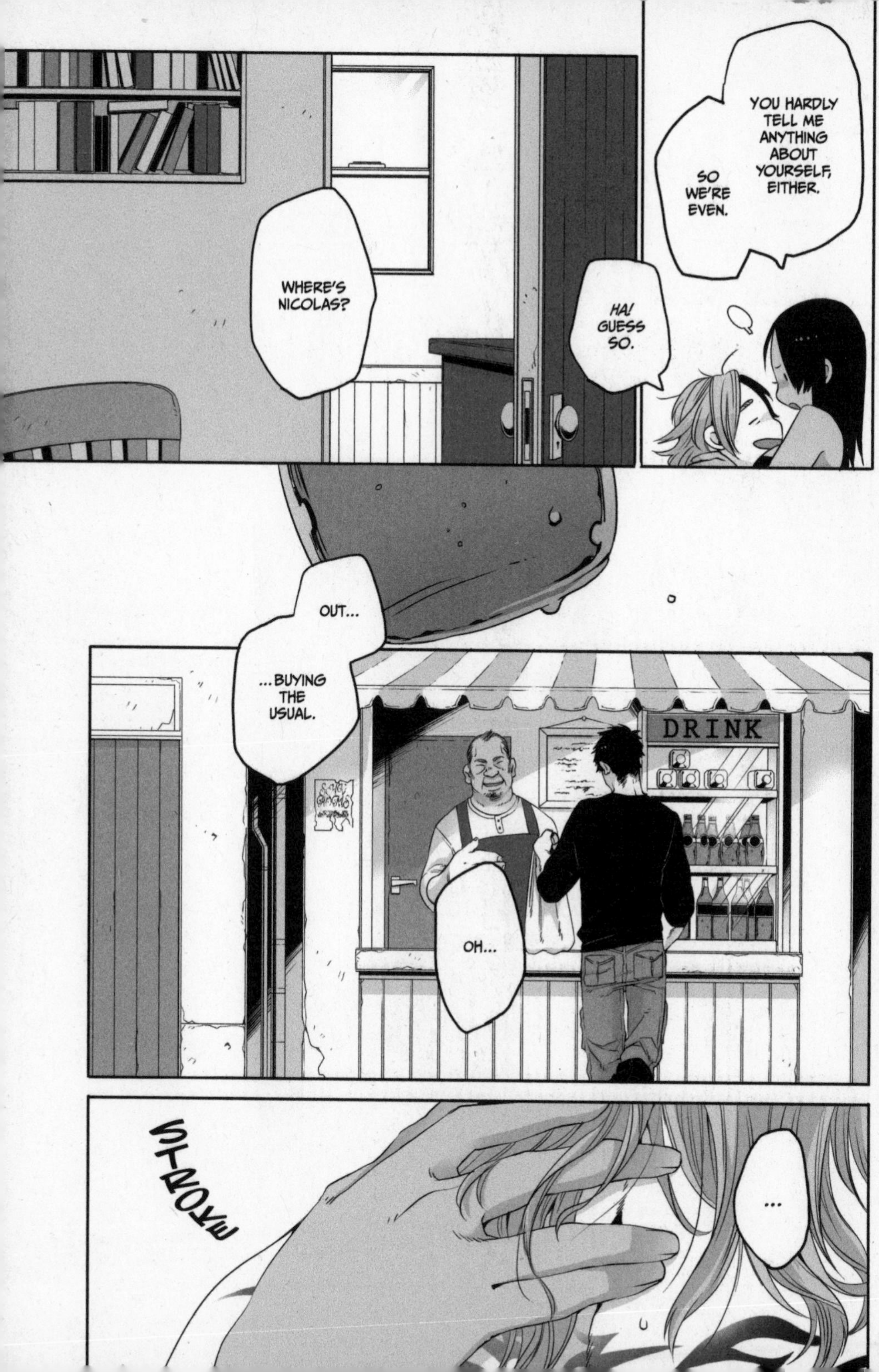
YOU HARDLY TELL ME ANYTHING ABOUT YOURSELF, EITHER.
SO WE'RE EVEN.
HA! GUESS SO.
WHERE'S NICOLAS?
OUT...
...BUYING THE USUAL.
DRINK
OH...
STROKE
...

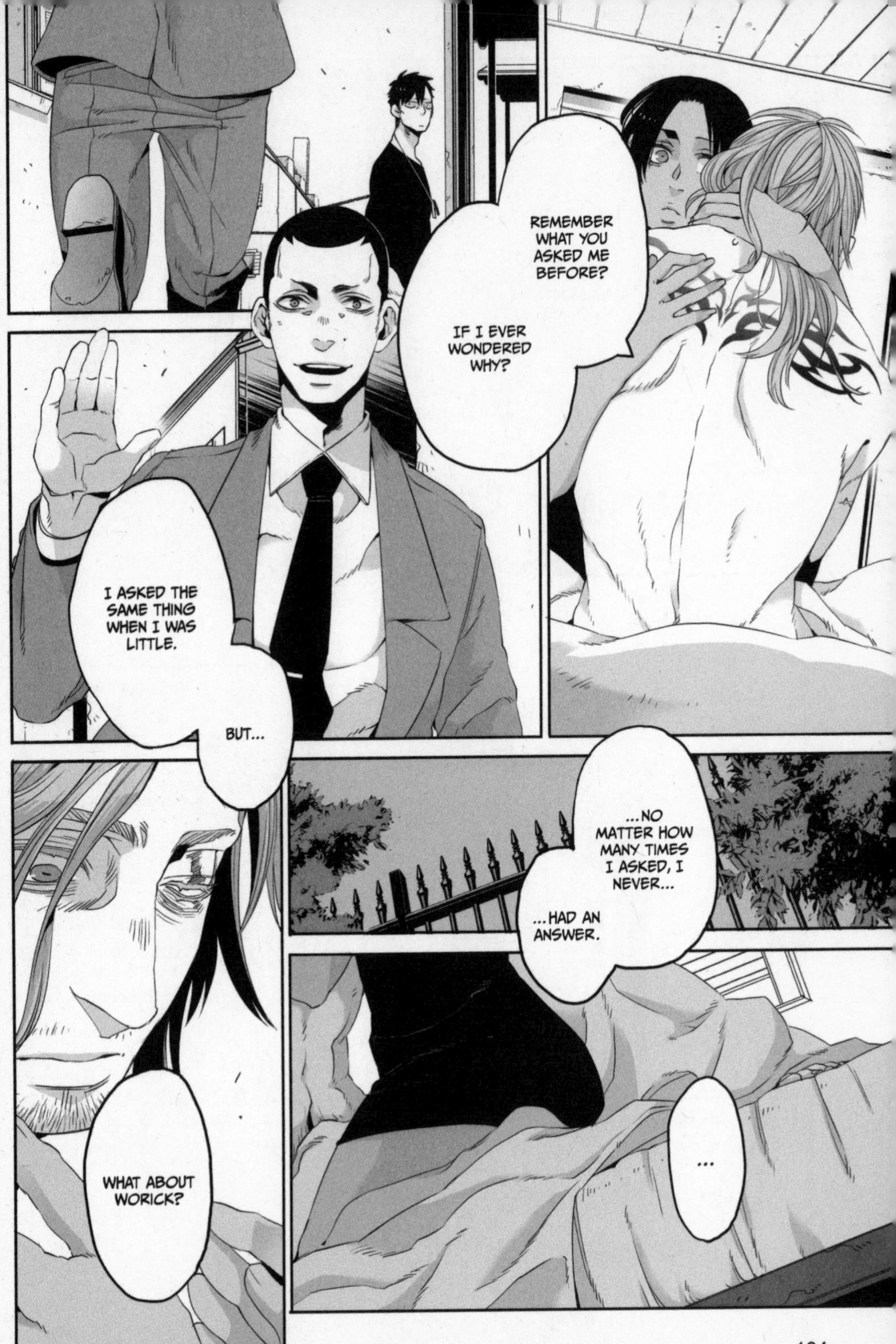
REMEMBER WHAT YOU ASKED ME BEFORE?
IF I EVER WONDERED WHY?
I ASKED THE SAME THING WHEN I WAS LITTLE.
BUT...
...NO MATTER HOW MANY TIMES I ASKED, I NEVER...
...HAD AN ANSWER.
...
WHAT ABOUT WORICK?

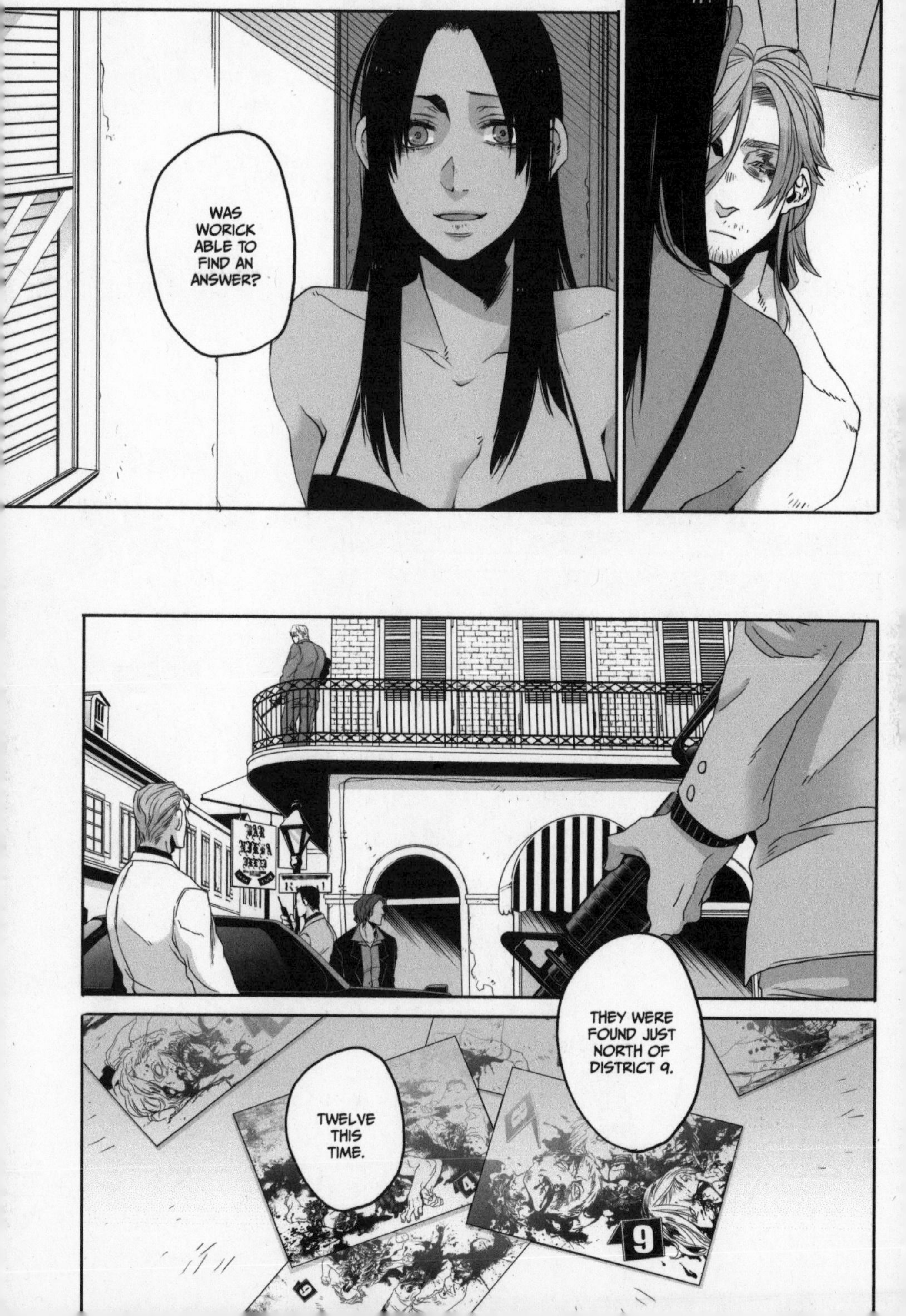
WAS WORICK ABLE TO FIND AN ANSWER?
THEY WERE FOUND JUST NORTH OF DISTRICT 9.
TWELVE THIS TIME.

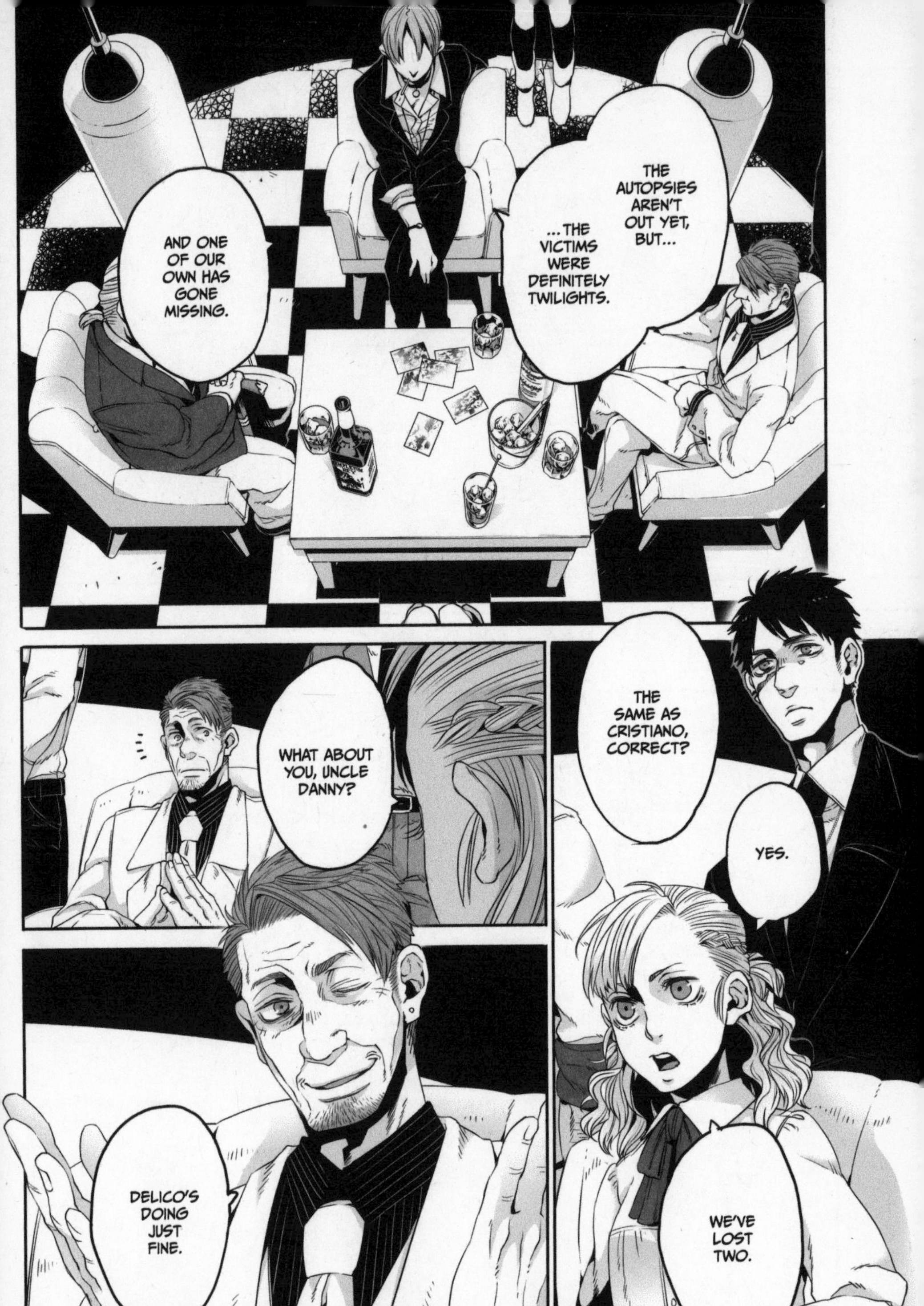

THE AUTOPSIES AREN'T OUT YET, BUT...
...THE VICTIMS WERE DEFINITELY TWILIGHTS.
AND ONE OF OUR OWN HAS GONE MISSING.
THE SAME AS CRISTIANO, CORRECT?
YES.
WE'VE LOST TWO.
WHAT ABOUT YOU, UNCLE DANNY?
DELICO'S DOING JUST FINE.

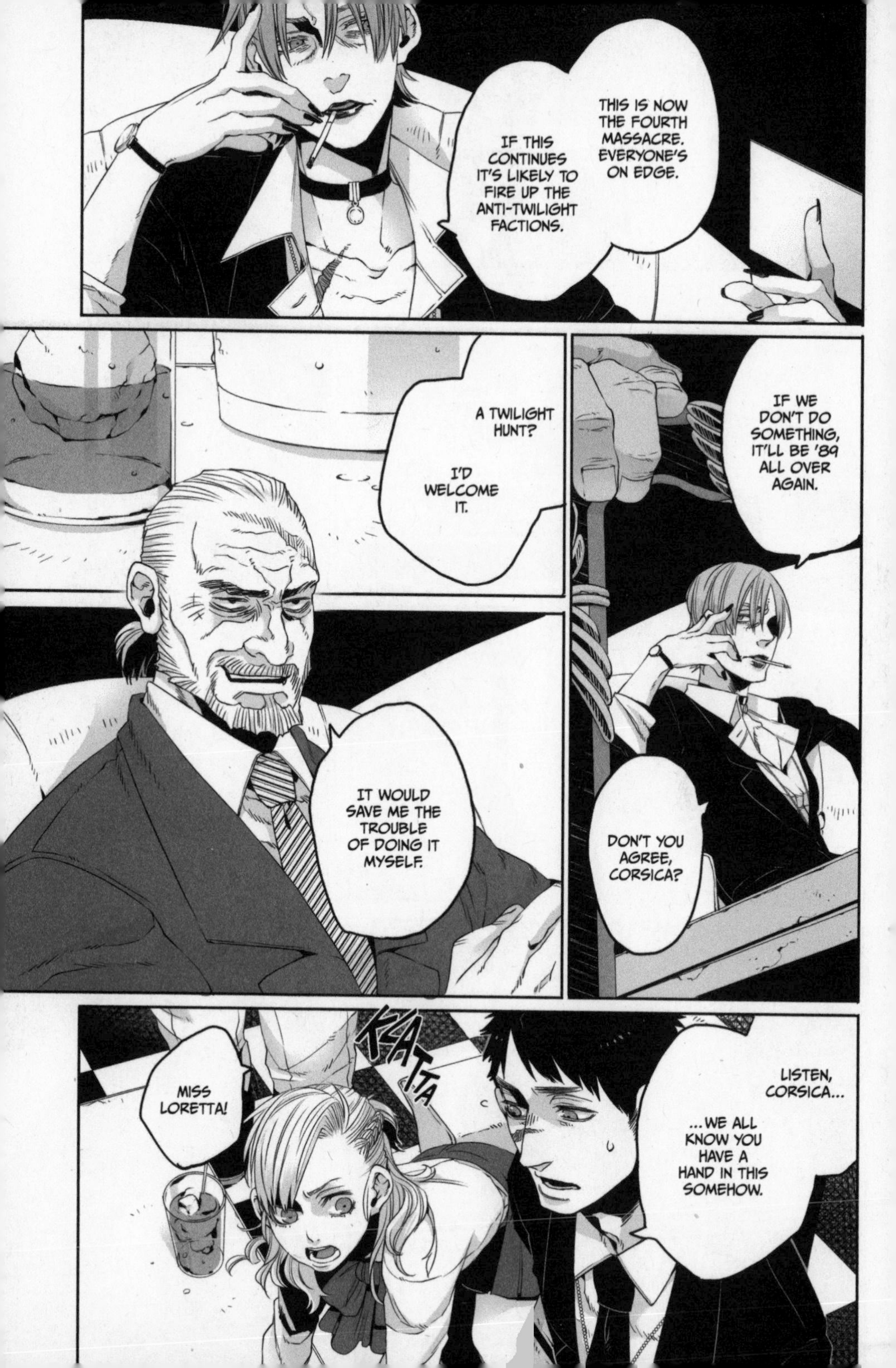
THIS IS NOW THE FOURTH MASSACRE. EVERYONE'S ON EDGE.
IF THIS CONTINUES IT'S LIKELY TO FIRE UP THE ANTI-TWILIGHT FACTIONS.
IF WE DON'T DO SOMETHING, IT'LL BE '89 ALL OVER AGAIN.
DON'T YOU AGREE, CORSICA?
A TWILIGHT HUNT?
I'D WELCOME IT.
IT WOULD SAVE ME THE TROUBLE OF DOING IT MYSELF.
LISTEN, CORSICA...
...WE ALL KNOW YOU HAVE A HAND IN THIS SOMEHOW.
KATTA
MISS LORETTA!

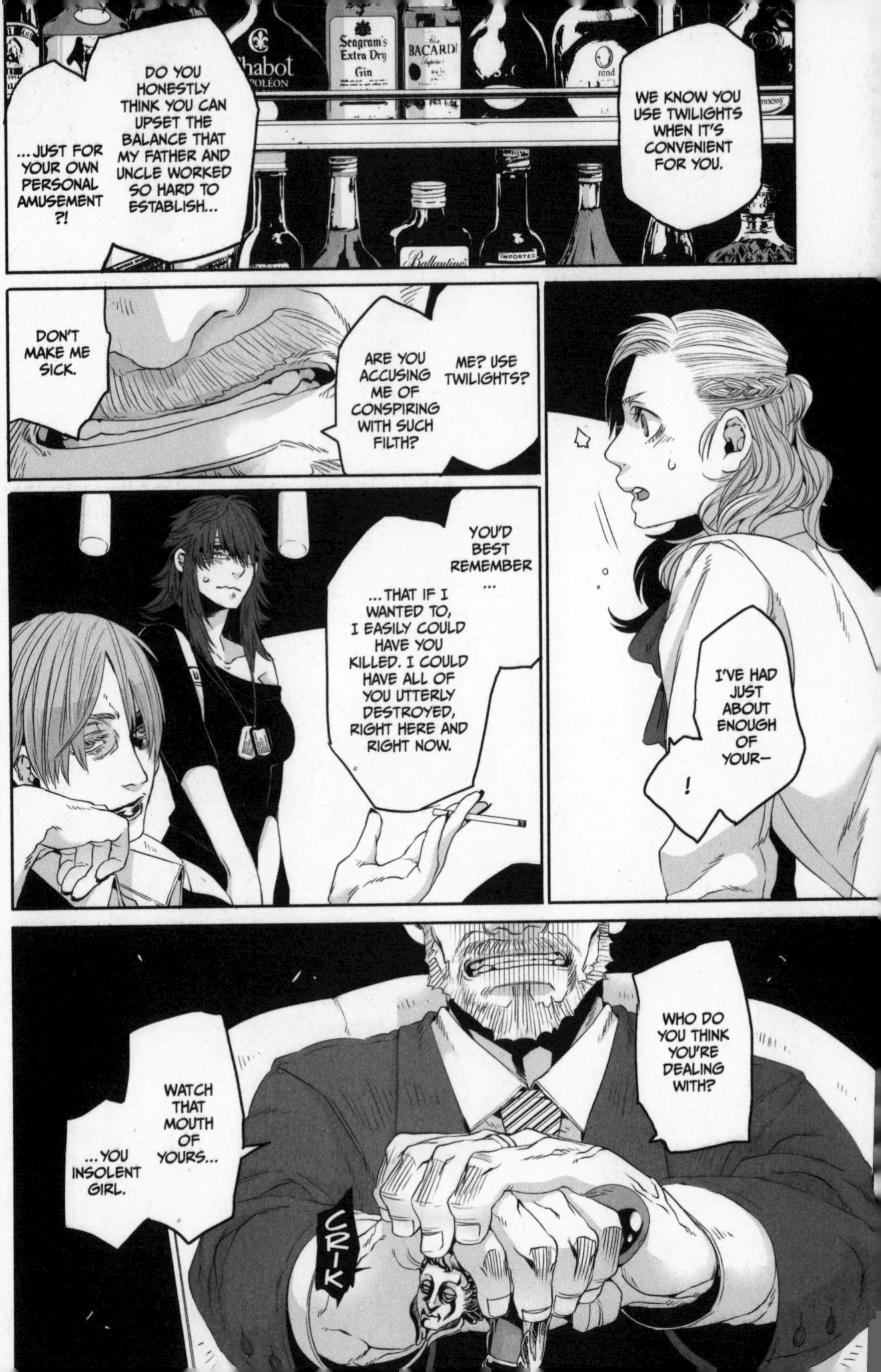

Seagram's Extra Dry Gin
BACARDI
WE KNOW YOU USE TWILIGHTS WHEN IT'S CONVENIENT FOR YOU.
DO YOU HONESTLY THINK YOU CAN UPSET THE BALANCE THAT MY FATHER AND UNCLE WORKED SO HARD TO ESTABLISH...
...JUST FOR YOUR OWN PERSONAL AMUSEMENT ?!
Ballantine's
IMPORTED
I'VE HAD JUST ABOUT ENOUGH OF YOUR—
!
ME? USE TWILIGHTS?
ARE YOU ACCUSING ME OF CONSPIRING WITH SUCH FILTH?
DON'T MAKE ME SICK.
YOU'D BEST REMEMBER...
...THAT IF I WANTED TO, I EASILY COULD HAVE YOU KILLED. I COULD HAVE ALL OF YOU UTTERLY DESTROYED, RIGHT HERE AND RIGHT NOW.
WHO DO YOU THINK YOU'RE DEALING WITH?
WATCH THAT MOUTH OF YOURS...
...YOU INSOLENT GIRL.
CRIK

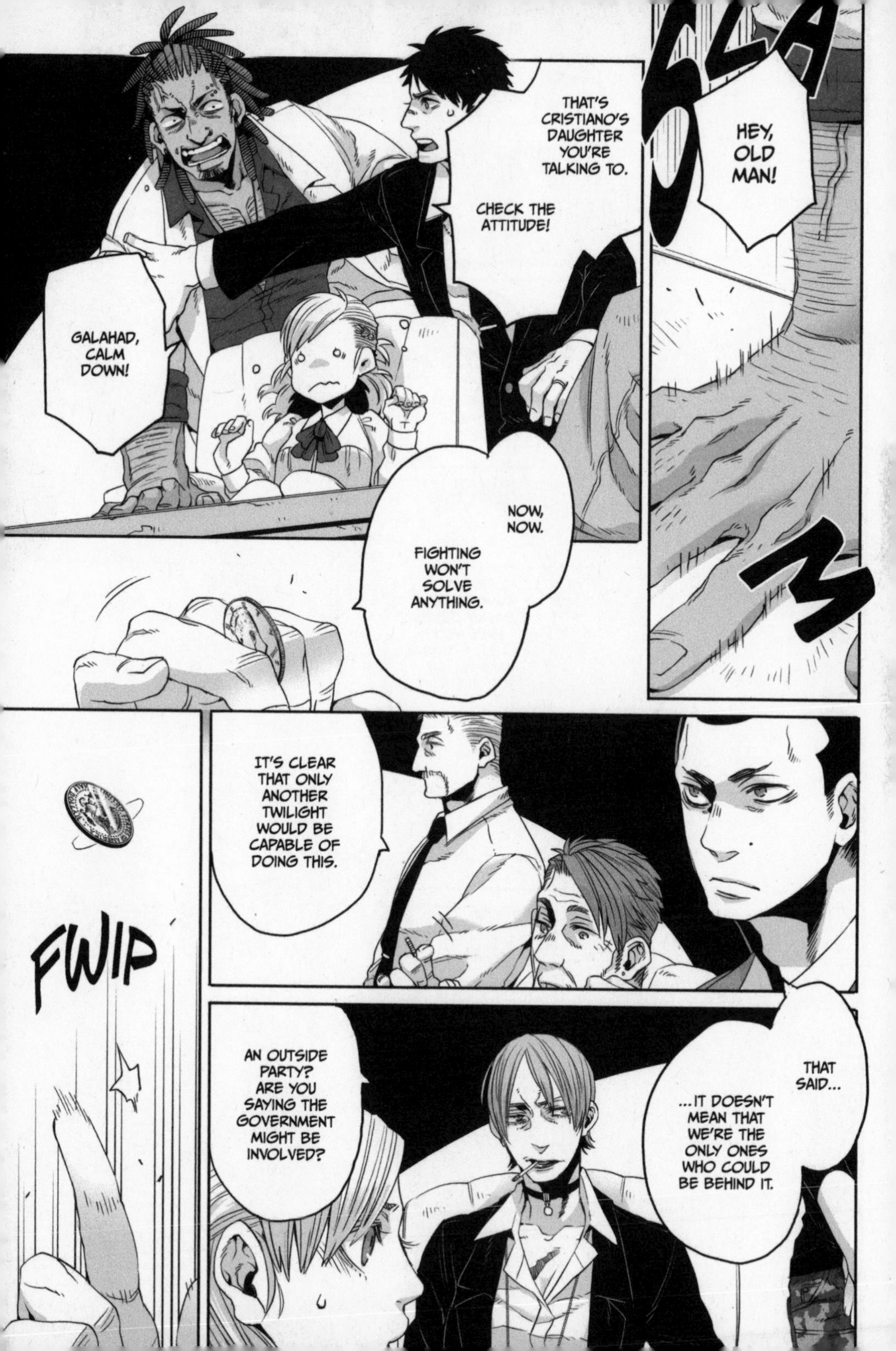
CLA
HEY, OLD MAN!
M
THAT'S CRISTIANO'S DAUGHTER YOU'RE TALKING TO.
CHECK THE ATTITUDE!
GALAHAD, CALM DOWN!
NOW, NOW.
FIGHTING WON'T SOLVE ANYTHING.
IT'S CLEAR THAT ONLY ANOTHER TWILIGHT WOULD BE CAPABLE OF DOING THIS.
THAT SAID...
...IT DOESN'T MEAN THAT WE'RE THE ONLY ONES WHO COULD BE BEHIND IT.
AN OUTSIDE PARTY? ARE YOU SAYING THE GOVERNMENT MIGHT BE INVOLVED?
FWIP

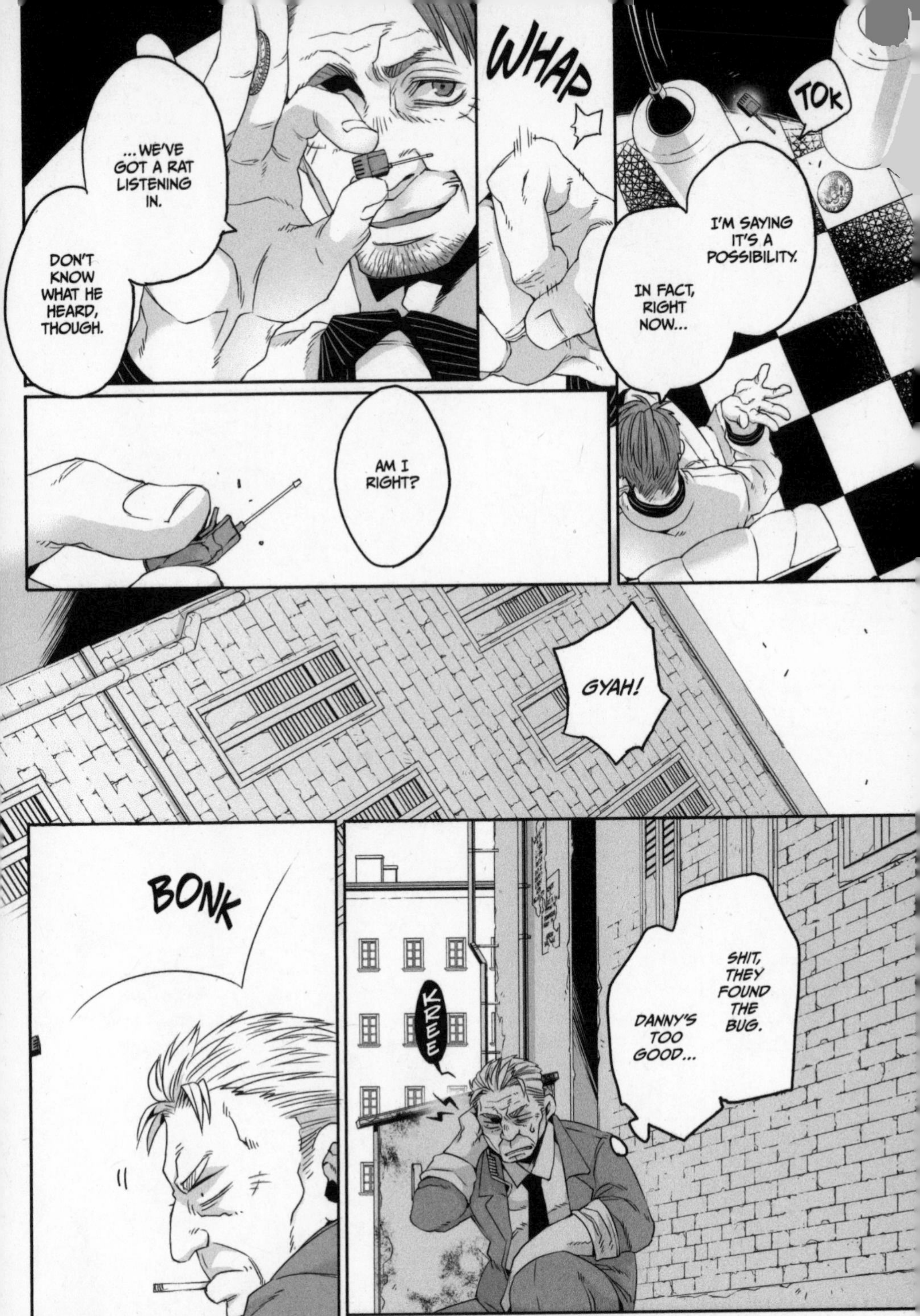
TOK
I'M SAYING IT'S A POSSIBILITY.
IN FACT, RIGHT NOW...
WHAP
...WE'VE GOT A RAT LISTENING IN.
DON'T KNOW WHAT HE HEARD, THOUGH.
AM I RIGHT?
GYAH!
SHIT, THEY FOUND THE BUG.
DANNY'S TOO GOOD...
KREE
BONK

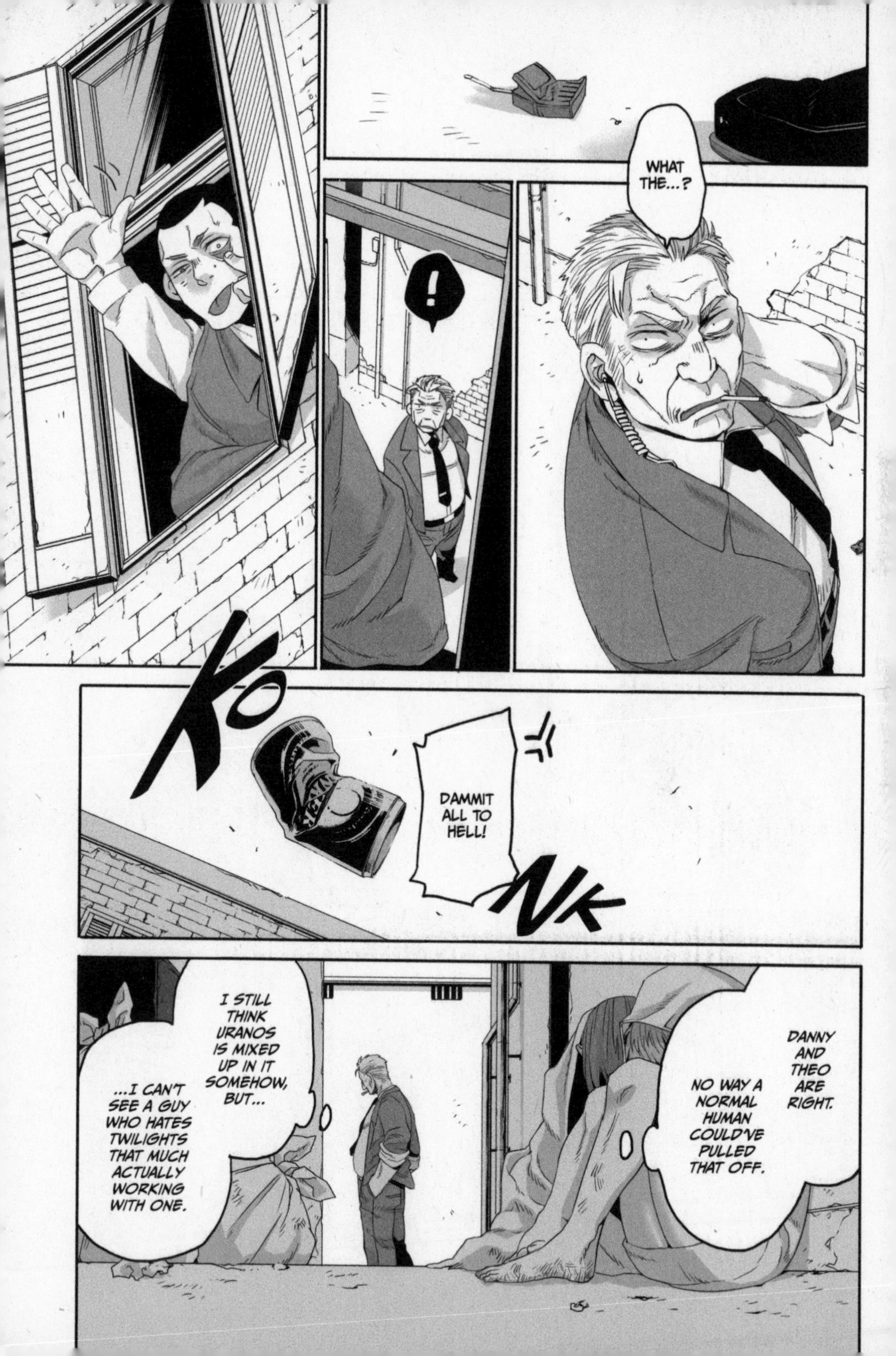
WHAT THE...?
!
KONK
DAMMIT ALL TO HELL!
DANNY AND THEO ARE RIGHT.
NO WAY A NORMAL HUMAN COULD'VE PULLED THAT OFF.
I STILL THINK URANOS IS MIXED UP IN IT SOMEHOW, BUT...
...I CAN'T SEE A GUY WHO HATES TWILIGHTS THAT MUCH ACTUALLY WORKING WITH ONE.

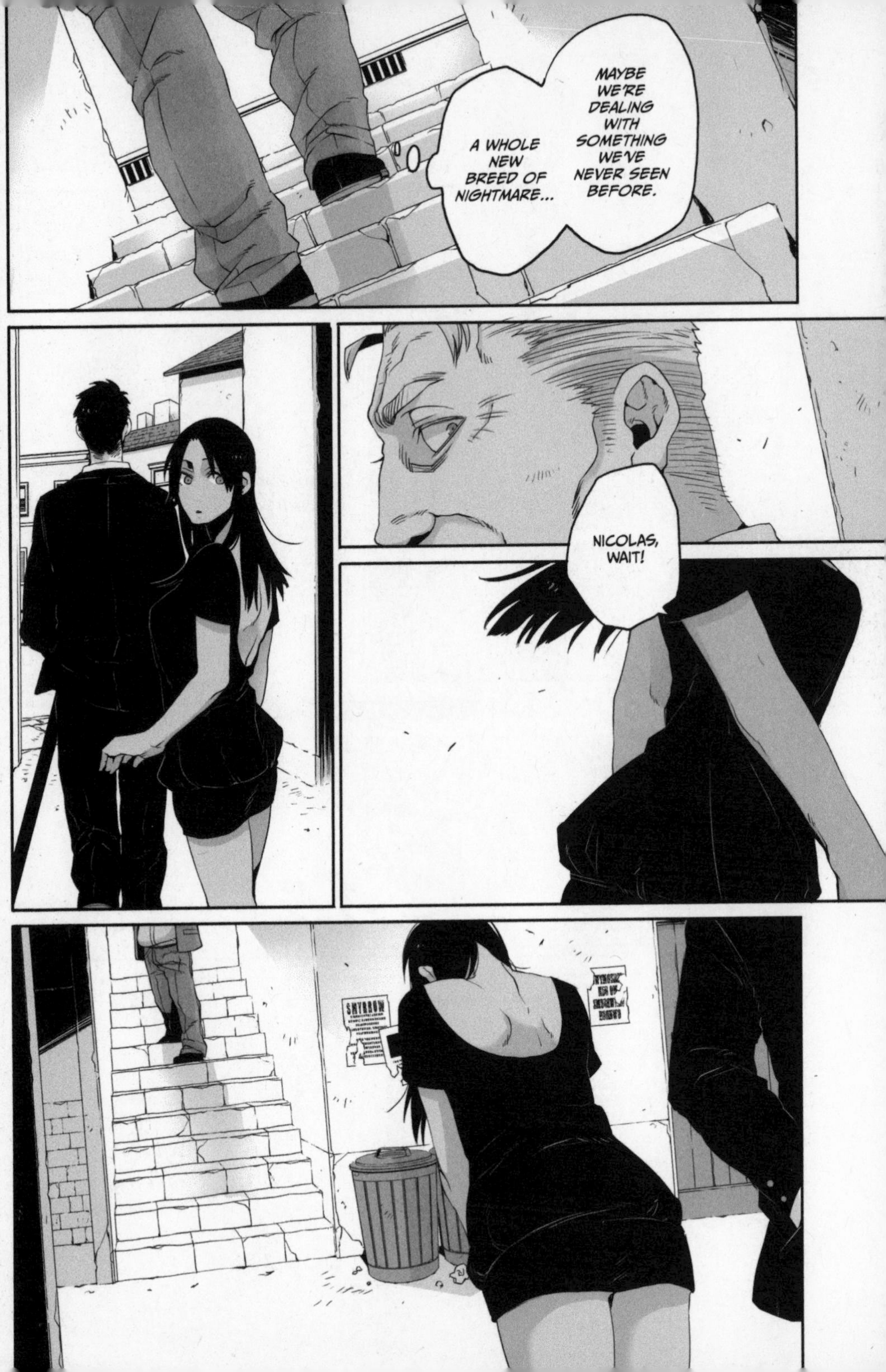
MAYBE WE'RE DEALING WITH SOMETHING WE'VE NEVER SEEN BEFORE.
A WHOLE NEW BREED OF NIGHTMARE...
NICOLAS, WAIT!

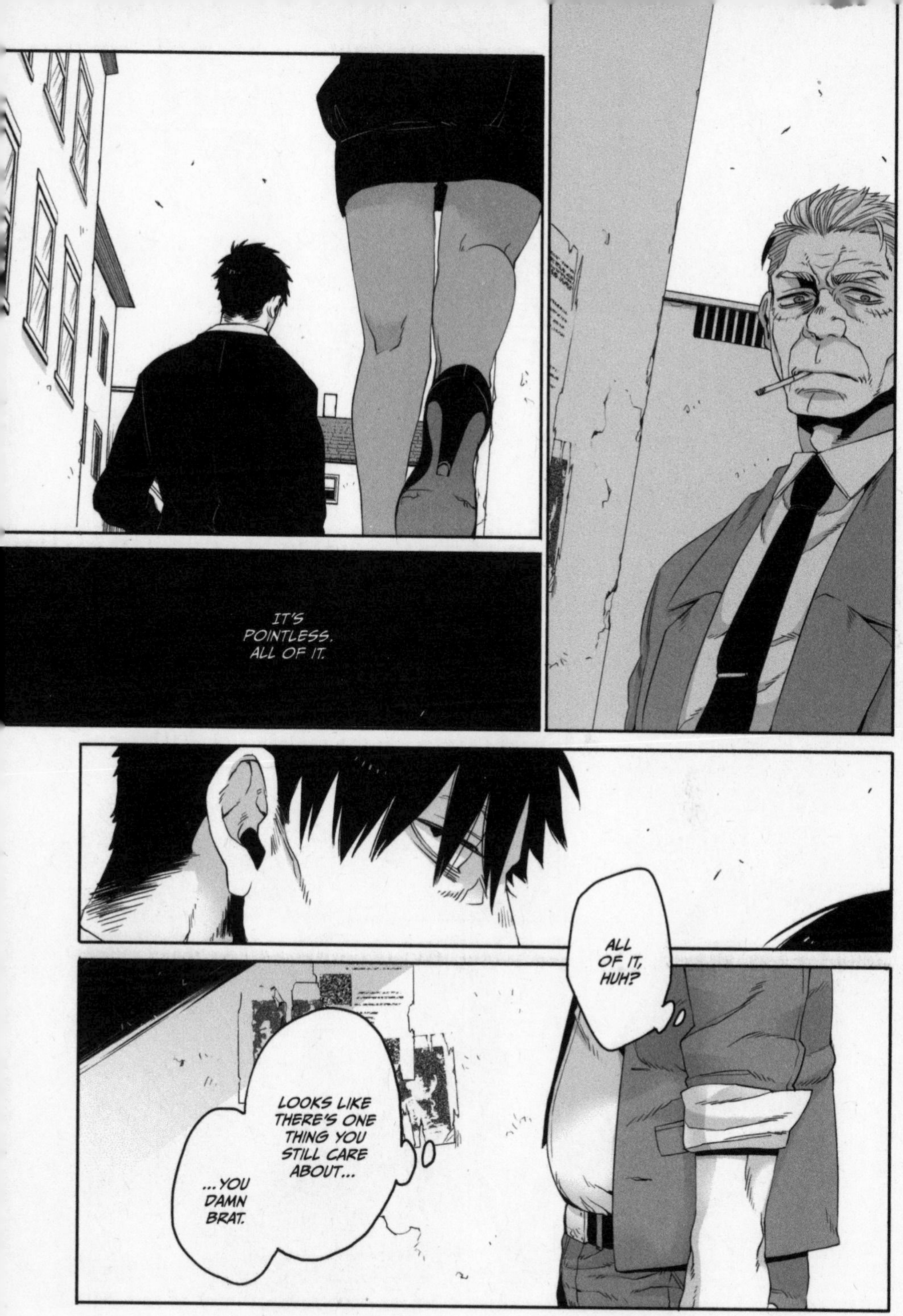
IT'S POINTLESS. ALL OF IT.
ALL OF IT, HUH?
LOOKS LIKE THERE'S ONE THING YOU STILL CARE ABOUT...
...YOU DAMN BRAT.

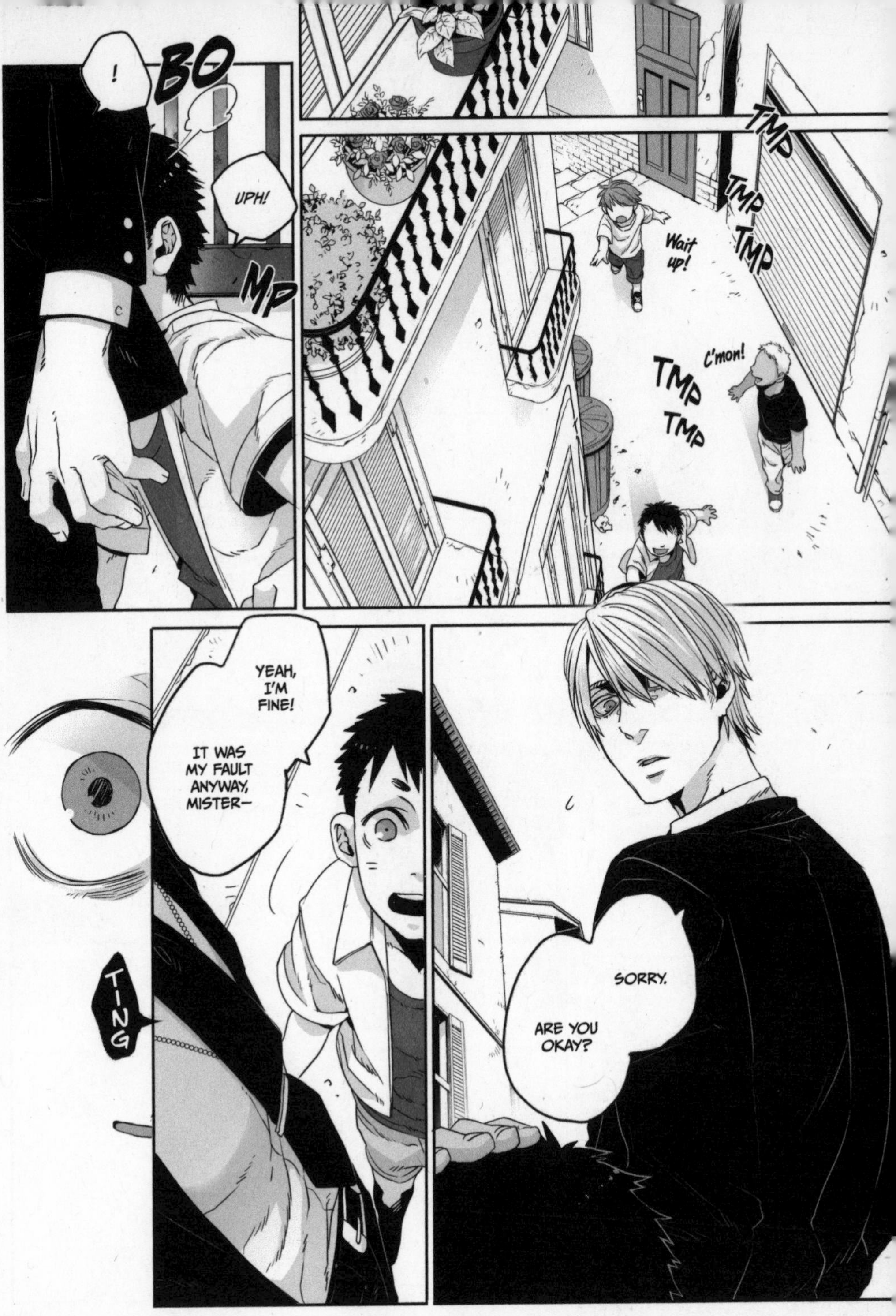
TMP
TMP
TMP
Wait up!
C'mon!
TMP
TMP
!
BO
UPH!
MP
SORRY.
ARE YOU OKAY?
YEAH, I'M FINE!
IT WAS MY FAULT ANYWAY, MISTER—
TING

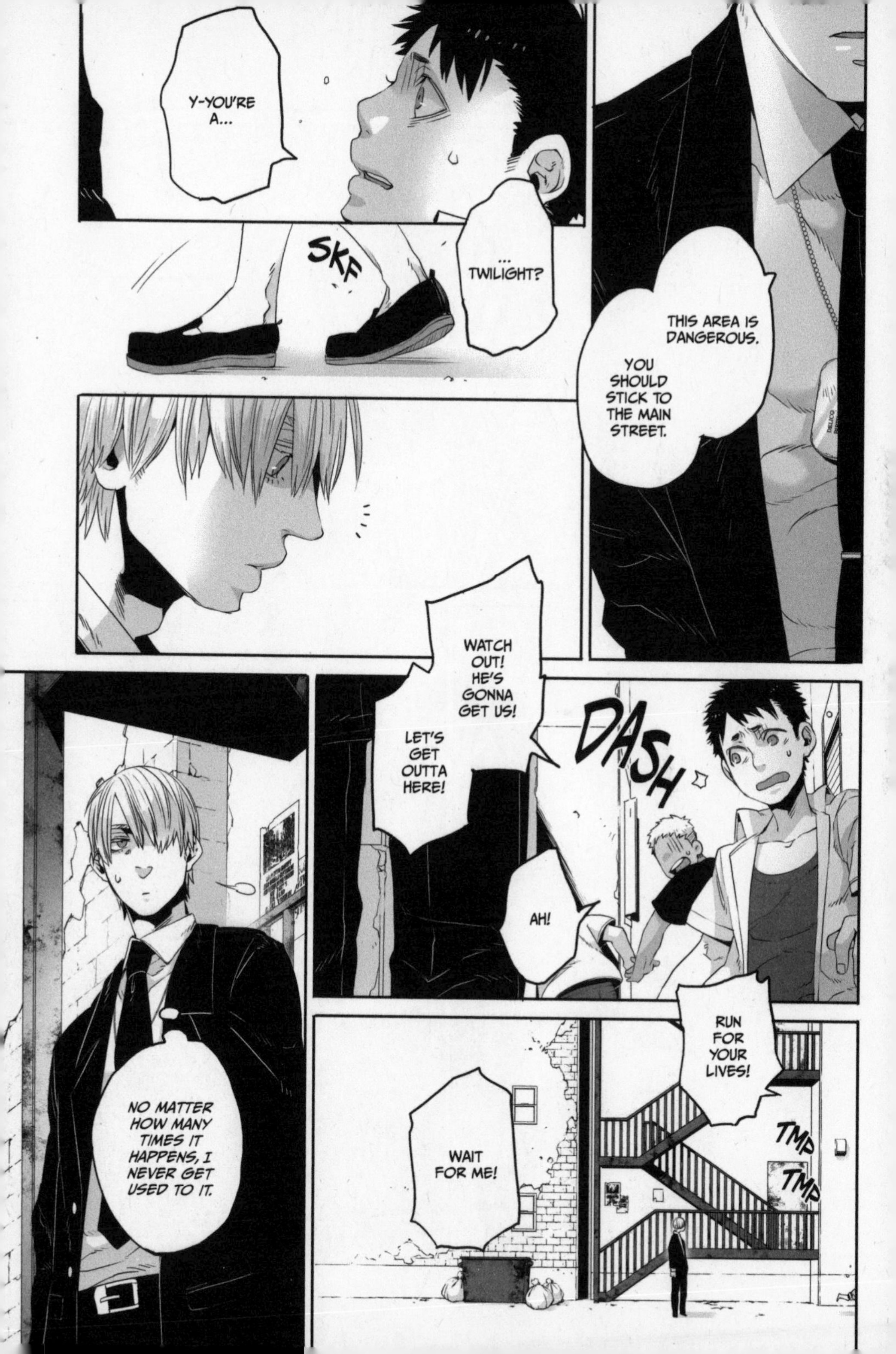
THIS AREA IS DANGEROUS.
YOU SHOULD STICK TO THE MAIN STREET.
Y-YOU'RE A...
SKF
...TWILIGHT?
WATCH OUT! HE'S GONNA GET US!
LET'S GET OUTTA HERE!
DASH
AH!
RUN FOR YOUR LIVES!
TMP TMP
WAIT FOR ME!
NO MATTER HOW MANY TIMES IT HAPPENS, I NEVER GET USED TO IT.

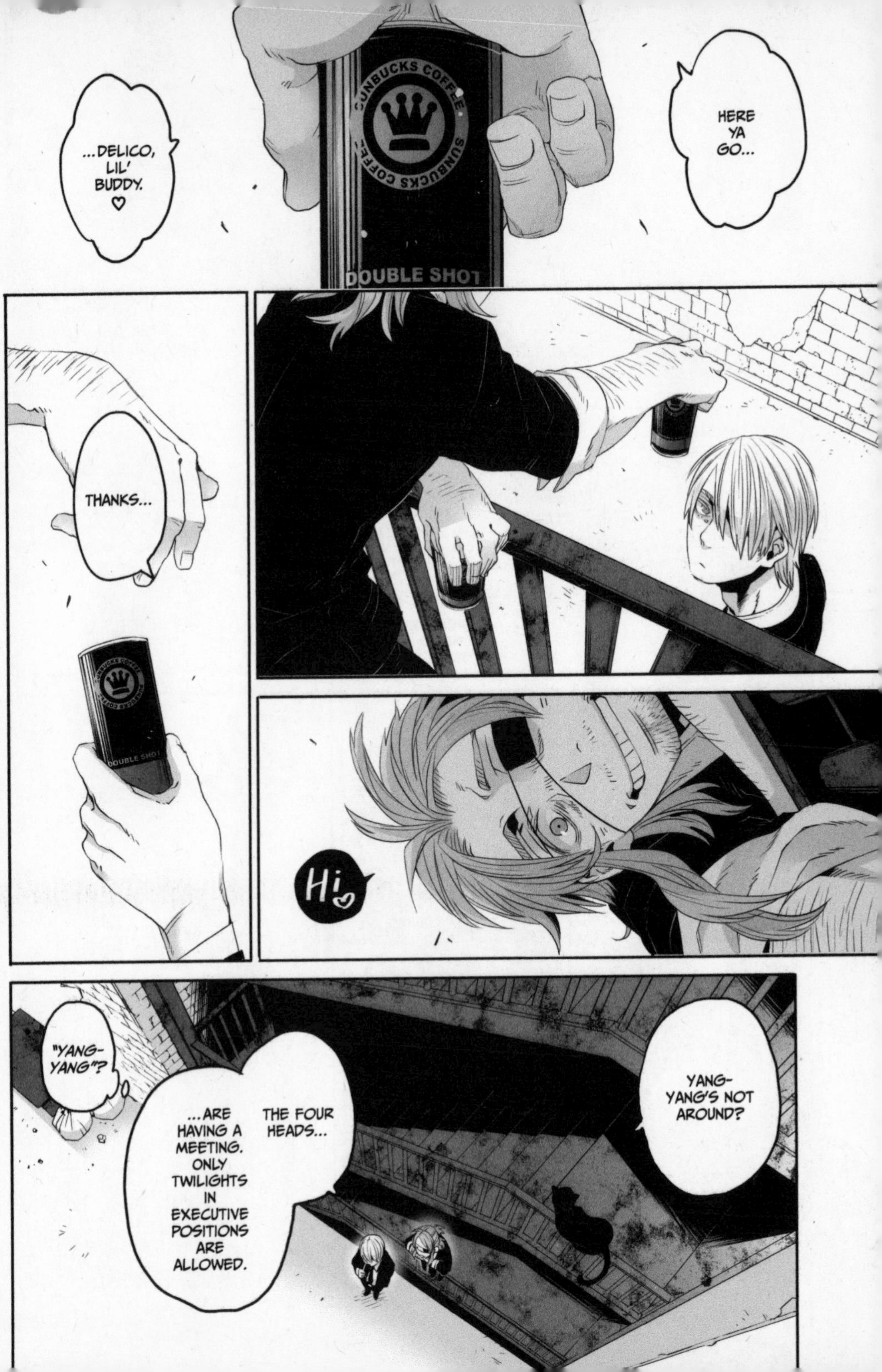
HERE YA GO...
SUNBUCKS COFFEE
DOUBLE SHOT
...DELICO, LIL' BUDDY. ♡
Hi♡
THANKS...
SUNBUCKS COFFEE
DOUBLE SHOT
YANG-YANG'S NOT AROUND?
THE FOUR HEADS...
...ARE HAVING A MEETING. ONLY TWILIGHTS IN EXECUTIVE POSITIONS ARE ALLOWED.
"YANG-YANG"?

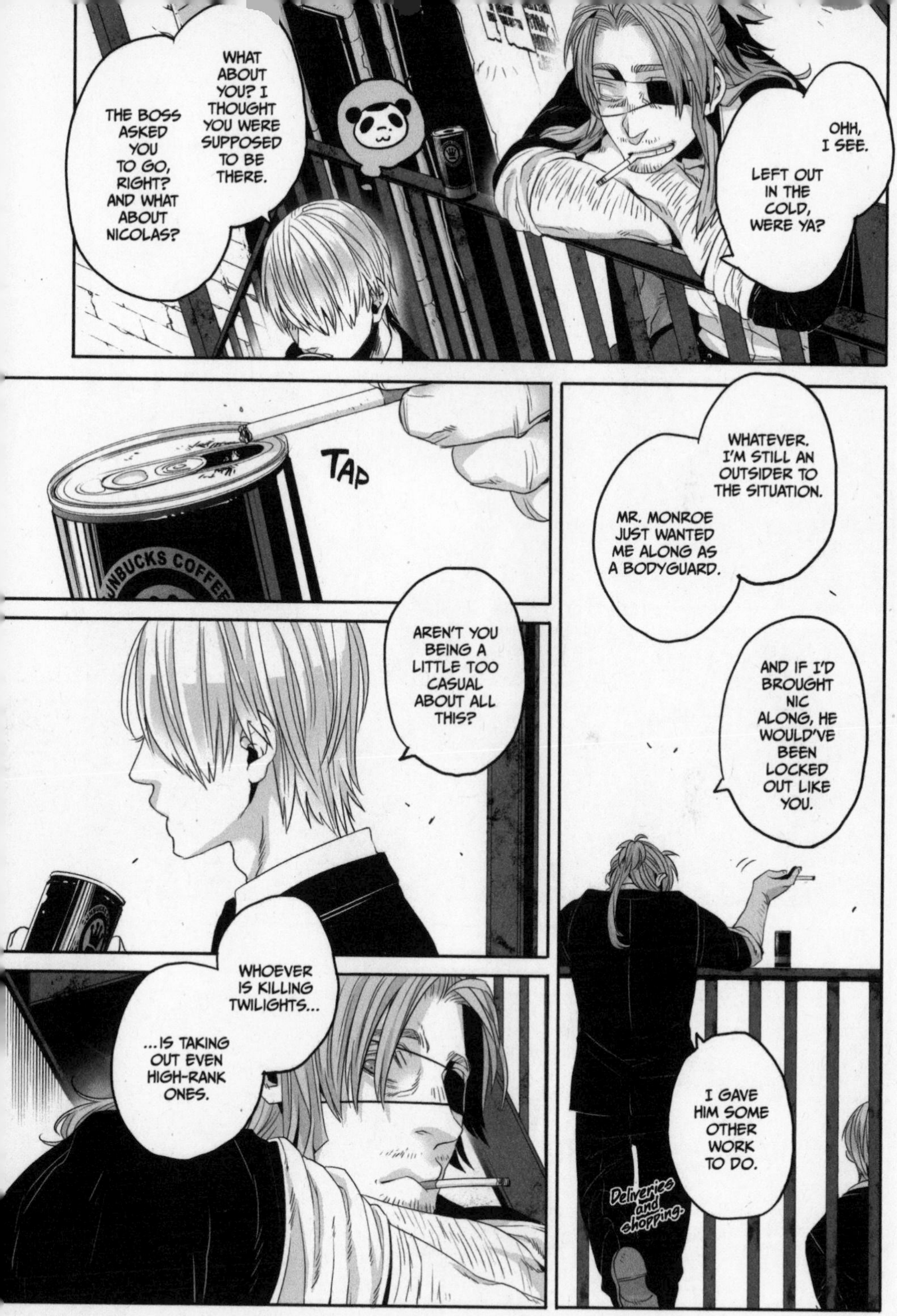
OHH, I SEE.
LEFT OUT IN THE COLD, WERE YA?
WHAT ABOUT YOU? I THOUGHT YOU WERE SUPPOSED TO BE THERE.
THE BOSS ASKED YOU TO GO, RIGHT? AND WHAT ABOUT NICOLAS?
WHATEVER. I'M STILL AN OUTSIDER TO THE SITUATION.
MR. MONROE JUST WANTED ME ALONG AS A BODYGUARD.
AND IF I'D BROUGHT NIC ALONG, HE WOULD'VE BEEN LOCKED OUT LIKE YOU.
I GAVE HIM SOME OTHER WORK TO DO.
Deliveries and shopping.
TAP
UNBUCKS COFFEE
AREN'T YOU BEING A LITTLE TOO CASUAL ABOUT ALL THIS?
WHOEVER IS KILLING TWILIGHTS...
...IS TAKING OUT EVEN HIGH-RANK ONES.

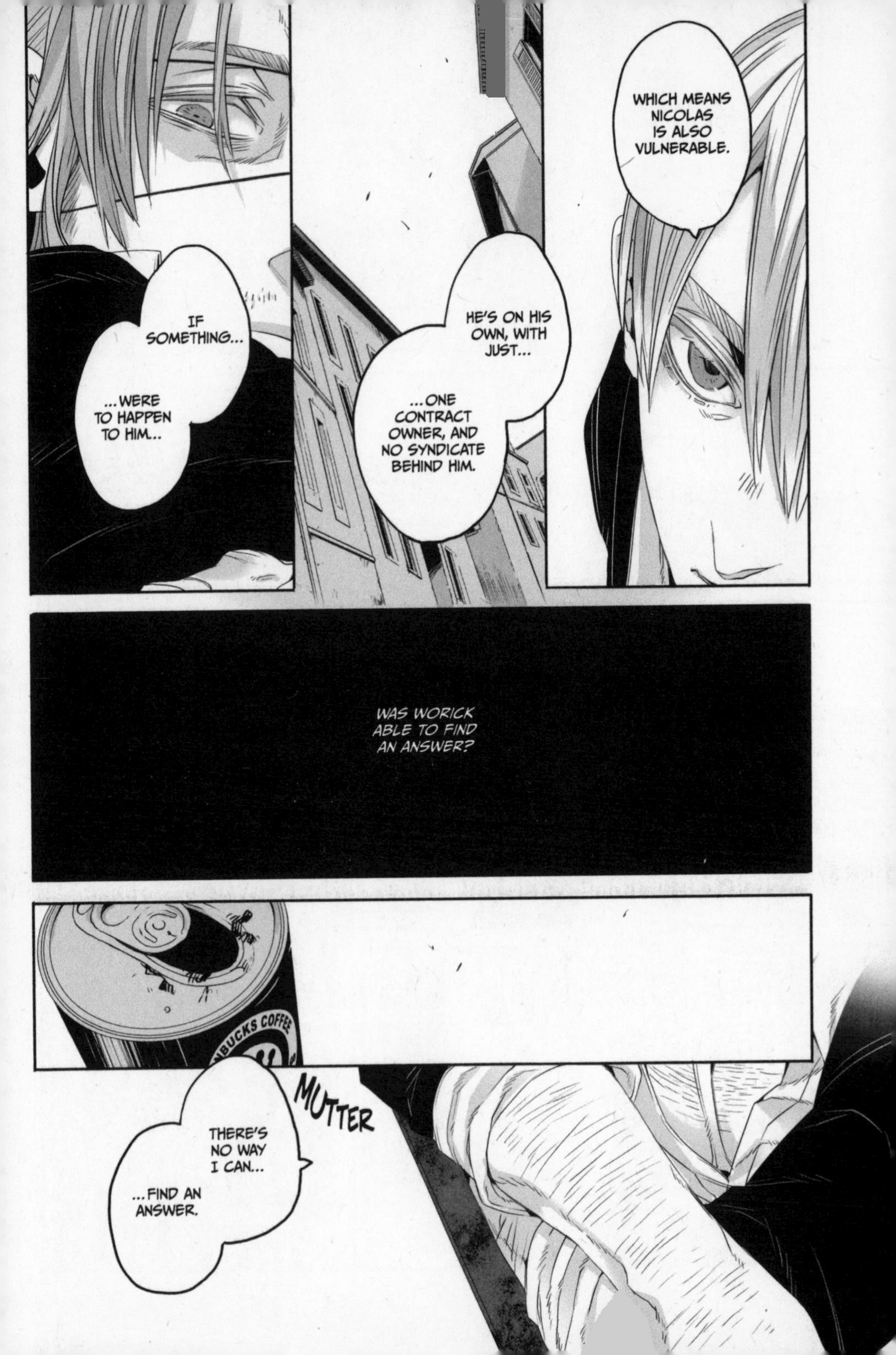
WHICH MEANS NICOLAS IS ALSO VULNERABLE.
HE'S ON HIS OWN, WITH JUST...
...ONE CONTRACT OWNER, AND NO SYNDICATE BEHIND HIM.
IF SOMETHING...
...WERE TO HAPPEN TO HIM...
WAS WORICK ABLE TO FIND AN ANSWER?
MUTTER
THERE'S NO WAY I CAN...
...FIND AN ANSWER.

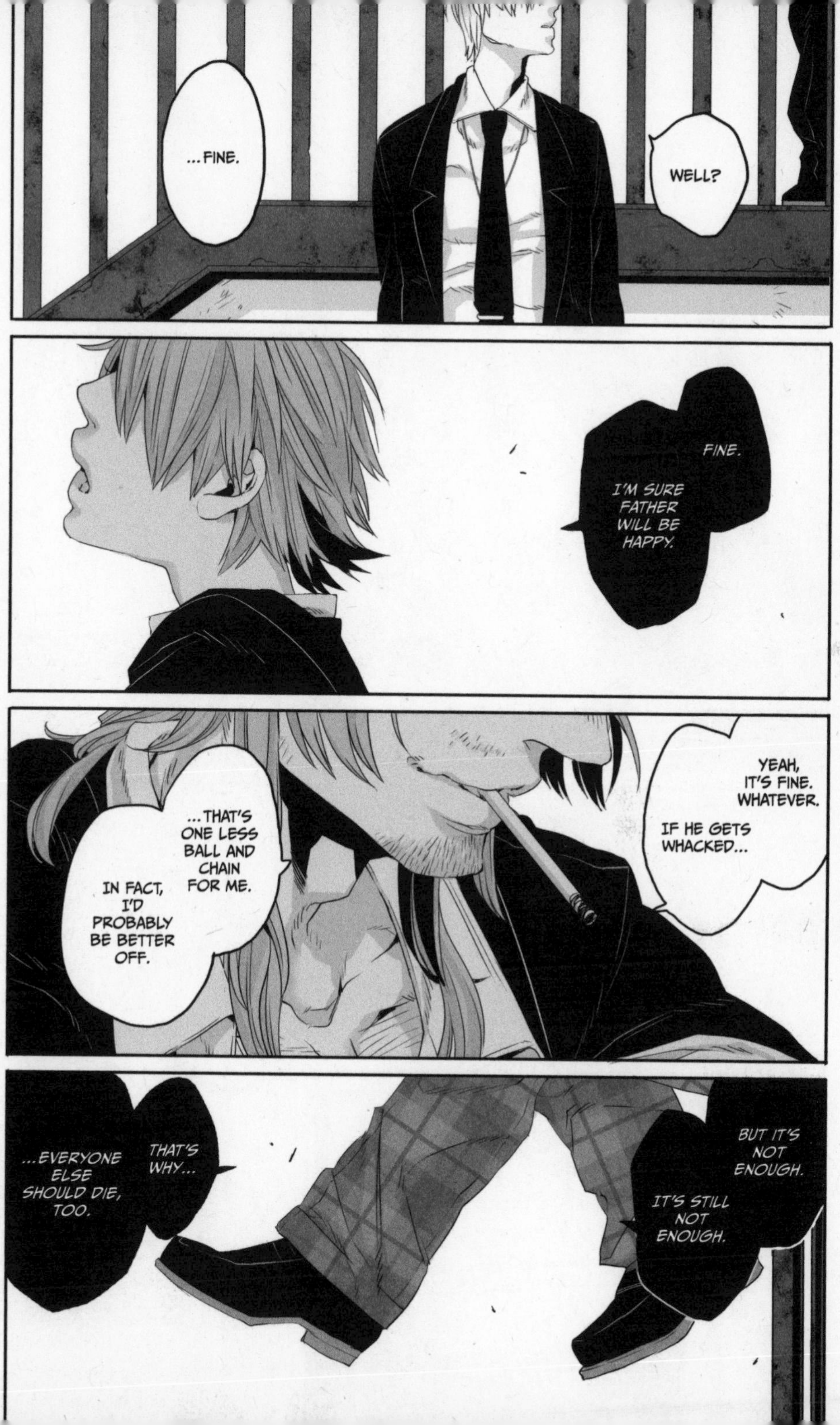
WELL?
...FINE.
FINE.
I'M SURE FATHER WILL BE HAPPY.
YEAH, IT'S FINE. WHATEVER.
IF HE GETS WHACKED...
...THAT'S ONE LESS BALL AND CHAIN FOR ME.
IN FACT, I'D PROBABLY BE BETTER OFF.
BUT IT'S NOT ENOUGH.
IT'S STILL NOT ENOUGH.
THAT'S WHY...
...EVERYONE ELSE SHOULD DIE, TOO.

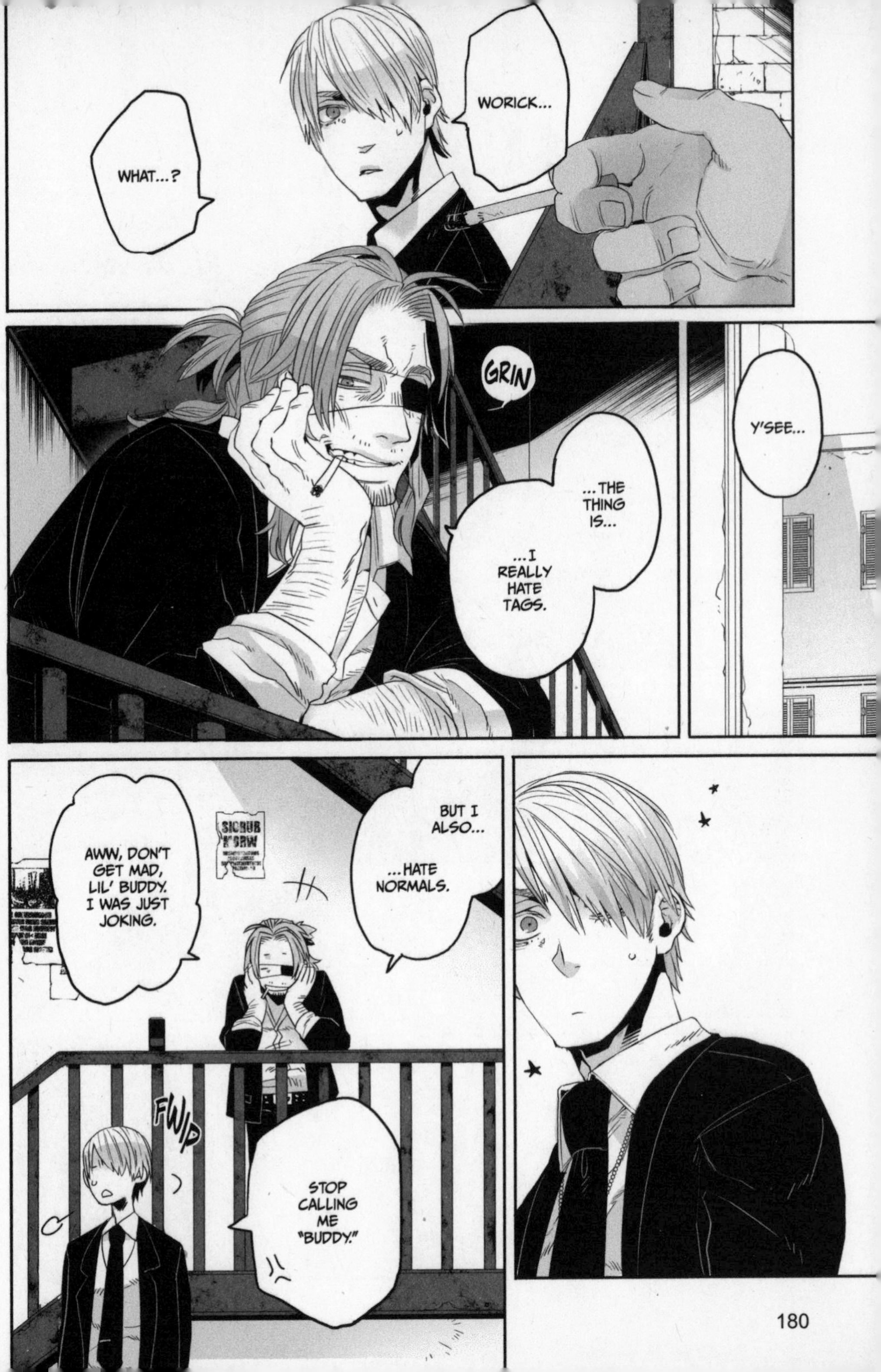
WORICK...
WHAT...?
Y'SEE...
GRIN
...THE THING IS...
...I REALLY HATE TAGS.
BUT I ALSO...
...HATE NORMALS.
AWW, DON'T GET MAD, LIL' BUDDY. I WAS JUST JOKING.
FWIP
STOP CALLING ME "BUDDY."

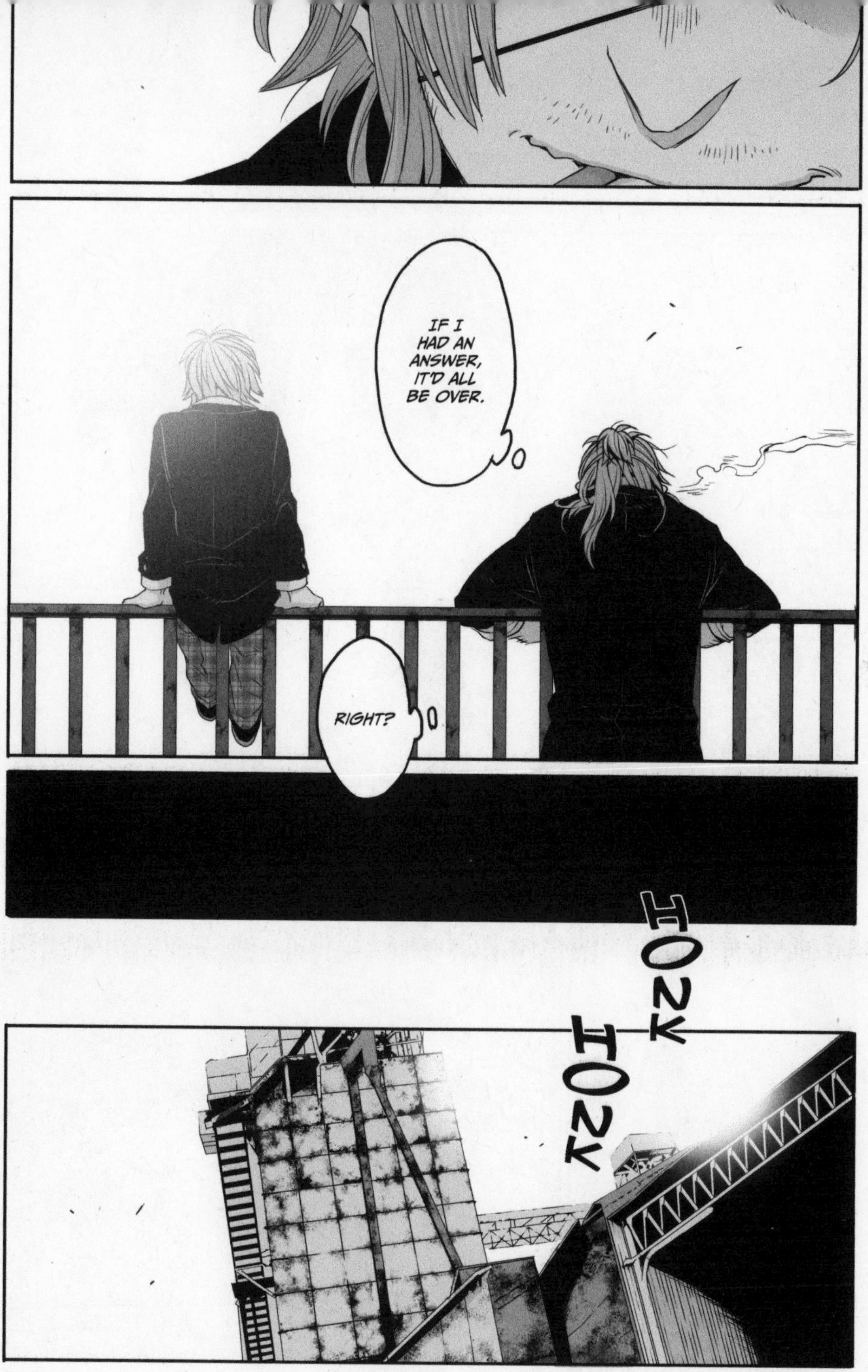
IF I HAD AN ANSWER, IT'D ALL BE OVER.
RIGHT?
HONK
HONK

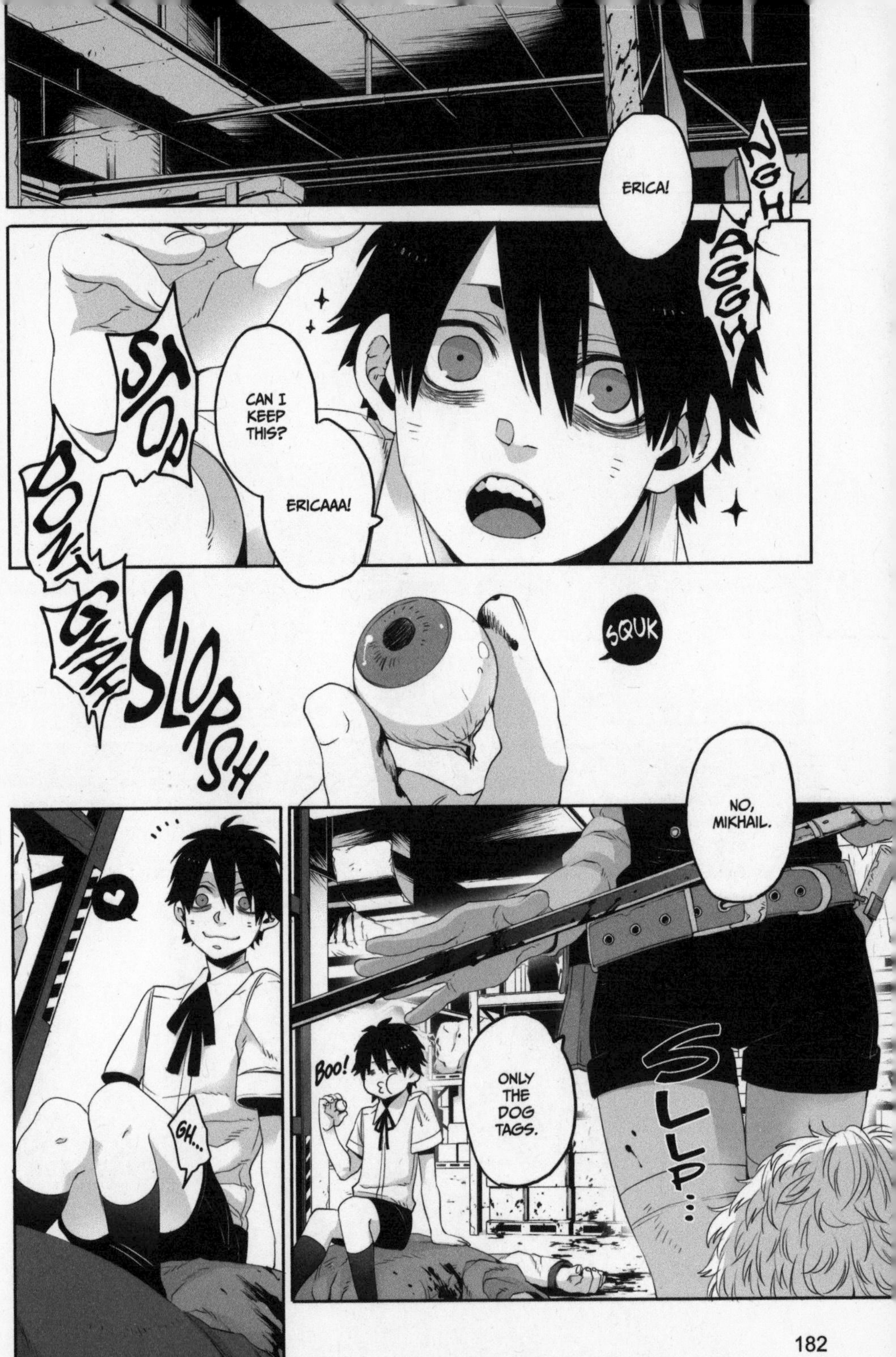

ERICA!
NGHAGGGH
CAN I KEEP THIS?
ERICAAA!
STOP
DON'T
GYAH
SLORCH
SQUK
NO, MIKHAIL.
ONLY THE DOG TAGS.
BOO!
SLLP...
...
GH...

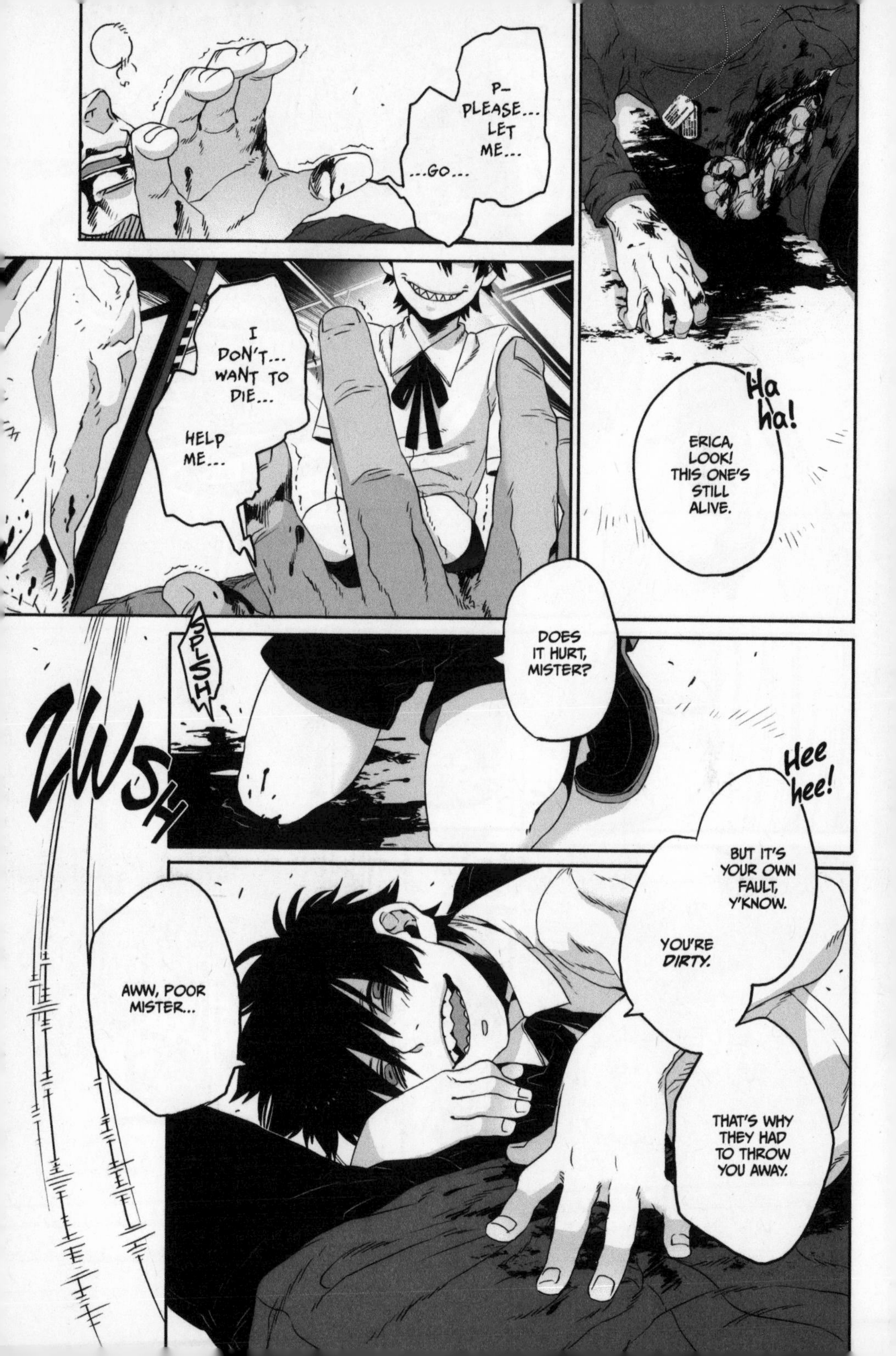
Ha ha!
ERICA, LOOK! THIS ONE'S STILL ALIVE.
P-PLEASE... LET ME...
...GO...
I DON'T... WANT TO DIE...
HELP ME...
DOES IT HURT, MISTER?
SPLSH
ZWSH
Hee hee!
BUT IT'S YOUR OWN FAULT, Y'KNOW.
YOU'RE *DIRTY.*
THAT'S WHY THEY HAD TO THROW YOU AWAY.
AWW, POOR MISTER...

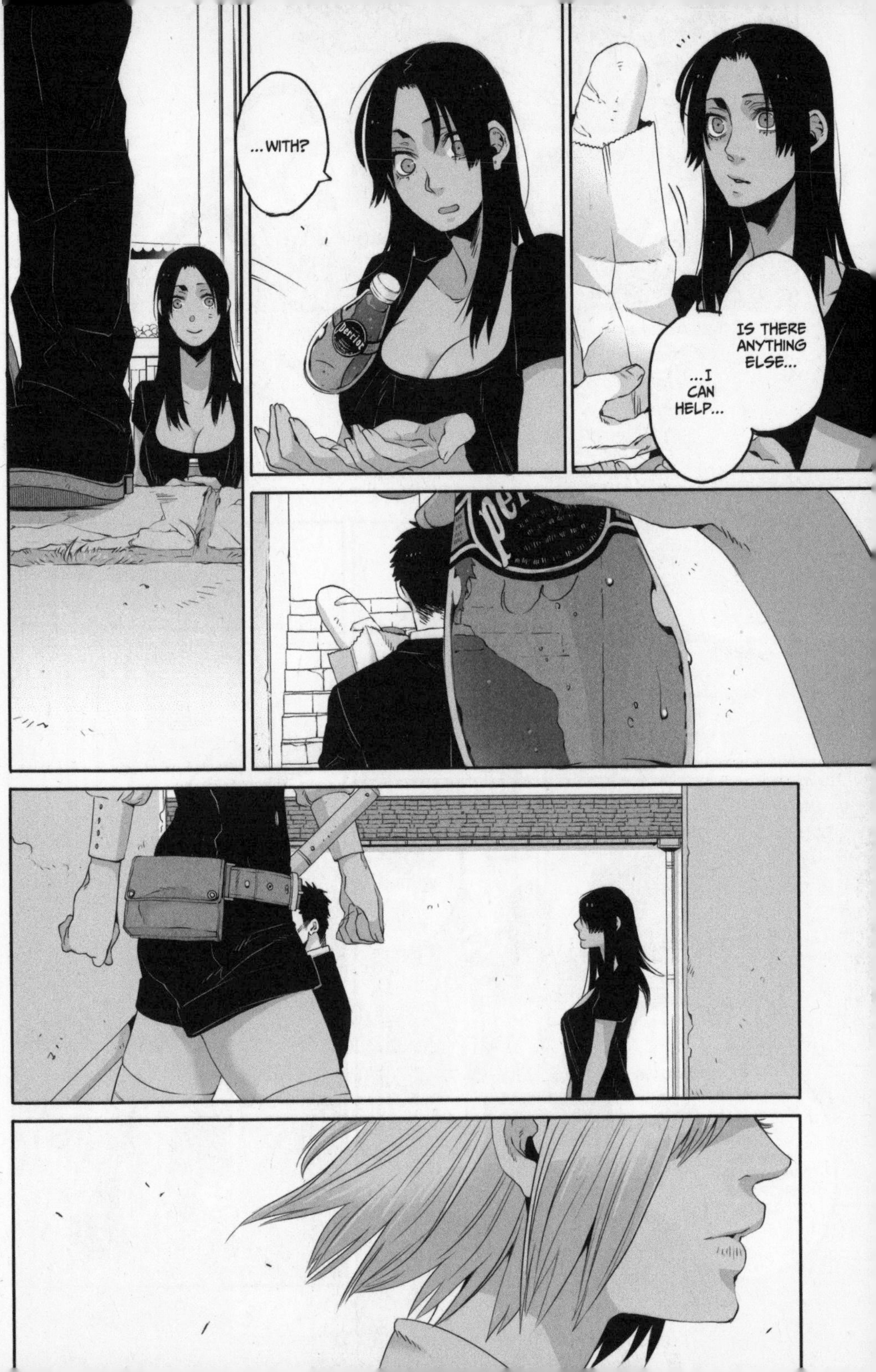
IS THERE ANYTHING ELSE...
...I CAN HELP...
...WITH?
Perrier

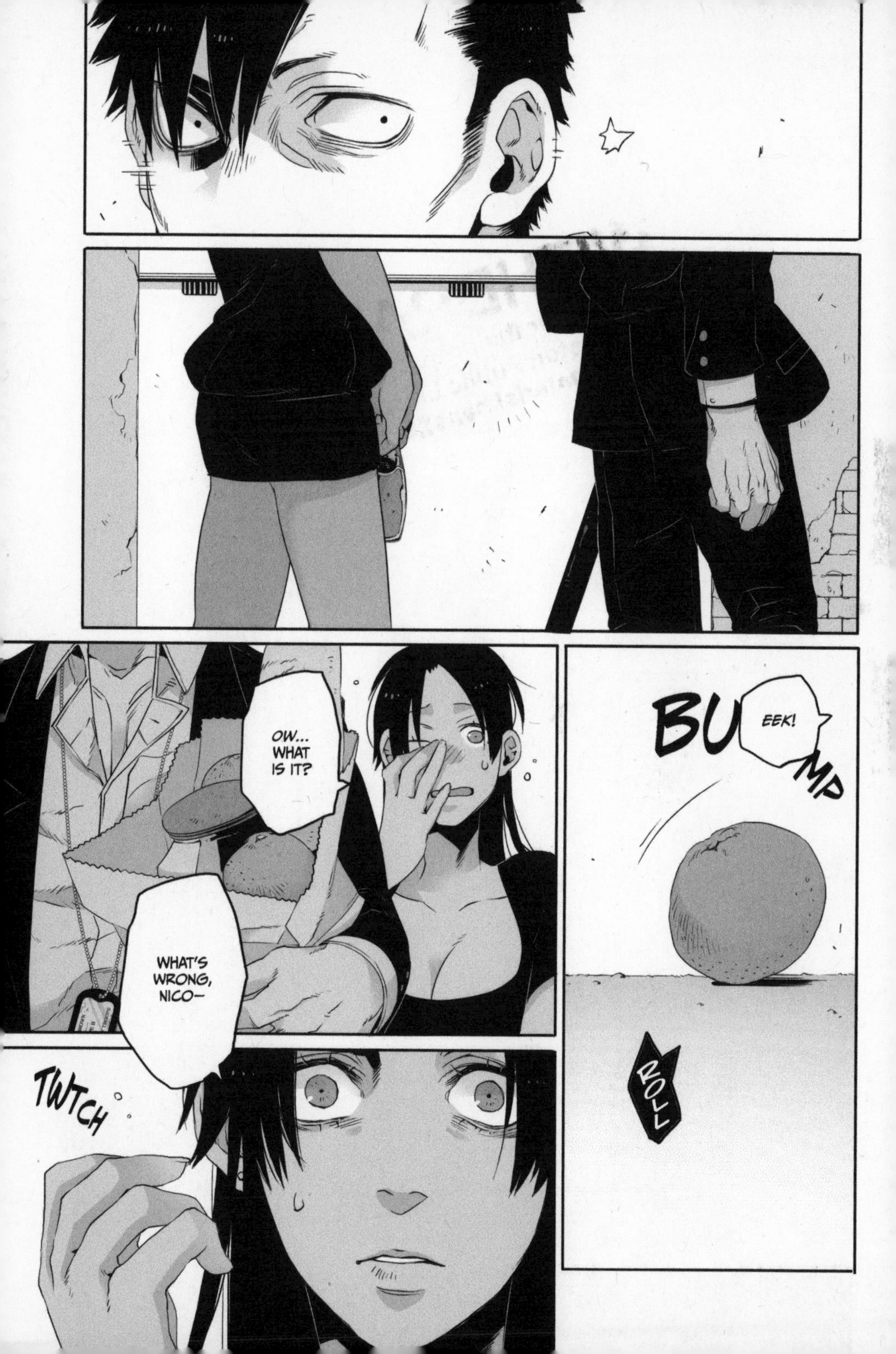
BUMP
EEK!
ROLL
OW... WHAT IS IT?
WHAT'S WRONG, NICO—
TWTCH

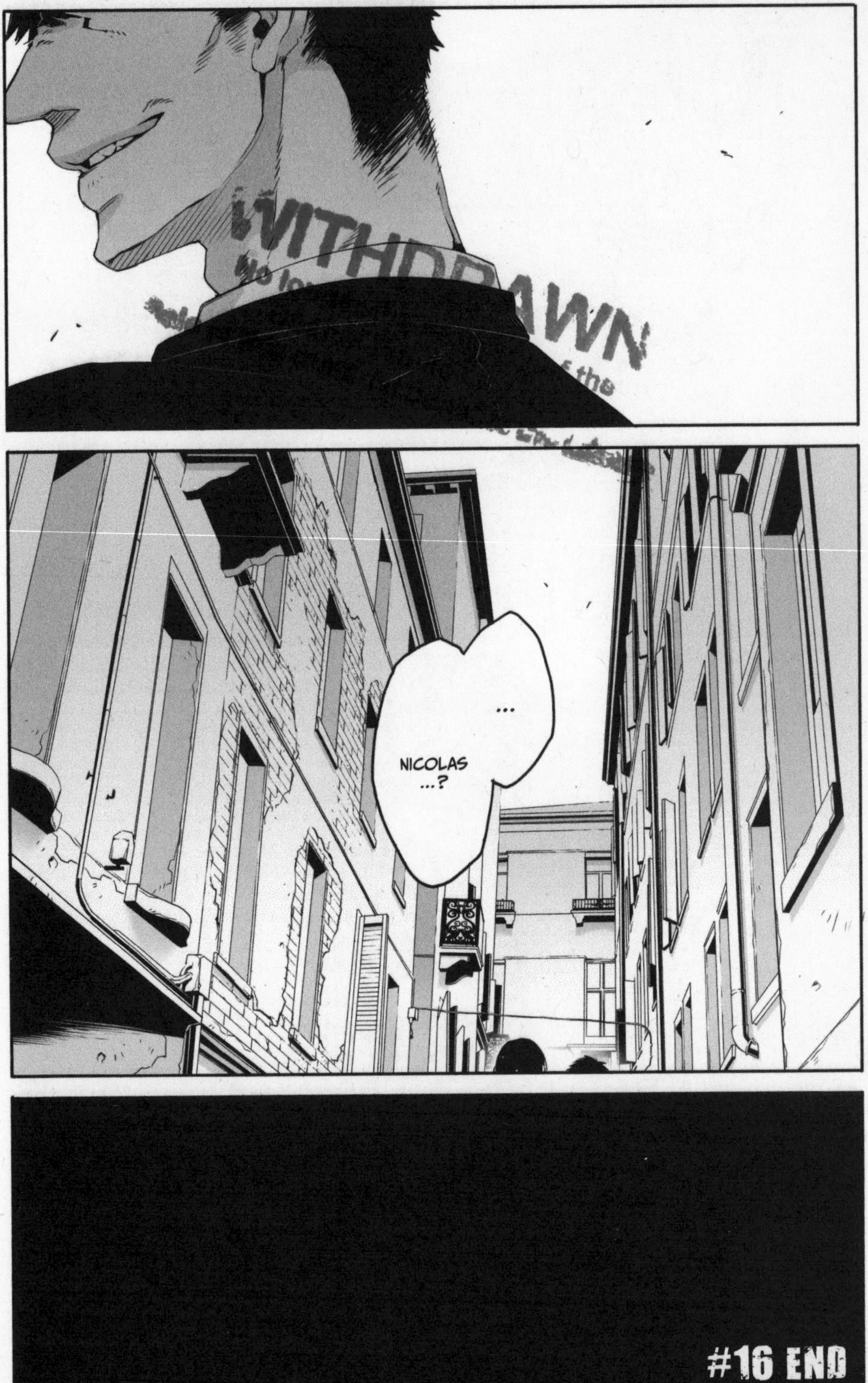
...
NICOLAS ...?
#16 END

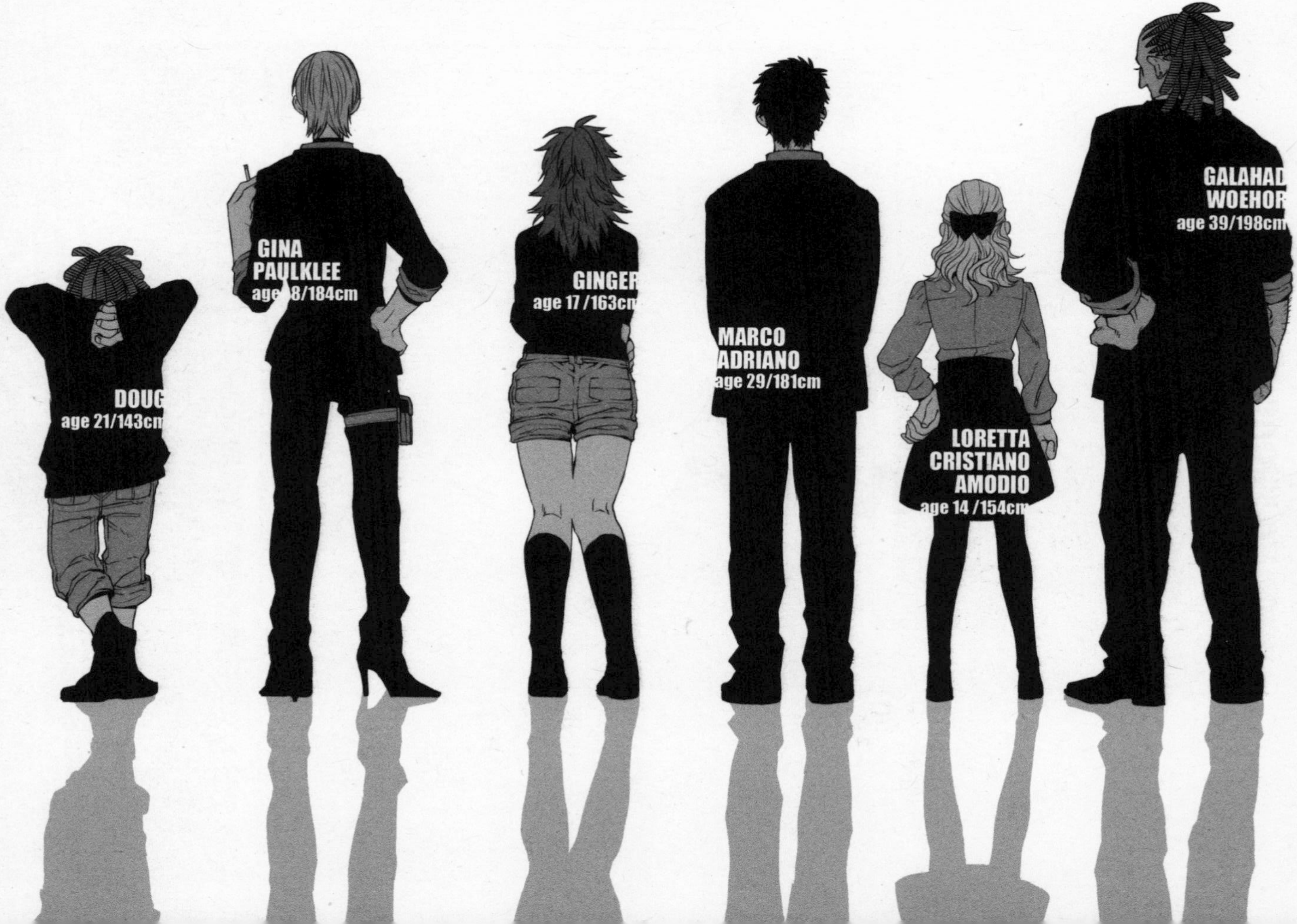
GALAHAD
WOEHOR
age 39/198cm
LORETTA
CRISTIANO
AMODIO
age 14 /154cm
MARCO
ADRIANO
age 29/181cm
GINGER
age 17 /163cm
GINA
PAULKLEE
age 8/184cm
DOUG
age 21/143cm

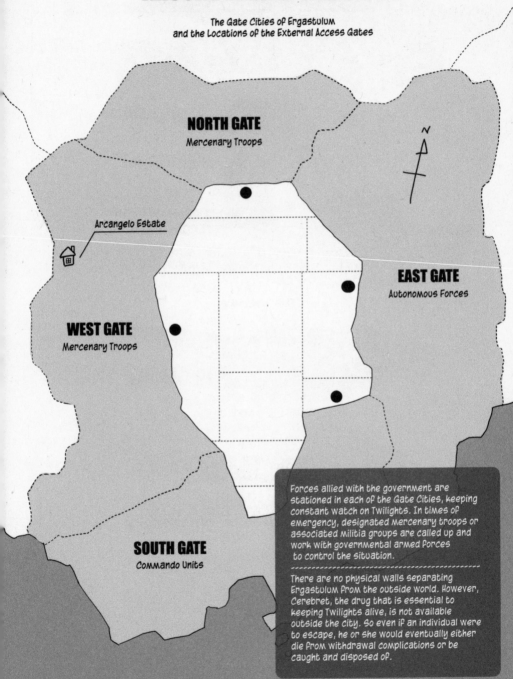

AROUND ERGASTULUM CITY

The Gate Cities of Ergastulum
and the Locations of the External Access Gates

NORTH GATE
Mercenary Troops

Arcangelo Estate

EAST GATE
Autonomous Forces

WEST GATE
Mercenary Troops

SOUTH GATE
Commando Units

Forces allied with the government are stationed in each of the Gate Cities, keeping constant watch on Twilights. In times of emergency, designated mercenary troops or associated militia groups are called up and work with governmental armed forces to control the situation.

There are no physical walls separating Ergastulum from the outside world. However, Cerebret, the drug that is essential to keeping Twilights alive, is not available outside the city. So even if an individual were to escape, he or she would eventually either die from withdrawal complications or be caught and disposed of.

THIRD GREETING

I was just mistaken for Josh Holloway. It's tough to be so handsome.
Oh, yeah?
PHEW
I was also mistaken for a celebrity recently.
Really? Who?
TADA
Nagura*, is that you?!

*Jun Nagura is a Japanese comedian.

Hello. This is Kohske.

I like little girls more than I like little boys. I was getting pretty tired of drawing guys and old men all the time, so I decided to give one of them a sex change. From here on out you'll be seeing a female Mafia head. I like fiery women.

Also, my work set-up wasn't that great, so I splurged on a high-quality German ergonomic chair. It's soooo comfortable.

See you in the next volume!

Thanks always (abridged):
Mom / My assistant Kamo / Saimoto / Ijihara / Fumi

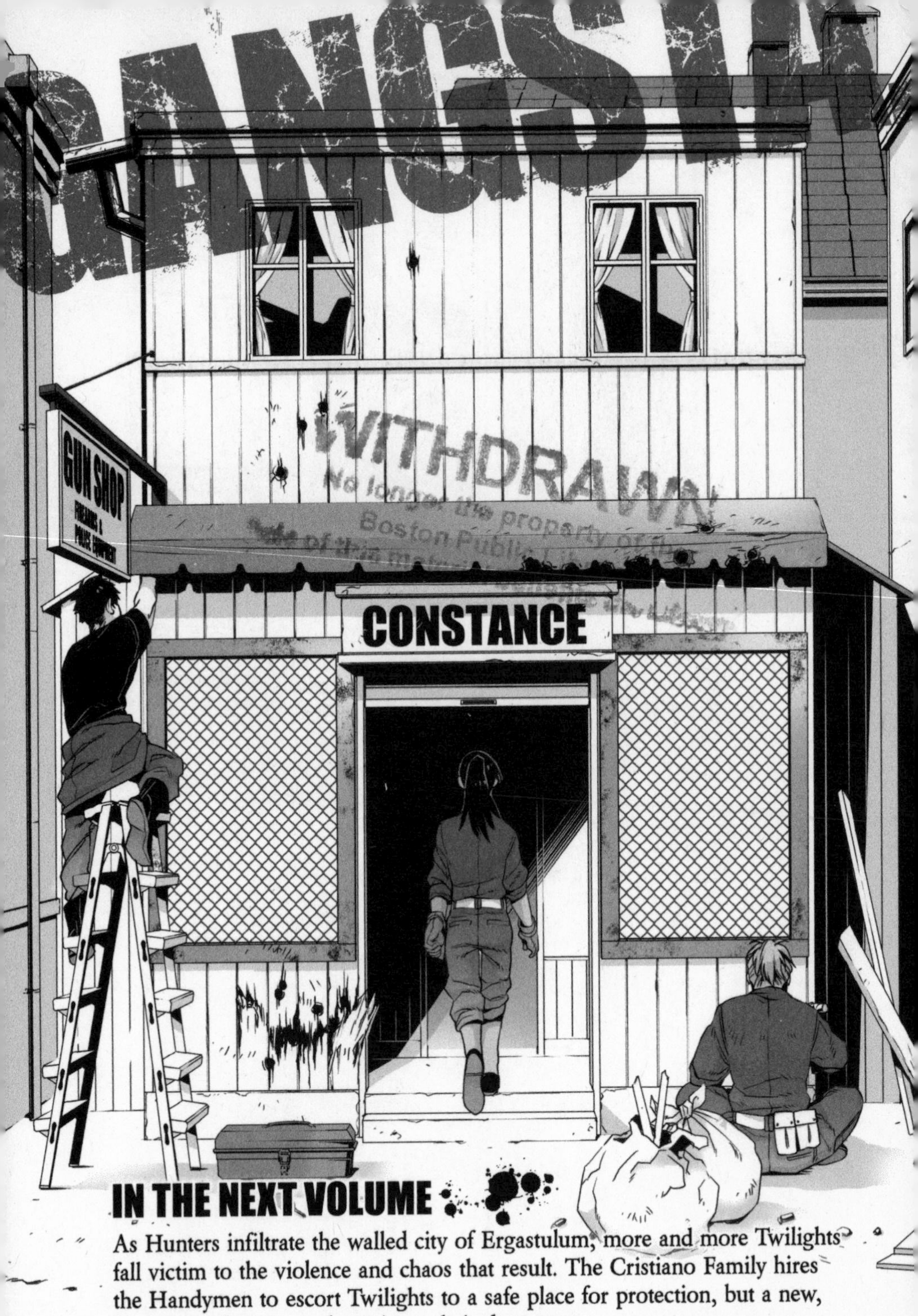
GUN SHOP
FIREARMS & POLICE EQUIPMENT
CONSTANCE

IN THE NEXT VOLUME

As Hunters infiltrate the walled city of Ergastulum, more and more Twilights fall victim to the violence and chaos that result. The Cristiano Family hires the Handymen to escort Twilights to a safe place for protection, but a new, even more dangerous threat is on their doorstep.

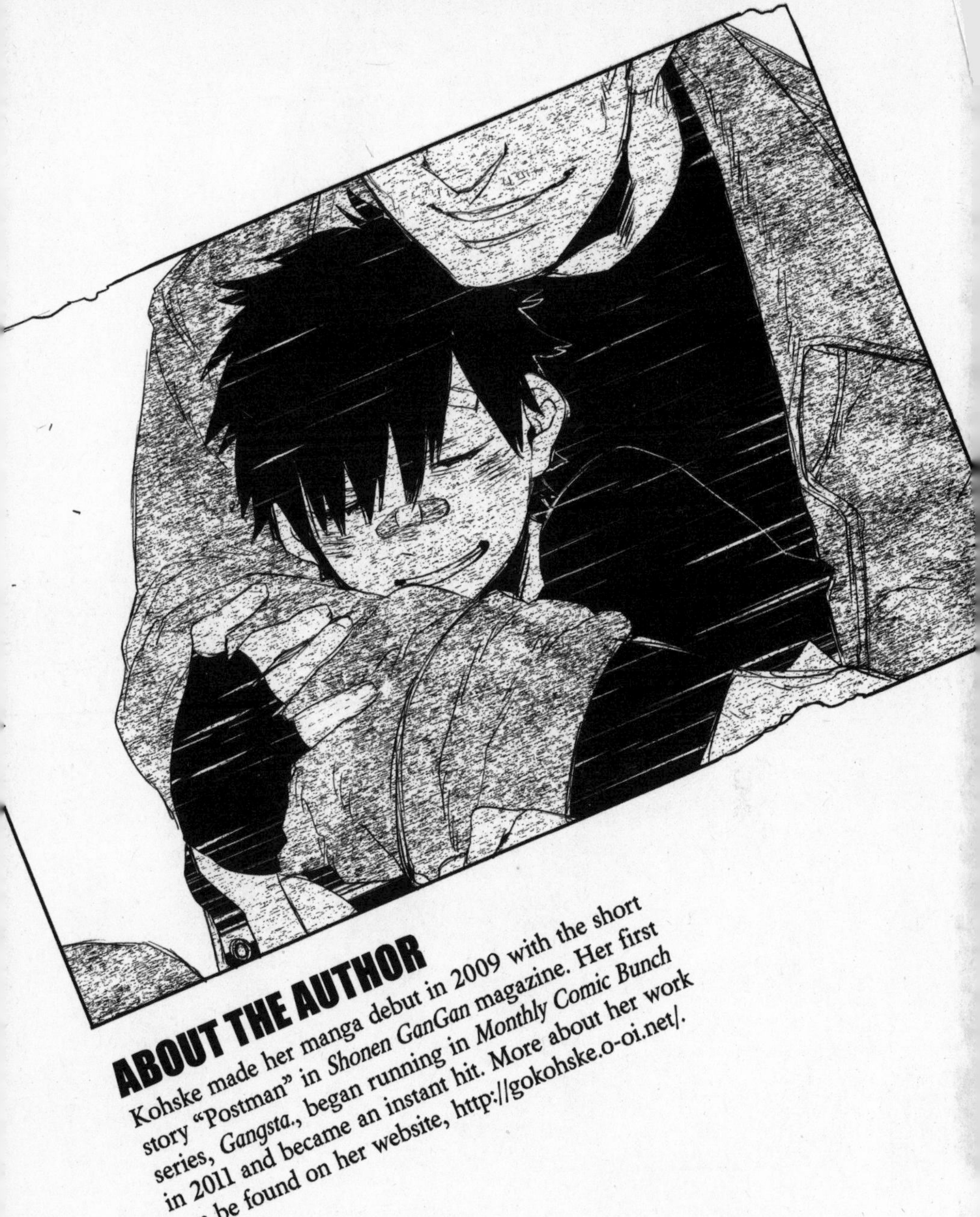

ABOUT THE AUTHOR

Kohske made her manga debut in 2009 with the short story “Postman” in *Shonen GanGan* magazine. Her first series, *Gangsta.*, began running in *Monthly Comic Bunch* in 2011 and became an instant hit. More about her work can be found on her website, http://gokohske.o-oi.net/.

GANGSTA.

Gangsta.
Volume 3

VIZ Signature Edition

Story & Art by Kohske

Translation & Adaptation/Katherine Schilling
Touch-up Art & Lettering/Eric Erbes
Cover & Graphic Design/Sam Elzway
Editor/Leyla Aker

Printed in the U.S.A.

Published by VIZ Media, LLC
P.O. Box 77010
San Francisco, CA 94107

10 9 8 7 6 5 4 3
First printing, August 2014
Third printing, July 2016

viz media
www.viz.com

RATED M FOR MATURE

PARENTAL ADVISORY
GANGSTA. is rated M for Mature and is recommended for mature readers. This volume contains graphic violence and mature themes.
ratings.viz.com

VIZ SIGNATURE